Late ancient Christianity

A PEOPLE'S HISTORY OF CHRISTIANITY

LATE ANCIENT CHRISTIANITY

A PEOPLE'S HISTORY OF CHRISTIANITY

Denis R. Janz
General Editor

Volume 1
CHRISTIAN ORIGINS
Richard Horsley, editor

Volume 2
LATE ANCIENT CHRISTIANITY
Virginia Burrus, editor

Volume 3
BYZANTINE CHRISTIANITY
Derek Krueger, editor

Volume 4
MEDIEVAL CHRISTIANITY
Daniel E. Bornstein, editor

Volume 5
REFORMATION CHRISTIANITY
Peter Matheson, editor

Volume 6
MODERN CHRISTIANITY TO 1900
Amanda Porterfield, editor

Volume 7
TWENTIETH-CENTURY GLOBAL CHRISTIANITY
Mary Farrell Bednarowski, editor

A PEOPLE'S HISTORY OF CHRISTIANITY

Volume 2

LATE ANCIENT CHRISTIANITY

VIRGINIA BURRUS
Editor

FORTRESS PRESS
Minneapolis

LATE ANCIENT CHRISTIANITY
A People's History of Christianity, volume 2

Cover art: Funeral portrait from Fayum, Egypt, second century CE. © Erich Lessing / Art Resource, NY.
Cover design: Laurie Ingram
Interior design: James Korsmo

Scripture quotations are from the New Revised Standard Version Bible, copyright © 1989 by the Division of Christian Education of the National Council of the Churches of Christ in the USA and used by permission.

Further materials on this volume and the entire series can be found online at www.peopleshistoryofchristianity.com.

Library of Congress Cataloging-in-Publication Data

Late ancient Christianity / Virginia Burrus, editor.
    p.   cm. — (A people's history of Christianity ; v. 2)
  Includes bibliographical references and index.
  ISBN 0-8006-3412-8 (alk. paper)
  1. Christian life—History—Early church, ca. 30–600. 2. Church history—Primitive and early church, ca 30–600. I. Burrus, Virginia. II. Series.
  BR195.C5L27 2005
  270.2—dc22   2005022290

Manufactured in Canada
09 08 07 06 05   1 2 3 4 5 6 7 8 9 10

CONTENTS

CONTRIBUTORS

Kimberly Bowes is Assistant Professor of Art History at Fordham University. She has published on a wide range of topics relating to late antique material culture, including Roman domestic architecture, the reuse of ancient monuments, and rural settlement topography, and is the co-editor of *Hispania in the Late Antique World: Current Perspectives*. She is currently completing a book on private chapels and private ritual in late antiquity.

Virginia Burrus is Professor of Early Church History at Drew University. Her scholarly publications in the field of late ancient Christianity center on issues of gender, sexuality, and the body; orthodoxy and heresy; and the literatures of martyrdom and hagiography. Her books include *The Making of a Heretic: Gender, Authority, and the Priscillianist Controversy* (1995), *"Begotten, Not Made": Conceiving Manhood in Late Antiquity* (2000), and *The Sex Lives of Saints: An Erotics of Ancient Hagiography* (2004). She is currently working on a book about ancient Christian views of shame.

Elizabeth A. Clark is John Carlisle Kilgo Professor of Religion at Duke University, a Fellow of the American Academy of Arts and Sciences, and founding editor of the *Journal of Early Christian Studies*. Her books include *The Origenist Controversy: The Cultural Construction of an Early Christian Debate* (1992), *Reading Renunciation: Asceticism and Scripture in Early Christianity* (1999), and *History, Theory, Text: Historians and the Linguistic Turn* (2004). She is currently working on a study of how "patristics" became established as a discipline in America.

Charlotte Elisheva Fonrobert is Assistant Professor of Religious Studies at Stanford University and specializes in Judaism, particularly talmudic literature and the construction of gender in this literature. She is the author of *Menstrual Purity: Rabbinic and Christian Reconstructions of Biblical Gender*

(2000) and co-editor of the Cambridge Companion to Rabbinic Literature. She is currently working on a book about Jewish self-definitions with respect to the late ancient polis and the relationship between Jewish communal boundary-making and the urban neighborhood.

David Frankfurter is Professor of History and Religious Studies at the University of New Hampshire. He is author of *Elijah in Upper Egypt: The Apocalypse of Elijah and Early Egyptian Christianity* (1993), *Religion in Roman Egypt: Assimilation and Resistance* (1998), and (ed.) *Pilgrimage and Holy Space in Late Antique Egypt* (1998), along with numerous articles on apocalypticism, magic, Christianization, and religious violence in the ancient Mediterranean world.

Cornelia B. Horn is Assistant Professor of Historical Theology at Saint Louis University. Her publications include *Asceticism and Christological Controversy in Fifth-Century Palestine: The Career of Peter the Iberian* (2006); *John Rufus: The Lives of Peter the Iberian, Theodosius of Jerusalem, and the Monk Romanus,* co-authored with Robert R. Phenix, Jr. (forthcoming); and *'Let the Little Ones Come to Me': Children in the early Christian Community,* co-authored with John W. Martens (forthcoming), as well as articles on a wide range of topics, including martyrdom, asceticism, pilgrimage, penitence, Mariology, female missionaries and patrons, and children in early Christianity. Her research continues to explore the intersection of theology/religion and social/cultural phenomena in the world of early Christianity, especially Eastern/Oriental Christianity from biblical times to the rise of Islam.

Robin M. Jensen is the Luce Chancellor's Professor of the History of Christian Art and Worship at Vanderbilt University Divinity School. Her books include *Face to Face: Portraits of the Divine in Early Christianity* (2005) and *Understanding Early Christian Art* (2000). She is currently at work on a study of the iconography and architecture of early Christian baptism and a co-authored work on the practice of Christianity in Roman Africa.

Rebecca Lyman is the Garrett Professor of Church History Emerita at The Church Divinity School of the Pacific in Berkeley, California. Her writings include *Christology and Cosmology: Models of Divine Activity in Origen, Eusebius, and Athanasius* (1993) and *Early Christian Traditions* (1999) as well as various articles on ancient Christian theology and dissent.

Harry O. Maier is Professor of New Testament Studies at Vancouver School of Theology. He is author of *The Social Setting of the Ministry as Reflected* *in the Writings of Hermas, Clement and Ignatius* (2002) and *Apocalypse Recalled: The Book of Revelation after Christendom* (2002), as well as numerous articles on topics related to the social world of early Christianity.

Andrew McGowan is Director of the Theological School and Munro Lecturer in Theology at Trinity College, University of Melbourne. His work on the social and intellectual history of early Christianity has often focused on food and meals, and he is the author of *Ascetic Eucharists: Food and Drink in Early Christian Ritual Meals* (1999).

Judith Perkins is Professor of Classics and Humanities at Saint Joseph College. She is the author of *The Suffering Self: Pain and Narrative Representation in the Early Christian Era* (1995) and numerous articles dealing with ancient novels. Her present project is an examination of resurrection discourse in the context of Roman imperialism.

Dennis Trout is Associate Professor of Classics at the University of Missouri-Columbia. His recent research and publications are focused upon the transformation of Rome in late antiquity from a classical to a Christian city. He is the author of *Paulinus of Nola: Life, Letters, and Poems* (1999).

Robin Darling Young is Associate Professor of Theology at the University of Notre Dame. Her chief interests lie in the languages and cultures of the ancient Christian East, viz. Greek, Syriac and Armenian. Her writings include *In Procession Before the World: Martyrdom As Public Liturgy in Early Christianity* (2001) and *Ephrem the Syrian: Hymns on Fasting, and on the Pasch: On the Unleavened Bread, On the Crucifixion, On the Resurrection,* trans. with G. A. Anderson and S. H. Griffith (2003).

ILLUSTRATIONS

Figures

Color Plates (following page 126)

FOREWORD

This seven-volume series breaks new ground by looking at Christianity's past from the vantage point of a people's history. It is church history, yes, but church history with a difference: "church," we insist, is not to be understood first and foremost as the hierarchical-institutional-bureaucratic corporation; rather, above all it is the laity, the ordinary faithful, the people. Their religious lives, their pious practices, their self-understandings as Christians, and the way all of this grew and changed over the last two millennia—*this* is the unexplored territory in which we are here setting foot.

To be sure, the undertaking known as people's history, as it is applied to secular themes, is hardly a new one among academic historians. Referred to sometimes as history from below, or grassroots history, or popular history, it was born about a century ago, in conscious opposition to the elitism of conventional (some call it Rankean) historical investigation, fixated as this was on the "great" deeds of "great" men, and little else. What had always been left out of the story, of course, was the vast majority of human beings: almost all women, obviously, but then too all those who could be counted among the socially inferior, the economically distressed, the politically marginalized, the educationally deprived, or the culturally unrefined. Had not various elites always despised "the people"? Cicero, in first-century BCE Rome, referred to them as "urban filth and dung"; Edmund Burke, in eighteenth-century London, called them "the swinish multitude"; and in between, this loathing of "the meaner sort" was almost universal among the privileged. When the discipline called "history" was professionalized in the nineteenth century, traditional gentlemen historians perpetuated this contempt if not by outright vilification, then at least by keeping the masses invisible. Thus when people's history came on the scene, it was not only a means for uncovering an unknown dimension of the past but also in some sense an instrument for righting an injustice. Today its cumulative contribution is enormous, and its home in the academic world is assured.

Only quite recently has the discipline formerly called "church history" and now more often "the history of Christianity" begun to open itself up to this approach. Its agenda over the last two centuries has been dominated by other facets of this religion's past such as theology, dogma, institutions, and ecclesio-political relations. Each of these has in fact long since evolved into its own subdiscipline. Thus the history of theology has concentrated on the self-understandings of Christian intellectuals. Historians of dogma have examined the way in which church leaders came to formulate teachings that they then pronounced normative for all Christians. Experts on institutional history have researched the formation, growth, and functioning of leadership offices, bureaucratic structures, official decision-making processes, and so forth. And specialists in the history of church-state relations have worked to fathom the complexities of the institution's interface with its socio-political context, above all by studying leaders on both sides.

Collectively, these conventional kinds of church history have yielded enough specialized literature to fill a very large library, and those who read in this library will readily testify to its amazing treasures. Erudite as it is, however, the Achilles' heel of this scholarship, taken as a whole, is that it has told the history of Christianity as the story of one small segment of those who have claimed the name "Christian." What has been studied almost exclusively until now is the religion of various elites, whether spiritual elites, intellectual elites, or power elites. Without a doubt, mystics and theologians, pastors, priests, bishops and popes are worth studying. But at best they all together constitute perhaps 5 percent of all Christians over two millennia. What about the rest? Does not a balanced history of Christianity, not to mention our sense of historical justice, require that attention be paid to them?

Around the mid twentieth century a handful of scholars began, hesitantly and yet insistently, to press this question on the international guild of church historians. Since that time, the study of the other 95 percent has gained momentum: ever more ambitious research projects have been launched; innovative scholarly methods have been developed, critiqued, and refined; and a growing public interest has greeted the results. Academics and nonacademics alike want to know about this aspect of Christianity's past. Who were these people—the voiceless, the ordinary faithful who wrote no theological treatises, whose statues adorn no basilica, who negotiated no concordats, whose very names themselves are largely lost to historical memory? What can we know about their religious consciousness, their devotional practice, their understanding of the faith, their values, beliefs, feelings, habits, attitudes, their deepest fears, hopes, loves, hatreds, and so forth? And what about the trouble makers, the excluded, the heretics, those defined by conventional history as the losers? Can a face be put on any of them?

Today, even after half a century of study, answers are still in short supply. It must be conceded that the field is in its infancy, both methodologically and in terms of what remains to be investigated. Very often historians now find themselves no longer interrogating literary texts but rather artifacts, the remains of material culture, court records, wills, popular art, graffiti, and so forth. What is already clear is that many traditional assumptions, time-worn clichés, and well-loved nuggets of conventional wisdom about Christianity's past will have to be abandoned. When the Christian masses are made the leading protagonists of the story, we begin to glimpse a plot with dramatically new contours. In fact, a rewriting of this history is now getting under way, and this may well be the discipline's larger task for the twenty-first century.

A People's History of Christianity is our contribution to this enterprise. In it we gather up the early harvest of this new approach, showcase the current state of the discipline, and plot a trajectory into the future. Essentially what we offer here is a preliminary attempt at a new and more adequate version of the Christian story—one that features the people. Is it comprehensive? Impossible. Definitive? Hardly. A responsible, suggestive, interesting base to build on? We are confident that it is.

Close to a hundred historians of Christianity have generously applied their various types of expertise to this project, whether as advisors or editors or contributors. They have in common no universally agreed-on methodology, nor do they even concur on how precisely to define problematic terms such as "popular religion." What they do share is a conviction that rescuing the Christian people from their historic anonymity is important, that reworking the story's plot with lay piety as the central narrative will be a contribution of lasting value, and that reversing the condescension, not to say contempt, that all too often has marred elite views of the people is long overdue. If progress is made on these fronts, we believe, the groundwork for a new history of Christianity will have been prepared.

The volume before us, *Late Ancient Christianity,* features a rich collection of original essays by prominent specialists in that era. It introduces us to new perspectives on issues of Christian identity, self-definition, and boundary creation. Insisting on the priority of the local and the particular, it explores, for instance, food and children at play and domestic piety. In the end it paints a portrait of a diversity so rich and vibrant that no institutional elite could finally tame it. For this volume we all stand in the debt of its editor, Virginia Burrus, and I am especially grateful to her for taking on the task. Its virtues are in large measure attributable to her tenacity in the face of formidable obstacles, her high professionalism, and her superb scholarly judgment.

Denis R. Janz, General Editor

North
Sea

ENGLAND

Lullingstone •

• Rouen

ATLANTIC
OCEAN

Tours •

GAUL

• Lyons

• Milan

• Ravenna

• Braga

IBERIA

Corsica

ITALY
• Rome

• Nola

• Merida

Sardinia

Sicily

Hippo
•

• Carthage

Mediterran

NORTH   AFRICA

0   500 Miles

Fig. 0.1. Map of the Mediterranean world of late antiquity. Map by Lucidity Information Design.

Caspian Sea

Black Sea

PONTUS

Constantinople

Thessalonica

Gordine

Caesarea

CAPPADOCIA

PHRYGIA

GREECE

Qalat Siman

Athens

Ephesus

Antioch

SYRIA

Corinth

Cyprus

Crete

PALESTINE

Sea

Jerusalem

Gaza

Mamre

Apollonia

Alexandria

Scetis

Atripe

EGYPT

Tabennisi
(Pachomian
Monastery)

Red Sea

Abydos

Fig. 0.2. Whereas historical studies have traditionally placed the leaders of the church in the spotlight, this volume shifts the focus to the lives of ordinary Christians, such as the one known to us only as "the woman with the issue of blood" (Matthew 9:20-22), depicted in this early fourth-century fresco. Catacomb of SS. Marcellino e Pietro, Rome, Italy. Photo credit: Scala / Art Resource, NY.

SHIFTING THE FOCUS OF HISTORY

VIRGINIA BURRUS AND REBECCA LYMAN

INTRODUCTION

What would it mean to conceive of the history of Christianity not as a *history of the church*, but rather as a *history of Christians*? This simple reframing immediately gives rise to further questions. How does one recognize a "Christian"? Is Christian identity a matter of self-profession, or is it inevitably also a social or collective phenomenon? What criteria are invoked, whether implicitly or explicitly, either by the one who makes the profession or by those who choose to acknowledge or deny it? Is "being Christian" fundamentally a matter of subcribing to certain teachings about God or Jesus, the natural world, and the "world" shaped by politics and culture? Is it, alternatively, less a matter of belief than of adopting a certain ethical stance or code of behavior, participating in specific rituals, gathering in certain places, belonging to particular communities, reading certain books, or sharing certain stories? How does a person's Christianity relate to other aspects of his or her identity, such as class, gender, age, race or ethnicity, and familial or sexual roles? To what extent does it entail not only the affirmation but also the exclusion or rejection of certain beliefs, practices, or affiliations? For students of history, the answers to such questions cannot be presumed in advance but must be sought in the records of the past. Our task, in other words, is to attempt to understand what being Christian meant to people living in contexts often very distant and different from ours.

The Roman imperial period, with which this volume is concerned, bequeathed to later generations codifications of doctrine, liturgy, and institutional structure that have proved remarkably enduring. More than that, the legacies of this era have been explicitly marked as authoritative, not only by the various churches but also by a practice of scholarship tellingly labeled "patristics," indicating the study of the "fathers" of Christianity, a group of authors whose writings were affirmed already by the end of antiquity as ecclesiastically legitimate expressions of apostolic tradition

1

and doctrinal orthodoxy. This conventional focus on the works of a designated theological and institutional elite complicates the task of those seeking a history not of the church but of Christians. When we view ancient Christianity through the lens of the fathers, we see what those fathers and their self-proclaimed successors wanted us to see—namely, a story of steady progress toward unity and clarity of belief and practice. This narrative culminates in the production of such foundational doctrines as the divine Trinity and the two-natured Christ, such carefully scripted rituals as baptism and eucharist, and such widely acknowledged authority as that of the pastoral leader who interprets God's scriptural Word and administers the affairs of God's household. The distinctions between true Christianity and heresy, Judaism, or paganism seem, moreover, reassuringly clear-cut from the viewpoint of traditional church histories.

To be sure, such perceived clarity and continuity of self-definition across space and time are not purely illusory: ancient Christians characteristically thought of themselves as members of a unified and universal community, as reflected, for example, in the early and pervasive practice of letter writing, through which dispersed local communities created networks of communication and alliance. Yet, at the same time, this inherited story, with its selected sources and assumptions, does not tell us nearly enough about how Christianity was actually experienced and practiced by the ordinary people to whom the writings of the fathers were often addressed and to whom they frequently referred. When viewed not from above but on the ground, Christian identity emerges as a far messier and more diverse, and also, we believe, a far more *flexible* and *creative* phenomenon.

It is the aim of the chapters in this volume to draw the reader's gaze away from the transcendent God's-eye view of Christian history, which is itself a product of human imagination as well as an assertion of power on the part of various elites. Instead, we will direct our eyes toward the complex negotiations of Christian identity revealed in the local and everyday practices of men, women, and children. Three themes that will recur throughout our chapters thus already emerge: emphasis on *diversity* rather than sameness, on the *local* rather than the universal, and on *practice* rather than doctrine. Some may see this turn to a "people's history of Christianity" as the secular study of a particular religion; others may experience it as the practice of a genuinely incarnational theology.

At the outset we must acknowledge, however, that "the people" have been assigned a distinctive role in the production of the God's-eye view of Christianity within patristic texts. From the earliest days, Christian writers exploited conventional techniques of rhetorical one-upmanship and social control exercised against rival missionaries and teachers. As charismatic leaders of small communities, the authors presumed spiritual unity with the members of their communities while also claiming authority by vocation as apostles, prophets, or teachers. A modern sensibility detects the irony in the stances of clergy who claimed they were protecting congregations by casting aspersions on those supposedly elitist intellectuals whom they accused of attempting to distort the simple faith of the people. Those who aspired to authority in ancient Christian communities, not unlike those who aspired to authority elsewhere in Roman society, tended to appropriate the voice of the people and to denigrate their rivals as divorced from the common ideals of the community. The rivals were portrayed as self-promoting members of a troublingly exclusive elite who cared more about developing their own ideas and reputations than about clarifying the contours of shared faith and values. One might thus receive the impression from ancient authors that the Christian people were a unified front, and unified specifically around a spontaneous orthodoxy of belief and practice, balanced against the esoteric innovations of philosophizing heretics and other overly inventive or troublingly ambitious freethinkers and false prophets.

Such an initial impression of popular simplicity or unity is contradicted by the historical evidence. First, we should note that the virginal purity of popular faith *seemingly* so readily embraced by the fathers is not consistent with the intricacies of theological and exegetical debate also clearly valued by those same Christian leaders—who were, moreover, quick to tell the people what they should and shouldn't believe or do! Even in the best of times, necessarily sophisticated theological discourse chafes against the ideal of plain speech embodied in the common Greek of the New Testament. Second, the values attaching to communal debate were not strictly confined to religious professionals. Witness the tireless attempts of Irenaeus to equip the laity of second-century Lyons to distinguish between the "true faith" and "knowledge, falsely so-called," or Tertullian of Carthage's roughly contemporaneous insistence that debate with heretics about the scriptures could result only in a headache or nauseous stomach and thus should be avoided at all costs. In such cases, it is clear that local communities, whether in Gaul or North Africa or elsewhere, encompassed a diversity of interpretations of Christian teaching and practice and accommodated complex patterns of influence, discussion, and debate carried out in a popular arena. Robin Jensen's chapter in this volume provides an illuminating window onto differences surrounding baptismal practice in Tertullian's community, while Judith Perkins explores conflicting opinions regarding the nature of Jesus' body as well as of Christian community in the pre-Constantinian era. Negotiated tolerance was also part of this emerging Christianity. As Irenaeus insisted when addressing the date of Easter, "Our diversity shows our unity."

For the later imperial period, we have more explicit evidence of popular participation in theological debate, not always to the liking of the leaders.

The broadening of Christian community after the end of persecution may have increased the level of popular discussion while also bringing it into line with existing civic models of public debate. Writing in the fourth century, Bishop Athanasius of Alexandria, for example, expresses his irritation at his theological opponents' penchant for quizzing children in the marketplace about the freedom and mobility of the divine Son and questioning "little women" concerning their memories of childbirth, while another bishop, Gregory of Nyssa, notes with disdain that one could scarcely buy a loaf of bread without discussing the nature of the Trinity during the heat of the Arian controversy. Clearly, the people were no more unified in their positions or practices than were their bishops. The differences among bishops as well as within their congregations surfaced embarrassingly as sharp public disagreements in the period of the ecumenical councils, which were initiated with the fourth-century conversion of the Roman emperors to Christianity. Ultimately, the efforts of the bishops to define and enforce an "orthodoxy" left its mark on imperial as well as ecclesial legislation, as registered in the edicts collected in the Theodosian Code, discussed in the chapters by Kimberly Bowes, David Frankfurter, and Harry Maier.

The era of the imperial councils not only exposes the webs of communication, alliance, and enmity among clergy but also reveals the complex social dynamics operating within tight-knit, if frequently contentious, local communities. Religious leaders were the patrons—and thus the designated representatives—of their people, and they were closely constrained by the religious sensibilities of those people, sensibilities that they no doubt largely shared. In the early centuries of the Christian era, distinctions between clergy and laity, as well as relations among various competing figures of authority (prophets, martyrs, teachers, bishops), were frequently both ambiguous and fluid. The theological controversies of the later imperial period, when ecclesial office was more sharply demarcated, provide instructive examples of the degree to which even bishops attending councils of their peers were still pressured by the desires and expectations of the folks back home.

Symptomatic is Eusebius of Caesarea's letter to his congregation following the famous Nicene Council of 325, in which he attempts anxiously to convince them that the controversial creed to which he had appended his signature was truly the same as the local Palestinian profession of faith. Slightly later, Leontius, bishop of Syrian Antioch, resorts to mumbling the doxology inaudibly in order to avoid outbreaks of conflict among his sharp-eared and sharply divided congregation. More sinisterly, the mob violence accompanying the Council of Ephesus in Asia Minor, considerably exceeding the control of the attending bishops as well as of the emperor's police force, reminds us that the people had their stake in theological disputes:

the women of Ephesus, in particular, were not about to countenance any perceived slights on the exalted status of Mary the God-bearer.

As the last example already hints, with reference to the emerging cult of Mary, doctrinal debates were just the tip of the iceberg. When we examine the constellation of practices that emerge with the cult of the saints, for example, it becomes even more difficult to separate the perspectives of social or ecclesial elites from those of the common people—a point that has been emphasized by such influential Roman historians as Arnaldo Momigliano and Peter Brown, who have questioned the usefulness of the distinction between "popular" and "elite" culture as applied to ancient Christianity. (Of particular relevance here are the chapters by Bowes, Frankfurter, and Dennis Trout.)

The telling of a people's history requires that we read old sources in new ways while also attending to sources that have frequently been ignored, not least the rich realm of material culture. Only recently have scholars of ancient Christianity taken up this challenge, however. For much of the modern period, historians, whether religious or secular, have by and large remained constrained by the monolithic and polemical terms of debate first laid out by the fathers themselves, alternately defending Christianity as a laudably populist movement or critiquing it as the vulgarization of classical civilization. To recover a history of Christians, we must learn to interpret the surviving texts and other artifacts with less reliance on patristic categories and limits. We must develop an eye and an ear for differences that are not always oppositions. We must scrutinize the apparent unity of Christian life and thought in order to perceive the richness of its actual diversity. Christians of the Roman Empire did indeed tend to think globally in representing themselves quite innovatively as an ecumenical or world religion, but they also always acted locally. The local acts and embodied practices as much as the universalizing thoughts of ancient Christians therefore demand our close attention.

At the same time, with regard to a religion that placed a high value on word and book, we should not forget that speech and writing are also practices. Moreover, Christian talk issued forth from the very beginning in a babble of different languages, dialects, and accents, conveying a rich variety of distinctive narrative, doctrinal, and ritual traditions, each of which carried its own history of encounters with non-Christian neighbors, both Jewish and pagan, as is explored in the chapters by Charlotte Fonrobert and Frankfurter. In the multicultural mix of ancient Mediterranean society, these local Christian cultures frequently engaged one another in spirited dialogue—sometimes agreeing, sometimes cross-fertilizing, sometimes colliding violently—but they did not simply merge into a single undifferentiated whole. Indeed, the records of the very debates such as the gnostic,

Montanist, Arian, Nestorian, or Pelagian that frequently structure traditional accounts of the "rise of orthodoxy" indicate that the increasingly vigorous efforts of teachers or bishops, and eventually of emperors as well, to forge consensus and enforce unity on a diverse church often served to intensify awareness of the differences among Christians, differences mapped, for example, in Maier's chapter.

When we listen attentively to the ancient Christians, we do not, then, hear a single people speaking as if with one voice. Rather, our ears are filled with a multitude of voices, some synchronizing harmoniously, some clamoring contentiously, some simply following their own scripts as if oblivious to the strikingly different words issuing from other quarters. Admittedly, such an insistence on the many-voiced diversity of ancient Christianity still leaves an important question unaddressed: who precisely *are* the people who are to be the subjects of this explicitly revisionist "people's history"? Or, to put the question differently, who is *not* part of the people? Already, however, we can see why this question is difficult to answer: "the Christian people" is neither a unity nor an essence, not an "it" but a "they." Indeed, if this volume contributes to our sense of the infinite richness, complexity, and variety of Christian thought and practice in late antiquity—if it, in effect, refuses to give a definitive answer to the question of who the people are—it will have gone far toward achieving the goals of a people's history of Christianity.

Nonetheless, if we want to approach Christianity not from on high but from below, not from the center but from the margins, not from the abstract perspective of the church but from the concrete perspectives of Christians, it will be helpful to consider several possible ways of mapping the angles of our investigation. Specifically, we will here explore the usefulness of locating the people in relation to distinctions of social class, gender, age, lay or clerical status, ethnicity, and (most ambiguously) orthodox credentials of religious purity. Each of these distinctions, as we shall see, proves helpful in certain ways. No single one of them, however, will tell us all we want to know, nor can they simply be combined to produce a single, synthetic definition of "the people."

SOCIAL CLASS

Christianity, it is frequently emphasized, emerged as a movement of the disenfranchised. Jesus and his earliest followers were Galilean peasants, marginal in relation not only to the Roman Empire but also to the Jewish elite who exercised leadership over Judea and its environs in ambivalent collusion with the imperial rule of the Romans. In the course of two unsuccessful Jewish revolts, the first of which resulted in the destruction of the Temple and the second of which made clear that the Jewish state would not recover, the power of the priestly class, based in the Temple cult, came to an end, and Judaism underwent dramatic changes. One strand of Judaism began to reorganize along patterns that eventually gave rise to rabbinic Judaism. At the same time, the Christian movement within Judaism shifted its weight toward the Gentile mission, adopting a spiritual rather than genealogical understanding of its claims on the heritage of Israel. Partly as a result of marking their break with an ethnic, genealogically defined Judaism, Christians—now viewed as practitioners of a new religious movement whose founder had been crucified as a political criminal and whose adherents were deemed antisocial—became the target of intermittent persecution by a militarized imperial regime that desired both to keep the peace and to ensure the support of the gods by promoting traditional piety. Persecution created the context for the emergence of practices and ideologies of martyrdom that placed Christianity in a public stance of political resistance to empire. (See the chapters by Perkins and Robin Darling Young.) Only gradually, in the course of two or three centuries, did Christianity begin to encroach upon the class of civic notables, and it was not until the conversion of the Roman emperors themselves and the end of persecution that the paganism of the senatorial class began slowly to erode, as political favors and power went more and more to those identified with Christianity.

Yet certain sociological factors complicate this view of Christianity as a strictly "lower-class" or simply "anti-imperial" movement even in the period of persecution. Modern understandings of class correspond imperfectly to the realities of an intensely hierarchical ancient Mediterranean society in which relationships were most frequently defined on a vertical axis of patronage rather than on a horizontal axis of class solidarity. Even a slave or former slave might exercise significant powers of patronage, as well as profit from patronage: a vast gulf separated a well-educated slave or "freedman" of the imperial household, for example, from a slave consigned to physical labor or subjected to an owner ill-positioned to award social, economic, or political favors. The earliest-known Christian communities included many of low social status, whether slave or free, but they also enjoyed the support of men and women who were well enough placed, socially and economically, to provide meeting places that could accommodate small congregations as well as food for shared meals, care for the poor, and at least minimal political protection.

At the same time, Christianity—not unlike other schools of Judaism, mystery cults, and philosophical sects—quickly attracted members of a mobile class of teachers and miracle workers, rhetoricians, and philosophers, who traded on the opportunities for social advancement created by the empire while seeking ways to disrupt the innate privileges of ethnicity and aristocratic class through a persuasive display of acquired skills. The earliest writings produced by Christians, written predominately in Greek, are not high literature, but they do reflect access to literacy, familiarity with rhetorical convention and hermeneutical practice, and general affinities with contemporary cultures of performance and spectacle. Moreover, to the extent that such literature was culturally or politically subversive—and in many respects it was, as Perkins, for example, highlights—it tended to effect its subversions subtly, frequently questioning the dominant culture by slyly invoking or appropriating the values and habits of that very culture. Within Christian communities characterized not only by their social inclusiveness but also by a certain fluidity with regard to social status, class tensions are nonetheless frequently manifested: in the early third century, Hippolytus of Rome, for example, sneered at an episcopal rival, Callistus, for being a former slave.

Such factors not only complicate our view of Christianity as a lower-class or politically radical movement but also help explain the spread of the religion. The conversion of the emperor Constantine, on which a class-based analysis of the growth of Christianity inevitably and appropriately turns, is not merely an explanation for Christianity's success but is itself an event that calls for historical explanation. If Constantine converted to Christianity and if this conversion proved significant, it is in part because Christianity had demonstrated itself marketable to late Roman society. Christianity as a universal and inclusive religion appealed to the social realities of the Roman Empire, even if it violated many of its cultural ideals. The triumphal as well as universalizing worldview of Christians not only provided ongoing sources of resistance to imperial authority but also proved remarkably adaptable to the context of an imperial church, some of whose bishops had also been powerful players in the Roman political system—Ambrose of Milan being an oft-cited example. At the same time, the alliance of the church with the class interests of the political elite was scarcely uniform or stable, even in the late imperial period. Christian episcopacy provided a power base for a new elite whose interests did not always coincide precisely with the goals of their emperors: even Ambrose, who had held the office of consular governor under the emperor Valentinian, perceived in his new role as Christian bishop of Milan the social opportunity not merely to match but to exceed the claims of political office; he is famous for his audacity in instructing and chastising even emperors and empresses.

Then, too, the rising popularity of the ascetic movement continued to create opportunities for both women among the elite and men and women of the sub-elite to exercise power outside the church's hierarchy, whether through charismatic leadership or sheer strength in numbers and zeal. Indeed, as Elizabeth Clark argues, ancient Christians, despite their egalitarian aspirations, had always produced their own internal social differentiations, articulated not only through ecclesial rank but also through the more ambiguous measure of holiness. As Andrew McGowan points out, meal practices evidence a similar tension between egalitarianism and the replication or production of hierarchies within the Christian community. Sometimes these hierarchies aligned with the class distinctions of the broader Roman world, and sometimes they dramatically disrupted such distinctions. However, the notion of a strictly egalitarian Christian community is as questionable as is the notion of Christianity as a distinctly low-class or proletarian movement. A people's history must thus take account of both the ways in which ancient Christian practices challenged social hierarchies by privileging the unprivileged—the ways, in other words, in which ancient Christianity may be broadly construed as a popular movement—and the ways in which it simultaneously reaffirmed existing class distinctions and gave rise to new ones.

GENDER AND AGE

Ancient Christianity was typically discredited by pagan critics as a religion of gullible women and children. In this way it was also represented as a movement that gravitated toward the suspiciously shadowed spaces of the private sphere—a sphere particularly well illumined by Bowes and Maier. Indeed, despite the patriarchal impulses and anxieties that are present in the earliest layers of documented Christian history, there are indications of a relative gender egalitarianism prevailing in early Christian communities: women as well as men were followers of Jesus, patrons of house churches, presiders at eucharistic meals, acknowledged prophets, venerated martyrs, and ascetic saints. The initial location of Christianity in the domestic sphere seems to have furthered such flexibility, as women typically operated with more freedom and authority in the domestic than in the political arena.

While the extent of women's "liberation" within Christian circles should not be exaggerated, the very evidence of *resistance* to practices such as women's prophesying, teaching, or administering sacraments (and the ability of Christians to draw upon rhetorical convention to express it) suggests that some Christian communities did indeed challenge prevailing gender hierarchies. Paul had famously proclaimed that "in Christ there is no male and female" (Gal. 3:28), though he elsewhere set limits on women's rights to prophesy or speak up in the Christian assemblies (1 Cor. 11:3-16;

14:34-35). Seeming to affirm one aspect of the Pauline tradition while questioning another, the second-century *Acts of Paul and Thecla* represents its first-century heroine as a cross-dressing missionary who baptizes herself after the apostle Paul has refused to do so. Tertullian, writing near the end of the second century, opposes the use of Thecla's example to support women's right to baptize, indicating that such issues were controversial in his own community, as both Jensen and Perkins note. Martyrdom literature furthermore suggests that the context of persecution might frequently allow for a loosening of gender roles: male martyrs, embracing their own suffering as an opportunity to imitate Christ, took on passive roles that jarred contemporary ideals of masculinity; at the same time, female martyrs like Blandina of Lyons or Perpetua of Carthage were represented not only as Christlike figures but also as triumphant athletes and gladiators, roles strikingly unconventional for women. The early third-century *Passion of Perpetua*, moreover, preserves a sample of Perpetua's own writing, rare in a culture that tended to deny women access to publication. (On martyrdom and its literature, see Young.) A particularly intriguing instance of apparent ritual innovation on the part of women is evidenced in the third-century Syrian *Didascalia*, addressed to a community in which at least some women are following practices relating to menstrual purity, despite their bishops' objections, as discussed by Fonrobert. The diversity of women's roles and attitudes toward them within early Christianity reflects the complexity of the ideas and ideals of gender as lived out in varied communities of the radical sectarian movement.

When Christianity took on a more public face in the post-Constantinian period, the hierarchy of the church as well as the language of theology was decisively masculinized, and the position of women likewise shifted significantly. In this era the Trinitarian nomenclature of Father, Son, and Spirit triumphed, replacing and partly suppressing earlier, more fluid, and less decisively gendered metaphors for God and Christ. Also at that time a clerical hierarchy now allied with emperors took on a more political profile. If some Christians in the third century had begun to express the opinion that women could not hold church office because Jesus had chosen exclusively male disciples (a debatable point, of course), by the fourth century, as the official church was invested with the pomp of public ceremonial rites and architectural monuments, women's institutional leadership became simply unimaginable. Bishops, tellingly, began to be styled "fathers" of the church, in rather literal confirmation of the church's increasingly patriarchal constitution, as reflected, for example, in Athanasius's habit of designating the bishops who attended the Council of Nicea as "fathers."

Nonetheless, the simultaneous rise of asceticism, which permeated Christian culture in this period, disrupted the long-standing cultural authority of the patriarchal family and thereby extended traditions that, like martyrdom earlier, allowed for considerable flexibility of gender roles. Some men now actively shunned public roles, and even powerful bishops might find it advantageous to represent themselves as humble and retiring figures, while many women—especially elite women—gained unprecedented power and visibility, as is detailed by Clark. In addition, the fourth century witnessed the emergence of a remarkable new literary phenomenon, namely, the production of female biographies, launched with Gregory of Nyssa's hagiographical tribute to his sister Macrina. Thus, even in the post-Constantinian period, attitudes toward women remained diverse and contested.

If the history of women has for some decades attracted much attention, the history of children within early Christianity is only beginning to be explored. It is well known that ancient Christians made much use of the language of birth and infancy to describe the experience of conversion and resocialization. This image of Christians as children was conveyed pedagogically through catechesis and performed liturgically in rites of baptism, which marked even adults as newborn infants, and in the feeding of the postbaptismal eucharist, which in at least some places included a cup of milk and honey. (See the chapters by Jensen and McGowan.) Less clear, however, is how childhood, understood in a more literal sense, was configured socially within the Christian community. In this area, Cornelia Horn's chapter on the toys, games, and play practices of Christian children breaks important new ground. The not-infrequent representations of young girls and boys in martyrdom accounts as well as in ascetic lives suggests both that children were understood to partake fully in the life of Christian witness and that their accomplishments were particularly valued precisely because they were unexpected and thus all the more potent testimony to the power of the Christian God. It is far less surprising, for example, that the mature Alexander steps forward voluntarily to confess his Christianity, as depicted in the *Letter of the Martyrs of Vienne and Lyons* than that the fifteen-year-old boy Ponticus has the courage to face torture without wavering. It is less surprising too, perhaps, that the adult ascetic Antony persevered in his fights with the demons than that, already as a young boy, he eschewed dainty foods or other material comforts, as well as the pleasures of sociality.

Turning from the young to the elderly, we note that widows held a significant, albeit distinctly ambiguous position in early Christian communities. Privileged recipients of charity within Christianity as within Judaism, they also appear to have exercised quasi-clerical authority in many communities. In addition, there is frequently a blurring of distinctions in our sources between women who were widowed and those who actively chose

a life of celibacy, whether by avoiding or leaving marriages—a fact that further challenges any view of Christian widows as simply recipients of charity. Older men were not typically marked with similar vulnerability but rather profited from their venerability as communal elders—as is indicated by the term "presbyter" or "elder," which is among the earliest titles of ecclesial office. Nonetheless, there are indications that elderly men, as well as women, could be viewed with a certain tender compassion by their Christian communities. One thinks, for example, of the eighty-six-year-old bishop Polycarp of Smyrna, represented as bruising his shin and fumbling awkwardly with his shoes in the course of his martyrdom, or of the frail ninety-year-old Pothinus of Lyons, who did not survive the tortures of prison life to make his witness in the arena. Overall, we detect within ancient Christianity many signs of the poignant attraction and resultant authority exerted by figures of vulnerability—women, children, the elderly. Such sensibilities in the ancient sources provide a fertile resource for a people's history.

LAY STATUS

"Laity" is the traditional technical term by which ancient Christians themselves named the people, thereby setting up a contrast between the people and the clergy. However, the progressive clarification, elaboration, and intensification of clerical authority, tightly linked with both the protection of doctrinal orthodoxy and the restriction of sacramental powers, emerged more gradually and unevenly than is usually imagined. In addition, and still more significant, clerical authority remained haunted by competing claims to authority at or beyond the margins of the institutional hierarchy. As is typical of emerging sectarian movements, earliest Christianity accommodated a complex ecology of authority and power, encompassing diverse models of organization and participation, some more centralized and others more diffuse. All appealed to charismatic authority, and disputes over leadership and authenticity were intense; in the early centuries, the roles of bishops, teachers, presbyters, prophets, martyrs, and others often overlapped. The earlier uses of terms like "holy ones" or "people" were, more-over, not markers of difference between clergy and laity but inclusive terms for the community as the people of God.

The very fact that bishops found it necessary throughout the ancient period to ally themselves with the social authority of more charismatic figures highlights the continuing ambiguity that characterized the distinc-tion between clergy and laity. Ignatius of Antioch, frequently (but perhaps misleadingly) hailed as the first bishop, could only persuade his early second-century audience of his authority by speaking in the "loud voice" of a prophet (his words, tellingly: "obey the bishop!") and making the most of his status as a soon-to-be martyr. The distinction between the laity and the order of the clergy only emerged forcefully in the third century with the consolidation of the office of the monarchial bishop. Nonetheless, in the fourth century Bishop Athanasius of Alexandria (to take only one exam-ple) was still marshaling the same resources as Ignatius in order to buttress his own episcopal authority. He represented himself, via his disputes with heretical opponents and their imperial backers, as a persecuted martyr for orthodoxy while borrowing the aura of sanctity of desert holy men like the ascetic Antony, a participant in what was a popular lay movement in its origins. To Roman eyes, the combination of a permanent elected office and the undergirding of that office by charismatic authority made bishops an odd social phenomenon. Furthermore, aristocratic men were not used to mixing with women or lower-status people on any sort of equal terms, and the frequency of conflict in fourth-century Christian communities in part reflects the clash of religious and social customs and ideals. The efforts of well-educated bishops such as Ambrose and Augustine to incorporate popular practices into official worship and to integrate ascetic women and other powerful members of the laity into ecclesial life exemplify the ideal of the spiritual unity of the community as well as the shrewd leadership exercised within a socially diverse movement.

When we turn our attention away from issues of leadership to matters of practice, both the limits of clerical authority and the blurring of bound-aries between clergy and laity become still more evident. Private prayer, love feasts, saints' cults, practices of menstrual purity, icon veneration, magical rites, ascetic disciplines—thus unfurls the expansive realm of lay piety, largely uncontrolled by the clergy yet always interfacing with the realm of official liturgy and the concerns of institutional leadership. The point is not merely that the clergy's ability to impose discipline on extra-ecclesial ritual was limited—though clearly it was—but that the lived expe-rience of Christian communities gave rise to a diversity of religious practices that spanned the boundaries between ecclesial and extra-ecclesial realms, even as the public and private arenas of ritual performance overlapped and bled into each other at multiple points. One cannot, in other words, make easy distinctions between official liturgy and popular cult. Even baptism might be administered by a layperson, as Jensen's treatment of Tertullian reminds us. Cultic meals were a still more mobile and malleable phenomenon, taking place not only on the bishop's altar but at the tombs of martyr saints and in the homes of Christians (sometimes, but not always, utilizing elements sanctified at the bishop's altar), as discussed by McGowan, Bowes, and Trout. Relics, and the rites and miracles associated with them, might similarly be found under the altar, in saints' shrines, in homes or private chapels, preserved in small caskets or bottles, or worn as a protective amulet around the neck, as Bowes, Frankfurter, Horn, Trout, and Young all demonstrate. The efficacious magic of words might be accessed by priests in the official liturgy or by a holy man or woman appealed to for help with a specific problem, as Frankfurter shows. And the empowering life of ascetic discipline described by Clark was equally accessible to a bishop, whose authority would be thereby enhanced, and to an uneducated monk or nun.

Lay piety opens an extremely important window onto the history of the Christian people, and it is no accident that many of the chapters in this volume deal, in one way or another, with this phenomenon. At the same time, it must be acknowledged that in late antiquity, if not also in other periods of Christian history, the notion of a realm of religious practice that is separate from or simply outside the institutional church is as untenable as is the notion of a realm of popular religion that is distinct from or even opposed to the religion of the elite. Despite the many instances and indicators of clerical disapproval of certain extra-ecclesial rites, detailed in Frankfurter's explorations of language censuring popular ritual, bishops and aristocrats were as likely to participate in saints' festivals or traffic in relics as were the common people. Laity and leaders alike were caught up in the complex choreography of processions, festivals, cultic meals, and other performative rites that established the distinct rhythms of time and mappings of space that structured Christian identity in late antiquity.

ETHNICITY

From the command of the risen Jesus to the disciples to go to all nations and baptize all people (Matt. 28:19) to the descent of the Spirit manifested in the varied tongues of the Jewish diaspora (Acts 2), the earliest Christians claimed to embrace all places and peoples. In antiquity one's *ethnos* or "race" was an essential marker of culture and religion as well as regional identity, so that the Christian rejection of traditional ethnic identity or its replacement by the concept of an inclusive third race was a way to declare this religion universal, thereby erasing such social or geographical boundaries. To a great degree this claim was realized, as Christianity spread rapidly throughout the culturally diverse cities and towns of the Roman Empire and beyond to regions such as India. The traffic and dialogue between cultures that was already mobilized by the empire was intensified in local Christian communities that ascribed to the ideal of ethnic inclusiveness while also understanding themselves as participating more broadly in a universal church that incorporated still greater differences.

At the same time, ethnic distinctions inevitably persisted, as is evidenced in the rich variety of forms Christianity took in different locales. In addition, the dynamics of power as well as the specific polemics invoked in situations of conflict reflected contemporary ethnic categories and prejudices, many of which were tied to the power of the literary and political elite. The Greek speakers, and later also the Latin speakers, living in the urban centers of the empire claimed the authoritative voice of an ecumenical Christianity, whereas Christians in more remote or rural sites were correspondingly marginalized or even, on occasion, viewed with suspicion. As was the case with gender or class status, the ancient Christian redefinition and negotiation of ethnic identity preserved the tension between the reach for a radically egalitarian inclusiveness and the stubborn tug of hierarchical distinctions.

Historically, "barbarian" was a Greek category of denigration that applied to all non-Greek speakers, and thus the term carries an assertion of cultural superiority on behalf of Greeks. However, the extension of Greek language and culture around the eastern Mediterranean under Alexander the Great (fourth century BCE) and his successors had long since created complex fusions of local (or "barbarian") cultures and Hellenic ideals in such regions as Egypt, Syria, and Palestine. At the same time, non-Greek cultures exerted a particular attraction for their Greek colonizers: Egypt was especially alluring because of its venerable antiquity, as was Judaism. As these Mediterranean areas subsequently became subject to Roman power, another layer of imported culture and politics was added to the mix. Religiously, therefore, people of the Roman Mediterranean inhabited a rich and eclectic world of local and regional traditions while also enjoying varied degrees of access to and acceptance of broader, universalizing political, philosophical, and cultic affiliations. Cities in particular offered a display of Greek ideals visible in architecture or social institutions like the gymnasium, layered over and blended with prior, non-Greek cultural values and practices. The extent of Hellenization in the countryside was uneven and must be carefully examined with reference to particular cases. Some religious cults remained highly local, if also often extremely eclectic. Others were both more mobile and more explicitly universalizing, such as the cult of Isis, which drew on the cultural authority of ancient Egypt while claiming that its goddess—who was worshipped in Rome and Carthage as well as Alexandria—represented the sum of all local deities and powers. Thus ethnicity was an essential and pervasive aspect of identity in late antiquity, yet scarcely simple or stable.

As Christianity, like the Isis cult, spread through the towns and cities of the Mediterranean, communal debates and disputes reflected the tensions arising out of such complexly layered and continuously negotiated ethnic identities. Judaism in the first centuries was a widely respected ancient *ethnos;* notable for its exclusivity, it also accommodated aspects of cultural adaptation and mission activity. The emergence of Christianity is therefore an extension of the adaptive development of Jewish identity in late antiquity. Outside observers initially understood early Christians as part of the Jewish *ethnos,* as did many Christians themselves. The canonical book of Acts preserves a narrative in which Paul's controversial vision of a radically universalizing Judaism includes Gentiles (that is, non-Jews) without the requirements of circumcision or observance of traditional dietary laws. This perspective is echoed in Paul's letters, such as that to the Galatians, which states explicitly, "In Christ there is no longer male or female, Jew or Greek, slave or free" (3:28). The ethnically mixed communities of Christians, including both Jews and a variety of non-Jewish ethnicities, were in conflict with other communities that continued to observe traditional Jewish practices. Such conflicts continued, moreover, well into the fourth century, as Fonrobert demonstrates. As Christianity and Judaism developed more separate identities, the emerging requirement of rabbinic Judaism for matrilineal descent may reflect a reaction to the inclusive Christian practices of conversion and baptism.

Geographical mobility enabled by the empire simultaneously disrupted and intensified the significance of a shared ethnic identity, and this is powerfully reflected in the early history of Christianity. The earliest mission communities took root in ethnically distinct sections of urban centers, so that the first Christians in the predominantly Latin-speaking city of Lyons, for example, were Greek speakers with strong ties to Asia Minor. In Rome, Christian teachers arrived from all parts of the empire, including Alexandria, Pontus, and Palestine, and their ethnic origins remained a significant part of their identity, even as they participated in a shared Hellenistic rhetorical and philosophical culture. However, when asked to divulge their political status or ethnic background in the context of persecution, Christians would typically refuse, declaring instead their new identity: "I am a Christian." The *Epistle to Diognetus* notes that to Christians "every foreign land is a homeland, every homeland a foreign land." Some Christians defined themselves as a third race distinct from either Hellenism or Judaism. The Syrian author Tatian claimed the Greeks had in fact stolen their culture from the barbarians and that Christians represented the original wisdom that underlay these barbarian cultures.

If such universalism was appealing, tensions between localities, as well as between different ethnic groups within a given locale, also frequently surfaced, as in the debate regarding the difference in calculations for the date of Easter in Rome and Asia Minor. Polemical categories invoked by ancient Christians also reflected common patterns of ethnic competition and insult, as revealed, for example, in the depiction of the controversial Christian leader Marcion as a gloomy teacher from Pontus, of the Montanists of Asia Minor as rural "hicks," or of the Ethiopians as culturally marginal and dark with sin. Such evidence calls attention not only to the geographical diversity and inclusiveness of the communities but also to the vulnerability of members to the prejudices and polemics of mainstream society during conflicts.

With the establishment of the imperial church in the fourth century, the role of ethnicity in Christian communities shifted. The voices of the rural communities began to emerge in indigenous Christian literature in Coptic and Syriac as Christianity spread slowly into the countryside. Monastic literature often represents these voices. The relation of the urban leaders to such local traditions and identity was extremely important. Increasingly, the social status of church leaders rose so that they were often part of the provincial elite who received Hellenic education or *paideia* while also retaining their local identities, the traces of which could produce tension or even embarrassment. Augustine, for example, worried about his African accent when he went to Italy to seek his fortune as a rhetorician. When Gregory of Nazianzus became bishop of Constantinople, he was ridiculed by the crowd for his provincial dress and manner, even though he had been educated in Athens. Athanasius was the first Alexandrian bishop whom we know to have preached in Coptic as well as Greek; John Chrysostom preached in both Greek and Syriac. Urban leaders therefore were often the slender bridge between the empire-wide ecclesiastical community and the local congregations and Christian cultures of their regions.

The continual doctrinal debates of the fourth and fifth centuries likewise reflected aspects of emerging ethnic and regional diversity within late ancient Christianity. Part of Bishop Athanasius's passion to enforce the Nicene Creed during the so-called Arian controversy was fueled by his desire to preserve the orthodox credentials of his episcopal predecessor Alexander in the context of the Alexandrian church. Other places and people properly claimed not to be a part of this doctrinal fight between an Alexandrian bishop and his presbyter Arius, but their local dispute was eventually judged by the ecumenical councils and the universal creeds and canons that they produced. The interaction between local and translocal theaters of debate and adjudication meant not only that regional pieties could be disciplined by the decisions of bishops from elsewhere but also that labels of heresy could be dislodged from their original contexts and used to discredit Christians who had no relation at all to the beliefs and practices initially targeted by such labels.

Thus, Ambrose of Milan accused certain Western bishops of Arianism and named others "Egyptian heretics." The Donatist controversy reflected even more clearly the tension between regional or ethnic Christianities and widespread desires to institutionalize a catholic or ecumenical orthodoxy that would encompass all Christians. In the course of bitter and sustained conflict between Christians rooted in traditional North African piety and those more influenced by Roman theology and practice, the North African traditionalists mocked their opponents as Romans, implying that they were both persecutors and foreigners. The split of the Eastern church between Chalcedonian and Monophysite parties, as well as the eventual split of the Western church from the Eastern churches, was again tied to regional cultures, genealogies, and loyalties that appeared to be compromised by imperially backed theological legislation. The strength of local ethnic identity and tradition is furthermore evident in the autocephalous, or institutionally independent, churches of Eastern Orthodoxy, which continue to be defined by separate languages and regions, if also bound together by doctrinal definitions. The spur to a lasting universal orthodoxy ironically mirrors the realities of local diversity.

Ancient Christianity therefore always located itself in the tension between the lived religion of local cultures and the universalizing, transethnic aspirations of believers. By late antiquity, however, the Christianization of the countryside, where highly dynamic localized cultures flourished, as Frankfurter shows, combined with heightened pressures to conform to a universalizing imperial church, producing both an intensification and an increased visibility of ethnic and regional differences in the churches. With the erosion of Roman imperial power, much of the institutional infrastructure of an ecumenical church likewise disintegrated, even as ethnic differences increased. Nonetheless, the ideal of unity and universalism was never abandoned: in the medieval and Byzantine periods, as in the Roman era, Christian identity would rest on the particular, local interpretations of a common gospel issuing from a variety of places, cultures, and linguistic traditions.

ORTHODOXY AND HETERODOXY

Does "orthodoxy" include the voice of the people? As we have already seen, ancient orthodoxy did indeed claim to represent the doctrinal voice of *all* Christians, articulated through the legislation of clergy and other elites. As the congregants of their institutional leaders, the people, therefore, are assumed to be included in and protected by the voices of those traditionally designated the fathers of the ancient church. Yet there is a problematic circularity attending any definition of "the people" in which the only people who count are those already counted among the faithful—that is, those who are within a community limited and defined in advance by its agreement with the definitions of the authorized leaders. By opening the view to embrace a larger population and realm of practices as Christian, we are here shifting the criteria invoked to identify Christians and thus to evaluate and interpret the historical practices and beliefs of an ancient people of faith.

The earliest Christian communities included a variety of voices and testimonies as preserved in the numerous gospels, letters, and other writings of the first two centuries of Christian history. These documents include references to charismatic practices accessible to all members of the communities, such as healing or speaking in tongues. Spiritual discernment in relation to these often controversial gifts frequently focused on ideals of unity: were they offensive to some members of the community, even if otherwise lawful or appropriate? Theological questions such as those addressing the physical resurrection of Jesus, as discussed by Perkins, were also used as measures of identity and unity, but no central authority or source of definitions existed. Thus, in the Epistles of John, members are advised to test travelers before offering hospitality; presumably those rejected found another more welcoming community. Given the popular level and appeal of much early Christian literature, which included tales of miracle-working apostles, riveting accounts of "witnessing" deaths, and collections of pithy and repeatable wise sayings, together with the ethnic, class, and gender diversity of characters represented therein, we can infer the presence of wide and varied audiences. The charismatic basis of the early Christian communities as well as their geographical and cultural diversity encouraged both theological breadth and internal controversy, as is already evident in Paul's letters, the earliest surviving literary witnesses to ancient Christianity.

In the second century, leaders like Irenaeus and Tertullian began to argue for the existence of an orthodoxy that was articulated in a rule of faith representing the universal and apostolic teaching of the gospel purportedly discoverable in every authentic Christian community. They asserted that this shared faith was not merely the creation of the leaders but also the voice of the people: even those who were not literate, they claimed, could both recite and affirm the foundational beliefs in God as creator and Jesus as divine. The identity and stability of the community rested on corporate faithfulness to these beliefs, though the guaranteed authenticity of teachers now located in the succession of bishops ensured the continuity of Christian faith. These early manifestos on behalf of orthodoxy were issued in response to competing teachers, especially the so-called Gnostics, who were considered to be innovative and elite and who diverged from traditional doctrines and met separately from the apostolic churches.

Given that our map of heterodoxy is provided by polemical literature written by elites, it is extremely difficult to judge the popularity of theological movements as they were once encountered on the ground. How many people, and what manner of people, adhered to gnostic rather than orthodox beliefs? Would the differences between the two have been apparent to most? Such questions are not easy to answer. A rule traditionally invoked for identifying popularly affirmed piety is *lex orandi, lex credendi,* meaning "the rule of prayer is the rule of belief." However, the matter is not so simple: the pressure for a rule of faith was exerted precisely because even those participating in a shared liturgy could do so with differing theological understandings. Moreover, the fine, albeit significant, distinctions of theological debate are quite difficult to discern in the recorded confessions of the martyrs or the preserved prayers and epitaphs of early Christians.

In the first three centuries Christian practice and belief remained therefore local and subject to the authority acknowledged within a particular community. Authors circulated letters to advise about dangerous opinions or teachers, but orthodoxy was enforced only by local leaders. Controversial individuals such as Origen of Alexandria could simply move. Although his own bishop condemned him, neighboring bishops welcomed and even ordained Origen as a revered teacher and exegete. Tertullian in North Africa reflected both a strong defense against heresy and a willingness to debate controversial questions with clerical authorities. As late as the third century, Dionysius of Alexandria reported that a longstanding lay member of his community had only recently realized that he had been baptized in a heretical group. When a synod of bishops condemned Paul, a popular bishop of Antioch, he refused to give up his church and, presumably because of his congregation's support, could only be put out by a change in imperial authority. Christian leaders and people therefore operated on a map of diverse, and often diverging, beliefs and practices.

The fourth-century emergence of imperial councils to define and enforce doctrinal consensus gradually changed this diffuse orthodoxy. Fragile literary networks of agreement now could acquire the backing of imperial enforcement, with the result that bishops vied with one another to convince the emperor of their orthodoxy—as well as to persuade the emperor of what version of Christianity should be upheld as orthodoxy. Emperor Constantius could be David or the Antichrist to Athanasius, depending on his agreement with the Nicene formula. Legislatively and rhetorically articulated, imperial orthodoxy created a map of identity that eventually labeled all other ancient religions as well as varied theological errors "heresy." The function of such exhaustive cataloging and enforcement was to stabilize and exclude whatever was outside the hard-won consensus of Christian truth. The result was labels that could be applied pejoratively to any suspect theology or practice and therefore subject such beliefs or rites to ecclesiastical control or political discipline. Cyril of Alexandria could thereby, for example, release the laity of Constantinople from obedience to their bishop Nestorius, on the grounds that his Antiochene Christology was really adoptionist heresy. Ascetic women were particularly vulnerable to charges of Gnosticism or Manichaeism, as prior polemics against heretical women were invoked and intensified. Many traditionalists in the fourth century found themselves labeled "Arians" because of their subordinationist Christologies. If heresy was now made a matter of public security for the imperial church, orthodoxy thrived less by the articulation of clarity at the center than by the proscription of error at the edges.

This new centralization of authority still functioned in tension with and by consent of local communities and leaders. We have evidence of public demonstrations and debates around doctrinal issues, as would be usual in antiquity. Whether the resulting acclamations of consensus were spontaneous or orchestrated is difficult to judge, though it is clear that clerical and doctrinal authority rested to a great degree on popular acceptance. Ambrose wrote hymns to encourage his congregation to resist Arians in Milan. Theophilus of Alexandria changed his theological position on the image of God when confronted by hundreds of monks who flooded in from the desert. Donatists in North Africa celebrated martyrs who would not submit to imperial orthodoxy. The people of Alexandria lynched a bishop who had signed an imperial creed that they felt compromised their local theology. The Monophysite churches embraced the Nicene Creed liturgically as a means of rejecting the decisions of the council of Chalcedon. Ancient orthodoxy therefore was a public and contested matter, which only allowed enforcement if the local bishop had the consent of the populace.

Nestorius alienated the emperor and factions within Constantinople by his attempts to enforce orthodoxy in the city and thus ended up exiled as a heretic himself. Yet how successfully such power reached into private space remains debatable. The regulation of private reading by Athanasius and the later condemnations of Priscillian's use of the Apocrypha were attempts to create an orthodox practice, as was the emphasis on public liturgy as opposed to private ritual. Yet, as Augustine warned a colleague, all theological mistakes are not heresy: thus we see a curious hierarchy of doctrinal unity defended by leaders who acknowledge a diversity and popular practice beneath. The language of orthodoxy was an essential marker of identity, but it often remained a prescriptive rather than a descriptive religious dialect.

CONCLUSIONS: WHAT IS A PEOPLE'S HISTORY OF CHRISTIANITY?

Traditionally, ancient Christianity has been approached as either a religious institution or a doctrinal orthodoxy defined by the tension between a center and its unruly margins. A people's history, in contrast, invites us to view Christianity in the Roman period as the complex social and cultural product of multiple, dynamic local communities of practicing believers linked to one another (sometimes very tenuously indeed) by long-standing habits of communication and communion undergirded by ideals of universality and unity. These ideals, of course, simultaneously criticized, competed with, and imitated the ambition of the Roman Empire itself to conquer the world and thereby constitute an ecumenical society. The dialectic of diversity and unity mobilized by the Christianity of the Roman Empire entailed both an ongoing, even restless process of communal self-definition and a near-constant shifting of boundaries of identity that together account for much of the vitality and creativity, as well as the staying power, of the movement.

Attention to the factor of social class allows us to acknowledge the variety of ways that Christianity effectively subverted elite privilege and imperial authority, even in the post-Constantinian period; ancient Christianity may thus be seen as a broadly popular and democratizing movement. Yet we also cannot overlook the ways in which Christian communities actively embraced imperial patronage and affirmed class privilege while generating their own class distinctions along a variety of gradients, including ranks of church office and attributions of holiness. Perhaps the most notable characteristic of ancient Christian communities, from such a social perspective, is the instability and flexibility of social hierarchies, rather than their absence. Similarly, attention to factors of gender or age does not so much produce a picture of Christianity as a movement of women, children, and the elderly—or alternately, as a movement in which distinctions of gender or age did not matter—as allow us to appreciate the ways in which flexibility was introduced.

At first glance, one of the areas of relative *in*flexibility within ancient Christianity is exposed by the incessant clerical monitoring of doctrine and liturgy, best exemplified by the institution of the ecumenical council. Yet, here too, focus on local communities—and we should not forget that there is no Christianity that is *not* embedded in a local community, whether urban or rural—betrays the vast diversity and ongoing malleability of practices of piety as well as articulations of belief only loosely woven into the fabric of a unified, ecumenical church. If certain practices and beliefs were periodically excised via disciplinary processes, frequently by being branded either "pagan" or "Judaizing," these heresies not only left their traces on the patterning of orthodoxy but also often persisted in private pockets of worship and communal life, sometimes reconverging subsequently with the broader church. As antiquity neared its end, with the waning of the power of the Roman Empire, regional Christianities shaped by ethnic and linguistic differences and divided by political boundaries began to diverge further, even as the ideal of Christian universalism or ecumenicity was never relinquished. The spontaneous emergence of distinctive Syrian, Armenian, Coptic, Gallic, and Celtic traditions, for example, only heightens our awareness of the ways in which ancient Christianity had always manifested itself as and in the interweaving of multiple, differentiated local practices arising at the borders of religious and cultural exchange.

A people's history is not, finally, an optional addition or supplement to traditional histories of the church that emphasize doctrinal, liturgical, or institutional unity and stability. Rather, it contributes to a thoroughgoing revision of our understanding of late ancient Christianity as a whole.

HIERARCHY
AND SUBVERSION

Part 1

Late Ancient Christianity

ASCETICISM, CLASS, AND GENDER

ELIZABETH A. CLARK

By late antiquity, asceticism was a popular option for Christians, admired and idealized even by those who themselves did not choose a life of renunciation. But was it a movement of "the people"? Yes and no. Some decades ago, Ramsay MacMullen put forward three criteria for determining high social status in the Roman Empire: "the farther back ..., the more ..., the closer to Rome," that is, the antiquity of one's ancestors, the extent of one's wealth, and one's proximity to the distinguished city of choice.[1] What, by contrast, might constitute the defining characteristics of "the people?" Often cited are the necessity to work for a living, especially by manual labor (those falling in this category are deemed "the poor"),[2] and lack of literacy in Greek or Latin. Christian asceticism, I argue, complicated these differentiations. As a result, class distinctions produced and maintained by Roman society were partly leveled by a renunciation that was open to the common people, laborers, the poor, and the illiterate, as well as to men and women of privilege. Yet, paradoxically, ascetic practice also created a new elite within Christianity. Exploring the complex interaction between worldly and ascetic status, with special attention to the different positionings of female and male ascetics in relation to social class, will be the task of this chapter.

At the outset we should note that some scholars dispute whether the term "class" can truly be applied to ancient Roman society. In an era in which labor remained uncommodified, in which the use of money was "unproductive," and in which surplus value was extracted from workers by pressures other than monetary ones, should the relations of production be described as economic? Marxist historian Geoffrey de Ste. Croix has argued that if "class" is defined primarily as "the collective social expression of the fact of exploitation (and of course of resistance to it),"[3] then the term fits societies in which the relations of production differ from those of capitalism. Others, perhaps wishing to sidestep the Marxist framework, opt for the softer concept of "status." I will refer to "class" and "status" in this looser sense.

Christianity itself (whether in more ascetic or less ascetic forms) complicated the usual status markers of Roman society. In this, it drew inspiration from its central theological confession: if God had lowered himself to become human, then humble abasement received divine sanction. The apostle Paul taught that Jesus, though "in the form of God, did not regard equality with God as something to be exploited, but emptied himself, taking the form of a slave" (Phil. 2:6-7). Likewise, Jesus promised that "the poor" (or "the poor in spirit") would inherit the kingdom of heaven (Luke 6:20; Matt. 5:3). And had not Jesus chosen Palestinian fishermen rather than Roman senators as his disciples (Augustine, *Sermon* 87.10.12)? Moreover, the presence of women among Jesus' followers could be taken as a sign of his condescension to the lowly (Jerome, *Ep.* 127.5). The church fathers often appealed to this blessing on the humble when faced with hostile critics who construed Christianity's esteem for the lowly as a sign of moral degeneracy (for example, Origen, *Celsus* 1.27; 3.44), countering that Christianity improved the morals of even the most disreputable (Origen, *Celsus* 1.9; 1.26; 3.56; Athenagoras, *Apol.* 12; cf. 32–33). Nobility of ancestry, wealth, and residence in Rome counted—in theory—for nothing in the new Christian dispensation.

The poor indeed played an important role in Christian practice and discourse: according to some church fathers, their essential function was to pray for the salvation of their better-off benefactors.[4] Giving to the poor enabled the rich to "wash away" their post-baptismal sin (Cyprian, *On Works* 1–2). Some went beyond advocating charity and endorsed (at least in their rhetoric) a form of "primitive communism," teaching that at the time of humans' creation God had intended the world's goods to be shared in common; private property, of which some now claimed a disproportionate share, constituted in itself a form of injustice (Cyprian, *On Works* 25; Gregory Nazianzus, *On Love* 14.25; John Chrysostom, *To the People* 2.6, *Hom. John* 15.3, *Hom. 1 Tim.* 12.4; compare Lactantius, *Div. Inst.* 5.5).

Bishops sharply denounced the arrogant rich in sermons, painting graphic portraits of the lot of the suffering poor. Basil of Caesarea, for example, writing in the later fourth century, describes the plight of a poor man who in his wretchedness contemplates which son to sell first. In Basil's heartrending depiction, the man asks himself, "Can I become as brutish as the beasts? Can I forget nature? If I try to keep all of them, I envision them all perishing with hunger. If I sacrifice one, how can I look at the others?" In scathing terms, Basil pictures the wretched man offering his own flesh and blood in order to live, while "you"—the rich hearer of this sermon—

haggle about the price, trying to buy the dearly beloved son for less (*Hom. "I Will Pull Down My Barns"* 4; see also Chrysostom, *Hom. 1 Cor.* 11.5). Christian writers of still more radical opinion (such as the author of an anonymous treatise *On Riches*) argued that since nothing unjust comes from God and that common property was the original state at creation, the acquisition of riches is necessarily sinful. In this line of argument, poverty exists only because some are rich. If God at the time of creation had meant for there to be an unequal distribution of the world's goods, he would not have given the air, the sunlight, the rain, the moon, and the stars for the benefit of all creatures (8–9, 12).

Despite their praise of humility and lowliness and their advocacy of economic justice, early Christian writers also (and somewhat contradictorily) attempted to claim the powerful, wealthy, and well-educated as a sign of the religion's success in proselytizing. As William Countryman has detailed, ecclesiastical leaders depended on the rich to support the extensive charity operations of the church; without them, the church could not fulfill its mission.[5] Simultaneous claims on the poor *and* the rich coexisted in some tension in early Christian discourse.

Like wealth, literacy was rendered more complex in its function as a status marker because Christians who were not literate in Latin or Greek (though perhaps able to read in a local language, such as Coptic) often knew considerable portions of scripture: a biblical culture could be shared even among those who could not read and write.[6] Given the prevalence

Fig. 1.1. Although few in antiquity could afford the privilege of a formal education, even illiterate Christians could listen to Scripture or tales of martyrs and saints being read aloud. This stele, dating from the 2nd or 3rd centuries CE, portrays a teacher and two pupils. Rheinisches Landesmuseum, Trier, Germany. Photo credit: Erich Lessing / Art Resource, NY.

of reading out loud in antiquity, the technically illiterate might participate to a limited extent in a book culture. "Low" literature (such as the New Testament itself and later martyr tales and hagiographies) could be consumed by people of all social levels and could serve as an equalizing factor among Christians in a way that complex theological treatises might not.[7]

Christianity in general, then—in its theology, its ethics, its worship, and its practice—unsettled ancient Roman status markers. Asceticism, we shall see, did so even more.

ASCETICISM AND STATUS IN THE ROMAN WORLD

Askesis had a long heritage before the advent of Christianity. Originally signaling the physical discipline undertaken by athletes, its meaning expanded to include the discipline of self-restraint that any "rational man" might strive to practice.[8] In Christian usage, however, ascetic renunciation was not understood as a means of personal enhancement or a route to mental equanimity, but as a way to bring the devotee closer to God. Correct motivation was necessary if ascetic renunciation was to be lauded; non-Christians who "renounced" would receive no reward (Clement of Alexandria, *Strom.* 3.1.1; 3.1.4; 3.3.24; 3.6.48; 3.6.50; 3.7.60). Although older textbooks often describe early Christian asceticism in dualistic terms—soul versus body—this understanding runs counter to the affirmations of ascetics themselves as well as to their more recent interpreters: despite the temptations that bodily desires might pose, soul and body were taken to interact mutually, bodily discipline serving to strengthen the soul.

What did early Christian ascetics renounce? The typical focus on their renunciation of marriage, sex, and reproduction is one-sided. Ascetic devotees renounced money, property, and possessions, curtailed their intake of food and drink, and restricted the amount and manner of sleep; more important, they struggled against the intangible vices of anger, avarice, sloth, vainglory, and pride. Contact with the secular world was to be avoided—a difficult feat for those ascetics whose labors brought them into close association with worldly people. In extreme forms of asceticism, restriction of bodily movement (by standing on pillars, confining oneself within cramped spaces, or covering oneself with heavy iron chains) was deemed by some a sign of special devotion, as were practices such as homelessness (in imitation of Jesus), not cutting one's hair and nails, roaming naked like the wild animals, or inflicting pain upon oneself to curtail desire.[9]

The wide variety of literary genres promoting or defending ascetic practice testifies to its importance in early Christianity: in addition to New

Testament injunctions (found especially in the Gospels and Paul's letters), there are theological and ethical treatises, hagiographies, monastic rules, letters, sermons, and decrees of church councils. Important for this chapter's discussion are the *Lausiac History,* the *Sayings of the Desert Fathers,* the *History of the Monks of Egypt,* various early monastic *Rules,* hagiographies of important renunciants, and letters and sermons by various early Christian writers.

Scholarship on early Christian asceticism in recent decades has stressed the geographical specificity of its practices.[10] Sources pertaining to early Egyptian monasticism claim that the earliest form of asceticism in Egypt involved an individual's retreat to the desert: Antony's renunciation in the late third century provided a pattern for monks who came to reside at Scetis, Nitria, and "the Cells," even though the *Life of Antony* itself makes clear that Antony was not the first to adopt the hermit life (3). Several decades after Antony's ascetic profession, communal monasteries were formed in Egypt under the leadership of Pachomius and his followers.

In Syria, single ascetics often practiced their renunciatory devotion within the structures of church life, while in Palestine, solitaries might live alone in caves but engage with other ascetics in communal worship and food production. By contrast, urban ascetics might live either in their own houses or in communal settings in the midst of city life. Sometimes a male and a female ascetic (or groups of such) would reside together—a flourishing practice that was roundly condemned by church authorities throughout the patristic and medieval periods. Climactic and geographical conditions also influenced what was deemed appropriate for ascetic living: Upper Egypt and Gaul, for example, necessitated different practices regarding clothing, food, and work (Cassian, *Institutes* 1.10). But wherever and however renunciation was undertaken, the desire to shape a life of more perfect devotion to God lay at the heart of Christian ascetic practice.

Ascetic practice tended overall to strengthen the Christian notion of "leveling." Christian ascetics claimed that they were imitating the virtuous form of life practiced by the early Christians in Jerusalem, who, according to Acts 2, 4, and 5, shared their possessions (see Athanasius, *Life of Ant.* 2; Basil of Caesarea, *Longer Rules* 7, 32; John Cassian, *Institutes* 7.19; *Conferences* 12.2; 18.5-6; 21.30; John Chrysostom, *Hom. Acts* 11). In a monastic community no one was to deem himself or herself better than others on the basis of social status, wealth, or place of origin. Numerous tales signal the rebuke of ascetics who imagined themselves of superior holiness (for example, Jerome, *Life of Paul* 7; Palladius, *Laus. Hist.* 34). Ecclesiastical leaders frequently held up renunciants as models to shame the laity, who were chided for not "giving more" (Cyprian, *On Works* 18–19). Yet here lay spiritual danger: the sheer fact of renouncing family and possessions, which enabled ascetics to manifest their sacrificial devotion more fully than married laypeople, might encourage pride.

Indeed, the attempt to create for oneself a more perfect life militated against the ascetic's striving for lowliness and humility: Christian asceticism, by definition an attempt to mark oneself off from *hoi polloi,* carried the danger of promoting pride. Émile Durkheim, reflecting on the role of abstinence and interdiction in religion ("the negative cult"), argued that the "excessive disdain" that ascetics show for all that ordinary people treasure is necessary if the general populace is to be encouraged to recoil from "an easy life and common pleasure": "it is necessary that an elite put the end too high, if the crowd is not to put it too low. It is necessary that some exaggerate, if the average is to remain at a fitting level."[11] When thousands of lukewarm converts flocked to the church after the cessation of the persecutions in the early fourth century, ascetic rigor might have distinguished a more ardent Christian from this mass. Thus the fourth-century ascetic enthusiast Jerome famously wrote to the adolescent devotee Eustochium, who had recently renounced, "learn from me a holy arrogance: you are better than they" (*Ep.* 22.16). Asceticism's promotion of "distinction" could run up against its command of lowliness.

Another complicating factor concerns the exchange of kinds of capital that asceticism encouraged: wealthy aristocrats who became ascetics retained their status capital in terms of influence (and sometimes portions of their real money as well) but acquired as surplus the symbolic capital that Christians bestowed on ascetic virtuosi. Ascetics from lower social backgrounds could also acquire symbolic capital, although for them it was not a matter of exchange or of surplus, but of simple acquisition. Here, Geoffrey Galt Harpham's witticism that asceticism's structure of investment and reward might be defined as "capitalism without money" seems appropriate.[12]

In addition, MacMullen's status criterion of "how close to Rome" was complicated when high-status aristocrats *left* Rome (and Alexandria, Constantinople, and so forth) to practice ascetic renunciation in deserted areas in a manner that dramatically exceeded the customary aristocratic quest for *otium,* or "leisure." The highly international character of late ancient Christian asceticism suggests that devotees sought out monasteries or ascetic companions in places far removed from the prestigious cities—a fact further encouraged by Roman aristocrats' flight from Rome at the time of the Goths' sack of the city in 410 CE (see *Life of Mel.* 19–20, 34–35). The desert itself could become a city, ascetic enthusiasts claimed (*Life of Ant.* 14).

Still another form of leveling attended Christian asceticism: ascetic practitioners were enjoined to work with their hands (a marker of lowly social status) whether as an economic necessity, to support themselves or their communities, or as a sign of their deep humility. Ascetic devotees of the upper classes were exhorted to engage in manual labor along with those for whom such work would have been their necessary lot in the larger world. We shall see below numerous examples of this attempt at leveling.

Nevertheless, we should question the extent to which asceticism succeeded in breaking down the status barriers of late antiquity. Despite the fact that asceticism could be considered a "career open to talents,"[13] Christian writers lavish praise on the "high" who become "low" (such renunciants receive disproportionate attention in hagiographical literature), but they also manifest considerable anxiety that the "low" who adopt the ascetic life might inappropriately claim a newfound superiority. Despite Paul's injunction in Gal. 3:28, the distinctions between "slave and free" and between "male and female" were only partially erased.

MALE ASCETICS AND SOCIAL CLASS

The sources regarding male renunciants of the desert are much fuller than those pertaining to women, perhaps because their male authors did not visit women's monastic communities frequently, if at all, and hence had fewer stories and sayings to report. What do we learn about the class backgrounds of Christian ascetic men from these sources?

Palladius's *Lausiac History,* the *History of the Monks of Egypt,* and the *Sayings of the Desert Fathers* provide many examples of ascetics from lower-class backgrounds: Paul the Simple, who had been a herdsman; John of Lycopolis, formerly a builder or carpenter; Sisinnius, a slave; Amoun of Nitria, a balsam grower; and Moses the Ethiopian, a houseman and a robber.[14] Macarius the Younger and Apollo had been shepherds; Paul and his brother Timothy, barbers; Patermuthius, a brigand chief and tomb robber; Silvanos, an actor (*Laus. Hist.* 15.1; *Sayings Alph.,* Apollo 2, Paul the Barber 1; *Hist. of Monks of Egypt* 10.13; *Paralipomena* 2.2). The emphasis upon the ascetic's humble background suggests that the writers of these accounts wished to signal that the ascetic life was open to all and that it "ennobled" even the lowly: Christianity's superiority as a religion is shown in its ability to bring the dissolute to a moral life.

As for the status marker of illiteracy, the sources' frequent mention of an ascetic's inability to speak or read Greek or Latin is designed either to show that God gives wisdom even to the illiterate or to humble those of higher status who might be tempted to parade their learning. The desert father Or,

Fig. 1.2. Some ascetics came from humble backgrounds, having worked as farmers, carpenters, barbers, or shepherds. This marble relief from the early Roman imperial period depicts a herdsman watering a cow that is feeding its young calf. Vatican Museums, Vatican State. Photo credit: Alinari/ Regione Umbria / Art Resource, NY.

although illiterate, was given (the sources allege) the ability to recite the scriptures by heart and expound them to fellow ascetics. When some brothers brought him a book to test his ability, he, miraculously, read (*Hist. of the Monks of Egypt* 3 [Syriac version]). To Paphnutius is attributed the ability to expound the Old and New Testaments, although he had never read commentaries (*Laus. Hist.* 47). The desert father Theon is said to have been given by God's grace knowledge of Greek and Latin (*Hist. of Monks of Egypt* 6.3), as is Pachomius (who knew only Egyptian) when he needed to hear the confession of a "Roman" who spoke Greek (*Paralipomena* 11.27).

Other male ascetics came from mercantile backgrounds. The desert father Apollonius, formerly a businessman, was too old to learn a craft or work as a scribe, but he supplied the community with medicine and groceries brought from Alexandria, especially appreciated by brothers who fell ill. When he died, he left his wares to another, who carried on the trade. Palladius comments on the necessity of this service for the five thousand monks living in the desert of Mount Nitria (*Laus. Hist.* 13).

The brothers Paesius and Isaias also came from a mercantile background. Upon their father's death and the receipt of their inheritance, one sold all and gave to the poor, to monasteries, and to prisons, while the other used his share to build a monastery and take in strangers, invalids, and the poor, offering meals for many on Saturdays and Sundays. When the brothers themselves died, Abba Pambo pronounced both of them to be equally virtuous—a pronouncement confirmed by a vision he received of the brothers standing before God in paradise (*Laus. Hist.* 14).

At other times, monastic literature portrays well-born heroes and heroines who abandoned comfortable, even affluent, lifestyles. The desert father Isidore is alleged to have been both rich and generous and to have met "the entire Roman senate and all the wives of the great men" when he visited Rome in the company of Athanasius during the latter's exile (*Laus. Hist.* 1). Amoun of Nitria is described as "of noble birth and rich parents" (*Hist. of Monks of Egypt* 22). Innocent the priest is alleged to have served as a palace dignitary during the early reign of Constantius (*Laus. Hist.* 44), while the monk Cronius is credited with having formerly been "head of the administration" (*Sayings Alph.*, Cronius 5).

Of the monks who came from situations of wealth, Arsenius is especially celebrated. He is said to have lived for forty years in the palace of Theodosius I (*Sayings* 15.10). Several of the forty-four sayings of and stories about him in the *Sayings of the Desert Fathers* signal his high status. Like other high-status desert fathers who had renounced much, he is applauded for his humility. When a brother asked Arsenius why as a scholar of Latin and Greek he took counsel with an old Egyptian, Arsenius replied, "I indeed know the worldly learning of the Greeks and the Latins, but I have not yet been able to learn the alphabet of this countryman" (15.7). When an Egyptian who had formerly been a shepherd tried to "out-asceticize" Arsenius (who slept with a head rest and had clean, sandal-clad feet), Arsenius's questioning led the man to confess how much softer his life as a monk was now, in contrast with Arsenius's renunciation of "high glory and riches" (10.76). And when Arsenius, destitute, fell ill at Scete, he accepted a single coin as alms, thanking God for making him worthy "to have come to this, that I must ask for alms" (6.6). (Hugh Evelyn White notes that Arsenius and the other early higher-class ascetics in Egypt were all foreigners; there is no record, he claims, of an upper-class Egyptian— presumably as contrasted with a cosmopolitan resident of Alexandria— becoming a monk in this early period.)[15]

Elsewhere, ascetic enthusiasts and monastic founders came from either high or middling backgrounds. Paulinus of Nola, who abandoned a prominent secular career for ascetic retreat, was a member of the senatorial aristocracy.[16] Basil of Caesarea and his sister Macrina, founders of monasteries in Cappadocia, were members of a provincial aristocracy.[17] Augustine of Hippo, on the other hand, whose father had been a minor official of the Roman government in North Africa, claimed that as bishop of Hippo Regius he controlled twenty times more property than he had derived from his own inheritance (*Ep.* 126.7).

Others, however, deemed aristocrats' renunciation disgraceful. Ambrose, bishop of Milan in the later fourth century, described the shock with which the Roman nobility greeted the senator Paulinus of Nola's renunciation:

"It is unbearable that a man of such a family, such a lineage, such talent, endowed with such great eloquence, should retire from the senate and break the succession of a noble house" (*Ep.* 27.3). Fifth-century Gallic Christians (so we read in Salvian of Marseilles) believed an ascetic profession to be socially debasing, claiming that "when a man changes his garb, he immediately changes his rank" (*On the Governance* 4.7.32–33). Yet some monks from high-status backgrounds, after lowering themselves to a humble station in ascetic renunciation, went on, by lateral transfer, to become bishops (*Life of Martin* 10; *Life of Aug.* 11, 31)—an example of how capital of one kind could be traded for another.

THE EXAMPLES OF ANTONY AND PACHOMIUS

Antony, often touted as the founder of anchorite asceticism, provides an interesting (and disputed) test case regarding social status. Athanasius's *Life of Antony,* written in the fourth century some years after the events described and by an author with limited knowledge of his subject, provides several (albeit conflicting) clues to Antony's social status. Although Athanasius claims that Antony's parents were "well-born and prosperous," leaving him around 207 acres of land (1–2), other features of the text shed doubt on this assessment: as a child, he refused to "learn letters," and, later, he required a translator in order to converse with Greek-speaking visitors (1, 3, 72, 74). He taught his followers that desert ascetics, unlike the Greeks, do not need to go abroad for education; they can learn of the kingdom and practice virtue at home (20). When Antony was reputedly ridiculed for his illiteracy, he responded that if the mind is sound, a person has no need of letters (73). Such is Athanasius's version of Antony's status.

This assessment, however, has been complicated by recent scholarship: in a detailed study, Samuel Rubenson argued that the epistles attributed to Antony (the authenticity of which had been discounted) should be considered genuine. Countering the picture of an "unlettered" Antony is the fact that these letters brim with theological points derived from the third-century church father Origen, whose complex theology heretofore was deemed accessible only to those of considerable education.[18] If Rubenson's claim is upheld (and many scholars find his arguments convincing), we would have to question why Athanasius construes Antony as "unlettered." Did he wish to show that even those of humble backgrounds can possess "wisdom" and manifest the "philosophic life"? This suggestion accords well with Athanasius's desire to portray Antony's virtue as a gift from God, not acquired by his own effort.[19]

Pachomius's *Life* reports that he was born of pagan parents and was converted to Christianity in early adulthood (3, 7 [Bohairic]). Upon discharge from the army in which he had served as a recruit, Pachomius gathered disciples (at first native Egyptians) around him (8, 10, 23), for whom he prescribed "absolute equality in clothing and food, and decent sleeping arrangements"(23). Clergy who wished to enter the monastery were told that they must agree to "the rules laid down for the brothers, like everyone else" (25). As the monastery's fame grew, others—with Greco-Roman names like Paulus and Cornelios—joined up (24, 89). Pachomius's *Life* reveals that he did not speak Greek (89), and interpretation between Greek and Egyptian appears to be a regular feature of life in the Pachomian monasteries (91, 196): the international character of Pachomian monasticism is here signaled. Only the Greek (not the Bohairic) version of Pachomius's *Life* suggests that Pachomius enjoyed a higher degree of theological literacy in its claim that he knew, but rejected, the theology of Origen, whose book he threw into the river (31).

WOMEN ASCETICS AND SOCIAL CLASS

Stories about and sayings of women are considerably fewer in monastic sources, excluding hagiographies. Some monastic collections contain no chapters on women (for example, *History of the Monks of Egypt*). The Alphabetical Collection of the *Sayings of the Desert Fathers* includes only three out of 120 chapters on women (Sarah, Syncletica, Theodora) and gives no status markers for any, although the *Life of Syncletica* reports that she distributed her "abundant wealth" and property to the poor after her parents' death (7, 12). In the collections that detail the lives and sayings of women—for example, Palladius's *Lausiac History*—few of the women are identifiably of "the people." It is tempting to speculate that Palladius includes many more stories of women because he, presumably unlike many of the collectors of monastic tales, personally knew more ascetic (and aristocratic) women, such as Melania the Elder and Melania the Younger; in addition, he composed his work for Lausus, count of Constantinople, who was well connected with aristocratic circles that included women devoted to asceticism.[20]

Some women Palladius simply groups together in a chapter titled "The Women's [Pachomian] Monastery," which he reports numbered "some four hundred women" (*Laus. Hist.* 33). This monastery was built by the brothers for Pachomius's sister, Mary, who served as its first head. Pachomius appointed an old ascetic, Apa Peter, to be their father and to preach to them, and sent for their use the *Rules* that had been devised for the men's monastery (*Life of Pach.* 27 [Bohairic]). Palladius's description of the women's monastery, nonetheless, is largely taken up by the tale of an unnamed sister who was falsely accused of sexual misconduct, and the shocking suicides that stemmed from this incident (33). In another tale, a young woman, feigning madness, accepted the lowliest jobs in the monastery's kitchen and was known as "the sponge" (or "the broom") of the monastery, but in the end she was declared to be holier than the hermit Piteroum himself (34). This story illustrates how tales of women ascetics could be used as shaming devices for their male counterparts. A tale in the *Lives of the Fathers* also supports this point: the monk who turned aside when he noticed nuns coming along the road was rebuked by the abbess: "If you had been a perfect monk, you would not have looked so closely as to perceive that we were women!" (4, 62). As the Bohairic *Life of Pachomius* exhorts, if women can conquer their nature by virginal asceticism, how much more should virile men (107)!

When Palladius devotes whole chapters to women ascetics, however, it is striking that most of them, with a few exceptions,[21] are identified by upper-class status markers. In his chapter on the topic "Saintly Women," Palladius mentions the Roman matron Paula, her daughter Eustochium, and the Roman virgin Asella (all aristocrats famed for association with Jerome); Veneria, wife of a count; Theodora, wife of a tribune; Basianilla, wife of a general; and Avita and her daughter Eunomia (relatives by marriage of Melania the Elder) (42). Palladius devotes chapters 46, 54, and part of 55 to the exceedingly wealthy Melania the Elder, who was also his informant for some other stories he reports (see 5.2; 9; 10.2). Other chapters he devotes to Silvania (55), sister-in-law of Rufinus, formerly prefect of the East; to Olympias (56), granddaughter of a former prefect of Constantinople and briefly married to another prefect; to Candida, daughter of a general, and Gelasia, daughter of a tribune (57); to an unnamed virgin (60) who transferred a copy of Clement of Alexandria's work on the prophet Amos to (presumably) Palladius himself; to Melania the Younger (61); to an unnamed virgin (63) who provided for Athanasius's "bodily needs and personal affairs" and obtained books for him for six years while he was in hiding; to a virgin Juliana (64), who sheltered Origen and provided for him "at her own expense for two years"; to Magna (67), a virgin or widow of Ancyra, head of some houses of virgins, who gave money for hospitals, the poor, and bishops going on pilgrimages. And what is the moral of the story? To achieve renown as a female ascetic, it helped to be from a wealthy or prestigious family.

Palladius presents more detailed accounts of the wealthy aristocrat Melania the Elder and her granddaughter Melania the Younger, whom he knew personally. Melania the Elder, widow of a high-ranking Roman official, sheltered exiled Nitrian monks in Palestine and appealed to her family status to threaten the meddling consul of Palestine; she built a monastery in Jerusalem that housed fifty virgins, and she endowed it upon her death. For twenty-seven years she and her monastic companion, Rufinus of Aquileia, entertained bishops, monks, and virgins who visited Jerusalem (46, 54). Her impressive capacity for reading Greek theological literature, especially that of an Origenist cast, provides another status marker (55). Her granddaughter Melania the Younger renounced the world at the age of twenty, distributing much of her enormous fortune to churches and monasteries, freeing eight thousand of her slaves, and selling her property in Spain, Aquitania, Taraconia, and Gaul (but not that in Sicily, Campania, and Africa, which she used to endow her monasteries) (61; see also *Life of Mel.* 19, 20).

Accounts of these aristocrats are paralleled in the letters that Jerome and John Chrysostom wrote to women. The closest we come to "the people" in these accounts are hints that they took their slaves with them into the monasteries they founded. Jerome's friend Paula, who founded a monastery for women in Bethlehem, divided the nuns in her monastery into three groups, presumably on a class basis: Jerome reports that some were of "noble birth while others belonged to the middle or lower classes." Paula forbade the virgins to keep the same slaves who had previously attended them (note that they might have others). She insisted that all the sisters be clothed alike and renounce private possessions (*Ep.* 108.20). John Chrysostom had a large circle of women supporters, most notable among whom was Olympias; Palladius credits her with virtually supporting the operations of the church of Constantinople.[22] According to her *Life*, Olympias took fifty of her own slaves with her into the monastery she built in Constantinople, which came to house 250 women (6). And Palladius reports that Melania the Younger made some of her slave women "associates in her ascetic practice" (*Laus. Hist.* 61). Although such notices are doubtless designed to show ancient readers how ascetic renunciation broke down social barriers, to modern readers, they more likely signal the class distinctions that remained.

MONASTIC RULES AND MANUAL LABOR

The writers of early Christian monastic rules aimed to promote equality within the monastery, and they often cited passages from Acts 2 and 4 regarding the communal sharing of the early Jerusalem Christians. According to Jerome's preface to his Latin translation of the *Rules of Saint Pachomius*, hierarchy in Pachomius's monastery derived not from family or class status, but from the date of the monk's profession: who had joined first and who later (1, 3). All the brothers were to eat the same food, receive equal amounts of any extra treats, and have no possessions except "what is prescribed for all together by the law of the monastery" (*Rules* 35, 38–39, 81).

In the *Rules* Basil of Caesarea formulated for his monastery, communal living is given a philosophical justification: since man is a sociable animal, not a "solitary and fierce" one, he needs to associate with and love others.[23] Communal living is justified on the grounds that no person is self-sufficient. In community, monks can reprove and correct one another, and numerous commandments can be kept at the same time, so that the private gift or virtue of one monk becomes the property of all. Moreover, attacks of "the enemy" can be better warded off in a group (*Longer Rules* 7). The communal life, Basil continues, enables the monk to practice the perfect humility of the Lord, who washed the feet of his disciples; to "have all things in common," as did the early church described in the book of Acts (2:44); and to carry out Paul's injunction (1 Cor. 12:12-27) that the various members of one body must cooperate for harmonious living (7, 24). Those who wish to enter the monastery must be tested to see whether they will accept the lowliest tasks (*if* such work is deemed useful, Basil adds, thus providing a loophole for those for whom such tasks might be deemed "not useful") (10). Basil accepted male and female children, including orphans, into the monastery, and made special provisions for their living arrangements and studies (15).

Fig. 1.3. Benedict of Nursia was the founder of a monastic style of life in which manual labor played an important role. The Rule of St. Benedict was immensely influential in medieval Europe. This portrait of Benedict is found in a manuscript of the Liber moralium of Pope Gregory, housed in the Library of the Abbey, Montecassino, Italy. Photo credit: A. M. Rosati / Art Resource, NY.

Augustine's monastic *Rules* likewise stress the communal aspects of renunciation: "no one is to claim anything for his own," but is to live as the Apostles allegedly did according to Acts 4.[24] The monks' motivation in living together is to seek God with "one heart and one soul" (*Rule* 1.1). They are to call nothing their own, but "possess everything in common" (Acts 4:32, 35); those who had possessions in "the world" must "freely consent to possess everything in common in the monastery" (1.3–4).

Yet in Augustine's *Rule (Praeceptum)*, concern for class divisions surfaces more visibly than it does in (for example) Pachomius's *Rules*. Augustine admonishes those from humble backgrounds not to seek possessions in the monastery to which they would not have had access in their previous lives, nor to become proud that they now associate with men whom they would not have dared to approach in the world: if the rich are enjoined to become humble, the poor are exhorted not to become proud (1.5–6). Those from higher backgrounds, on the other hand, are not to look down on those from the lower orders; their donations to the monastery should not promote pride (1.7). Those monks of robust physique (seemingly from the lower classes) who do not require the special arrangements made for those from softer backgrounds should not grumble, but consider how much more the rich have renounced in order to embrace the monastic life. The monastery would defeat its purpose, Augustine argues, if while the wealthy engage in work, the poor become "pampered" (2.4). And the same principles apply to the women's monastery (*Rule for Nuns* 1; 3.3–4). The communal spirit here emphasized also informs the later *Rule of St. Benedict* (58).

It is not surprising that manual labor becomes an important site for both maintaining and disrupting class distinctions within the monastery. A central distinguishing characteristic that separated the higher orders from "the people" in antiquity was the necessity for the latter to engage in productive labor. The very definition of an aristocrat assumed the ability to be at leisure. Thus ascetics' attitudes toward and practices regarding manual labor reveal the disjuncture—clear but not absolute—with the standards of the world.

Both anchorites and Pachomian monks engaged in manual labor.[25] According to the *Sayings of the Desert Fathers*, Agathon made wicker baskets, selling the small articles he produced in town, as did Isidore the Priest at Scetis (*Sayings Alph.*, Agathon 7, 30, Isidore the Priest 7). Pior worked at the harvest, as did Serinus, who also sewed and wove (Pior 1, Serinus 2). And Abba Pistamon, advising a brother that he might lower the price on his goods for sale, added, "Even if you have other means to supply your need, do not give up manual labor" (Pistamon 1). Such was the intrinsic importance placed upon working with one's hands.

For monks in Pachomian monasteries, manual labor played a central role: the monastery sought to provide for the needs of the community by the monks' work in the fields, as herdsmen, and as weavers of ropes and mats for sale.[26] Transport of goods by boat on the Nile to markets in villages and cities required careful organization. Moreover, considerable work was entailed in feeding and clothing the thousands of monks who flocked to Pachomian monasteries (see Jerome, Preface to the *Rule of Pach.* 6; *Rule*

Fig. 1.4. This relief from a first-century Roman sarcophagus depicts a rope maker. Rope making was among the occupations pursued in Pachomian monasteries, where manual labor was both an ascetic practice and an economic necessity. Museo Nazionale Romano (Terme di Diocleziano), Rome, Italy. Photo credit: Erich Lessing / Art Resource, NY.

23, 24, 26, 68, 72, 76, 77, 80, 108, 116–18). Great care was to be taken with the tools provided for the monks' work; losing or damaging community property was a punishable offense (*Rule of Pach.* 66, 131, 125, 4). So prominent a feature of the monasteries was manual labor that (according to Jerome) the Pachomian brothers were even organized into houses by virtue of their trades (Preface 6). After Pachomius's death Abba Theodore claimed that he was distressed that the community had acquired "numerous fields, animals, and boats," a sign that the monasteries had flourished economically (*Life of Pach.* 197 [Bohairic]).

Basil's monastic *Rules* are less concerned about detailing issues of manual labor. Basil instructs the monks that they must "work diligently" and not use piety as an excuse to abstain from work (monks can pray and sing spiritual songs while they work with their hands). To Basil, however, work is not represented entirely as an economic necessity for the community, but as a means for learning patience and for showing "love to our neighbor." He cites various New Testament injunctions—such as Paul's command that he who does not work should not eat (2 Thess. 3:10)—to justify his requirement of work (*Longer Rules* 37). The type of work in which monks engage, Basil allows, will vary according to local business opportunities. Agriculture is the best type of labor, since it furnishes the necessities of life for the monks and prohibits excessive contact with the outside world (38–39). To be able to serve those in need and to promote brotherly love is the main goal of the monks' work (42).

In the sixth-century *Rule of St. Benedict* monks are to be occupied either in manual labor or in "holy reading." Here again, agricultural labor is the norm; several hours of the day are designated for work in the fields (48). But other crafts are pursued in the monastery as well, whose products are sold (although below the market price); Benedict worries, however, that craftsmen will judge themselves superior to common agricultural laborers (57). The *Rule of St. Benedict* set a pattern for monastic life that was widely adopted in early medieval monasticism in the West.

An especially interesting glimpse of problems occasioned by the demand for manual labor in monasteries is provided by Augustine's treatise *On the Work of Monks.* Disputes arose in a men's monastery in Carthage when some monks, citing Jesus' words on the birds of the air and the lilies of the field (Matt. 6:26-29) and interpreting New Testament verses referring to "labor" to mean "spiritual labor," tried to opt out of manual duties. Augustine rejoins with 2 Thess. 3:10, "If any man will not work, neither let him eat" (1.2), and argues that Paul performed manual labor in addition to his missionary activity, a task for which the complaining monks are not responsible (13.14–14.15; 19.22; 21.24). Nothing prevents the monks from singing and praying while they labor with their hands (17.20). Augustine insists that not all can write sermons (that is, not all stem from the educated classes), and even if there were more than one who could, they should take turns (18.21). Augustine implies that few monks in this monastery come from classes (and hence educational backgrounds) in which softer tasks, such as administrative work, might be assigned them. Have they as slaves, freedmen, or ordinary farmers and craftsmen, he asks, fled to the monastery in search of an easier life? Do they wish to dominate those by whom they were formerly despised and ill-treated? "In this Christian campaign for piety," Augustine concludes, "the rich are not humiliated so that the poor may be lifted up to *superbia* [pride]." He considers it "unfitting" that when "senators become laborers" in the monastic life, "peasants should be pampered" (22.25; 25.33).

Aristocrats who adopted lives of ascetic renunciation, however, seem either to avoid physical labor or to engage in lowly duties only to mark their humility, not to provide for their basic support. For ascetics such as Paulinus of Nola, Jerome's correspondent Pammachius, Sulpicius Severus, and others, labor consisted chiefly of worship, study, writing, and contemplation. Melania the Younger's now-ascetic husband Pinianus devoted his time to "reading, gardening, and solemn conferences" (*Laus. Hist.* 61). The aristocratic women who became ascetics undertook such tasks as scrubbing vegetables, nursing the sick, spinning, and weaving (Jerome, *Ep.* 66.13; 77.6; 108.20; 130.5). In a gesture calculated to shame men, John Chrysostom praises delicate young women from prestigious backgrounds who have adopted the ascetic life and "even" do their own cooking (*Hom. 13 Eph.* 3–4). Such work, however, was not economically necessary, as it was for the Pachomian monks: the funds for the upkeep of these aristocratic nuns and their monasteries came from inherited wealth. There were indeed nuns who worked to support themselves by their own labor, but these do not receive major attention in the sources that remain (Augustine, *On Morals* 1.31.68; 1.33.70; Ambrose, *On Virgins* 1.11.60). Even within the monastic life of supposed equality, it appears, class divisions remain.

CONCLUSIONS

Neither Christianity's more general praise of humility nor asceticism's leveling tendencies entirely broke the class and status codes of the late ancient world. Although Christian theology and practice in general, and ascetic renunciation in particular, were alleged to eliminate class differences among the religion's practitioners, achieving this ideal was harder in practice than in theory: old Roman notions of what was fitting to one's status continued to disrupt the call for equality. In sources pertaining to women ascetics in particular, their aristocratic backgrounds and wealth are frequently noted, even as the author stresses their voluntary debasements. In the process, "the people" receive scanter commemoration than we might expect based on the praise of "the lowly" in Christian rhetoric.

At the same time, we have seen that ascetic practice itself created new class distinctions within Christianity, by differentiating practitioners according to criteria of holiness. To be sure, the elitism of ascetic preference did not go unchallenged. We know from Jerome's literary battle with Jovinian in the early 390s that some within the church argued that ascetic renunciation was not superior to the married state, other virtues being equal.[27] The holy forefathers of the Old Testament, such as Sarah and Abraham, lived in the world, married, reproduced, and were blessed by God, Jovinian argued (Jerome, *Jov.* 5). Against Jerome's denigration of marriage and assertion of asceticism's superiority, Augustine's moderating stance has been called a defense of "Christian mediocrity."[28] Yet some thought that even Augustine had not sufficiently protected marriage: Augustine's Pelagian adversary Julian of Eclanum mounted a strong campaign against his doctrine of original sin, which implied (to Julian) that the sexual relations that created offspring were tainted, perhaps even the work of the devil. Is not holy matrimony, including sexual relations, a blessed way of life ordained by God? Julian asked.[29] Excessive praise for asceticism might suggest that a Christian harbored heretical views regarding the goodness of the created order, and hence of the Creator.

Thus, even within Christianity, at least two different models of egalitarianism vied with one another, as ascetics called for a radical restructuring of society in which (in principle, at least) distinctions of class and gender were eradicated, while others resisted the claims of the ascetics in order to assert the equality of all Christians, whether married or celibate.

FOR FURTHER READING

Brown, Peter. *The Body and Society: Men, Women, and Sexual Renunciation.* New York: Columbia University Press, 1988.

Burrus, Virginia. *The Sex Lives of the Saints: An Erotics of Ancient Hagiography.* Philadelphia: University of Pennsylvania Press, 2004.

Clark, Elizabeth A. *Ascetic Piety and Women's Faith: Essays on Late Ancient Christianity.* Lewiston, N.Y.: Mellen, 1986.

———. *Reading Renunciation: Asceticism and Scripture in Early Christianity.* Princeton, N.J.: Princeton University Press, 1999.

Countryman, L. William. *The Rich Christian in the Church of the Early Empire: Contradictions and Accommodations.* Texts and Studies in Religion 7. New York: Mellen, 1980.

Elm, Susanna. *"Virgins of God": The Making of Asceticism in Late Antiquity.* Oxford Classical Monographs. Oxford: Clarendon, 1994.

Goehring, James E. *Ascetics, Society, and the Desert: Studies in Early Egyptian Monasticism.* Harrisburg, Pa.: Trinity Press International, 1999.

Rousseau, Philip. *Basil of Caesarea.* Transformation of the Classical Heritage 20. Berkeley: University of California Press, 1994.

Rubenson, Samuel. *The Letters of St. Antony: Monasticism and the Making of a Saint.* Studies in Antiquity and Christianity. Minneapolis: Fortress, 1995.

Wimbush, Vincent L., ed. *Ascetic Behavior in Greco-Roman Antiquity: A Sourcebook.* Minneapolis: Fortress, 1990.

FICTIONAL NARRATIVES
AND SOCIAL CRITIQUE

JUDITH PERKINS

CHAPTER TWO

The early Christian centuries were a period of significant social change and restructuring, witnessing the spread of Roman power across the Greek East as well as the emergence of Christianity and rabbinic Judaism. The period also gave rise to a literary innovation—namely, the increasing use of prose for the writing of fictional narratives. Here, as so often, the emergence of a new cultural form both indicated and enabled broader societal transformations. In the changing matrix of the early Roman Empire, inhabitants turned to prose fiction as a vehicle for rethinking and renegotiating their cultural identities. Christians participated in this process, and this chapter will look at early Christian fictions, stories about the apostles Peter, Paul, John, Andrew, and Thomas that survive—for the most part, sadly, only in fragmentary state—from the second and early third centuries CE.[1] These stories, traditionally referred to collectively as the *Apocryphal Acts of the Apostles,* were apparently written from a range of geographical locations across the Roman Empire: Asia Minor, Egypt, Syria, and Rome have all been proposed as likely places for the composition of various *Acts.*

As must be the case for all written productions in this period of very low literacy, one can only conjecture how much access these stories give to the sentiments of the people. But the generally simple language and literary style of all the *Acts,* the evidence they give of incorporating oral stories, and their inclusion of motifs that cross-culturally have popular appeal (romance, our-guy-against-their-guy face-offs, marvels and wonder-working, and talking animals) indicate they may have targeted a popular audience.

Whether or not the *Acts* can claim with certainty a popular perspective, they do display the perspective of voices that were later marginalized as Christianity evolved toward institutional orthodoxy. The very first reference to any of the *Acts* occurs in a condemnation of its viewpoint. At the end of the second century, the African church father Tertullian rejects the use by certain women of "the falsely written *Acts of Paul* to defend the freedom of women to teach and baptize." Tertullian explains that the presbyter (a church official) in Asia Minor who wrote the *Acts of Paul* was removed from his office, though he claimed to have written out of love for Paul.[2] This reference is useful not only for dating the text but also for showing its author's status as a Christian presbyter and its audience's use of the text as a warrant for their behavior. Clearly, for certain Christians in the second century, a pastoral and sacramental role for women was plausible. Competing authorities like Tertullian might reject their stance, but the reference provides evidence that some Christians entertained this position.

Because the *Acts* were already rejected as heretical in late antiquity, their testimony for Christian

Fig. 2.1. The adventures of Jesus' apostles provided the plotlines for many ancient Christian novels. This sixth-century Coptic fresco reminds us of the enormous popularity of the apostles, who were not only the objects of devotion but also the subjects of story. Coptic Museum, Cairo, Egypt. Photo credit: Borromeo / Art Resource, NY.

perspectives and beliefs in the early centuries has been neglected. But as François Bovon has pointed out, canonical texts "were declared legitimate more for doctrinal than historical reasons," and a "more comprehensive historical understanding of the beginnings of Christianity" would use evidence such as that provided by the *Apocryphal Acts*.[3] That certain Christian writings were later rejected should not subvert their valuable testimony for the kinds of self-understandings, beliefs, and attitudes motivating Christians in an earlier period. Both the persons who wrote the *Acts* and the people for whom they wrote considered themselves Christians. Furthermore, although condemned, the *Acts* never lost their potential for engaging Christian imaginations: their continued presence in the representational life of the church testifies to their resilience. Their themes and dramatic highlights appear in Christian iconography and literary texts for centuries. The use of "apocryphal," meaning "hidden and covered over," is thus a misnomer for describing these narratives whose stories long continued to shape Christian thinking. Two fourth-century fathers, Gregory of Nazianzus and Gregory of Nyssa, for instance, held out as an example Thecla, the virgin heroine of the *Acts of Paul* (*Oration* 24.10; *Commentary on the Song of Songs, Homily* 14, respectively). The sections of the *Acts* describing the apostles' martyrdoms were read publicly on their saint's days in many locations for centuries, and the *Acts*' translations into Latin, Syriac, Coptic, Ethiopic, and Armenian versions likewise attest to their ongoing influence.

The Apocryphal Acts of the Apostles can help us understand how some Christians in the early centuries positioned themselves in their society and worked to forge and articulate an emerging social identity in a period of rapid change for both Christianity and the Roman Empire of which it was a part. In this chapter we will first examine the *Acts*, taken collectively, in dialogue with the Greek romances, in order to show how the *Acts* worked to interrupt their society's traditional structures of privilege and power. However, treating the *Acts* together and focusing on what they share mutes their individual perspectives. Each of the *Acts* has its own agenda and differences of perspective and emphasis. The chapter's second major section will compare the *Acts of John* and the *Acts of Peter* to show that, in spite of close similarities of plot, these narratives differ at fundamental points and project very different social statements. Comparing these two narratives helps, moreover, to clarify the social ramifications behind one of the most contentious issues dividing Christians during the early period—namely, the nature of Jesus' body and, by analogy, the nature of human resurrection. In the first centuries, Christian debate raged around the composition of Jesus' body. Proponents vehemently defended positions ranging across a spectrum from claims that Jesus possessed an actual material human body to arguments that Jesus had a wholly spiritual body that only appeared to be human. The comparison of the *Acts of John* and the *Acts of Peter* will suggest that a correlation exists between a group's attitude toward Jesus' bodily nature and its challenge to contemporary structures of privilege.

IDENTITY AND SOCIAL CRITIQUE IN THE *APOCRYPHAL ACTS OF THE APOSTLES*

The *Acts* play a particularly significant role for understanding Christianity in the early centuries because they offer an opportunity to view how Christians understood and positioned themselves vis-à-vis and in dialogue with other members of a complex and highly mobile society. As the multicultural inhabitants of the early empire worked to redefine themselves and reimagine their social and cultural identities in the face of social, cultural, and political changes effected by Roman domination, they appear to have turned to the prose story to help them articulate their self-understandings.

Prose fictional narratives, highly flexible, reflect no single perspective. Rather, they arise from a number of different cultural positions during the period. In the so-called Greek romances, the elite of the Greek East used prose fiction to display and assert their cultural identity and position over against their Roman conquerors. Around the same time, "subcultures within the Roman empire,"[4] including Christians and Jews, were also turning to the novelistic narrative form to tell their stories of identity. The *Acts* therefore ought not to be viewed simply as religious writings with a restricted relevance; rather, they should be seen to participate in a dynamic and competitive culture-wide articulation of social identity—or rather, of identities. Comparing the fictions of different social groups should bring into sharper focus what separated these groups, at what points their perspectives differed, and what was at stake in these differences. Christians functioned in and fashioned themselves within a larger social dynamic and as members of a larger social and cultural polity. The *Acts* provide a site for observing Christians' interactions with the cultural productions of their contemporaries.

Marriage

The *Apocryphal Acts*, like so much popular literature, are at one level formula stories. All share a number of plot and thematic similarities. Each of the *Acts* describes an apostle's arrival in a city, his preaching, and the subsequent conversion of many to his message and its call for sexual renunciation. Each of the *Acts* emphasizes the apostle's conversion of a woman connected to one of the city's important men. In all but one of the *Acts*, this woman's embrace of the apostle's call to renounce all sexual unions so infuriates her husband or lover that he has the apostle sentenced to death. Only the *Acts of John* ends with the apostle's natural death, although this narrative also presents John's preaching as disrupting relations between husbands and wives. It describes, for example, how Andronicus, one of the leaders of Ephesus, before his own conversion by John, shuts his wife up in a tomb and threatens her: "Either I'll have you as wife, as I had you before, or you must die!" The text continues, "She preferred to die" (63).[5]

The call to sexual continence and its fallout for the apostle is one of the central conflicts in each of the *Acts*. So Paul preaches, "There is no resurrection unless you remain chaste and do not pollute the flesh" (12), and a rejected husband in the *Acts of Thomas* describes how Thomas taught, "It is impossible that you enter into eternal life which I preach to you unless you give up your wives and the wives also give up their husbands" (101). The *Acts* testify that it was this message that provoked the opposition to the apostles. Thus, in the *Acts of Peter*, a husband, described as so in love with his wife that he was raging like a beast, confronts the prefect and demands, "Let us seize him and kill him [Peter] as a trouble maker, so that we may have our wives back and avenge those who cannot kill him but whose wives he has alienated" (34). The writers of the *Acts* explicitly focus on the power of the Christian message to disrupt this social bond. The apostles are persecuted not for overtly religious or political reasons but for their interruption of the relationship between a husband and a wife.

The *Acts'* focus on a marriage and its interruption locates their plots in a larger matrix of narratives that similarly revolve around a couple's relationship. Like the *Acts,* the five surviving Greek romances thought to have been written between the first and fourth centuries CE are formula stories of a sort. They all treat a beautiful and wealthy young couple's falling in love, subsequent separation, trials and tribulations, and marriage or final reunion. The centrality of marriage in both sets of narratives highlights the importance of this relationship as a symbolic focal point for both social change and resistance to change.

The Greek romance, with its emphasis on the highborn young couple's marriage and its endurance, can be read as an endorsement of social stability. Marriage in such literary works traditionally functions as the happy ending. In the union or reunion of the happy couple, audiences can see the protagonists successfully integrated into normative social structures and experience an affirmation of society, both its present and its anticipated future in the children expected from the marriage. During this historical period, not only was marriage a focus in the romance, but it had become an important topic for philosophical and political attention elsewhere; in Peter Brown's words, marriage functioned symbolically as a "reassuring microcosm of the social order."[6]

In the Greek East, where the romances were likely written, it is tempting to read them as manifestos of social identity in the face of Rome's increasing power, as narratives projecting the continuing vitality of Hellenic and ethnic social life and identity.[7] Through the figure of the loving couple who manage to stay true to each other and fend off every assault to their chastity and commitment, the romance offers the dream of a social unity able to overcome every eventuality of fate or fortune. So Anthia, the heroine of Xenophon's romance, proclaims her perseverance through constant and gruesome challenges: "I have found you again, after all my wanderings over land and sea, escaping robbers' threats and pirates' plots and pimps' insults, chains, trenches, fetters, poisons and tombs. But I have reached you, Habrocomes, lord of my soul, the same as when I first left you" (5.14). The message of Anthia's speech and of the romance plot in general is endurance, the ability to survive intact in the face of sustained jeopardy. This message would likely appeal to the wealthy urban elite of the East, as they maneuvered to reposition themselves and their cities in the changed circumstances of Roman supremacy. The elite could read into these texts their hope for the survival of their social positions and culture.

One warrant for giving the romances such a political reading is the care with which the narratives keep Rome offstage. A fear of anachronisms cannot account for how conspicuously the protagonists of the romances crisscross extensive territories controlled by the superpower without a sign of Rome. The romances would seem to provide a fictive social space free from the intrusion of Roman realities, in which the elite could write their own story. By ignoring Rome and foregrounding the beauty and social unity of their wellborn protagonists' cities, whether Ephesus, Syracuse, Tyre, or Meroe in Ethiopia, the romances register a resistance to Rome's influence.

If the Greek-speaking elites used the romance's married couple as an image for their idealized social order and employed the romance's fictive prose form for a subtle resistance to Roman control, the *Apocryphal Acts* usurped both the image and the form to represent a more explicit and extensive resistance to normative social and political structures. Contemporaries would have read the attitude toward sex and marriage expressed in the *Acts,* for example, as radically antisocial. In the philosophical and political context of the period, an attack on marriage was an attack on the social polity. So the philosopher Musonius Rufus in the first century CE could write, "Whoever destroys human marriage destroys the home, the city, and the whole human race" (Fragment 14). The *Acts* in their rejection of sexual unions—of "horrid intercourse," as the *Acts of Thomas* says, or a "loathsome and unclean way of life" in Andrew's words—testify that some Christians in the early centuries were very willing to embrace such a thoroughgoing destruction of dominant social institutions.

Elite Privilege

Ancient society was starkly divided between haves and have-nots, and cultural practices inculcated and normalized this divide. The haves unabashedly and publicly flaunted their power in their dress, special insignia, retinues, and public inscriptions proclaiming their honor, good deeds, and ancestry. Derogatory references to the have-nots as the "sordid" or the "common" were standard. So Cicero refers to low-status persons as the "filth and dregs of the city." Close in time to the writing of the *Acts,* the imperial government further codified inequity in a new legal distinction between the *humiliores* ("more humble") and the *honestiores* ("more honorable"). Judicial penalties became legally calibrated to social status, whereby the "more humble" became liable to harsher judicial treatment than the "more honorable."

The *Acts'* opposition to the social status quo appears to target exactly those practices that support elite privilege. On the basis of their attack on marriage, Andrew Jacobs has described the *Acts* as examples of "class based resistance": "Men and women giving up *sex* tell the story of asceticism and subversion, but men and women giving up *marriage* tell a story . . . along social status lines."[8] As Jacobs notes, marriage in antiquity was not for everybody; people of the servile class could not marry, and people without much property would have had little cause to. Marriage was for passing on property and was very much a prerogative of the propertied class. Jacobs makes a compelling argument that the *Acts* disrupt the idealized partnership of the loving elite couple and replace it with a new social model, that of a Christian "kinship" group comprising mixed statuses, "a brotherhood of slaves, kings and women." In some of the *Acts,* preaching against marriage displays a Christian resistance to elite ideology and its exclusionary practices.

The nature of this resistance emerges in a comparison of the *Acts'* treatment of elite male desire with that of the Greek romances. The "construction of a desiring subject" might almost serve as a definition for the romance plot. The story begins when two young, beautiful, wellborn people become mad with desire for each other. The plot continues by presenting various obstacles that teasingly delay the successful resolution of this desire. This resolution, every reader knows, must occur in the end because, as the romance reiterates, the elite deserve to get what they want on the basis of their outstanding beauty and background. The romance concludes with a citywide festive celebration of realized elite desire, either a marriage or a reunion of a married couple. The narrative world of the romance, just as the social world it reflects and endorses, privileges elite desire and its consummation as natural and inevitable.

The *Apocryphal Acts,* on the contrary, quite blatantly subvert and challenge the romance's message that elites get what they want and deserve. A central feature of their plots is the representation of an elite male's passion and devotion for his beloved and the repeated thwarting of his desires. Each of the *Acts* presents a scenario that would be highly unlikely in this society founded on hierarchy and elite privilege: an elite male, often a leader of his city, is persistently denied what he wants. In the *Acts of Andrew,* for example, Aegeates, a proconsul (that is, the representative of Roman rule) is depicted as a loving husband. Returning from a trip, he rushes in to embrace and kiss his wife, Maximilla, but she denies him, saying, "After prayer, a woman's mouth should never touch a man's" (14). Aegeates sustains his loving attitude, even after his wife tricks him by sending a substitute to sleep with him (22). Weeping, he begs her to return to him: "I cling to your feet, I who have been your husband now for twelve years, who always revered you as a goddess and still do" (23). His devotion is all in vain. The narrative offers a denouement very different from that of the romance: not the elite man's desire finally realized, but rather his destruction. After the apostle Andrew's death, Maximilla chooses to live chastely among her Christian community, even as Aegeates continues to implore her to return. In the end, brokenhearted, he "threw himself from a great height and died" (64).

The narrative conveys its resistance to elite privilege not only through this high-status male's ignominious death, but perhaps even more tellingly by making Aegeates appear ridiculous throughout the narrative. On one occasion, he is delighted when he overhears his wife mentioning his name and thinks she is praying for him, but the narrative supplies her actual thoughts: "Rescue me at last from Aegeates' filthy intercourse" (14). The narrative mocks his self-delusions. In another episode, Aegeates returns home unexpectedly and almost discovers a Christian meeting going on in his house. But the apostle prays that the Christians may all escape undetected, and the Lord answers his prayer: "As the governor, Aegeates, came in, he was troubled by his stomach, asked for a chamber pot, and spent a long time sitting, attending to himself. He did not notice all the brethren exit in front of him" (13). The humiliation implicit in this scene cannot be unintentional; the narrative, by including it, reveals as one of its targets the pretensions of high-status males.

> For when the wretched man overtook her at prayer, he supposed she was praying for him and was delighted to hear his own name mentioned while she prayed. This is what Maximilla actually said: "Rescue me at last from Aegeates' filthy intercourse and keep me pure and chaste, giving service only to you, my God." When he approached her mouth intending to kiss it, she pushed him back and said, "Aegeates, after prayer a woman's mouth should never touch a man's...." Taken aback by the sternness of her face, the proconsul left her.... Maximilla then told Iphidama, "Sister, go to the blessed one so that he may come here and lay his hand on me while Aegeates is sleeping." ... Andrew laid his hand on Maximilla and prayed as follows. "... May your word and power be strong in her and may the spirit that is in her overcome even Aegeates, that insolent and hostile snake. O Lord, may her soul remain pure, sanctified by your name. In particular, protect her, Lord, from this disgusting pollution [of intercourse]."
>
> —*Acts of Andrew* 14–16

The *Acts* incorporate a message of social resistance to the hierarchical social structures operating in their contemporary society by repeatedly insisting that elite males, even Roman proconsuls, cannot necessarily have things the way they want them. Charisius, in the *Acts of Thomas*, correctly interprets this message in his lament that his wife, Mygdonia, no longer loves him: "Who can bear it when his treasure is taken from him.... All my glory has been taken away. And I am a prince, second in authority to the king. All this Mygdonia has taken from me by rejecting me" (115). Charisius specifically reads Mygdonia's rejection as an assault upon his honor, his authority, and his power. Mygdonia's reply confirms this power shift: "He whom I love is better than you and your possessions" (117). In the

Fig. 2.2. This flask, dating from the sixth or seventh century, depicts the popular saint Thecla. In the second-century *Acts of Paul*, Thecla is sentenced to fight the beasts in the arena, where a lioness sacrifices her life defending Thecla against a lion. Here Thecla is depicted between two lions. Photo: Hervé Lewandowski. Louvre, Paris, France. Photo credit: Réunion des Musées Nationaux / Art Resource, NY.

paradigm provided in the *Acts,* the espousal of Christianity functions as a rejection of contemporary structures of elite privilege figuratively played out in the female convert's refusal to satisfy the high-status male's desire.

Through their depiction of the remarkably unsympathetic attitude of wives to their devoted husbands, the *Acts* also challenge the romance's representation of the shared mutuality binding the loving couple and, by analogy, their community. After Charisius, for example, finishes professing his love to his wife, he piteously begs her to return to married life with him. The narrative records her response: "Mygdonia sat like a stone. She prayed, however for daylight, that she might go to the apostle of Christ" (97). Her unfeeling rejection perhaps replays Christian attitudes toward the pretense of mutuality in the civic social structures of the period.

Another vignette hints at the social aggression underlying this Christian resistance. In the *Acts of Paul,* a certain Alexander, described as an "influential citizen of Antioch" and "being of great power," attempts to embrace Thecla, the virgin heroine of the *Acts,* on the street. She, like the *Acts* themselves, challenges his belief that he is powerful enough to do whatever he wants, no matter at whose expense: "She tore his cloak and pulled off his crown and made him a laughing stock" (26). The narratives of the *Apocryphal Acts* offered their Christian readers a fictional space to challenge and contest their society's structures of privilege and domination; into the figure of the resisted male they might read their own resistance to contemporary elites and the structures that supported them.

Apostolic Power

The challenge to contemporary social structures continues in the depictions of the apostles. Again, given their different narrative agendas, individual *Acts* do offer different conceptions of the apostle. Paul and John, for example, are described as itinerant missionaries, moving between communities as they win converts, whereas Peter works to establish the church in Rome on a firm basis of structural hierarchy and fund-raising. But the apostles do share important characteristics in all the *Acts*. They are all depicted as powerful Christian champions, wonder-workers, healers, and exorcists, and they embody the proof that Jesus and his power remain with his community. Furthermore, they all testify that this power is located in the figure of a nonelite male.

An episode in the *Acts of John*, for example, illustrates the apostle's power. John travels to Ephesus explicitly to challenge the great goddess Artemis on her feast day at her ancient and prestigious shrine. He confronts the Ephesians: "What now, men of Ephesus? I [John] have ventured to come up even into this idol temple of yours. I will convict you of being completely godless and dead to human reasoning. Behold, I stand here. You all say that you have Artemis as your goddess; pray then to her that I alone may die. Or if you are not able to do this, I will call upon my God, and I will kill every one of you for your unbelief" (39). John immediately makes good on his challenge; he does not die, but the altar of Artemis splits in half. Its statues are thrown down, and the roof falls in, killing the goddess's priest. The people immediately recognize the superior power of John's God, and all convert. Later in the narrative, John raises up Artemis's priest, who then also "believed in the Lord Jesus and followed John" (47). The Christian apostle is represented as a powerful man, using Jesus' power to challenge and defeat opposing powers and win converts to the Christian message.

"What now, men of Ephesus? I [John] have ventured to come up even into this idol temple of yours. I will convict you of being completely godless and dead to human reasoning. Behold, I stand here. You all say that you have Artemis as your goddess; pray then to her that I alone may die. Or if you are not able to do this, I will call upon my God, and I will kill every one of you for your unbelief." Since they already knew him and had seen the dead raised up, they cried out: "Do not kill us like that, we beg you, John. We know that you can do it...." And with these words of John the altar of Artemis suddenly split into many pieces and the offerings put up in the temple suddenly fell to the ground, and its arch broke, and so did more than seven of the idols. And half of the temple fell down, and the priest was killed at one stroke, as the pillars fell. And the people of Ephesus cried, "There is only one God, that of John; only one God has compassion for us, for you alone are God. We have become converted, now that we have seen your miraculous deeds."
—*Acts of John* 39–42

The *Acts of Peter* similarly includes a very public display of the apostle's power in a face-off with Simon Magus, the arch-magician. Simon first exhibits his power by flying into Rome and drawing many away from the Christian community to be his followers. When Peter arrives to challenge him, the prefect of the city arranges a contest between the two in the Forum. Again the issue is whose god is the more powerful, and the contest is in raising the dead. Peter is the clear winner, raising three men in quick succession,

Fig. 2.3. The temple of Artemis at Ephesus was famous throughout the Mediterranean and would have housed many statues of the goddess, such as this one. The *Acts of John* portrays the apostle destroying the altar and overturning the statues in the temple. Museo Archeologico Nazionale, Naples, Italy. Photo credit: Alinari / Art Resource, NY.

while Simon can only get one corpse to open his eyes and bow before slipping back into death. Again the apostle's manifest power wins converts: "From that hour on they worshipped him like a god, and the sick, whom they had at home, they brought to his feet to be cured by him" (29). The *Acts* portray the apostles as strong leaders allied to a powerful deity, unafraid of confronting opposing powers and able to heal and help their community.

Another shared motif emphasizes the strong identification between Jesus and his apostles. In the narratives Jesus sometimes appears in the exact form of an apostle, vividly conveying their close correspondence. This feature is very common in the *Acts of Thomas,* as might be expected, since this text, written very probably in Syria, draws upon the tradition according to which the apostle Judas Thomas was the twin brother of Jesus (in Aramaic "Thomas" means "twin"). In one episode, for example, a bridegroom enters his bridal chamber and sees someone he thinks is Thomas talking to his bride. But the Lord explains, "I am not Judas Thomas, I am his brother" (12). Like the apostles, the Lord preaches continence and persuades the young couple to leave their marriage unconsummated. Paul is not Jesus' twin, but the Lord also takes on his likeness when Thecla faces persecution and death in the stadium at Iconium. The text describes how the Lord comes to comfort Thecla: "Thecla kept searching for Paul. And having looked into the crowd she saw the Lord sitting in the likeness of Paul and said, 'As if I were unable to endure, Paul has come to look after me.' And she gazed upon him in great eagerness, but he went up to heaven" (21).

In the *Acts of Peter* Jesus in the form of an apostle again brings reassurance to his followers. On the night before Peter's contest with Simon, Marcellus dreams he sees Christ as Peter defeat a monstrous dancing black woman containing "the whole power of Simon and his god" (22). Marcellus describes his dream: "A man who looked like you, Peter, came with a sword in his hand and cut her into pieces. And I looked at both of you, at you and at him who cut up the demon, and to my astonishment you were both alike" (22). Peter interprets this dream to mean that the "Lord always takes care of his own." This identification with the apostle symbolizes how fully present Jesus is for his community; he is there for them in the person of the apostle as he was for Thecla and Marcellus.

The *quo vadis* ("where are you going?") scene offered in both the *Acts of Paul* and the *Acts of Peter* suggests that this identification extends beyond the apostle to every Christian, especially when he or she suffers. In the scene in the *Acts of Peter,* the apostle, learning he is about to be persecuted, flees Rome and meets Jesus coming into the city. He asks the Lord where he is going *(quo vadis?),* and the Lord answers he is going to Rome to be crucified. Peter questions further: "'Lord, are you being crucified again?' And he said, 'Yes, Peter, again I shall be crucified.' And Peter came to himself; and he saw the Lord ascending to heaven. Then he returned to Rome rejoicing and praising the Lord because he had said, 'I am being crucified.' This was to happen to Peter" (35). This image of identification with the divine and the implicit promise of divine support suggests an important source of strength for Christians' commitment to the Christian message: Jesus in the form of his successors was with his community.

For Jesus to be in the form of the apostle was for him to take the form of a lower-status person. One function of these narratives is to identify divine power with the nonelite. All the apostles, except perhaps John, who is described as leaving money at his death (59), are represented explicitly in the *Acts* as belonging socially to the have-nots. In this status, they again are identified with their Lord, as a demon confirms in the *Acts of Thomas.* The demon describes how Jesus came to overpower him and the other demons: "He . . . left us under his power, because we knew him not. He deceived us by his unattractive form and his poverty and want" (45).[9] The demon's words express how very improbable the coincidence of poverty and power was in this society. How could a real threat be expected from a seemingly poor and unattractive person? In the society of the period, good looks, good breeding, and wealth were the overt signs of power. A conventional feature of the Greek romance is how constantly the young elite lovers are compared to gods and goddesses, usually on the basis of their beauty. The *Acts* invert this image: here the divinity is compared to a low-status person, poor and without beauty.

On the model of their Lord, the apostles display none of the signs of high status. In the *Acts of Andrew,* for example, Andrew, summoned by Maximilla to heal a sick slave, arrives at the praetorium, or governor's palace, where the slaves of the household attack him, taking him for a "common" person (3). When Aegeates first meets Andrew, he comments on his menial appearance: "You appear in this manner like a poor, simple old man" (26). Similarly in the *Acts of Thomas,* Charisius is incredulous that his wife could prefer a man like Thomas: "Look at me. I am far more handsome than that sorcerer. I have riches and honor, and everybody knows that none has such a family as mine" (116). Charisius lists all the qualities of high status: good looks, wealth, elite family. Thomas falls far below this standard, as his description of himself to Tertia, the king's wife, shows: "What have you come to see? A stranger, poor and despised and beggarly, who has neither riches nor possessions" (136). Earlier Charisius had dismissed Thomas's fasting as not a religious or philosophical practice, but rather real poverty. Thomas neither eats nor drinks, Charisius claims, "because he has nothing. For what should he do who has not even his daily bread? And he has only one garment because he is poor" (96). The *Acts'* emphatic presentation of both the apostle's real power *and* his poverty and unprepossessing appearance again demands a social reading. The narratives convey a message that the seeming powerlessness of those who have been traditionally discounted on the basis of their lack of wealth, good looks, or status may be an illusion.

The *Acts of Andrew* provides evidence that the have-nots recognized how the elite looked down upon them. After being converted by Andrew, Stratocles, Aegeates' brother and a former soldier and philosopher, embraces the Christian lifestyle. A servant tells Aegeates of his brother's "repulsive" behavior. The servant explains that Stratocles, although wellborn, now walks through the streets carrying his own belongings, doing his own chores, and buying his own food (25). Stratocles' Christian behavior, reflecting a nonelite lifestyle, is defined as repulsive and degrading from this elite perspective. Contemporary evidence supports this disdain as an accurate representation of the elite's attitude. As Paul Veyne comments, "The ancients did not scorn labor; they did scorn those who were compelled to work in order to live."[10] The *Acts,* with their depictions of the apostles' poverty, challenge this contempt for the have-nots and interrupt the cultural prejudices that legitimated it.

Some of the *Acts* extend their critique of contemporary society by expressing concern for slaves. The *Acts of Peter* includes what Dimitris Krytatas has called "the strongest statement in favor of manumission in Christian Literature."[11] Peter is depicted as refusing to raise a young senator from the dead until his mother promises to keep the pledge she made at her son's death to manumit his slaves:

> Before raising him he said to his mother, "These young men, whom you have set free in honor of your son, can as free men obey their living master. For I know that the spirits of some of them will be wounded when they see your risen son and serve again as slaves. But let them all be free and receive their subsistence as before—for your son shall rise again—and let them be with him." And Peter looked at her for some time awaiting an answer. (28)

The narrative both recognizes and comments upon the slaves' aversion to their slavery; elite literary productions usually mask this reality. Peter's concern for how the slaves would feel and his refusal to raise the boy until their potential hurt is addressed reflect a perspective not often articulated in literary productions of the period.

An episode involving slavery in the *Acts of Thomas* conveys the stark status polarities of the period. Before Mygdonia's conversion, she tries to approach the apostle to hear him preach: "She was being carried by her own slaves, but because of crowds and the narrow space they were not able to bring her up to him. So, she sent to her husband for more servants. They came and went ahead of her pushing away the people and striking them" (82). Contemporary testimony confirms that Mygdonia's violence toward the crowd was not unusual, but typical of her rank, the wife of a high official. Thomas's concern for her litter bearers is more unusual. Thomas first rebukes Mygdonia and quotes Jesus' words "Come to me all who labor and are heavily laden, and I will give you rest" (see Matt. 11:28). He then turns to the men bearing her litter and explains that these words apply to them because "although you are men they lay burdens upon you, as upon the irrational beasts, because your lords think you are not men like themselves" (83). Thomas challenges the contemporary paradigm that categorized slaves and others who labored with their bodies as animals; instead he affirms the slaves' humanity and comforts them.

Talking Animals

When Thomas protests that masters treat their slaves like animals, he uses the Greek word *alogos*, meaning "without speech" as well as "without reason," to specify the difference between animals and humans. Thomas objects that the slaves, these men, are treated like speechless, reasonless animals. This context may help to elucidate the examples of talking animals that occur in the *Acts of Paul*, *Acts of Peter*, and *Acts of Thomas*; when such voices speak, they stand in for all the others left voiceless in society. Talking animals likely perform a range of functions in the texts. They may serve to indicate that the narratives did aim in some sense at a popular audience. Quintillian, the first-century CE

> And it happened that a woman whose name was Mygdonia, the wife of Charisius, the close relative of the king, came to see the new phenomenon of the new god who was being preached and the apostle who had come to stay in their land. She was being carried by her own slaves, but because of crowds and the narrow space they were not able to bring her up to him. So, she sent to her husband for more servants. They came and went ahead of her pushing away the people and striking them. But when the apostle saw it, he said to them, "Why do you push upon those who come to hear the word and are eager for it? But you wish to be near me, when you are yet far off—as it was said of the crowd who came to the Lord... 'Come to me all you who labor and are heavily laden, and I will give you rest.'" And looking at her litter bearers, he said to them, "This beatitude that was given to them is now given to you who are heavy laden. You are those who carry burdens grievous to be borne, and are driven onward by her order. And although you are men they lay burdens upon you, as upon the irrational beasts, because your lords think that you are not men like themselves.... But we received the commandment from the Lord, that what is displeasing to us when it is done by another, we should not do to another human."
>
> —*Acts of Thomas* 82–83

rhetorician, attests that animal stories had a special appeal for the less-educated and simple audiences (*Institutio Oratoria* 5.11.19). Christopher Matthews, in his excellent overview of the talking animal motif in the *Apocryphal Acts*, argues that the examples display their authors' conviction "that animals possess an innate sense of the divine and a desire to serve God and the servants of God" and are thus appropriately included "in Christian salvation."[12] It would seem that this device, by emphasizing the expansive inclusiveness of salvation with such charm and humor, also asserts the worth of all those in society who are devalued as animals.

The *Acts* offer a number of examples of talking animals playing active parts in the narratives. Wild asses and an ass colt (a descendant, he announces, of Balaam's speaking ass in Numbers and of the ass that Jesus rode into Jerusalem) speak in the *Acts of Thomas*. They perform a variety of roles. Some offer transport for the apostle, and one of the wild asses confronts a demon, urges Thomas to action, and preaches (39–41, 74–81). In the *Acts of Peter* (9–11), a dog and a speechless seven-month-old child berate Simon and order him to come out and stand up to Peter's challenge.

A talking lion is featured in the *Acts of Paul*; recent papyri finds have significantly expanded the testimony for this lion's role. Sentenced to fight with the beasts in Ephesus, Paul thinks he recognizes the fierce lion sent out against him as an animal he had baptized. Paul asks him how he was captured, and the lion answers, "Just as you were." His response highlights the symmetry between the apostle and the animal. This symmetry continues as both man and lion, aided by a violent hailstorm, manage to escape from the stadium. A recently discovered papyrus section of the *Acts* shows the scene of the lion's baptism and emphasizes his active integration of the Christian message. Agreeing to the baptism, Paul takes him by the mane and immerses him three times in a river in the name of Jesus Christ. The lion then runs off, and Paul relates that "a lioness met him, and he did not yield himself to her."[13]

> Peter turned to the people that followed him and said, "You are about to see a great and marvelous sign." And Peter saw a large dog tied by a big chain. He went to the dog and let him loose. When the dog was free, he took on a human voice and said to Peter, "What do you order me to do, servant of the ineffable and living God?" Peter said to him: "Go inside and say to Simon in the midst of his followers, 'Peter says to you to come outside; because of you I have come to Rome, you most wicked man and deceiver of simple souls.'" Immediately the dog ran and rushed into the midst of the people around Simon, raised his front legs and said in a very loud voice. "Simon, Peter, Christ's servant, who stands at the door says to you, 'Come out in public, for because of you I have come to Rome, you most wicked man and deceiver of simple souls.'" When Simon heard this and saw the incredible sight, he forgot the words with which he deceived those who surrounded him and all of them were amazed.... But Simon said to the dog, "Tell Peter I am not in." And the dog answered in the presence of Marcellus. "You most wicked and shameless man, you enemy of all who live and believe in Christ Jesus. A dumb animal talking in a human voice has been to you to convict you and prove you a cheat and deceiver. Have you thought for all these hours, to say, 'Say that I am not here?' Are you not ashamed to raise your feeble voice against Peter, the servant and apostle of Christ, as if you could hide from him who commanded me to speak against you?"
>
> —*Acts of Peter* 9–12

This Christian lion, as do all the Christians depicted in the *Apocryphal Acts,* avoids sex.

A later narrative, the *Acts of Phillip,* likely written near the end of the fourth century, represents an even more active participation of animals in the Christian community. Phillip and his companions encounter a leopard and a goat kid in their travels. The leopard rushes up to Philip and tells his story. The leopard says he had caught the kid and was just about to eat it, when, in a human voice, the kid persuaded him to give up his savage ways, as apostles were about to arrive with the word of God. Phillip accepts the animals into his traveling party. A recently recovered manuscript continues the story and shows the animals begging to receive the eucharist. Phillip agrees that God through his son has come to all, "not just humans, but beasts and every animal species" (12). The goat and the leopard rejoice and look forward to their bodies changing into human form "to the end that we might become partners of your evangelists" (12).[14] In this scene the *Acts of Phillip* endorses the portrayal of animals in the earlier narrative; they all testify to the conviction that Jesus by his saving action has effected the integration and community of all living creatures. All have entered into a new partnership. This message of universal inclusiveness and equal participation by all species can be read to challenge a social hierarchy that devalued some persons as too akin to animals.

DIVERGENCES AMONG THE *ACTS*

The commonalities of the *Apocryphal Acts* support the social challenge implicit in these narratives and their construction of a resistant Christian identity. A number of the *Acts* share emphases on a rejection of marriage, a thwarting of elite desire, a correlation of power and nonelite status in the figure of the apostle, a concern for slaves, and the use of talking animals to point toward a more inclusive community. These themes illustrate the ways in which the *Acts* are resistant to their contemporary society and its structures. But the *Acts* in no sense present a unanimous perspective at all points; they diverge on many other crucial issues, including conceptions of church organization, the position of women, degrees of egalitarianism, and attitudes toward Roman authorities. Their differences reflect the diversity of Christian thinking in these early centuries.

The different perspectives of the *Acts* may in fact help to clarify what was at stake in some of the intra-Christian polemics of the period. In the second century, for example, heated dispute concerned the nature of Jesus' body—whether it was a truly human, material body or had a more spiritual nature. The *Acts of John* and *Acts of Peter* hold different positions on this point, and interestingly, this difference appears to relate directly to divergent attitudes toward social hierarchy. Theological issues, it seems, have social implications.

Views of Incarnation

The distinction between the mind or soul and the body provided the foundation for ancient hierarchical thinking. Elite Greco-Roman ideology held that the opportunity for living a truly honorable human life was not open to people compelled to work with their bodies or to support bodily necessities. Plato maintained in the *Republic* (590c) that bodily labor was debasing and rendered both slaves and laborers incapable of mastering themselves or controlling their natural animal instincts. Both Cicero and Seneca, following earlier Greek models, divided occupations into "respectable" and "sordid"; to the latter category belonged not only laborers but also retailers and certain artisans. As Dale Martin aptly observes, "The ancient form of the body/soul dualism thus, not coincidently, reflects the class structure of society."[15] A comparison of the *Acts of Peter* and the *Acts of John* will suggest that those Christians who advocated for a fleshly, material, bodily Jesus worked to interrupt the ideological system that disdained the body and the people traditionally associated with it and projected a more inclusive community. In contrast, Christians who held that Jesus' body was immaterial, spiritual, or otherwise different, in their disavowal of the material body continued their culture's dismissal of those traditionally associated with the body—the nonelite.

The *Acts of John* consistently downplays the materiality of the body of Jesus, containing no mention of the incarnation or the birth or passion of Jesus and stressing Jesus' nonhuman qualities and immateriality. Although a number of the *Acts* feature Jesus' polymorphy (his ability to be perceived in different forms by different people at the same time), only the *Acts of John* describes a polymorphous Jesus before the resurrection, thereby emphasizing a consistent and continuous unreality for Jesus' human body in its earthly appearances. When John describes Jesus' call to him and his brother, he tells how his brother saw a child beckoning, but he saw a young man, and later, when he saw an old bald-headed man, his brother saw a young man (88–89). In John's account, Jesus' body presents like a mirage, appearing at the same time in different physical images to different perceivers.

John recounts how Jesus' eyes never closed and how, when John reclined upon Jesus' breast at table, it sometimes felt "smooth and tender, and sometimes hard, like stone" (89). Jesus also levitated off the ground, leaving no footprints (93). In the *Acts of John*, Jesus never had a real human body, so he never died and thus was never resurrected. In a section of the *Acts* that was likely added to the original text, this point is made explicit: "Neither am I he who is upon the cross" (99); "therefore I suffered none of the things that they will say of me" (101). John's Jesus is not human: "That is no man I preach to you to worship, but God unchangeable, God invincible.... If then you abide in him, you shall possess your soul invincible" (104).

The *Acts of Peter*, in contrast, asserts that Jesus had a human body, was born from a woman, ate and drank, suffered, died, and was resurrected. Peter stresses the physical reality of Jesus: "He ate and drank for our sake, although he was neither hungry nor thirsty. He also endured and suffered shameful things for us. He died and rose again because of us" (20). In his first address to the Romans, Peter proclaims Jesus' real birth, death, and resurrection: "God sent his son into the world ... brought forth by the Virgin Mary" (7). And he warns his listeners "not to look for another besides ... this crucified Nazarene who died and rose again on the third day" (7). The *Acts of Peter* depicts Jesus with a specific human identity, a Nazarene, who was truly born and truly died (23). Indeed, it is just on these points that Simon Magus attacks Peter, for believing in "a human being, a Jew and a carpenter's son" (14). This taunt does not trouble Peter; he accepts its truth. The *Acts of Peter* explicitly represents Jesus as having a human body, a human identity, even a human occupation.

Views of Social Hierarchy

The *Acts of John* appears to reflect the contemporary society's hierarchical convictions that some persons are inherently more worthy than others. This hierarchical stance is particularly evident in what have been called the interpolated chapters (94–102, 109), but the attitude pervades the *Acts*.[16] The Lord himself is depicted instructing John in hierarchy when, supposedly hanging on the cross, he appears to him. The Lord emphasizes John's privileged knowledge: "John, to the crowd below I am being crucified ... but to you I am speaking" (97). The Lord explains that he [Jesus] is not what they call him, "which is lowly and not worthy of me" (99), that is to say, a human body. Jesus explains that those in the crowd around the cross of light are of a lower nature (100) and tells John to ignore "the many" and disdain those outside the mystery (100). The Lord's words assert John's superior insight and position and imply a hierarchical community structure. The Lord explains that those who would know him know him as a kinsman (101). John later describes himself laughing at the multitude because of what the Lord has told him.

It is well attested that some second-century Christians, just as John did, held themselves to be superior to the general Christian community. Irenaeus, the church father, explains that the Valentinians classified people into three groups, the hylic (material), the psychic (souled), and the pneumatic (spiritual). Only the latter two divisions could attain salvation. The hylic could not be saved; regular Christians, according to the Valentinians, belonged to the middle group and must prove themselves worthy of salvation. The pneumatics' superior nature assured their salvation, and only they achieve the final grade—reunion with the Fullness (*Against the Heresies* 1.8.3). Scholars suggest that Irenaeus may overstate the determinism of the Valentinian scheme, but its intrinsic hierarchical nature is obvious. The Valentinian paradigm offers another example of the Greco-Roman drive to construct social categories that depend on the devaluation of the material and most likely, through long-established analogy, of those persons associated with providing material necessities. With such an attitude, these Christians would seem simply to remap upon the Christian community the traditional hierarchal assumptions holding that some in a society, those less associated with material life and its work, are innately superior to others.

In contrast, the *Acts of Peter* emphasizes not the kinship of some humans with the divine, but rather the universal and inherent weakness of the human condition. Peter explicitly presents himself in such a way as to ensure that no one mistakes him for a divine figure. Before his contest in the Forum, Peter asserts both his humanity and his failures: "Romans, I am one of you; I have human flesh and am a sinner" (28). Peter emphasizes his material being and his sins. Indeed, sins and their forgiveness provide a major theme in this narrative. The plot develops from Peter's mission to come to Rome to win back to the faith the Pauline Christians who have apostatized because of Simon's inducements. When he first addresses these Christians, he reminds them of God's mercy. God, moved by compassion for humankind, had sent his Son into the world (7). Peter also reminds them of his own failures; although he himself had witnessed miracles, nevertheless he denied the Lord, not once but three times. He reassures them, "But the Lord did not blame me. . . . He had mercy for the weakness of my flesh" (7).

Peter's vision of God's compassion comforts these fallen Christians, and they repent. In his address Peter also recalls his own miracle experi-

> Almighty God, moved by compassion, sent his son into the world and I was with him. And I walked on the water and survive as a witness. I confess I was there when he was at work in the world performing signs and wonders. Dearest brothers and sisters, I denied the Lord Jesus Christ not once but three times, for those who ensnared me were wicked dogs, just as the prophets of the Lord said. But the Lord did not blame me, and he turned to me. He had mercy for the weakness of my flesh, so that I wept bitterly, and I mourned for my little faith, having been deceived by the devil, and did not keep in mind the word of my Lord.
>
> —*Acts of Peter 7*

ence of walking upon the water. Later Marcellus mentions that Simon used this very episode and Peter's doubt upon the water to challenge his faith. Such reiterated references to Peter's failings permeate the narrative and work to present him as an example of God's persistent compassion. Marcellus, the senator, also fails in this narrative. Seduced by Simon, he withdraws his support from the Christian community, but the talking dog persuades Marcellus of the apostle's power, and he subsequently begs for forgiveness (9–10). Peter forgives and embraces Marcellus (11). The liberality of the Lord's and Peter's forgiveness and compassion for human weakness are touchstones in the *Acts of Peter*. No one is exempt; there is no hierarchical ordering. The apostle and the senator are as vulnerable to failure as others. The *Acts of John* proposes that some Christians are superior to others on the basis of a superior spirituality, but in the *Acts of Peter* all are equalized in their common fallibility.

A scene in the *Acts of John* featuring multiple resurrections shows how this narrative retains its society's inherently hierarchical perspective. The action begins when Callimachus, a wellborn Ephesian (73), becomes consumed with desire for Drusiana, the ascetic wife of Andronicus. Learning of his passion, Drusiana is so distraught at being the cause of sin that she sickens and dies. Callimachus's desire, however, does not abate, and after her burial, he bribes Fortunatus, Andronicus's steward, to open Drusiana's tomb so that he can defile her. On the third day after her death, John and Andronicus come to the tomb and find a strange sight: Callimachus lying with a huge snake sleeping upon him and, next to him, Fortunatus dead (73). John orders the snake off the man and prays, and Callimachus rises up and describes how he was undressing Drusiana when a beautiful youth covered her with his cloak and said, "Callimachus, die, that you may live" (76). Then the snake killed Fortunatus and terrified him [Callimachus] into a lifeless state.

Callimachus interprets his resurrection from the dead as a kind of spiritual conversion. He tells John that the command he heard (that he must die to live) is already fulfilled: "For that unbeliever, godless, lawless man is dead; I am raised by you as a believer, faithful and godly." Next Drusiana is raised up, and she asks that Fortunatus also be raised. But once raised, Fortunatus runs off, complaining of the Christians' power: "O how far the power of these awful people has spread! I wished I were not raised but remained dead, so as not to see them" (83). John, declaring that neither Fortunatus's soul nor his nature is changed, begins an extended anathema of Satan and all his issue. John concludes by foretelling a second death for Fortunatus, a death that, the reader soon discovers, has already occurred (86).

The action of this scene reiterates the naturalness of the elite's prefer-
ment. Two men were resurrected, Callimachus and Fortunatus, but only
one is saved. Both men were clearly sinners. Callimachus, described as one
of the most prominent young men of Ephesus (73), had desired necrophilia
with Drusiana, and Fortunatus, the steward, had abetted him. After Callimachus is raised, he tells about the voice he heard declaring his resurrection to a new life, and then he repents, falls at John's feet, and is embraced
by the apostle (76–78). But the case is quite different for the second sinner.
When Drusiana first proposes that Fortunatus be raised, Callimachus
objects, as the voice he heard did not mention Fortunatus. Callimachus
concludes, "If he were good, God out of mercy would have certainly raised
him through the blessed John. He knew that the man should have a bad
death" (81). Fortunatus is raised, but he wishes he were still dead and runs
away.

John announces that Fortunatus has not changed for the good (84)
and condemns him as Satan's offspring. His words suggest that Fortunatus
by his very nature was never capable of repentance: "O nature, naturally
unsuited for the better" (84).[17] The message in this vignette appears to be
that some humans by their very nature are prohibited from repentance
and salvation. This explains why, as Callimachus said, the voice never mentioned Fortunatus to Callimachus during his death experience. Resurrection from physical death would be wasted upon Fortunatus, as he is
incapable of spiritual life.

In contrast, Peter lays a much less adamant denunciation upon Simon,
who is called a child of the devil (28). Peter hopes he will repent, "for God
does not remember evil deeds" (28). When Simon does not repent and
threatens the faith of the Roman converts by flying over the city, Peter
appeals to the Lord to stop him. In his prayer Peter carefully specifies that
he does not want Simon killed but simply disabled. Peter's attitude toward
Simon keeps open a possibility for his repentance. Neither Peter's words
nor his actions suggest he believes that Simon is incapable of salvation. By
describing Fortunatus as by his very nature unsuited for becoming better
(84), the *Acts of John* reinscribes the hierarchal thinking of the contemporary society that restricted some people from a full moral life.

In fact, the scene at Drusiana's tomb can be read as one more refigura-
tion of the most conventional of the elitist social paradigms of Greco-
Roman society. Two sinners are raised; one proves worthy of salvation,
one does not. The worthy man, Callimachus, also happens to be wellborn,
one of the most prominent men of his city. The unworthy man, Fortunatus, is a servant, almost certainly a slave. This episode not only does nothing to challenge the society's traditional hierarchical assumptions, but

actively reinforces them. Characters assume their conventional social roles. The elite turn out to be naturally more suited to be better than their social inferiors. The wellborn Callimachus is able to use his second chance, even though as the necrophiliac he seems most guilty. But Fortunatus, the servant, is proved to be naturally unsuited for a better life. The episode, in fact, could be read to imply that favor and kindness are wasted on the lowborn; Fortunatus just throws away his second chance.

A multiple resurrection scene in the *Acts of Peter* offers resurrections from diverse status positions: a slave, a poor youth, and a rich one are each raised up. In this scene in the *Acts of John*, in contrast, two of the three raised are wealthy, and the other, a servant, proves unworthy of his resurrection. The two texts reflect inherently different positions toward social hierarchy. The *Acts of John*, with its spiritual Jesus, disavows the body and those connected to the body's work. The narrative displays the same justification and bias for hierarchical thinking characteristic of the society as a whole, and again a servant turns out to be innately less worthy than one of the elite. The *Acts of Peter*, with its material, bodily Jesus, refuses its culture's contempt for the body and those traditionally associated with it—the nonelite—and moves toward a less exclusionary perspective.

> The lover of Drusiana, inflamed with lust through the influence of the many-formed Satan, bribed the greedy steward of Andronicus with much money. And he opened Drusiana's tomb and left him to accomplish the forbidden thing on her body that was once denied him. Since he had not had her during her life, he continually thought of her body after she was dead and exclaimed, "Although alive you refused to join with me in love, after your death I will dishonor your corpse." With this intention, he had arranged the wicked deed with the accursed steward, and he burst into the tomb with him. When they had opened the door, they began to remove the grave clothes from the corpse, saying, "Miserable Drusiana, what have you gained? Could you not have done this while alive? It need not have grieved you if you had done it willingly." When only her undergarment remained to hide her nakedness, a serpent appeared from somewhere, bit the steward, and killed him. The serpent did not bite the young man, but wound itself around his feet, hissing terribly, and when he fell, the serpent sat on him.
> —*Acts of John* 70–71

In this context it is interesting to recall that while the *Acts of Peter* feature a powerfully articulate talking dog, the animal scene in the *Acts of John* depicts the apostle asking bedbugs to vacate his bed so that he may have some rest. In the morning his companions discover all the bugs collected in a mass at the door. They return to the bed only at John's permission: "Since you have been wise to heed my warning, go back to your place" (61). Like *John's* resurrection scene, this scene also reflects an inherent hierarchy in the narrative's social thinking about the lower orders. The obedient bugs do not get to speak, but only to listen, obey, and know their place.

The *Acts of Peter* and *Acts of John* exhibit different degrees of resistance to contemporary social structures. While they both challenge their society through their rejection of marriage, the *Acts of Peter* projects a more inclusive Christian community.

CONCLUSIONS

The early Roman imperial period was one of dynamic change, as Rome extended its power into communities across the Greek East. In this time of ongoing transition, different cultural, social, and ethnic groups maneuvered to articulate their own positions and cultural identities in the new context. Identity, as we know, is often largely a product of rhetorical self-fashioning. Groups come to understand and assert themselves through techniques of self-display. In the early Christian period, various groups across the empire were using fictional narratives to construct and position themselves. A reading of the *Acts of John, Paul, Peter, Andrew,* and *Thomas* suggests that some Christians of the period criticized the ideology of marriage out of their resistance to the wider culture's structures of power and privilege. In varying degrees, all the *Apocryphal Acts* challenge their society's hegemonic claims that the elite have an uncontested right to all they desire. The forms of social critique mobilized within this ancient body of Christian fiction sometimes differed significantly, however. The contrast between the uncompromising incarnationalism and corresponding egalitarianism of the *Acts of Peter* and the more transcendentalizing theology and relatively elitist politics of the *Acts of John* reminds us of the diversity of perspective encompassed by the early Christian communities.

FOR FURTHER READING

Bovon, François, Ann Graham Brock, and Christopher R. Matthews, eds. *The Apocryphal Acts of the Apostles: Harvard Divinity School Studies.* Cambridge: Harvard University Center for the Study of World Religions, 1999.

Bremmer, Jan N., ed. *The Apocryphal Acts of John.* Studies on the Apocryphal Acts of the Apostles 1. Kampen: Kok Pharos, 1995.

———. *The Apocryphal Acts of Paul and Thecla.* Studies on the Apocryphal Acts of the Apostles 2. Kampen: Kok Pharos, 1996.

———. *The Apocryphal Acts of Peter: Magic, Miracles and Gnosticism.* Studies on the Apocryphal Acts of the Apostles 3. Leuven: Peeters, 1998.

Burrus, Virginia. *Chastity as Autonomy: Women in the Stories of the Apocryphal Acts.* Studies in Women and Religion 23. Lewiston, N.Y.: Mellen, 1987.

Hock, Ronald F., J. Bradley Chance, and Judith Perkins, eds. *Ancient Fiction and Early Christian Narrative.* Atlanta: Scholars, 1998.

MacDonald, Dennis Ronald. *The Legend and the Apostle: The Battle for Paul in Story and Canon.* Philadelphia: Westminster, 1983.

Pervo, Richard. *Profit with Delight: The Literary Genre of the Acts of the Apostles.* Philadelphia: Fortress, 1987.

Thomas, Christine M. *The Acts of Peter, Gospel Literature, and the Ancient Novel: Rewriting the Past.* Oxford: Oxford University Press, 2003.

Wills, Lawrence M. *The Jewish Novel in the Ancient World: Myth and Poetics.* Ithaca, N.Y.: Cornell University Press, 1995.

MARTYRDOM AS EXALTATION

ROBIN DARLING YOUNG

CHAPTER THREE

Sometime around the year 390, Eulalia, a Spanish girl martyred ninety years earlier, was commemorated in a lyric poem written by her countryman Prudentius, a lawyer and administrator in the now-Christian imperial court at Milan. He had composed the hymn for an annual festival in her honor, a public liturgical ceremony in a yearly cycle of saints' days, in which the city's residents could praise their saint as a powerful intercessor in the court of heaven. From her station in heaven, Eulalia was still close enough to earth to hear a Christian congregation in Merida singing her praises. Eulalia was like other martyrs whose enshrined remains lay near or in cities throughout the Greco-Roman world. She had died a violent death—having been scourged before being burned—but was now promoted to the rank of powerful patron.[1]

How did her violent death result in her exaltation to a position of superhuman power? To answer that question, the historian must inquire into the previous two hundred years of documented Christian history. Several developments help account for the broadly held early Christian conviction that lay behind Eulalia's elevation: the interpretation of voluntary death as a witness benefiting both the Christian and the community, the acknowledged power of intercessory prayer joined with sacrifice, the equality of women martyrs with their male counterparts, and the illegality and consequent persecution of Christianity under the early Roman Empire. The main development behind the veneration of martyrs, however, was the understanding that the death of Jesus, a divine–human being, offered a pattern for martyrdoms. Jesus was interpreted as both the priest and sacrifice of the (new) Temple in Jerusalem, and his death was replicated in the performative rites of a Christian assembly whose members were understood simultaneously as priests, sacrifices, and temples of God.[2]

Early Christians shared with other Jewish dissenters of the first century, such as the Qumran community, a belief that the discredited Temple of

Jerusalem had its veritable existence in the human beings of their own community. Already in the Epistle to the Hebrews and in the book of Revelation, Jesus was construed as the High Priest bringing benefits formerly confined to the Temple to his followers in Judaea.[3] First-century texts support the widespread existence of such beliefs within Judaism and help to explain the strong presence in the literature of second- and third-century Christianity of the assumption that the Temple lives on in Christians and their rituals.[4] Such a continuity is not surprising, but if it is just beginning to be explored in New Testament studies, it still remains to be investigated in the study of early Christianity and of early Christian martyrdom. Yet the evidence of contemporaneous Judaism supports the claim that the early church contained a robust theology of sacrifice, communal and personal, and likewise that martyrs were interpreted through that lens.

Already by the end of the second century, Christians cherished their martyrs as saints, or "holy ones." They gathered at the graves, or *martyria*, of these saints on the anniversaries of their death, with processions, hymns, and ceremonial meals. The saints' relics had the power to heal and protect, and they also kept the saint close to those who venerated them, making it likely that their repeated praises would result in further favorable treatment.

Clearly, the veneration of the saints constituted, in part, an exaltation of the saint by means of a ritual. In late antiquity, veneration consisted of more than just a ritual, however. A martyr was venerated by means of the composition of his biography or the deeds of her martyrdom as well—the act of writing down and interpreting the actions that guaranteed the memory of the community in which she had lived, or of other more far-flung communities that heard about and honored the saint as well. Because these martyr acts were interpretations that aimed to connect the life of the martyr with the life of Christ or others who had died for God, they were quasi-scriptural; they aimed to be a sacred kind of text as well.

The number of saints' lives is large, and because Christians continued to characterize the church by its association with martyrdom, producing works to promote the martyrs' veneration, the number of later interpretations of saints' lives is even larger. Martyrs become the ideal for the Christian, in a kind of interpretive overlay upon the life of Christ, who could not as a divinity be perfectly imitated. The martyrs started low—low as human beings, and low in relation to the power of the broader society of the Roman Empire. Their acts are written up specifically to show how it is that a human being can be exalted, if God wishes that she or he become a martyr.

The goal of this chapter is to examine how, already in an earlier period and not just in the later cult of the saints, commemorative veneration in written form portrayed the very acts of trial, suffering, and death as a ritual of exaltation in itself. The acts of the martyr, formalized as they are, attest to the way in which the early Christian authors who composed the texts understood suffering and death as a ritual exaltation that raised the martyr from human to semidivine or angelic status. Only thus could human beings become guardians and guides.

Two points need to be emphasized here: first, as we have already seen, martyrdoms are rituals of exaltation—exaltation of the divinized human being—that draw upon the conceptions of the Temple as a place of sacrifice and identify the martyr's death as a sacrifice, not as a suicide. If it is a sacrifice, it is efficacious for something. Second, martyrdoms permit the exaltation of women, who are equally a sacrifice. Martyrs' acts generally overlook the broader cultural assumption that women can neither be nor offer a sacrifice, because women are shown to do both.

The newfound suitability of women to become sacrifices (and even priests of their own offering) and hence to be exalted above their stations appears very clearly in Prudentius's poem, although presumably it was not his direct intention to exalt women as such. His hymn to the twelve-year-old virgin and aristocrat Eulalia of Merida, victim of the great persecution under Diocletian, dwelt, in a thoroughly conventional way, on the dramatic contrast between Eulalia's girlish weakness and her heroic bravery. Prematurely wise, composed, and brave, ascetically contemptuous of feminine ornaments, Eulalia's spirit had rebelled at the order that Christians offer incense to the emperor's image. Eluding her parents' guard, she escaped from her home on a winter night and hurried into the city to confront the Roman praetor, denouncing Maximian and the pagan worship of his empire. By legal proceeding she received the death she had known already to expect.

In keeping with a prior tradition that depicts the martyr vaulting from defeat and death to a supercosmic position of power and honor not depending upon the official honors of the political world, but apparently overturning those honors, Prudentius composed a hymn that celebrates the paradoxical exaltation of dramatic reversal. Scourged and burned, Eulalia's body was covered by the falling snow as her spirit flew heavenward in the form of a dove, a visible rebuke to her tormentors and a sign of her innocence. Dying for God and his anointed king, as a witness to the victories and holy name of Christ against idolatry and imperial might, she now interceded for her city, to whose greatness and wealth she had become the most important contributor. Her own political allegiance had become that of her city, and she had become the city's protector: invisibly she had defeated the empire while helping to convert it and leaving its power intact. At her annual feast day, the Christians of the city could borrow Prudentius's words to ask for the aid of the little girl whose testimony earned her the highest place in the universe. The hymn's last stanza reads:

> It is thus pleasing to honor her bones,
> The altar, too, raised over them—
> She, placed at the feet of God,
> Looks out from a distance at these things
> And propitiated by this hymn
> Sheds favor on her people.

From Prudentius's perspective, Eulalia had a double station. Her heroic act of martyrdom established her as a member of the heavenly court. She had helped to overturn pagan rule and was a reliable benefactor of the city whose "illustrious honor" she had increased by her martyr's blood and the *martyrium,* the martyr's tomb, inscribed with her name. For this she became a kind of invisible mayor or member of the city council, dispensing favors in proportion to the flattery she gained.

> Eulalia, nobly born
> Yet nobler in the style of her death
> Holy virgin of her own Merida,
> Born from the city's breasts,
> She crowns her with her bones
> And protects her with her love.
> Near the far West is the place
> That has borne an exemplary glory—
> A mighty city, richly populated,
> Yet far mightier for the blood of the martyrdom
> And for the inscription on the virgin's tomb.

Embellished by the poetic craft of Prudentius, the Eulalia of the hymn was at the same time a creation of the common Christian imagination, well stocked with biblical and poetic references and reflective of a long-established Christian practice of interpretation and worship. The deed of martyrdom and its subsequent celebration were both quasi-sacramental actions habitual to Christianity from its earliest days. To this religious tradition Prudentius added his own literary skill in depicting, for an eager audience of Merida's Christians, the pathos of a slaughtered girl whose potential mercy mirrored Christ's own. He gave them a hymn to sing on the day that they remembered her and sought her aid, at the same time congratulating their city on possessing her relics and power. Like other fourth-century authors, Prudentius here skillfully combined an ancient pagan tradition with a distinctively Christian one when he promoted a city by reciting the heroism of one of its citizens at the same time that he helped that city's church venerate its native martyr.

What accounts for the emergence of this particular kind of civic drama—the veneration, in hymn and ritual, of a weak female child on the part of a poet and the inhabitants of the city of Merida? Prudentius's hymn serves as a ritual of exaltation, and it is the aim of this chapter to sketch the origins of that ritual as expressed in the earlier acts of the martyrs. The chapter first discusses the general characteristics of martyrdom in early Christianity. It then turns to an account of the complex cluster of traditions that constituted an interpretive field in which martyrdom gained meaning. Finally, it examines two particular examples of the use of those traditions in the creation of a ritual of exaltation, that is, the formalization of a means in which the deeds of one particular person are publicly celebrated as an example of a religious act of the highest value both to that person and to her or his admirers.

MARTYRDOM IN THE EARLY CHRISTIAN CONTEXT

"Martyrdom" is the usual English translation of the Greek term *martyria*, meaning the state of being a witness to someone or something, as well as the witness itself. Yet the connotations of the English term are both broader and more specific, because they reflect the development of both the practice and the concept within early Christian history. There is only incomplete scholarly consensus about the origin, elements, and character of martyrdom, but early Christian texts use the term in connection with a series of events and dispositions: the occurrence of persecution, often understood as the operation of demonic opposition to God; the refusal to renounce Christianity or offer sacrifice to the emperor that is construed as blasphemy or religious infidelity; the willing sacrifice of the publicly witnessing Christian as a means of appeasing divine anger; the revelation of heaven, or ascent to heaven, on the part of the martyr; the veneration of the martyr by her or his local church; and the composition of accounts of the martyrdom itself in order to increase that veneration.

Not all martyrdoms were recounted in the particular literary form of acts; since martyrdom was the culmination of Christian life, according to most early Christian authors, it is mentioned in numerous contexts. Nonetheless, the act of witness itself, either recounted, interpreted, or hoped for and appearing in letters, poems, treatises, or histories (such as the Acts of the Apostles or apocryphal acts), as well as martyr acts proper, led to a concentration upon the biography of the martyr and an exaltation or magnification of the martyr's person and deeds.

Of all early Christian practices, the veneration of the martyr-saints was the most popular and accessible. With a unanimity that eluded them in other matters of belief, Christians repeatedly gave three reasons for honoring these women and men as the most admirable and intensely exemplary of believers. First, the imitation of Christ enjoined on all believers appeared most visibly in their triumphant deaths. Second, in reward for their faithfulness, the martyrs now in heaven possessed special powers. And third, when Christians praised and supplicated them, the martyrs would return the favor in the form of visible assistance. This complex rationale appears either implicitly or explicitly in numerous forms of literature attesting to early Christian martyrdom.

This rationale was also the common belief upon which Prudentius drew. His art was not unlike that of the iconographers who had already "written" the deeds of saints in painted icons or mosaic panels to be placed for devotion in the large churches built in the fourth century. Like the creators of visual images, Prudentius could heighten his readers' wonder at the martyrs' deeds by vivid portraiture, contrasting their common human weakness and fear or their low social position with their determination and courage in the face of torments administered by imperial persecutors. At the same time, this accomplished lawyer and bureaucrat crafted liturgical offerings in the form of lyric poetry. Prudentius could do this because the Christian church for which he wrote unanimously believed that honoring the martyrs, whose bones lay in their tombs while their spirits interceded in the court of heaven, resulted, in this intense exchange of commodities, in the protection and favor of the saints.

Yet to list the three features above—imitation of Christ, possession of power, and distribution of favors—as common to the veneration of martyrs in early Christianity merely results in pointing out a recognizable feature of the religious landscape. Why and how did Prudentius, among many others of his era, come to possess the ability and the imperative to provide for popular appetite for hearing about, praying to, and imitating the martyrs?

An answer lies in the obscure period of the formation of the church itself, when the practice of martyrdom was already spoken of as if it were taken for granted, and not from any formal decision taken by a specific teacher, bishop, or council. And the reasons for this, in turn, are two: first, the lack of a centrally organized church, and second, the preexistence of the ideal of martyrdom itself.

During its first three centuries, the Christian community was insufficiently solidified to have been brought to a collective decision by means of any single authority. From the mid-first to the early fourth century, the church was a confederation of communities in different locations. Universalizing in their self-presentation, following the preaching of early teachers such as Paul, they were still small, local, and weak with respect both to each other and to the urban worlds in which they were located. These communities could command obedience locally within their congregations, by means of effective instruction before initiation and after baptism by penitential discipline and persuasion of full members, but their often-attested sense of themselves as belonging to a catholic, or universal, body resulted mainly from agreement with common tradition and increasing habit of communication by visits and exchanges of letters. They knew from the letters of Paul and John, from the Gospels, and from the first chapters of the book of Acts that they were meant to be one flock, but until the rise of the powerful metropolitan bishops of the late third century and the general councils of the fourth, the union of the Christian communities that represented the ideal single church of Christ depended upon extended negotiations and the intelligent arguments of teachers and interpreters.

If no one leader of the church promoted and spread a belief in the value of martyrdom, what would then explain its nearly universal acceptance among Christians? Even groups later identified as dissidents prized their martyrs, Montanists and Donatists, for instance, when they might disagree with other Christians on central beliefs or practices of the faith. Only a few teachers despised martyrdom; following the opinions of ancient authors, contemporary scholars have generally identified these Christians as Gnostics, holding to a dualism that led them to discount the importance of the body and the corporeal offering of martyrdom and its analogue, the eucharist. Its nearly universal admiration among early Christians suggests either that martyrdom predated the moment of separation between Christianity and Judaism or that martyrdom—or the expectation of it—was a catalyst for that separation and hence a constitutive part of the religion itself, a given.

UNDERSTANDING THE BEGINNINGS OF MARTYRDOM

All too often, scholars have analyzed the literature and practice of martyrdom as if they resulted primarily from Roman persecution of an illegal religion. Such a perspective, however, makes martyrdom almost an extrinsic, temporary feature of Christianity—the accidental effect of purely external factors. In this view, martyrdom is understood to result from the clash between Christianity and its opponents and thus to have developed among early Christian communities as a response to opposition from groups or governments that opposed and wished to control, damage, or suppress Christianity.

Yet martyrdom was not merely the result of a clash between the early church and the laws and officials of the Roman Empire. It was an ideal that derived much of its power from prior tradition. In late Second Temple

Judaism, several strands of interpretation initially emerge that are later adapted in early Christian writings. The view that the Temple is now represented by a righteous community, which itself offers sacrifices of praise that expiate sins, appears in Daniel (LXX), 1, 2, and 3 Maccabees, and the Qumran texts, for example. The revelation of the throne of God, to which a righteous person has ascended, becomes part of the tradition of ascent and apocalyptic vision, seen, for instance, in the Books of Enoch and the *Testaments of the Twelve Patriarchs*. These revelations often occur in the context of conflict, in which there is warfare on heaven and earth between the servants of God and the evil forces opposing God. Such visions and revelations are commonly associated with prophecy.

Moreover, the expectation of suffering on the part of those faithful to God appears already in ancient Jewish scripture and becomes a more prominent part of Jewish religious culture with the exile and the later occupation of the land of Israel by Greeks and, later, Romans. The history of Jewish thought about suffering and martyrdom in the Second Temple period is complex, and its subsequent development by the early rabbis reveals both similarities and differences with parallel Christian developments. For our purposes, however, it may suffice to consider two sets of scriptural texts from the earlier period that show how the figure of the martyr was already beginning to take shape. The first is Second Isaiah; the second is the book of Daniel.

Beginning, then, with Second Isaiah, we note that the "servant, [God's] chosen" of Isa. 42:1 and 52:13—53:12 is portrayed as an innocent sacrifice, a royal and prophetic person who suffers for the entire people of Israel: "he was wounded for our transgressions, he was bruised for our iniquities; upon him was the chastisement that made us whole, and with his stripes we are healed." Later he "shall prosper; he shall be exalted and lifted up, and shall be very high" (52:13). In Isa. 53:11 he is said to have borne "the sin of many, and made intercession for the transgressors."

Later, the book of Daniel will reinterpret this view of the servant of God's vicarious suffering in a context where the opponents of Hellenization in the second century BCE are regarded collectively as the servant. (Later still, of course, the authors of two Gospels—Matthew and Luke—and other early Christian literature apply the verse to Christ.) The author of Daniel elaborates the tale of the trials of Daniel and his companions in the Persian court, a coded reference to the trials of the Jews of Palestine under Antiochus IV Epiphanes in 167–164 BCE. In view of the interpretations that would subsequently draw on Daniel, the book's important features are the roles of the prophet and the three young men, understood as representatives of the entire people of Israel; the eschatological insistence upon the nearness and victory of God and his kingdom; and the promise

Fig. 3.1. Early Christian ideas about martyrdom were powerfully influenced by the story of the three Jewish youths sentenced by the Persian King Nebuchadnezzar to be burned to death, as recorded in the book of Daniel. Catacomb of Priscilla, Rome, Italy. Photo credit: Erich Lessing / Art Resource, NY.

of the vindication of the Jewish people via a return from exile. It is a vivid story of persecution, righteous sufferers, and the intervention of God to rescue them. Interestingly, Daniel and his companions do not actually die as a result of their fidelity and their trials, but they nevertheless become eloquent symbols of martyrdom and resurrection. In fact, the contest between the three boys and the Persian ruler Nebuchadnezzar in chapter 3, in which the boys are apparently protected by an angel inside the furnace into which they are cast, makes it clear that they are rewarded for their faithfulness with a kind of protection against death, that is, immortality: "the fire had not had any power over the bodies of those men" (3:27). When the willingness of the four to die rather than transgress Jewish law is added to the final story of the deaths of many in Israel, the entire book has become a charter for martyrdom. Eventually, the book predicts a triumphant end to the persecution of Israel (11:21-35). After a "time of trouble" those "written in the book" will be resurrected. Those who are resurrected to eternal life seem to become angels: "those who are wise shall shine like the brightness of the sky, and those who lead many to righteousness, like the stars forever and ever" (12:3).

For the later interpreters of Daniel who read the Greek version of the Aramaic text, the significance of personal martyrdom and sacrifice followed by exaltation was even clearer. In a long liturgical section appended to Daniel 3, the three boys make a progression from supplication through deliverance to thanksgiving and worship—that is, they ascend from danger into a kind of anticipation of presence at the spiritual Temple or court of God. In these Greek additions to the text, they are walking freely "in the midst of the flames, hymning God and blessing the Lord." Publicly affirming the power and justice of God, and in particular his judgment against Jerusalem, they also lament the absence of the Temple—a fictional device suitable to the book's setting in Persia. They describe Israel's predicament thus: "For we, O lord, have become fewer than any nation, and are brought low this day in all the world because of our sins. At this time there is no prince, or prophet, or leader, no burnt offering, or sacrifice, or oblation, or incense, no place to make an offering before you or to find mercy" (3:14-15). In the absence of a place or means to worship, the boys themselves become virtual temples: "Yet with a contrite heart and a humble spirit may we be accepted, as though it were with burnt offerings of rams and bulls, and with tens of thousands of fat lambs; such may our sacrifice be in your sight this day, and may we wholly follow you, for there will be no shame for those who trust in you" (3:16-17).

Thus, within Second Temple Judaism, beginning in the second century BCE, there emerged an emphasis on suffering both as a result of opposition and as propitiation for the sins of Israel. These themes were continuously reworked, as faithful Jews responded to the occupation and profanation of their land by offering their lives as propitiation for the sin of those Jews who cooperated with the pagans. Indeed, some Jewish thinkers had come to understand that the Temple in Jerusalem was itself compromised as a place of sacrificial worship of God, so that the sacrifice that God required of his people could now only be accomplished outside that Temple, but in imitation of what it was supposed to be. The Qumran community viewed itself as a replacement for the Temple, its members as priests or angels accomplishing the Temple sacrifices in an alternative way. Other Jews viewed the persecutions and deaths of those faithful to the law as the equivalent of Temple sacrifices (thus 2 Maccabees 7, as well as Daniel). Likewise, other Jews—the first followers of Christ—viewed the community of those baptized as an alternative Temple and understood their deaths in persecution to be an imitation of the death of Christ, the supreme Temple sacrifice. The birth, life, trial, execution, and triumphant resurrection of Christ they understood to conform to the pattern of a sacrificial death in the Temple, and they perceived baptism and the eucharist to be signs and extensions of his death. They could do this because they understood that the resurrected Christ lived in every baptized believer, making imitation of Christ in baptism, eucharist, and persecution to be the foundation of a widening sacrificial system.

The calling of Israel, the giving of the Law, and the worship of God in the Temple were all reinterpreted. Not only were they the foundations of the Jewish people in pre-Hellenistic times, but they were also the prediction of the life of Christ and the calling of his disciples, as well as the ongoing access to Christ and to God through Christ by means of sacrifice, imitation, and interpretation. What must be emphasized in taking the measure of this reinterpretation following the appearance of the Messiah is the apocalyptic, eschatological, and strongly otherworldly aspect of its aims.

Early Christians were all supposed to be martyrs—witnesses—although not all were expected to die. Paul instructed the recipients of his letters that they would suffer, and the writers of the Gospels recorded it as a central feature of the teaching of Jesus. All were expected to give public testimony (martyria) to a supremely political and public fact: that the kingdom of God had already arrived in the person of his Anointed, Christ, and that this kingdom trumped all others. Although proselytizing, conversion, and catechesis could be private in this early period, this did not negate the necessity for public testimony. It was only in the experience of decades of sporadic conflict that Christians began to set terms and conditions for giving public witness, so that, for example, the testimony would be successful as indicated by the endurance of the martyr.

Nevertheless, the eagerness with which many early Christians sought a public occasion to give witness indicates that they had already been primed, indeed trained, for the opportunity. It is also likely that they already understood this giving witness in sacrificial terms, so that their witness became a ritual occasion—a sacrificial liturgy parallel to, and with some of the same effects as, the eucharist. Out of this ritual of exaltation in which a martyr became a saint grew the devotion to the saints in early Christianity, along with their relics and the public cycle of ceremonies devoted to their memories.

MARTYRS AS EXALTED VICTIMS

Early Christian authors, and the martyrs themselves, thus followed Jewish precedent when they construed martyrdoms as liturgical acts, offerings of themselves to God as redemptive sacrifices on their own behalf and on behalf of their congregation (and, indeed, of all humanity) that likewise provided a means for ascending to the throne of God in the manner of previous Jewish prophets and visionaries. What is new in early Christianity is the way in which these martyrdoms are understood as the appropriation of the identity of another through mimesis, thus accomplishing a mass or common exaltation in Jesus. The way of ascent and exaltation is thereby opened not just to a priesthood or restricted class of trained visionaries, but potentially to every Christian. Whether this differed in practice is another matter. While this chapter does not argue for the "democracy" of early Christian martyrdom, it does argue that the extension of sacrificial opportunities to all within the Christian community made for a tradition in which the elite of a community were also the nonelite. Martyrs, through their actions and the narratives about them, became the quintessential representatives of Christian identity. They blazed a trail into death and the kingdom of God and were understood to mediate God's favors while they served the community and stood as exemplars of brave faith. It was the martyrs who had fulfilled the obligations of their baptismal contract, as Origen wrote in his *Exhortation to Martyrdom*. They stood in the place of the ancient priesthood.

Yet in this the martyrs competed with others. In early Christianity, an ordained ministry of trained leaders and interpreters gradually emerged and ruled the church in an increasingly hierarchical way, eventually coming to see themselves as heirs of the Levitical priesthood. The unordained, sometimes unlearned martyrs were frequently viewed as direct rivals of the bishops, as we see in the works of Cyprian of Carthage, whose authority was challenged by those preparing for martyrdom,[5] or in the dream of Perpetua, in which the bishop abases himself before her as a sign of her higher authority as martyr.[6] The social position of the martyrs, therefore, could be described as inherently ambiguous: selected by the divine will rather than by membership in a socially restrictive association, not required to be learned or even literate, not restricted to wealthy male citizens, martyrs were still, in most Christian textual sources, regarded as the most completely or faithfully Christian members of the church. On the other hand, the martyrs' authority was necessarily temporary, their immediate power restricted to certain occasions, and their stories controlled by interpretation.

This ambiguous position often received a theological explanation that followed from the portrait of Christ as the Suffering Servant or that drew from the New Testament writings the assertion that social divisions had been overcome "in Christ," that is, by the presence of Christ in the church. It is interesting to note that the deaths of martyrs were famously puzzling to non-Christians, including the officials of the empire who sent them to their deaths as a penalty for illegal activity. Christian texts play on the stupefaction of the persecutors, their apparent victory but hidden defeat, and their theological theme conditions the perspective of the Christian authors who chronicle and celebrate martyrdom. In addition, there was some opposition in early Christianity to dying for Christ, and some questions about whether martyrdom should not be avoided, and so Christian

Fig. 3.2. The North African martyr Perpetua left a remarkable journal of her time in prison in which she recorded the visions she received in the days before her death. In one of these visions, she sees herself transformed into a naked young man who wins a wrestling match with a formidable opponent. In this mosaic portrait, however, she appears demurely clad. Archbishop's Palace, Ravenna, Italy. Photo credit: Scala / Art Resource, NY.

authors themselves had to explain their interpretation and advocacy of such combat.

Martyrdom was, in theory, enjoined upon all, but it also required extreme virtue and courage. One expositor and cautious apologist for martyrdom, Clement of Alexandria, approached the egalitarianism of martyrdom by citing as precedent for early Christian martyrdom the deaths of more ancient and brave people, as evidence of a general human ability, when informed by reason, to strike an attitude of contempt toward suffering in view of a higher or more permanent state of happiness: "Neither, then, the hope of happiness nor the love of God takes whatever happens ill but remains free, although through among the wildest beasts or into the all-devouring fire; though racked with a tyrant's tortures. Depending as it does on the divine favor, it ascends aloft unenslaved, surrendering the body to those who can touch it alone" (*Miscellanies* 4.8). Here Clement reflects a culturally elite view of martyrdom, wherein the most highly trained person is the one who can approach a painful death calmly; the Thracian god Zalmoxis, he continued, was an example of a person "who is judged of the most sterling worth [and] is put to death, to the distress of those who have practiced philosophy, but have not been selected, at being reckoned unworthy of a happy service."

However, when Clement turns to the church's martyrs as an authentic instance of these ancient heroic deaths, he vacillates between holding that this kind of death is available to all and arguing that its heroic virtue is really only a trait of a cultivated person (typically an elite male). His ambivalence is part of the church's ambivalence, as part of an ancient society that took gradations of human value for granted. Here, perhaps thinking of the story of the mother of the Maccabees, Clement writes, "So the church is full of those, as well chaste women as men, who all their life have practiced for the death that rouses up to Christ. For the one whose life is framed as ours is, may philosophize without education, whether barbarian, whether Greek, whether slave—whether an old man, or a boy, or a woman. For self-control is common to all human beings who have made choice of it." Clement uses this dictum, Stoic in origin, to orient his discussion of martyrdom, and in particular his views about the relative positions of men and women, divided into superior and inferior in this world by their possession of bodies, but in the next equal because they are all humans and rational. Although part of a larger discussion about the worth and the proper preparation and conditions for martyrdom, his statement can stand here to indicate that already in the late second century an established tradition viewed martyrdom as the common destiny of Christ's disciples, predicted by Christ: "So it was not that he wished us to be persecuted, but he intimated beforehand what we shall suffer by the prediction of what would take place, training us to endurance, to which he promised the inheritance" (4.11).

Clement's view of martyrdom represents one elaboration of a much more ancient tradition that regards suffering and death out of allegiance to God not only as part of the public confession to him that arises from study and devotion, but also as a rebuttal of God's opponents and a sanctification of the sufferer. The act of faithful suffering is understood to redeem the sins of others and to attest to the holiness of the witness. As we have seen, this view first appears clearly in Second Isaiah and the book of Daniel, both of which present figures of holy people who suffer in Israel's stead.[7] Extended consideration of two examples of Christian martyrdom literature will further illumine the distinctly Christian interpretation of martyrdom as a rite of exaltation while also demonstrating the continuity of themes over the space of two centuries. The first is from the letters of Ignatius, bishop of the church of Antioch in the first years of the second century, and the second is from an anonymous account of the martyrdom of a group of women in the early fourth century.

The Letters of Ignatius

Ignatius of Antioch was arrested, tried, and sent to Rome for execution somewhere between the years 110 and 117. Thus he was a convicted criminal under Roman law and expected to meet his death in a public spectacle in Rome, where he would be put in the role of a gladiator before being mauled and killed by wild animals. As bishop of the church of Antioch and leader among the other churches, Ignatius wrote seven letters to guide Christian congregations faced with persecution. As his letters make clear, Ignatius expects that future martyrdoms will occur soon and that the support of congregations for their martyred members will take the form of concord and prayer, as well as training in scriptural interpretation and Christian teaching.[8]

Although each letter is directed toward the immediate and urgent situation of his correspondents, and therefore is little more than a series of notes or reminders to those already familiar with Christian teaching at significant depth, Ignatius has obviously become a master of an already-established tradition. He is familiar with the Gospels and the letters of Paul, and he knows the prophetic and legislative writings of the Old Testament, as well as the wisdom literature. He has worked out a principle of interpretation, and he is well aware of the opposing interpretations of "Judaizers" and other heretical teachers. Therefore he urges his congregations not only to be faithful to the pattern of Christian teaching but also to avoid particular misinterpretations of religious behavior and thought. His

Fig. 3.3. As he anticipated his own death in the Roman arena, Ignatius imagined himself a gladiator and referred to the soldiers who had arrested him as leopards. This Roman mosaic of a leopard and a gladiator seems to open a window onto Ignatius's fantasy. Galleria Borghese, Rome, Italy. Photo credit: Scala / Art Resource, NY.

own uncertainty about how he will meet his destiny colors his letters and gives them an additionally urgent character, as many commentators have noted.

However, underpinning the uses to which his letters are to be put by the recipients lies a pattern of thought about Christian worship in the "last times" that draws very deeply from the traditions of the Temple and ascent to the Temple found already in Second Temple Judaism and in the thought of Jesus and Paul and other writers of the New Testament. For Ignatius, the Temple, now identified with the church, stands as the center and portal of the world, and devotion to the Temple marks every letter he writes. Ignatius understands the Temple as the entry to the heavenly court, and he believes that within that Temple Jesus, whom he understands as the wisdom of God the Creator, had already initiated apt sacrifices before the beginning of the world. To participate in those sacrifices is to gain entry to the world of invisible realities that control this visible world; actually, to become a sacrifice is to become identified with Jesus and to become oneself a portal to salvation.

This interpretation of the cosmology of the earthly Temple and its sacrifices of blood, transposed in Christianity to martyrdom and eucharist (thanks to the cessation of animal sacrifices in the Temple, which ended, at least in principle, with the crucifixion of Jesus), requires that both the communal action of the church and the person of the martyr, or indeed of any Christian, be interpreted in a certain way.

Ignatius discusses the church and the Christian martyrs in terms of a reinterpreted Temple most concentratedly in two letters, those to the Ephesians and the Romans. He uses the language of temple sacrifice in Ephesians 8, for instance, when he says, "I have been consecrated an offscouring [outcast]" or expiatory victim and tells his readers, "You are as stones of the Temple of the Father. . . . You are also then all roadmates, God-bearers and temple-bearers, Christ-bearers, holiness-bearers, and in every way adorned with the commandments of Jesus Christ." Here Ignatius has already worked in an extended metaphor of the construction of a temple "made ready for the house of God the father, carried up to the heights by the engine of Jesus Christ, that is the cross, and using as a rope the Holy Spirit." This metaphor reflects the art of the architect as well as the heavenly temple, where the Son and the Spirit are at the same time material and spiritual rope and engine, and Ignatius has imagined the cross as a structure to hold a pulley bearing heavy stone. Ignatius also lays out a theme of exaltation by means of suffering, and he extends to his readers the qualities of the martyr: "Let us be found to be their brothers by gentleness; let us be zealous to be imitators of the Lord, and seek who might suffer the more wrong, be the more poor, the more despised; that no diabolical plant may be found in you, but that in all purity and temperance you may remain spiritually and bodily in Jesus Christ."

Although the next example comes from a different genre and a later time period, it, too, continues to pursue the theme of martyrdom as a ritual exaltation. In this case, however, the exaltation is not that of a suffering bishop, but of a group of women who have no claim to authority in the church beyond that of their willingness to be offered as a sacrifice.

The Martyrdom of Agape and Eirene

According to a document of the fourth century, seven women were arrested in Thessalonika during the persecution of the emperor Diocletian, on the charge of refusing to eat sacrificial food. Subjected to interrogation, two were sentenced and executed by burning, and four were sent to prison. Later, a third was executed, also by burning. According to the anonymous author of their *martyrion*, the dictated *hypomnemata*, or notes on the judicial transcript, formed the material basis for the account. The officiating *hegemon*, or prefect, in the case was one Dulcitius.

Whether the author of the *martyrion* actually based the account on official court records, however, is almost beside the point. For the written document is a skillful composition that shows how these three women and their deaths were conformed to a long tradition of sacrificial death that accomplished several specific goals: victory over the devil, redemption of the chosen people, glory for the local city, and transformation of the sacrificed person to the status of victims, priests, temples, and angels. The author has created a story that operates on several levels: on the cultic level, in the way just specified; on the liturgical level, in being an annual memorial text; and on the exegetical level, in linking the actions of the martyrs to specific biblical texts that make clear how scripture aims to promote both martyrdom and asceticism. This short story portrays not only the spectacular and public suffering and death of three holy women, but also their ascetic combat, sacrificial roles, and intercessory action as agents of the exchange of heavenly for earthly benefits. In so doing, it includes women within the sacrificial and sacramental system of early Christianity and provides another observable link between monasticism and martyrdom.[9]

The *martyrion* has three parts. A long, three-paragraph introduction initially presents the seven women—in particular, the three martyrs—setting their sufferings in the context of sacred history beginning with the "ancient holy men" and ending specifically with the events taking place in Thessalonika. The second part purports to be the court record. This itself has two parts. In the first, all seven women are interrogated and divided according to punishment; in the second, Eirene is subjected to a long interrogation about her activities and those of her associates, two of whom are already dead. The third part, a short conclusion, closes the story with a description of Eirene's death and finishes with an interesting invocation, worth citing in full for its scriptural and historiographical ambitions: "It was in the ninth consulship of Diocletian Augustus, in the eighth of Maximian Augustus, on the first day of April, Jesus Christ Our Lord being eternal king, with whom glory is to the Father, with the Holy Spirit, unto ages of ages, Amen." The entire *martyrion* claims to be set, therefore, in a temporary reign within an eternal one, since it had begun with a reference to the "parousia and *epiphaneia* of our Lord and Savior Jesus Christ," claiming for Jesus the attributes of the emperor himself in his arrival and glorious appearance.

The author's reference to the civic pride of the Thessalonian Christian community suggests the great local attention paid to the martyrs, although in the Latin version the site was shifted to Aquileia. The author remarks, "Such were the three holy women sprung from the city of Thessalonika glorified by the all-wise Paul when he praised its faith and love, saying 'To every place your faith has gone out,' and again about [Thessalonika's] brotherly love, 'There is no need for me to write about your love for each other, you who are taught by God'" (1 Thess. 1:8; 4:9). From this framing device it is clear that the *martyrion* was written to glorify the city as well as its women martyrs and that it presupposes the overarching reign of Jesus as superior despot to Diocletian and Maximian. As we shall see, the true enemies are the rebel angels, "those that are devoted to fire, the Devil and all his sub-heavenly host of demons," and through the young women and their combats the city and its Lord achieve a victory. Roman officials are portrayed as neutral and willing to grant a stay of execution; in other words, their authority is not directly contested.

The text is composed in a plain, narrative style that would have made it easy to understand in a recitation on the anniversary of the martyrs' deaths. As a self-consciously historical work, however, it is supplied with the technical vocabulary of the Roman *imperium* and its courtroom. Much more important than these touches of verisimilitude, though, is the way in which the composition constantly cites biblical texts in order to show how the martyrs occupy a place in sacred history. In doing this, the author can anchor in the scriptures a set of themes that are characteristic of the theology of martyrdom: *askesis* (asceticism) and spiritual warfare; the precedent of the patriarchs, prophets, and apostles; the imitation of Christ as type and fulfillment; and the continuing presence of the church as the Temple of the Lord in which beneficial sacrifices are offered and accepted, heaven and earth being joined precisely upon the altar.

Indeed, one of the unusual features of this text among martyr acts is the prominence accorded to the reading and preservation of Christian writings by the women martyrs. Evidently these women, whose families were pagan, were considered "sisters," perhaps bespeaking their status as an ascetic community. They were also readers and librarians. Moreover, so dense is the thicket of scriptural quotations that express their actions that the martyrs can themselves be regarded as living books, on the model of the scriptures themselves. Their actions are so thoroughly tied to verses from the scripture that they cannot be understood apart from them.

As much as the words of scripture are unmistakably present, startlingly absent is any human authority guiding the women. No mention is made of any ecclesiastical figure, although numerous bishops suffered in this particular persecution and despite the fact that a bishop might have been expected to exercise guardianship of some kind over female ascetics. A husband is mentioned only once, and he is said to have died and left Eutychia pregnant, for which reason she is sent back to prison. Families are portrayed as pagan enemies. Only the women and their books, and the grace of Christ and the Holy Spirit, stand against the power of the empire and its demon-inspired religion.

These two strands are first manifest in the testimony of Chione, in a dialogue with the *hegemon*:

> The *hegemon* said: What do you say, Chione?
>
> Chione said, No one can change my mind.
>
> The *hegemon* said: Do you have in your possession any notes or parchments or books of the impious Christians?
>
> Chione said: We do not, Lord. Our present emperors have taken these from us.
>
> Who was it who gave you this idea? asked the prefect.
>
> God almighty, said Chione.
>
> The prefect said: Who was it who counseled you to commit such foolishness?
>
> It was almighty God, answered Chione, and his only begotten Son, our Lord Jesus Christ.

The point becomes much clearer, however, with the later interrogation of Eirene, to whom Dulcitius says, "It is clear from what we have seen that you are determined in your foolishness, for you have deliberately kept even until now so many tablets, books, parchments, codices, and pages of the writings of the former Christians of unholy name; even now, though you denied each time that you possessed such writings, you did show a sign of recognition when they were writings." Later, Eirene tells Dulcitius that "we did not dare to be traitors, but we chose to be burned alive or suffer anything else that might happen to us rather than betray the writings."

It is clear from the first lines of the *martyrion* that the concerns of ascetics dominate in this account. Like the opening lines of Hebrews, the ancients are contrasted to the recent events connected with Jesus: "as great as the grace was of the ancients, so much better was the victory of the holy ones." The use of *hagioi,* or "holy ones," here reflects the double character of the martyrs as saints and angels, and recalls the combat of good and bad angels when the author asserts, "Instead of those visible enemies [fought against by the ancients], we have now begun to conquer invisible enemies, and the invisible hypostasis of the demons has been handed over to the flames by pure and holy women, filled with the Holy Spirit." Right away the author enlists the apostle Paul to reinforce the idea that Christians fight not against flesh and blood, but against the superior and more terrifying force of Satan—a battle anticipated anciently, but achieved victoriously after the advent of Christ, and achieved, moreover, by women "filled with the Holy Spirit."

The reference to being filled with the Spirit reminds the reader first, of course, of the precedents of the prophets, and more recently of Zechariah, Mary, and Jesus, and finally of the followers of Jesus in Jerusalem at Pentecost. But the underlying type of all of them is the tabernacling presence of God in the Temple in Jerusalem, and all of the previously mentioned persons are themselves also associated with the Temple. Where there is Temple, of course, there are both sacrifice and the vision of God, a tradition that is a millennium old when our author composes this account of the martyrs.

In order to reinforce the comparison of the martyrs with the visionaries who saw or spoke to God, the author emphasizes that the martyrs were like Abraham and Moses and, finally, Christ, leaving "city, family, property, and possessions because of their love of God and their expectation of heavenly things." They did "works worthy of their father Abraham" and went to a mountaintop like Moses and Jesus. Their exile and ascent is a trope for the departure from the world, admittedly, but it is also an extension of the withdrawal of the high priest behind the veil and into the Holy of Holies. This is possible because the martyrs had "clothed themselves with virtue, following the Gospel laws," and because they had fled persecution following those same laws. Ritual flight was not impermissible for the performance of the sacerdotal duties they were about to undertake.

Like Jesus in the garden, however, the young women were apprehended in the high wilderness, so "that thus fulfilling the rest of the divine commands and loving unto death their master, they might bind upon themselves the immortal crown." Like Jesus and the priests of the Temple, then, they were clothed and crowned. But the author adds another feature to the description: they have names that, given their pagan families, cannot have been their birth names but might be names taken in the religious life. Citing the biblical texts from which the names come, the author says of Chione that she "had preserved the pure shining [robe] of baptism," and therefore was called (whiter than) snow. Eirene contained the Holy Spirit: "The gift of our God and Savior [is] within herself and manifested it to all according to John 14:27, and she was called Eirene by everyone." The final one of the threesome had the name Agape, because "she possessed the perfection of the gospel, loving God with her whole heart and her neighbor as herself." The progression of the three names—"Snow-white," "Peace," and "Love"—can be seen as a variant of the Pauline "faith, hope, and love," with a movement from the baptismal robe of purification through the peace established by the blood of the cross and finally to the love established in the Christian community.

But more important than their names is the way in which the text next focuses upon the two courses of events coming, first, from the imperial regime and, second, from the reign of Christ. For although the prefect believes that he is carrying out religious duties by sacrificing the three martyrs to the flames, he is actually assisting in the final, millennial victory of Christ by offering a sacrifice that ensures the peace of the world.

The author introduces his main theme, the refusal of the women to cooperate in pagan worship and their victory over the demons, after giving their religious names with scriptural citations. The *hegemon* is at that point rendered powerless, because even though he will order their execution, the effect of his sentence is to make them an efficacious sacrifice for the defeat of the demons: "When the three were brought to the ruler, and willed not to sacrifice, he sentenced [them] to the fire, in order that through the temporary fire they would overcome the devil and all of his subheavenly army devoted to the fire, and, putting on the incorruptible crown of glory they might praise always the God who gave them this grace." This sentence is tightly constructed, turning on the linked phrases "and since they did not wish to burn [a sacrifice] he condemned [them] to fire." Later the *hypomnemata* list the names of the seven women, adding, "they did not wish to eat [meat] consecrated by the fire." This refusal to eat, although it is a conceivable enough episode, points backward to the Maccabean martyrs, by now one of the original types of martyrdom thanks to the preservation of the books of the Maccabees among Christians and the adulation accorded them due to their resemblance to later Christian martyrs.

Following the interrogations of the prisoners, during which each prisoner replies to the ruler's question about religious belief with a ritual response, two of the martyrs are sentenced: "Since Agape and Chione have with unholy intent acted against the divine decree of our lords the Augusti and Caesars, and because they adhere to the worthless and obsolete worship of the Christians which is hateful to all holy people, I sentence them to be burned." Here the ruler characterizes the imperial decree as divine in itself and Christianity as an out-of-date sect, while the author of the *martyrion* refrains from labeling the ruler as the agent of the devil, although it is arguable that the hearer is meant to draw that connection.

As we have seen, the charge against Eirene is not only the refusal to sacrifice but also the harboring of Christian writings. "Will you perform the order of our kings and caesars and prepare to eat the consecrated meats and burn the sacrifice to the gods?" Eirene refuses, of course, and to the ruler's question about who had ordered the women to keep Christian writings, Eirene responds, "God the pantocrator, who told us to love him unto death. This is why we were not bold to hand over, but chose to be burned alive or suffer *[paschein]* whatever might happen, rather than betray the writings." Direct communication from God, Eirene further says, determined the pattern of the women's lives while they were in exile. They lived, "in the mountains, in the open air . . . in various places among the mountains." Asked where they got their bread, Eirene responded, "From God, who supplies everyone." Here the author is surely recalling both the feeding miracles of the Gospels and, behind them, the manna in the wilderness that fed Israel, along with the eucharistic reference involved in both.

The ruler's frustration is evident in the different sentence that he imposes upon Eirene: "I do not wish you to die immediately in the same way. Instead I sentence you to be placed naked in the brothel with the help of the public notaries of this city and Zosimus the executioner, and you will receive merely one loaf of bread from our residence, and the notaries will not allow you to leave." Here it is plain that the author is contrasting Dulcitius with God: God's grace had preserved the women from hunger when they roamed on the mountains, while the ruler confines Eirene and reverses her asceticism, by placing her in a brothel. Eirene, who apparently owns the writings and the "cabinets and chests" in which they are stored, nevertheless remains chaste in the brothel "by the grace of the Holy Spirit, which preserved and guarded her pure and inviolate for the God who is the lord of all things."

It is clear, then, that Eirene is about to become an acceptable sacrifice, while the ruler is prepared to execute her for refusing "to obey the command of the emperors and burn sacrifice." Two types of burning and sacrifice are here brought together, in an evocation of scriptural themes in which the false sacrifices of idolators are juxtaposed to the true sacrifices of Israel. "I sentence her to be burned alive as her two sisters previously." The final act of Eirene is thus both a voluntary sacrifice and one accomplished under the command of the emperors through their official. Like Christ, she is led out of the city of Thessalonika, but, like Isaac and the sacrifices of the ancient Israelites, she is burned on a mountain: "They brought her to a high place, where her sisters had been martyred before her. They ignited a great fire and ordered her to climb up upon it. And the holy woman Eirene, singing and praising God [Isa. 51:11] threw herself upon it and thus was perfected." Behind the entire text lies Phil. 2:6-11, to which the author alerts the hearer by his variations of the phrase "unto death," quoting the passage directly. In imitation of Christ, the humiliation of the women is followed by their exaltation to angelic status. Agape and Chione reach this position first, but Eirene is doubly exalted because she has spoken freely before the ruler, defending Christian holy books and the grace of God in feeding Israel in its exodus, and has refused again to eat sacrificial meat. Finally, she herself is sacrificed, achieving the victory over the devil that will, as the hearers know by now, replace his power with the power of God.

Fig. 3.4. Abraham's near sacrifice of his son Isaac, depicted in this early Christian painting, was understood by ancient Christians as prefiguring not only the passion of Christ but also the deaths of the martyrs who followed him. Ipogeo di Via Latina, Rome, Italy. Photo credit: Scala / Art Resource, NY.

CONCLUSION

In the literature of early Christianity, martyrs and the act of martyrdom occupy much more space than their small numbers might seem to merit.

This apparent discrepancy points toward the increasing importance that the idea of martyrdom, and its literary depiction, gained in early Christianity. Always interpreted through comparison with the imitation of Christ, they were attractive spectacles of the exaltation that extreme humiliation and violent death made possible. Scriptural interpretation made the martyr possible, and martyrdom reinforced scriptural interpretation, yielding a kind of continuous loop of performance and interpretation that has retained its theological potency to the present day.

FOR FURTHER READING

Bisbee, Gary A. *Pre-Decian Acts of the Martyrs and Comentarii.* Philadelphia: Fortress, 1988.

Bowersock, G. W. *Martyrdom and Rome.* New York: Cambridge University Press, 1995.

Boyarin, Daniel. *Dying for God: Martyrdom and the Making of Christianity and Judaism.* Stanford, Calif.: Stanford University Press, 1999.

Castelli, Elizabeth A. *Martyrdom and Memory: Early Christian Culture Making.* New York: Columbia University Press, 2004.

Droge, Arthur J., and James D. Tabor. *A Noble Death: Suicide and Martyrdom among the Christians and Jews in Antiquity.* San Francisco: HarperSanFrancisco, 1992.

Frend, W. H. C. *Martyrdom and Persecution in the Early Church: A Study of a Conflict from the Maccabees to Donatus.* Oxford: Basil Blackwell, 1965.

Henten, Jan Willem van. *The Maccabean Martyrs as Saviours of the Jewish People: A Study of 2 and 4 Maccabees.* Leiden: Brill, 1997.

Workman, Herbert B. *Persecution in the Early Church.* New York: Oxford University Press, 1990.

Young, Robin Darling. *In Procession before the World: Martyrdom as Public Liturgy in Early Christianity.* Milwaukee: Marquette University Press, 2001.

LOCAL PRACTICES

Part 2

Late Ancient Christianity

CHILDREN'S PLAY AS SOCIAL RITUAL

CORNELIA B. HORN

The experience of childhood is common to all human beings. Across cultures, childhood marks the processes of biological development and socialization that produce mature adults. For ancient Christians, however, childhood carried particular metaphoric overtones that both broadened its meaning and complicated the distinction between child and adult. Liturgical rite and theological language endowed the concept of childhood with comprehensive, even global dimensions. The term "child" was expanded to apply to every Christian, understood to be a "child of God." This identity was performed first in the ritual of baptism, characteristically described in the New Testament as a new or second birth through water and the Spirit. With this metaphor of spiritual rebirth into Christ, all believers became children of God and remained so for their entire lives. Baptismal identity was reinforced by broader theological and soteriological (salvation-oriented) models and tropes. The Christian was encouraged to understand himself or herself as a brother or sister of Christ (see Matt. 12:50; Mark 3:35), who was himself in the course of the doctrinal developments of the early Christian centuries first addressed as "child of God" and subsequently identified definitively as the Son of God par excellence. By virtue of their intimate connection with Christ, therefore, all Christians shared in a familial relationship with God as parent, a parent who in the early Christian tradition is experienced and referred to more often as father, sometimes as mother. As son or as daughter, adoptive or otherwise, every Christian was a child of God.[1]

However, Christian communities also, of course, included children in the more usual, nonmetaphorical sense. The concept of child always carries a twofold meaning in Christian discourse, dual significations that sometimes intersect, as is already reflected in some of the earliest Christian sacred texts that refer explicitly to children's playful experiences (see, for example, Luke 7:35). This chapter primarily traces aspects of the world of experience of children in the stricter sense of the term, addressing the larger context of their social initiation into the life of the Christian community. It also implicitly raises the question of how the idea of the Christian as a permanent child—enacted in eucharistic feedings as well as baptismal birth—influenced and was influenced by the rituals of play that prepared children to participate as adults in the liturgical life of their communities. Thus this discussion has relevance also for understanding the experience and self-definition of every Christian, ancient and modern, by virtue of that shared and all-pervading dimension of life at its early stages in the context of the service of God. Breaking open new ground in the study of early Christianity by uncovering a largely neglected segment of the Christian people, namely, children, this chapter considers select textual and archaeological evidence from the New Testament period through late antiquity.

A crucial place in the personal and societal development of the individual child is held by the individual's ability to play, though play in antiquity was scarcely confined to children. For the ears of young and old Romans, the term *ludus* described a wide range of games, many of them performed in the amphitheater. The better-known voices of ancient Christianity that have commented on games and play—for example, Tertullian in his *The Shows*—seem to condemn the activity and concept of *ludus* almost categorically. Nevertheless, careful explorations of alternative traces in patristic literature allow us to affirm the applicability to ancient Christians of Hugo Rahner's argument for the centrality of play to human identity, as well as for the desirability of a Christian life that consciously develops and furthers play as an aspect of personal identity.[2]

Premised on the assumption that religion cannot be separated from other aspects of culture, this discussion first approaches the world of early Christian children by looking at their toys, games, songs, and other forms of playful activities. Some of these items and rules for games children inherited as hand-me-downs from earlier generations. Textual and archaeological evidence yields insights into significant aspects of children's lives with regard to how they entertained themselves and how they were entertained by adults around them. Allowing children to do what they did naturally, that is, engage in play, often enough constituted for parents and other adults involved in their education and upbringing a suitable way to shape expected behavior. Early in life, children learned through play to enter into adult roles and become properly functioning members of society. The direction sought out by children on their own when playing, as well as the direction provided by adults, had its effect on the development of rules for games and of rituals for playing with other children. Given the religious overtones that playing with certain toys or playing on certain days carried, one may reasonably suggest that aspects of the participation of children in the liturgical life of the early church can be seen as a continuation and extension of that world of play.

CHILDREN AND TOYS

Biblical tradition preserves a powerful image of a child at play as a witness to God's creative presence. When Wisdom in the book of Proverbs speaks about her origins, she reveals that "the LORD created me at the beginning of his work, the first of his acts of long ago" (Prov. 8:22). Witnessing God's creation of the world, she "was beside him like a little child and . . . was daily his delight, playing before him always, playing in his inhabited world and delighting in the human race" (Prov. 8:30-31).[3] To investigate the specifics of such heavenly playful activity may be impossible. Some patristic authors, however, applying such wisdom imagery to the Logos, do provide a few details as to the nature of children's play when they discuss how the persons of the triune godhead relate to one another (for example, Gregory Nazianzen, *Carmina* I, 2, 2.589–90). More extensive evidence for children's play in the world of early Christianity comes from less theological references in Christian texts as well as from non-Christian sources, sources reflecting the cultural influences that formed the imaginations of Christian writers.

Before considering the substance of children's play, we might raise the question of who could count as a child, in the stricter, nonmetaphorical sense that here concerns us primarily. In the ancient world the transition from childhood to adult life generally occurred earlier than in modern-day Western societies. While the determination of the age of maturity was somewhat flexible, it could be as early as twelve. Luke's depiction of Jesus discussing Torah with Israel's elders in the Temple at the age of twelve (Luke 2:42) served as a point of confirmation and orientation for Christian audiences. Boys and girls entered adulthood between twelve and seventeen, with a certain preference for the younger age in the later part of the period under review. In the case of boys in Roman society, for example, the passage to adulthood occurred when the new young citizen received the *toga virilis,* an event that depended on the decision of the *pater familias.* With respect to marriage and coming of age, a boy, standing at the threshold to adulthood, did not have to commit himself to marriage. That same privilege was not extended with equal liberty to the opposite sex. Girls customarily entered adulthood when they were married off, sometimes at twelve, more often a few years later.[4]

Evidence for children's playful entertainment of themselves in Christian antiquity is, as we may readily note, supplied by both classical and

Fig. 4.1. The scenes portrayed on the sarcophagus of M. Cornelius Statius, dated to the mid-second century, offer us tantalizing glimpses of a child's experience. Louvre, Paris, France. Photo credit: Erich Lessing / Art Resource, NY.

Christian authors, writing treatises, histories, letters, and poetry for both public and private consumption. In these works, classical Latin authors like Cicero (106–43 BCE), writing to family and friends, Hellenistic authors like Epictetus (ca. 50–130/140 CE), pondering philosophical questions amidst life's daily activities, as well as Christian authors like Jerome (ca. 347–419/20 CE) comment in passing on children's games and toys (*Letters* 107, 108, and 128).[5] Concerned as ever to recruit young girls to the ascetic life by way of letters, Jerome provides instruction to their parents on the kinds of toys to be given to them to further such goals. More concrete glimpses of children at play can be gained from archaeological evidence of toys and other objects that may have functioned in the context of games and related activities, sometimes of a ritual or cultic nature. A significant amount of this type of archaeological data is drawn, for example, from reliefs on children's sarcophagi (fig. 4.1) and from excavations of children's burial sites. Through a process of carefully piecing together these widely scattered tidbits of information, a labor in which classicists and museum curators have taken the lead,[6] an informative, though unfortunately still incomplete picture of children at play emerges.

Among the earliest toys a child played with were different kinds of rattles, *crepundia* and *crepitacula,* names derived from the verbs meaning "to make noise," "to make noise by striking," and "to clap." *Crepundia* were made of little ornaments, charms, or mini-toys, shaped in the form of swords, axes, tools, animals, flowers, or half-moons; manufactured from clay, bronze, or, more rarely, gold or silver; and pierced to allow for stringing them together on a thread or a chain. Such *crepundia* could be hung around a baby's neck and shoulder, perhaps also in front of it. The jingling and rattling noise produced at every one of the child's movements kept the little one entertained, amused, and busy. These material artifacts give mute witness to the multiple functions they once fulfilled as toys, as indicators of wealth and status of the parents, and as personal identification of the child's family of origin. Should a child be abducted or otherwise get lost, inscriptions of the father's and mother's names on them helped ensure the child would be reunited with his or her guardians.[7]

Crepitacula, on the other hand, were rattles that could be large enough to fit into an adult's hand. They were instruments made of clay, wood, bronze, sometimes even the dried heads of poppy flowers, producing sound through the rattling or clattering of little pebbles or seeds placed inside. *Crepitacula* came in quite a range of shapes, including spheres, boxes, rolls, fruits such as pumpkins or pomegranates, as well as animals. Of the latter, hedgehogs, owls, or pigs were common. Examples have also been found of cradle-shaped, square clay boxes with a baby's body in relief depicted on top.[8] Such larger-sized *crepitacula* were likely the tools of the nurse's trade, used to calm a crying baby, attract its attention, or lull it to sleep.

In ancient Greece, such rattles also had apotropaeic (anti-evil) and cultic functions. As one of his labors, Hercules, for example, used rattles to drive off the Stymphalic Birds. Ancient Greek vases connected with funerary rites depict adults sitting opposite one another at a table or altar, holding rattles in their hands. At the very least, one may surmise that when nurses used rattles to lull the little ones under their care to sleep, they may also have intended to ward off demonic influences.

Ancient society had developed customs and rites that accompanied and marked the passage of a newborn into childhood. In ancient Roman society, for example, boys and girls could be identified as children by the *bulla,* a piece of jewelry made of leather in the case of plebeian children, or, if the parents could afford it and came from patrician ranks, of two concave pieces of gold fastened together by a spring. Shortly after birth or on the *dies lustralis,* the day of purification, the father placed the *bulla* around the little one's neck. It was worn on a cord, strap, or chain, and it contained an amulet, which also pointed to the object's religious purpose as a protective charm against evil. By hanging the *bulla* around the newborn's neck, the father recognized him or her as part of the family and thus established his or her rank as child. It would have been difficult, however, for a little baby boy or girl in the cradle to distinguish between the *bulla* and the *crepundia* that served for his or her entertainment. The child would have recognized both merely for their quality as toys. Being accustomed to wearing such *bullae* might have made it natural for Christian children to wear cross pendants as signs of recognition as well.

Fig. 4.2. In antiquity as now, children played many different games with many different kinds of balls. Juggling was both entertainment and a way for children to develop their motor skills. Staatliche Museen, Berlin. Photo credit: Bildarchiv Preussischer Kulturbesitz / Art Resource, NY.

As children were developing their motor skills (fig. 4.2), parents gave them a wider range of toys to play with, including dolls, tops, hoops, and balls. The variety among such items was vast. Latin-speaking children, for example, distinguished between five different types of balls: *paganica* (made of leather and feathers), *harpastum* (relatively hard and less elastic), *trigonalis* (small and very hard), *follis* (made of leather and inflated with air), and *folliculis* (a small balloon). Such toys were welcome gifts on feast days. For example, on Saturnalia, a seven-day celebration encompassing the winter solstice, all members of Roman society could freely engage with one another, without restrictions of status, rank, or rules otherwise in place between masters and slaves. Gift giving was one of the favorite activities during this feast, when schools closed and everyone practiced not-so-random acts of kindness. Children partook of their fair share of cakes and sweetmeats, which were attached to boughs and exchanged between visitors and guests. Yet the *sigillaria,* doll-like clay figures they received as gifts, were their favorites. Transitioning from Saturnalia to the Christian celebration of Christmas, observed at the same time of the year, would have been an easy task for children, given that they continued to receive the toys they so treasured.[9]

The ancient world knew of the use of objects that modern society recognizes primarily as toys but that in antiquity were closely connected with religious cult celebrations. The swing, in particular, is such an item. Vase paintings show a young woman, often a young girl, only infrequently a little boy, seated on a swing that a satyr or male adult keeps in motion.

Fig. 4.3. Knucklebones were used in games, similarly to dice. They also had cultic associations and are found along with whips, tops, and hoops as votive offerings in ancient sanctuaries. Photo: Herve Lewandowski. Louvre, Paris, France. Photo credit: Réunion des Musées Nationaux / Art Resource, NY.

These scenes have been interpreted as representing fertility rites or purification rituals at the Aiora feast, a celebration connected in Greek mythology to the suicide of Athenian girls in revenge for the death of a male adult. Songs sung at that feast were known as *katabaukalēseis,* the same name given to songs sung by nurses to lull children to sleep.[10]

When boys and girls happily whipped at tops, employed sticks to drive their hoops, or played with balls, such toys were not unconnected to the realm of religious life either. The Greek gods had played with them and, like Hermes depicted on a vase teaching Ganymede how to play with the top, had taught the divine offspring the necessary skills. In variations of the Bacchic mystery cult, the top was one of the identifiers of Dionysus's presence.[11] Along with whips, knucklebones (fig. 4.3), and tops, hoops are frequently found as votive offerings in ancient sanctuaries, pointing to their use as gifts given by boys and girls in connection with initiatory rituals. Christians were conscious of such cultic connections associated with specific toys and, given the everyday nature of the objects involved, may not have seen a need to despise their use as "un-Christian." However, their teachers and catechists attempted to break such habits. Clement of Alexandria's *Exhortation to the Greeks*, a second-century prospectus for potential converts to Christianity, ridicules the Dionysian mysteries and the central place that toys like tops and rattles held in it.

The perceived danger was that insufficiently educated new converts might continue to connect the toys and games of their own childhood with the services and rites of gods they were called upon to leave behind when joining the church. Moreover, these connections could be passed down to their children through the same toys bestowed on them as gifts. Such fear was not completely unfounded even into the fifth century, as a scene from Theodoret of Cyrrhus's *Ecclesiastical History* demonstrates. Theodoret's main concern at this instance was to blackmail his opponent Lucius and the city's Arian faction. On that occasion, Theodoret also recorded that a group of boys subjected the ball with which they were playing to an ancient pre-Christian fire-based purification ritual for fear that it might have been polluted.

> The mysteries of Dionysus are wholly inhuman; for while [Dionysus was] still a child, and the Curetes danced around [his cradle] clashing their weapons, and the Titans having come upon them by stealth, and having beguiled him with childish toys, these very Titans tore him limb from limb when but a child, as the bard of this mystery, the Thracian Orpheus, says:
>
> "Cone, and spinning-top, and limb-moving rattles,
>
> And fair golden apples from the clear-toned Hesperides."
>
> And the useless symbols of this mystic rite it will not be useless to exhibit for condemnation. These are dice, ball, hoop, apples, top, looking-glass, tuft of wool.
>
> —Clement of Alexandria, *Exhortation to the Greeks* 2.17.2–18

> Some lads were playing ball in the market place and enjoying the game, when Lucius was passing by. It chanced that the ball was dropped and passed between the feet of the ass. The boys raised an outcry because they thought that their ball was polluted. On perceiving this Lucius told one of his suite to stop and learn what was going on. The boys lit a fire and tossed the ball through the flames with the idea that by so doing they purified it. I know indeed that this was but a boyish act, and a survival of the ancient ways; but it is nonetheless sufficient to prove in what hatred the town held the Arian faction. (4.13)

In a town torn apart by internal Christian bickering and strife, hatred against the Christian "other" appears to have taken up more space than working toward reconciliation. That the catechesis of children with an eye toward Christianizing aspects of their everyday activities may have fallen to the wayside, or at least been neglected, is not surprising.

Fig. 4.4. This second-century Roman doll has jointed arms and legs. Museo Nazionale Romano (Palazzo Massimo alle Terme), Rome, Italy. Photo credit: Scala / Art Resource, NY.

Very popular with children who had grown out of infancy were dolls made from rags, clay, hardwood (such as ebony), bone, ivory, or wax (fig. 4.4). Some dolls had movable, jointed arms and legs. Although the literary references to dolls are relatively infrequent, the archaeological evidence is especially rewarding and may provide part of the answer to the question of who played with dolls.[12]

Children seem to have shared toys, and children of both sexes at times played with the same kinds of toys. Both girls and boys certainly played with nuts, pebbles, and knucklebones. Not even the ample evidence concerning dolls, one of the most popular types of toys, suffices to establish that they were used exclusively by girls.[13] Since dolls were found in temples of Apollo, one of the two gods to whom boys in the ancient world had dedicated their toys when entering adult life,[14] it is not unlikely that at least a few boys possessed and played with dolls. More often, however, dolls are found in tombs of girls and in temples and sanctuaries of female goddesses like Aphrodite, Venus, and Hera. That archaeological evidence for dolls is more plentifully available than literary evidence should not be much of a surprise, given that the authors of ancient texts, mainly men, knew relatively little about dolls, about the girls who owned and played with them, and about the domestic space in which the girls spent more time than the boys did.

Depictions of children with dolls on tombstones, reliefs on other types of monuments, and paintings only show the child holding the doll or looking at it; no scenes of children actually playing with dolls seem to be preserved. Christian references to girls and dolls furthermore suggest that little girls may have prized the doll more for its looks than for its potential as playing companion. In his advice on how to raise the little Pacatula, Jerome thought the doll an appropriate reward for her. He was sure she "will make haste to perform her tasks if she hopes afterwards to get some bright bunch of flowers, some glittering bauble, [or] some enchanting doll" (*Letter* 128.1). Scholarly discussions have been intense as to whether dolls were primarily toys or votive offerings to gods or goddesses that only secondarily functioned also as toys for children. The Greek word *korē*, which is employed in a fourfold meaning to describe a doll, the figurine that a priestess holds in hand as offering to the gods or nymphs, the young girl herself, or the *Theotokos* (Mary the Godbearer) is instructive.[15] Most, but not all, of the depictions of dolls, as well as physically preserved dolls, do not represent a baby's body but contain indicators of sexual differentiation and thus represent a young marriageable girl or an already married adult woman. Girls seemed to have looked at dolls as role models. Dolls made from precious materials or beautifully dressed presented to and modeled for the little girl her destiny and instilled desire in her to grow up and be a chaste bride. When that goal was reached, on the eve of the wedding day, the doll, together with other toys, was brought and offered as a votive gift at the shrine of a female goddess. Often referred to is the example of Timarete, who as "girl to the girl" dedicated her tympana, a ball, a hairband, her dolls, and her dolls' clothes to Artemis right before her wedding (*Anthologia Palatina* VI.280).

The evidence concerning the dedication of dolls from the classical and Hellenistic periods helps to augment and explain the limited Christian evidence. Not so different from other parents in the ancient world, Christian parents made decisions for their children's future. Such plans included at times the dedication of an infant to a religious life. Jerome noted that "some mothers when they have vowed a daughter to virginity clothe her in somber garments, wrap her up in a dark cloak, and let her have neither linen nor gold ornaments. They wisely refuse to accustom her to what she will afterwards have to lay aside." Such mothers manifested toward their daughters the same behavior they as girls would have shown toward dolls, dressing them in whatever outfit suited their fancy. In the Christian context, the chosen garments for the girls were appropriate to their destination for the ascetic life. Other Christian mothers adopted the exact opposite policy, realizing that "women are fond of finery and many whose chastity is beyond question dress not for men but for themselves." Thus the second group of mothers thought it better if they gave their daughters what they asked for so that they might "enjoy things to the full and so learn to despise them" (Jerome, *Letter* 128.2).

The question of what kinds of dolls either group of mothers would have given their daughters to play with is intriguing. One might assume that the first group considered giving them dolls dressed in simple and dark-colored clothes in order to reinforce the desired vision of the future ascetic life. Yet neither archaeological nor textual data support such assumptions. Many of the dolls for which accessories or indications of clothing survive project the image of a well-groomed young lady. This observation holds true for dolls from non-Christian and Christian settings spanning a time frame of several hundred years. Among the better-known examples are bone and ivory dolls of vestal virgins and child empresses. From the second century comes the example of an attractive jointed doll in bone, depicting a tall, elegant young woman, wearing a gold necklace as well as bracelets on wrist and ankle. The doll was found in the tomb of the Vestal Virgin Cossinia. Alongside the doll was also found a small jewel casket made of red glass.[16] The second example consists of the likewise second-century jointed ivory doll of Crepereia Tryphaena, which was found wearing two golden bracelets and a ring with an attached key. That doll displays an impressive, towering hairdo.[17] The third example is a clearly Christian one, consisting of two precious ivory dolls found in the coffin of the fifth-century Empress Maria, baby bride of Honorius.[18] Yet dolls belonging to children of less elite status likewise display no obvious signs of having once been dressed in simple outfits. It is plausible that the traditional usage of dolls elaborately adorned as brides continued because these dolls were understood as models of virginal chastity. Dolls presented girls with an image of the attractive wife,[19] to which they could become accustomed through play and for which they could prepare. Thus even a girl destined for a life of virginity, and perhaps especially such a girl, could, in the eyes of her parents and guardians, be encouraged to grow further toward internalizing and accepting the ideal of becoming the "bride of Christ" by playing with beautifully dressed and adorned dolls.

From the age of seven, playing and studying competed with one another for children's attention. Some Christian children appear to have been soberly aware of the seriousness of the new situation, as a late poem, possibly a child's prayer, indicates: "Today, dear God, I am seven years old, and must play no more. Here is my top, my hoop, and my ball: keep them all, my Lord."[20] To make the transition easier, toys and games were developed in the service of the educational goals of learning how to read and write at school. In order to render the children's earliest attempts at acquiring the basics of the alphabet more effective and enjoyable, parents and instructors invented visual and tactile teaching tools, such as large, carved letter blocks. Evidence of such letters carved from ivory also witnesses to the monetary resources parents were ready to invest in order to turn those reading lessons into pleasurable activities. Both Quintilian and Jerome spoke of such ivory letters made for schooling purposes (see Quintilian, *Institutio Oratoria* 1.1.26). Jerome recommended the use of such toy letters also for the education of girls when he instructed Laeta to

> have made for [little Paula] letters out of boxwood or ivory, and call each by its proper name. Let her play with these so that her play may also be instruction. And let her keep the letters in order in her mind, so that in her memory she may go over the names in a rhyme. However, often change the internal order and mix up the letters so that the last ones are in the middle and the middle ones at the beginning: thus she may know them not only by sound, but also by sight.

Jerome is clear about the purpose of using such playful methods. The learning process needed to "guard against her hating her studies, lest a bitterness toward them learned early in childhood penetrate beyond her young years." That such playful teaching could be placed at the immediate service of developing knowledge about the Christian faith was a welcome side effect for Jerome. The words and names little Paula was to spell with her toy letters were to be "those of the prophets and the apostles, or the list of the patriarchs descended from Adam, as in Matthew and Luke" (*Letter* 107.4).

During breaks, after school, and certainly during the holidays, as Jerome remembered, children played wherever space allowed, even if it was "among the offices where the slaves worked" (*Apology against Rufinus* 1.30). Primarily in the case of boys, such games included the pulling or pushing of small toy carts and carriages. Sometimes the boys caught mice and then reined them in to draw the carriage for them.

CHILDREN AND PETS

Children greatly enjoyed sharing their time with animal companions. Dogs indeed were among their favorite pets. From the first Christian century onward, evidence for cats as children's pets emerges, at least in larger cities like Rome, but the evidence on the whole suggests that dogs were much more common. In addition, children also played with other animals like goats and rabbits, indicators of a childhood in the country.

Neither were water animals or birds excluded from the range of animal companions for children. Pliny the Younger described how the children at Hippo in North Africa had once found a special friend in a tame dolphin, alongside of which they used to swim. That spectacle, however, led to such a stream of curious tourists visiting town that the city's administrators ended up killing the dolphin in secret to restore order (*Letter* 9.33). Abba Isaiah seems to give evidence based on his observations of children or from memories from his own childhood when he compares himself to "a little sparrow whose leg is held by a child; if he relaxes his hold, it immediately flies upward, thinking that it has been set free. If the child holds it down, again it is brought down" (*Asceticon*, Discourse 8).

The close bond that could develop between a child and its pet is also documented on tombstones, for example, that of Avita, a little girl who died at the age of ten years and two months. The sponsors of the monument, presumably her parents, eternalized her memory by depicting her sitting on a chair with an opened book on her lap and a dog sitting right behind her to the left and looking up at her.[21] A mid-first-century CE marble altar from Ostia depicts the five-year-old freeborn Egrilius firmly holding on to the left horn of a little goat to his right.[22]

A different side of the connection between children and pets emerges when one considers how children at times became either the object or the expression of the playfulness of adults in the ancient world. As literary sources attest, some members of the elite, for example, Livia, Domitian, and Commodus, thought of and treated little children, often very young slave girls or boys, as pets *(deliciae)*,[23] taking pleasure in their company. The nakedness of the child's body suggested fruitfulness, sensual pleasure, and playfulness in artistic depictions as well, as, for example, on a mid-second-century CE marble relief from Ostia that shows a couple with right hands joined in marital pose *(dextrarum iunctio)*, the wife leaning her left hand over her husband's right shoulder while holding a fruit or a ball in her left hand. The two are framed by three naked young boys, the one in front at the bottom of the picture representing a real child, the couple's young son, the two to the upper right and left representing *putti* (cherubs).[24] The naked body as such initially did not pose a moral problem for early Christians either, given that their central rite of initiation, baptism, required a full-body immersion and in distinct regions also the chrismation (anointing with oil) of the body, including the genitals. In the case of little children, such baptismal rituals continued well beyond the third-century turn to more body- and gender-conscious regulations, as church members increasingly felt the impact of concerns related to practices of ascetic renunciation, including renunciation of the naked body.

At times, Christian authors effectively exploited for polemical purposes the potential of cases of pedophilia or practices of displaying children playing and dancing for adult entertainment. Hints that a doctrinal opponent took prurient interest in provocatively cross-dressed prepubescent bodies could assist in blackening the image of that opponent. In his *Ecclesiastical History,* Theodoret of Cyrrhus, for example, accused the supporters of Lucius, his Arian competitor for the bishop's throne, of having set up "on the holy altar itself where we call on the coming of the Holy Ghost . . . a boy who had forsworn his sex and would pass for a girl, with eyes, as it is written, smeared with antimony, and face reddened with rouge like their idols, in woman's dress, . . . to dance and wave his hands about and whirl round as though he had been at the front of some disreputable stage . . . while the by-standers laughed aloud and rudely raised unseemly shouts" (4.19).

GAMES CHILDREN PLAYED

Few descriptions of the actual rules of children's games have come down to us. From the relatively little that survives, however, one gets the impression that some of the games children played were quite similar to games still common in modern times. Such games included blindman's bluff, hide-and-seek, and forms of tug-of-war. Board games were also quite popular, but instead of marbles children in the ancient world played with pebbles or nuts. These could also be used for playing without a prescribed or drawn board. The sarcophagus of the boy Aemilius Daphnus shows a dozen little boys playing in small groups with nuts on the ground.[25]

Very popular, and not only among children, was a game played with bones taken from the ankle joints of young calves, sheep, or goats. Those knucklebones (astris, astrichos) resembled dice and thus could be used in a similar manner, by assigning numeric value to the different sides (fig. 4.3). Variations of the games played with these bones were among the best-beloved and most widespread forms of entertainment, judging from the many depictions of scenes of children engaged in it on vases, in reliefs, in sculptures, and on paintings and the plentiful archaeological material discovered as evidence for it. In ancient times, knucklebones also served their users in petitioning an oracle or as votive offerings in sanctuaries, and they were understood to be closely connected with Eros, the god of love, and Aphrodite, whose chosen toy they were. The throw of knucklebones that achieved the highest number of points was named after her.[26]

> We came to a spot where some small boats had been drawn up and were resting on oak supports off the ground to prevent rot. There we saw some small boys eagerly competing with one another in a game of throwing shells into the sea. In this game you choose from the shore a shell that has been rubbed smooth by the action of the waves; this you hold horizontally in your fingers, and stooping at an angle and low to the ground you hurl it with all your might over the water. The object [of the game] is that as it spins, it should sheer and skim the surface of the sea, gliding smoothly all the while; or it can shave the tops off the waves, constantly springing up again in a series of leaps and bounds. Among the boys, the one whose shell had gone farther and skipped more times considered himself to be the winner.
>
> —Minucius Felix, *Octavius* 3

While knucklebones and games with dice were games of chance, early Christian authors do not appear to have advised their flock to avoid them. Rather, their texts witness to the still widespread use of those games. Intent on making Origen's vast knowledge accessible to a Latin-speaking audience, Rufinus witnesses to the popularity of playing with dice as a boys' pastime, asserting that the treatises he had in front of him were "Origen's recreation no less than dice are a boy's" (*Apology* 2.22).

Boys and girls played at times by themselves and at other times in groups, sometimes with members of their own sex and at other times in mixed company (fig. 4.5). A young boy might enjoy rolling his hoop, as depicted and remembered by his family on a sarcophagus.[27] While it may be presumed that a given little girl will at times have played with her doll or another toy by herself, depictions of such scenes are difficult to find. The late-second-century CE terra-cotta statue of a young girl playing knucklebones, preserved in the Staatliche Museum in Berlin (color gallery, plate G), is among the very rare exceptions.[28] Most frequently children at

Fig. 4.5. The scene depicted on this child's sarcophagus captures some of the tension and energy generated by a group of boys playing games. Kunsthistorisches Museum, Vienna, Austria. Photo credit: Erich Lessing / Art Resource, NY.

play are seen when they are part of a group. Minucius Felix preserves the rules for a game of throwing shells played by groups of boys.

A second-century CE painting from an underground tomb shows a group of boys hitting a ball to keep it up in the air and prevent it from touching the ground. A relief on a second-century child's sarcophagus depicts separate groups of boys and girls: three girls lined up behind one another, taking turns in throwing a ball against the wall; and a group of four boys, two rolling a nut down an inclined board, attempting to hit and demolish a tower built of nuts by two other boys. Ovid specified the rules for this and related games with nuts for future generations (*Nux*, 73–86). Other reliefs show groups of girls playing quoits (a game similar to horseshoes) or knucklebones with one another. Less common, but still occurring, are scenes that depict groups of children of both sexes playing together.[29]

Christian writers, however, warned parents against boys and girls playing together. Jerome, for example, was rather outspoken when in 413 he instructed Gaudentius, who had asked for advice on how to bring up his infant daughter, Pacatula. "A girl should associate only with girls; she should know nothing of boys and should dread even playing with them," Jerome opined categorically (*Letter* 128.3a; see also *Letter* 107.4). Given the contrast between the visual depictions and such prescriptive statements, one may readily assume that quite the opposite was typical.

CHILDREN AT WAR

As one might expect, then as now children could get rowdy and out of control when playing with one another. In the midst of a game, a fight would break out, and a boy, for example, might start tearing the hair from his former playmate's head, as depicted on a sarcophagus, now in the Museo Chiaramonti.[30] Not necessarily causing "torrents of blood nor dead bodies," children's sport and pastime nonetheless at times reminded the observer of scenes of battle and war. John Chrysostom employs this image when describing the struggles of the soul against vices, leaving it open whether or not children he watched intentionally "played war" (*On the Priesthood* 6.13). Among the Spartans, a military training game had taken place, set within the framework of a ritual celebration that was intended to eradicate any emotions and feelings of mercy for the opponent in the boys who played it. The game, known as *platanistas,* named after the grove of plane trees on the island that served as the battleground, required the sacrifice of a puppy to Ares on the evening preceding the battle. Each team drew lots, and in their fight for possession of the island the boys "were allowed to kick, bite, and even to gouge their opponents' eyes."[31] That early Christians were keenly aware of the tight connections among war, military service, and pagan rituals and cults is demonstrated in numerous texts from patristic authors and hagiographic accounts.

Children were also capable of using violence carelessly against other human beings, and especially so when in a group. This is graphically illustrated in martyrdom accounts, even if one discounts the occasional hagiographic exaggerations of such literature. In his *Ecclesiastical History* Sozomen gives us a glimpse of the sometimes wild and brutal ball games of young boys on city streets. When a group of schoolboys as part of a crowd had witnessed how Bishop Mark of Arethusa's ears had been severed by ropes, they took the old man for their ball and "made game of him by tossing him aloft and rolling him over and over, sending him forward, catching him up, and unsparingly piercing him with their writing utensils" (5.10). The boys' systematically violent moves blur the boundaries between game and battle. Then as now, schoolchildren could indeed be cruel and violent when their energies were not directed in fruitful ways.

SONGS AND STORIES

To prevent children's play from becoming too destructive, forms of control were considered necessary in the eyes of many a parent or instructor. People in the ancient world did not hesitate to exercise such control in the form of corporal punishment. To the children's advantage, however, other forms of control and guidance could be employed. In order to calm children down, at times to direct their energies in more creative ways, parents and educators promoted children's singing and playing music. It is rather difficult to reconstruct the songs children sang and listened to, not the least because material evidence that could point to that part of their life is scarce. A few traces of children's musical engagement are preserved in the literary record, however, sometimes even directly in the sacred texts. As portrayed in the Gospel of Luke, for example, Jesus availed himself of the image of "children sitting in the marketplace and calling to one another, 'We played the flute for you, and you did not dance; we wailed, and you did not weep,'" when chiding his audience for accepting neither John the Baptist nor the Son of Man (Luke 7:32-34). While children did not readily play all available instruments, some musical instruments elicited admiration and wonder from children, as Eusebius of Caesarea noted when he disapprovingly spoke of children who would "admire the seven-stringed lyre," but disregard the instrument's builder or the musician who knew how to play it (*Oration in Praise of Constantine* 11.9).

The energies needed for practice when children sang in choruses is not to be underestimated. The members of the virgin choirs who performed hymns that Ephraem the Syrian composed for liturgy and religious instruction needed not only good voices but also linguistic skill, a good memory, and physical stamina. The hymns, for which Ephraem availed himself of more than fifty different syllable patterns,[32] fill more than a dozen volumes in Dom Edmund Beck's modern editions. While the virgins certainly included "daughters of the covenant," who had committed themselves to a life of asceticism and whose circle consisted of women of a broad range of age groups, it is unlikely that girls at an early age would not also have joined, thus being introduced in an entertaining way to the service of the church. One hymn, now only extant as part of Ephraem's Armenian corpus, was even composed for the day of dedication of a young girl as a "daughter of the covenant."[33] In a similar vein, Jerome referred to the examples of Miriam singing to the virgin choir (Exod. 15:21) and of Paula's daughter Eustochium, who taught "her [young virgin] companions to be music girls but music girls for Christ, to be luteplayers but luteplayers for the Savior." The content of the music taught was also of great importance. When advising little Paula's mother, Laeta, on how to raise her daughter, Jerome was convinced that the girl who was to be shaped into a temple of God could dispense with the "knowledge of the world's songs." Rather, her "tongue must be steeped while still tender in the sweetness of the psalms." He advised Gaudentius to "reward [his infant daughter] for singing psalms that she may love what she has to learn." There could not be enough of the proper, religious singing with sweet children's voices for Jerome, who foresaw that little Paula, when visiting with her grandfather, would "leap upon his breast, put her arms round his neck, and, whether he like[d] it or not, sing Alleluia in his ears." As far as he knew, she had already started in the cradle singing "Alleluia" (*Letters* 54.13, 107.4, 128.1, 107.4, and 108.27).

Not only were children instructed and encouraged to sing select passages from the Scriptures, most prominently the psalms, but the whole Christian congregation would also regularly be reminded of the centrality of children's witness to the faith. Rufinus, for example, documented in his *Apology* that "the Hymn of the Three Children . . . is regularly sung in festivals in the church of God" and even "martyrs or confessors . . . have sung the Hymn of the Three Children" (2.33, 35). The reference in Susanna to Daniel as a "young lad" (1:45) supported the identification of the three young men in the fiery furnace, Shadrach, Meshach, and Abednego (Dan. 3:1-18), as young children, as an alternative to their representation as young men, found, for example on reliefs on sarcophagi.[34]

Ancient texts also provide relatively ample evidence for the importance and frequency of different forms of role-playing in children's upbringing. Tales, gender-typical toys, and the imitation of real-life roles played an important part in this process. By being encouraged to imitate aspects of adults' behavior, children's social imagination was cultivated, and early on they learned central features of future roles they might play in the world. That adults thought they could easily form children's minds and behaviors had positive and negative dimensions. Some parents worried about the effect on their children of listening to slave nurses or instructors *(paedagogi),* especially in cases in which such personnel came from rural or foreign areas. Tacitus, for example, considered that children's "impressionable and untrained minds are affected by their tales and nonsense" (*Dialogue* 29.1). In an attempt to encourage or persuade the children in their care to proper behavior, nurses and even parents would frighten the children with stories about monsters or wolves that could come and devour them. The resemblance of such stories to "Little Red Riding Hood" and similar fairy tales is too obvious to require detailed comment. Jerome knew that children enjoyed being entertained by nursery tales (*Letter* 128.1). Early Christian authors, who realized also that the mythological exploits and adventures of pagan gods could be put to the same use, disapproved of such storytelling. Clement of Alexandria, for example, documents the reluctance of early Christian parents, "who avoid the practice of soothing our crying children, as the saying is, by telling them fabulous stories," "old wives' talk . . . of fabulous and monstrous shapes," or the "terrifying apparition of strange demons," for fear "of fostering in [the children's] minds the impiety professed by those who, though wise in their own conceit, have no more knowledge of the truth than infants" (*Exhortation* 6).

BECOMING AN ADULT

Although many types of toys and games were common to children of both sexes, some of the toys children played with helped instill in them an idea of what their future roles and tasks in life might look like. The potential that dolls carried for such purposes has already been demonstrated. While some of the miniature furniture pieces and vessels that often accompany dolls found in sanctuaries and tombs could be interpreted as additional votive offerings or funerary objects providing for the children's necessities in the afterlife, they could also have functioned at the same time as accessories to dolls with which the girls played, inspiring and modeling demands for proper household equipment for a future lady. One also notices that children who raced in the ancient equivalent of a go-cart, that is, a fit-to-size version of a chariot or carriage hitched to a small animal, often a goat or sturdy pony, are depicted as male.[35] In addition to the enjoyment the boys gained from the ride, they also may have imitated the latest winner of the horse races in the arena. At the same time, and with a view toward their future life in public and on the road, they learned basic skills of how to handle such means of transportation.

Children's imitation of adult behavior was strongly encouraged and playfully introduced into child behavior in the ancient world. Across all strands of society, both among the elite and among the lower classes, the preferred roles for imitation were those of leadership and public office. Children played kings or judges.[36] Parents promoted the early display of oratorical skills in order to advance the child's chances for serving in public office. At family gatherings, on feast days, or at burial ceremonies for family members, a boy might well give a speech in honor of the occasion or the deceased relative. Among the best-preserved and most impressive statues of children in the Roman world is one in the Louvre in Paris of Nero in the pose of a young orator, identifiable as a child by the *bulla* he is still wearing around his neck.[37] In the case of Gaius Caesar Caligula, whose surname means "little boots," his early acquaintance with the training and dress of the soldier is retained in his very name (Suetonius, *The Life of the Caesars: Gaius Caligula* 4.9). Any office that was visually distinguished by a special garb was by that very virtue highly attractive for children's imitation. This playful simulation of adult behavior is likewise reflected in Christian sources and their presentation of individual young Christians. One of the better-known examples is the behavior of little Athanasius, the later bishop of Alexandria.

Socrates Scholasticus and Sozomen recount in their respective *Ecclesiastical Histories* a version of an incident that took place during the episcopacy of Alexander and on the feast of the commemoration of the martyr-bishop Peter (Socrates 1.15; Sozomen 2.17). According to Socrates, Alexander observed how a group of children, including the boy Athanasius, were engaged in a sacred game at the seashore, imitating the tasks "of the priesthood and the order of consecrated persons." The children had allotted Athanasius the bishop's throne, while each of the rest of the lads impersonated "either a presbyter or a deacon." Thus, according to Sozomen, the children were "imitating . . . the ceremonies of the church." For a while, Sozomen continues, Alexander thought of the mimicry as merely an innocent children's game and enjoyed watching and witnessing what was going on. He behaved not much different from a Roman father who, having bought his son a new soldier's uniform, now took delight in how his son practiced the role of military commander among his playmates. Yet when he realized that the children not only conducted the readings and prayers of the first part of the liturgy, but also performed in their play "the unutterable," as Sozomen called it, that is, the offering of the gifts and the consecration, a part not known to catechumens, he either became concerned, as Sozomen portrayed him, or suspected a portent, as Socrates would have it. Alexander had the children summoned and carefully questioned about the roles each one had played and what exactly they had done and said. The children confessed that Athanasius not only had fulfilled the role of being "their bishop and leader," but also had baptized many of them who had not yet officially become initiated members of the church. Alexander first satisfied himself that in their game the children had used and "accurately observed" "the exact routine of the church." Then he concluded in agreement with the counsel of his fellow clergy that the young Athanasius's baptism of his playmates was indeed valid. No rebaptism "of those who, in their simplicity, had been judged worthy of the Divine grace" was necessary. Bishop Alexander did, however, celebrate for them the mysteries, an indirect witness to the children's full participation at the eucharistic liturgy. While Socrates reports that Bishop Alexander "gave directions that [all] the children should be taken to the church, and instructed in learning," Sozomen includes a comment that incorporates the request for collaboration on the part of the children's relatives to "[bring them] up for the church and for leadership in what they had imitated," suggesting that all of them were destined to become officeholders in the church. Socrates states specifically only for Athanasius that Alexander "ordained him deacon on his becoming of adult age."

Portents of extraordinary behavior and future office to be held by an individual child are a quite common feature of ancient biography and panegyric. Herodotus's account of Cyrus's childhood (*History* 1.114) is the earliest example in Greek literary tradition of "the idea that the future king is made manifest by his role within the hierarchy of children at play."[38] Thomas Wiedemann refers to the future emperor Septimius Severus, who was reported to have played judges with his playmates. The late-fourth- or early fifth-century *Augustan History* tells that "he would come in with fasces and axes borne before him and sit down with the other children standing around in a circle and give judgment" (*Scriptores Historiae Augustae, Severus* 1.4). While the church historians' nuanced presentation of Athanasius's revelation as bishop is a literary construct, and while one encounters other examples of children acting out the roles of bishops in works of Christian hagiography, known for its embellishments, it is still conceivable that early Christian children may at times have added to their repertoire roles that reflected at least some of their experiences at church. Even Sozomen, who dramatized the events most elaborately, did not think it worthy of special note that some of the children, including Athanasius, had been baptized and had at least some general idea of "the ceremonies of the church." What he found remarkable was that they knew "the exact routine of the church . . . accurately." At the least, therefore, the description of the event by the church historians witnesses to a general familiarity of at least some Christian children with the basics of the liturgy. It also supports the fact that the ancient Christian audience would have been somewhat familiar with, and thus would have accepted the plausibility of, children reenacting the liturgy when they played with one another. One might add that an additional side effect of such playful liturgical imitation consisted in an increased, more active familiarity of the children with the liturgical routines.

CONCLUSIONS

Our sources on the whole are ambivalent about the value of toys and games for the development of Christian children. On the one hand, toys and games were often associated with the worship of Greek and Roman deities. On the other hand, it was important that children be positively enticed and rewarded with toys: the educational value of play was appreciated by Christian and non-Christian writers alike. We noted the significance of the Christian child's learning of Old and New Testament writings, particularly of those texts important for the performance of the liturgy, for example, the psalms. Here playful contexts appeared to have enhanced learning. Since the experience of the Christian liturgy as well as the acquisition of the faith was a lifelong matter, it was seen as important that children be able to associate amusement with learning in their earliest years.

Christian children played games and enjoyed toys just as non-Christian children did. Aspects of the Christian liturgy lent themselves readily to reenactment by younger children; this had parallels in children's playing with items that were significant for certain cults, such as that of Dionysus. Faint traces of such ancient customs seem to be preserved in modern times, both in the East and in the West, in the roles of young altar servants, who sometimes function alongside lectors and deacons, but at other times replace them.

Placing children and their toys and games into a historical account that has often ignored them enhances our understanding of the complex social world of late ancient Christians. It also gives us more concrete purchase on the metaphorical associations evoked by a tradition that emphasized the childlike character of all Christian initiates, followers of a Christ who proclaimed, "Unless you change and become like children, you will never enter the kingdom of heaven" (Matt. 18:3).

FOR FURTHER READING

Elderkin, Kate McKnight. "Jointed Dolls in Antiquity." *American Journal of Archaeology* 34/2 (1930): 455–79.

Hett, Walter S. "The Games of the Greek Boy." *Greece and Rome* 1 (1931): 24–29.

Hopkins, Keith. "The Age of Roman Girls at Marriage." *Population Studies* 18 (1965): 309–27.

Jouer dans l'Antiquité. Musée d'Archéologie Méditerranéenne. Centre de la Vieille Charité. Catalog of exhibition held from November 22, 1991, to February 16, 1992. Marseilles, France: Musées de Marseille—Réunion des Musées Nationaux, 1992.

Kastner, Marie-Odille. "L'enfant et les jeux dans les documents d'époque romaine." *Bulletin de l'Association Guillaume Budé* (1995): 85–100.

Plati, Marina. *Playing in Ancient Greece.* Athens: N. P. Goulandris Foundation, 1999.

Rawson, Beryl. "Adult-Child Relationships in Roman Society." In Beryl Rawson, ed., *Marriage, Divorce, and Children in Ancient Rome,* 7–30. Oxford: Clarendon, 1991.

Shumka, Leslie Joan. "Children and Toys in the Roman World: A Contribution to the History of the Roman Family." M.A. thesis University of Victoria, Canada, 1993.

Wiedemann, Thomas. *Adults and Children in the Roman Empire.* New Haven: Yale University Press, 1989.

Wright, David F. "Infant Dedication in the Early Church." In Stanley E. Porter and Anthony R. Cross, eds., *Baptism, the New Testament and the Church,* 352–78. Journal for the Study of the New Testament Supplement Series 171. Sheffield: Sheffield Academic, 1999.

BAPTISMAL RITES AND ARCHITECTURE

ROBIN M. JENSEN

Christian identity is claimed, developed, and reinforced through ritual practice as much as—or perhaps more than—by the doctrines articulated by theologians. Both day-to-day communal experiences of worship and seasonal rites and festivals are essential to the way ordinary believers understand their place in the social and cosmic orders. Among these practices, baptism is the special ritual of entry and identity. It simultaneously requires and creates explicit boundaries between insiders and outsiders—boundaries that the rite renders permeable, even as it reinforces and affirms them. And, like all rituals, the actions, gestures, symbols, physical environment, and images are the essential and efficacious elements that make the rite work—that make it happen in a particular place and time and with specific human participants.

To some extent, shared sacred texts and common performative elements underlie and thus unite all enactments of this ritual. Yet, regardless of its foundational mythology and idealized universality, Christian baptism, like all religious practice, can only be explained and understood as the expression of a particular community in a specific time and place. Despite a relatively high degree of coherence in its basic symbols, asserted origins, and explained significance, the rite of baptism always has a regional character, habitation, and language. In late antiquity, the boundaries established by local Christian communities—as expressed in words, actions, and material artifacts—often emerged in the midst of controversies over the essential character of the church's core values, organizing structures, disciplinary processes, and acknowledged markers of membership.

The shape, meaning, and context of Christian baptism in Roman North Africa were simultaneously affected by a desire to resolve conflicts, to discipline perceived deviance, and to forge and reinforce personal and communal identity. This chapter begins by considering three distinct cases, from three key periods in the history of African Christianity that also involved three of the most significant thinkers in the shaping of later Latin Christianity. In each of these cases, the ritual was delineated in response to challenges posed by particular persons, historical events, practical problems, and encounters with practices or teachings perceived to be foreign or even heretical. Although the arguments advanced in each case claimed to be consistent with ancient and changeless traditions, as well as acknowledged authorities, the rite as well as its explained meaning inevitably was adapted to accommodate new circumstances and needs. Furthermore, since the evidence for rituals includes the actual places, elements, and objects that the participants employed, a concluding examination of the extant material artifacts and physical environments of baptism in Roman Africa will help to illuminate the experience of Christian initiation for those who underwent or performed the rite. Attention to the baptismal chambers and fonts, as well as to their visual décor, provides a different kind of window onto a practice that cannot be understood solely by examining texts.

TERTULLIAN, HERETICAL WOMEN, AND THE IMPORTANCE OF WATER IN BAPTISM

Tertullian's treatise on baptism is the earliest known description of the rite and it attends, in particular, to the centrality of the symbol of water. At the beginning he claims to offer a "discussion of the sacred significance of that water of ours [*aquae nostrae*]" in the hope that it will equip persons "under instruction" (catechumens) as well as those among the already baptized who might find their faith tempted in regard to the sacrament (*Bapt.* 15). Thus, although his text provides a wealth of information about baptism in Carthage at the end of the second century, Tertullian's introductory remarks reveal that his impetus for writing was polemical rather than purely catechetical or theological. He was determined to eradicate a dangerous and heretical attack on baptism that apparently had already led a number of Christians astray, putting their salvation in peril. Clearly, a controversy of some kind provided the occasion for this document.

Tertullian, like most Christians of his time, believed that baptism inside the church was essential for salvation (see John 3:5). Unbaptized Christians, he says, are like fish out of water. Baptized Christians, however, are "little fishes," swimming after Jesus Christ, the "great Fish." Christians begin their life in the water, and—like all fish—must remain in water to stay safe and sound (*Bapt.* 1). The safety of the little fishes, however, is being endangered by a recent arrival—a "certain female viper from the Cainite sect"—who teaches a "pestilential doctrine" and wants to destroy baptism. In addition to her sex, which disqualifies her even from teaching (see 1 Tim. 2:12), this woman presumes to baptize, and moreover without water, for he adds that creatures of her kind, vipers, asps, and basilisks, frequent dry and water-less places (Matt. 12:43). Tertullian views this practice as a demonic perversion of the ritual (*Bapt.* 2). Waterless baptism was, to him, more than an oxymoron; it was a fearsome threat.

The ritual of baptism that Tertullian defended can be broadly reconstructed from this treatise. Prior to baptism, the candidates were expected to undergo an unspecified period of instruction and preparation that included fasting, all-night vigils, and confession of sin (*Bapt.* 20). They were required to have sponsors, who could vouch for their character and stand as guarantors of their postbaptismal good behavior (*Bapt.* 18). Pass-over and Pentecost were days more appropriate for baptism, but any day was acceptable (*Bapt.* 19). The rite itself began with the consecration of the water in the baptismal font, as the Holy Spirit was invited to rest upon and sanctify the water. Water, Tertullian points out, is especially able to "absorb the power of sanctifying" (*Bapt.* 4). After the water was prepared, candidates renounced Satan and confessed faith in the Father, Son, and Holy Spirit. In addition, they confessed their belief in the one church (*Bapt.* 6).[1] Their confession was probably interrupted by a triple immersion in the water that "corporally washed the soul, and spiritually cleansed the flesh" (*Bapt.* 4).[2] When the newly baptized emerged from the water, they received a postbaptismal anointing with blessed oil (like Aaron's anointing into the priestly tribe) and an imposition of hands that "welcomed the Holy Spirit" (*Bapt.* 7).[3]

Unlike the roughly contemporary baptismal ritual described by the *Apostolic Tradition* ascribed to Hippolytus, Tertullian's ritual lacks an exorcis-tic prebaptismal full-body anointing—an anointing also included in later Western rites, such as that of Ambrose of Milan (*Ap. Trad.* 21; *Sacr.* 1.4). Tertullian was, however, concerned about the evil spirits who became espe-cially active around those who were about to escape their power forever. One has to be vigilant, he comments, since unclean spirits seem to gravi-tate to watery places, and the unholy angels of the evil one often do business

> This discussion of the sacred significance of that water of ours in which the sins of our orig-inal blindness are washed away and we are set at liberty unto life eternal, will not be with-out purpose if it provides equipment for those who are at present under instruction, as well as those others who, content to have believed in simplicity, have not examined the reasons for what has been conferred upon them, and because of inexperience are burdened with a faith which is open to temptation. And in fact a certain female viper from the Cainite sect, who recently spent some time here, carried off a good number with her exceptionally pestilen-tial doctrine, making a particular point of demol-ishing baptism. Evidently in this according to nature: for vipers and asps as a rule, and even basilisks, frequent dry and waterless places. But we, being little fishes, as Jesus Christ is our great Fish, begin our life in the water, and only while we abide in the water are we safe and sound. Thus it was that that portent of a woman, who had no right to teach even cor-rectly, knew very well how to kill the little fishes by taking them out of the water.
> —Tertullian, *On Baptism* 1

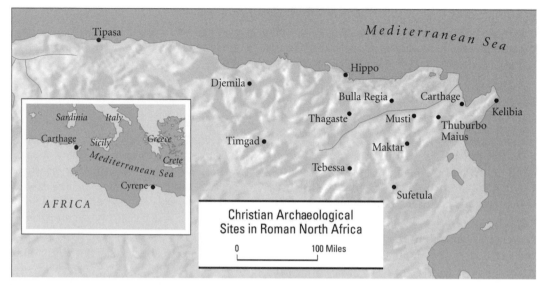

Fig. 5.1. Map of North Africa. Map by Lucidity Information Design.

with the same element (water), hoping to snatch the unwary into perdition. He reassures his audience, however, by reminding them that in the baptistery, just as in the pool of Bethsaida (John 5:4), a holy angel will set the water moving, thus rendering it safe and clean for its purpose (*Bapt.* 5). Although the water has been consecrated and already "conceived the power to make holy," the supplemental action of the angel is required to purify it of demonic contamination.

Water, then, is essential, and for that Tertullian offers scriptural evidence. Water was with God from the beginning: while the earth was a formless void, water was the naturally pure and "worthy carriage" for the Spirit (Gen. 1:2). God divided the water to establish the firmament of heaven and gathered the water into one place to spread out the dry land (Gen. 1:6, 7). From the very birth of the cosmos, water was the source of fertility, bringing forth living things upon the earth, and providing the necessary element of dust to form the human creature (Gen. 2:7). No one could doubt that God uses such an element to continue to form creatures through the sacrament of baptism. Water, Tertullian concludes, is the source of life, a material "always perfect, joyous, and simple and pure" (*Bapt.* 3). Even though Christians cannot be baptized in those same ancient waters of creation, the water of the font is of the same species, whether it comes from sea, pond, river, fountain, tub, or cistern. The specific places he mentions in this regard also indicate that baptism probably took place in a natural setting that provided plenty of water (*Bapt.* 4). Tertullian's panegyric on water, as he calls his treatise on baptism, continues with references to the many places where baptism in water is prefigured in the Hebrew scrip-

Fig. 5.2. Font from Bulla Regia/Hamman Djaradji (basilica I), sixth century. Photo credit: Robin Jensen.

tures, such as the Red Sea crossing and the miracle of water in the wilderness, as well as in certain New Testament stories, including the wedding at Cana, the woman at the well, and Pilate's washing his hands (*Bapt.* 3 and 9).

Who, then, was the viperous female from the Cainite sect who would deny the little fishes their water? According to Tertullian, she had already carried off a number of staunchly loyal Christians with her teachings. Reading between the lines of his vehement defense of water for baptism allows an imaginative reconstruction of her alternative baptism. Based on Tertullian's insistence on the necessity of water, we can surmise that she, and perhaps others of her group, offered a waterless baptism, perhaps denying the efficacy of baptism in water as too materialistic and even antiscriptural. Tertullian imparts a few concrete details about her ritual by drawing a contrast with the baptism he defends as simple in form, using few words and no unusual apparatus, and offered free of charge. Those administering the offending ritual, he says, charge a fee, since their rite promises marvelous outcomes and includes solemn ceremonies, secret rites, and "pretentious magnificence."

Tertullian allows that certain idolatrous groups, such as the devotees of Isis and Mithras, also use water for initiation, but they do so unaware that their water is "barren." Some even sprinkle water around their temples, houses, and cities and bathe images of their gods. Such practices, he insists, were designed by the evil one to deceive and confuse, by ritual similar to, yet essentially unlike, Christian baptism. Only that water appointed by God for a true salutary purpose can convey spiritual healing (*Bapt.* 5). Tertullian hints that the woman from the Cainite sect is aware that her ritual is demonic, which makes her even worse than the unenlightened pagans. She deliberately takes the little fish out of their water and knowingly leads them into perdition.

However, again reading between the lines, it seems clear that Tertullian's antagonist presented herself as a true Christian and not as an idol worshipper—which particularly galled him. He vehemently refutes interpretations of certain Gospel texts that must have been circulated by her or others like her. For example, he defends John's baptism as being from "heaven." He admits that John's baptism needed completion by the baptism of Christ, which confers the Holy Spirit (as asserted by the scriptures), but he utterly denies that John's was a basely material and merely provisional baptism (*Bapt.* 10). He objects to the argument that Jesus himself did not baptize and refutes the audacious claim that the apostles were never baptized, explaining why Jesus need not, could not, and even would not baptize. In his view, the ritual's efficacy was ultimately affirmed by Christ's passion, resurrection, and ascension—after he had entered into his glory (Luke 24: 26, *Bapt.* 11–12). Furthermore, he insists, the apostles must have been baptized, or Jesus' lines to Peter about not needing to be bathed again (John 12:10) would have been nonsensical (*Bapt.* 12).

We may conclude from his refutation that Tertullian's opponents asserted that John's baptism in water was earthly and preparatory only. Since Jesus' appearance on earth, it was, in their view, rendered ineffective and invalid—a point demonstrated by the fact that Jesus baptized no one (see John 4:2) and that scripture omits any mention of the apostles' baptism (*Bapt.* 11). Furthermore, these "thoroughgoing scoundrels and raisers of unnecessary questions" seem to have cited Hebrews 11 as evidence that Abraham pleased God by means of his faith, not through any sacrament of water (*Bapt.* 13). Tertullian responds by pointing out that Jesus after his resurrection had commanded baptism in the name of the Trinity (Matt. 28:19), and he insists that salvation is not a matter of mere belief but of a faith "sealed by the sacrament of baptism." In a final outburst, Tertullian cites the Epistle to the Ephesians to insist that there is only *one* baptism and *one* church (Eph. 4:5). These others cannot have the *one*, because they do not have the *same* baptism. Moreover, "as they do not have it in the proper form, without doubt they do not have it [at all]" (*Bapt.* 15).

Although not often noticed by historians, Tertullian's treatise actually describes an early struggle among different Christian groups, each defending a particular initiation ritual as efficacious and biblically justified. On one side was Tertullian's party, practicing a baptism in water that included a triple immersion and a postbaptismal anointing and laying on of hands. On the other side was a group that apparently allowed women to administer what may have been an initiation ritual that eschewed water, literally heeding John the Baptist's proclamation that the one who came after him would offer not baptism in water, but baptism with the Holy Spirit and—perhaps also—with fire (Matt. 3:22; Mark 1:8; Luke 3:16). Whether the particular woman whom Tertullian attacks was an actual member of the so-called Cainite sect is unclear, since that label may have been applied to discredit her.[4]

According to their ancient detractors, the Cainites venerated Cain as the divine power, rejected all traditional moral teachings, and defended Judas, either because Judas realized that Christ was a dangerous subverter of the truth or because he brought about the salvific benefits given by Jesus' crucifixion. However, little is known about Cainite ritual practices, and at least one modern scholar even doubts the actual existence of the sect.[5] It seems unlikely that Tertullian's "Cainite" was a member of a Valentinian sect, a group well established in Carthage, because, like the Marcionites, whom Tertullian also condemned, the Valentinians seem to have practiced a water baptism.[6] She may, however, have been a member of a gnostic group that practiced some kind of spiritual (and waterless) baptism, such as the Marcosians, who, according to Irenaeus, contrasted the "perfect" spiritual baptism inaugurated by the Divine Christ who descended upon the visible Jesus with the merely material or "animal" baptism offered by John the Baptist (*Her.* 1.21.2). Although some of these groups may have administered an initial water bath, others asserted that it was superfluous to bring candidates to water and, having rejected material elements, used only scented oil, maintaining that the "mystery of the unspeakable and invisible power" ought not to be perverted by the use of visible or corruptible things (*Her.* 1.21.3–4).[7] Alternatively, this woman may have been related to a "heretical" and "depraved" group described in a later African treatise wrongly credited to Cyprian that actually baptized with fire. This group, using some of the same arguments as Tertullian's opponents, argued that, since Jesus' appearance, baptism was incomplete without the addition of fire and the Holy Spirit (*Rebapt.* 16).

Toward the end of his treatise, Tertullian reminds his readers to observe the proper rules when giving and receiving baptism. The right to baptize belongs, first of all, to the bishop, then to those presbyters and deacons commissioned by him for this purpose, and finally—in emergencies—even to laypersons, since what is received may also be given (*Bapt.* 17). He insists, however, that laypersons must also remember the requirements of humility and not take to themselves powers rightly belonging to the bishop, because while some things might be lawful, they might not be beneficial (1 Cor. 6:12). Tertullian especially objects to women's baptizing, though they might well have understood themselves justified in doing so, since they too should be able to give what they had received. Lest anyone point to the example of Thecla, who was said to have baptized herself (according to the *Acts of Paul and Thecla* 34), to justify a woman's right to baptize in an emergency, Tertullian denounces the text as a forgery and points out that Paul would never have permitted a woman either to teach or to baptize. Finally, he insists, baptism should not be freely given to anyone who asks, but only to those who understand the requirements involved and the burdens entailed. Those who understand the significance of baptism as a life-changing experience, Tertullian asserts, will have more fear of obtaining it than of postponing it.

CYPRIAN, SCHISMATICS, AND THE GIFT OF THE HOLY SPIRIT IN BAPTISM

Tertullian's belief that salvation required valid baptism inside the one holy and pure church was shared by most early Christian theologians. Moreover, although Tertullian permitted emergency baptism by (male) laypersons, he worried that prerogatives of the bishop might be usurped, since opposition to the episcopacy is the "mother of schism" (*Bapt.* 17). Only martyrdom (baptism in blood) was recognized as a replacement for or equivalent of this otherwise clerically supervised and validated ritual (*Bapt.* 16).[8] A half-century later, however, the persecution of the Roman emperor Decius (250–51 CE) not only offered opportunities for Christians to undergo this "baptism in blood" but also presented a grave challenge to the North African church and gave rise to a new controversy, one that ultimately led to a reconsideration of the place of baptism in defining membership in the catholic community and guaranteeing salvation. This new controversy revolved around the questions of who (if anyone) had the power to forgive sin and where the church, as a single, pure body, was to be located. At the same time, responses to the crisis of the Decian persecution challenged the older (Tertullianist) point of view that serious sin committed after baptism must lead to expulsion from the congregation (see *Mod.* 3). While in the older, more rigorous Christian church excommunicated sinners' only hope lay in direct appeal to Christ himself in the last judgment, a church made up of persons facing daily and deadly peril from sin needed more immediate ways to negotiate its boundaries.

Christians in the mid-third century had to face two fearsome judges, one earthly, the other heavenly. The emperor ordered all citizens to sacrifice to the gods or face the penalties of prison, exile, loss of family property, or even death at the hands of the secular authorities. On the other hand, those who lacked the courage of martyrdom and lapsed into apostasy and idolatry faced expulsion from the church, the loss of the saving sacraments and intercessions of the saints, and eternal damnation at the judgment seat of Christ, who had proclaimed that anyone who denies him before others, he would deny before his Father in heaven (Matt. 10:33). Faced with this bleak choice, many Christians, afraid of leaving families destitute as much as of losing their own lives, complied with the imperial edict or found various ways to circumvent the process and obtain fraudulent documents that stated that they had sacrificed. Others, however, refused to sacrifice or resort to subterfuge, and some of

Fig. 5.3. Font from Sufetula/Sbeitla (basilica III, basilica of Servus, built into the cella of an earlier Roman temple), fifth century. Photo credit: Robin Jensen.

these were imprisoned or died under torture for their resistance. These "confessors" were subsequently seen as heroes and enlisted in the aid of those who had failed to withstand the imperial demand and succumbed under pressure. Confessors who died were regarded as saints who might intervene on their behalf from heaven. Those who survived their torment sometimes offered individual lapsed persons forgiveness in the form of a letter addressed to the bishop. These confessors believed they had the power to forgive sins, as well as the authority to readmit the fallen to the church, even after the lapsed Christians had been expelled for idolatry. The confessors compared themselves with the saints around the throne of God, crying out for vengeance, in the Apocalypse of John (Rev. 6:9-12; 7:13-14; 20:4).

Many bishops, Cyprian of Carthage among them, refused to recognize the forgiveness offered by the confessors or to readmit the lapsed solely on the basis of the intervention of martyrs, whether living or dead. In the face of practices that clearly challenged the bishop's role, Cyprian denied that sins could be forgiven by any human agents—even martyrs— since sins committed against God could only be forgiven by God (*Laps.* 17; see also Jer. 17:5, "Cursed are those who trust in mere mortals"). He also claimed that the threat of pollution was a primary motivation for his stern position. In an oration delivered after his return from self-imposed exile during the persecution, he warned his flock about the dangers arising from contact with the lapsed, describing cases of sinners being struck dumb, demonic possession, convulsions, or spontaneous vomiting when such sinners came forward to receive the eucharist (*Laps.* 23–26). Cyprian's hard line, however, resulted in the formation of an oppositional schismatic group made up of lapsed Christians and the bishops who absolved them, sometimes without any period of penance (*Ep.* 34, 42, 43). Thus Carthage came to have two Christian communities, one of them deemed impure by the other, since it included seemingly unrepentant idolaters. The split proved problematic for Christians who believed that only one church could be the true church, a situation that only worsened as bishops in each community administered baptism to new members. Valid baptism could not be obtained outside the one, pure, and holy catholic church; any other rite was (following Tertullian's terms) a demonically inspired imitation. Of course, each group claimed to be that one true church—the church of the martyrs—and identified their baptism as the sole gate of salvation.

The consequences of the split were made even more complex when baptized members of one communion converted and asked to be admitted to the other communion. Cyprian, in opposition to Stephen, his colleague in Rome, argued that the former ritual for reception of baptized heretics— the imposition of hands—was insufficient for those who had been baptized in schismatic communities that were additionally tainted by idolatry. He associated the laying on of hands with the reconciliation of penitents who had committed less serious sin. On the contrary, argued Cyprian, these converts would need to be baptized again, in a full ritual performed by a bishop within the church. While at first the issue revolved around the danger of being associated with the pollution of apostasy and idolatry (especially among the clergy), in time membership in a schismatic group was deemed to be equally threatening, since these groups were idolatrous per se. These schismatics sought to destroy the one, true church and, moreover, brought others into their self-made perdition. In Cyprian's view, since the church was one unified body with a single power to sanctify, an alternative body had no power either to forgive sins or to confer the Holy Spirit, nor could it offer the means for salvation through baptism (*Ep.* 69.10.2). In fact, the pseudo-baptisms administered by such a group would contaminate instead of cleanse—much like the rites offered by the viperous female

Fig. 5.4. Font from Thuburbo Maius/Henchir Kasabat (in former Temple of Baal and Tanit), fifth/sixth century. Photo credit: Robin Jensen.

Plate A. Christianity attracted many women, some of whom abandoned their traditional roles in the family so as to dedicate themselves to lives of prayer and study. This Roman painting of a woman writing reminds us that some women in antiquity were scholars, even theologians. Private Collection. Photo credit: Art Resource, NY.

Plate B. Jesus chose not Roman senators but Palestinian fishermen as his disciples, as fifth-century bishop and theologian Augustine pointed out. This sixth-century mosaic from the Church of S. Apollinare Nuovo in Ravenna, Italy, depicts Peter and Andrew fishing. Photo credit: Erich Lessing / Art Resource, NY.

Plate C. Another mosaic portrays a procession of saints led by Martin, whose tomb at Tours was the site of pilgrimage, cultic devotion, healings and other miracles. Church of S. Apollinare Nuovo, Ravenna, Italy. Photo credit: Erich Lessing / Art Resource, NY.

Plate D. The Cubiculum of Leo, a small room built in the late fourth century to serve as the tomb of a Roman official, is decorated with murals that attest to the important place of the saints in the drama of salvation as this was understood by ancient Christians. On the back wall is a painting of the martyr-saints Felix and Adauctus, who gesture towards a young Christ holding an open book. The side walls show episodes from the *Acts of Peter*, while a bearded Christ, flanked by an alpha and an omega, gazes down from the ceiling. Catacomb of Commodilla, Rome, Italy. Photo © Pontificia Commissione di Archeologia Sacra. Used by permission.

Plate E. This fifth- or sixth-century baptismal font recalls the shape of a woman's vulva, symbolizing the neophytes' birth from the fertile womb of the mother church and their status as infants entering a new family. Sufetula/Sbeitla, basilica II, basilica of Vitalis, Tunisia. Photo credit: Robin Jensen.

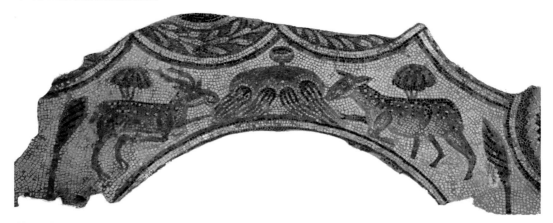

Plate F. This sixth-century mosaic depicts deer coming to drink at streams of living water, in an allusion to Psalm 42 that evokes the joys of Paradise promised to the baptized. From the baptistery attached to the basilica at Bir Ftouha (near Carthage), the mosaic is now in the Bardo Museum. Photo credit: Robin Jensen.

Plate G. Christian children would have played the same kinds of games with the same kinds of toys as did non-Christian children, despite tension surrounding the cultic associations of some of these toys and games. This late-second-century marble sculpture portrays a young girl playing knucklebones. Photo: Juergen Liepe. Antikensammlung, Staatliche Museen, Berlin, Germany. Photo credit: Bildarchiv Preussischer Kulturbesitz / Art Resource, NY.

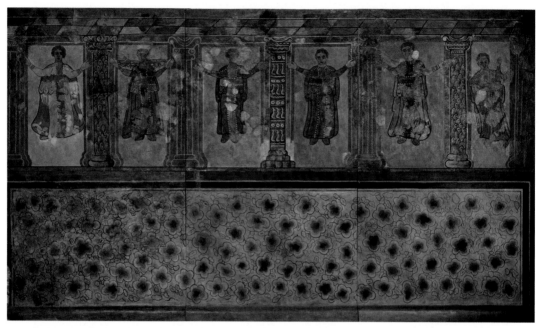

Plate H. On the west wall of the private chapel of a villa at Lullingstone, England, a frescoed "congregation" raised their hands in prayer, mimicking the actions of the worshippers. Photo credit: Wall painting of Orants from wall of chapel, Lullingstone villa. Photo © The British Museum. Used by permission.

Plate I. This sixth-century ivory pyxis depicts the Miracle of the Loaves and Fishes, a particularly apt image for a eucharistic container. While many such containers were used to hold the Eucharistic bread during the public mass, it has been suggested some were commissioned by members of the aristocracy to hold the reserved eucharist in the home. Photo credit: Pyxis with multiplication of loaves and fishes. The Metropolitan Museum of Art, Gift of J. Pierpont Morgan, 1917. Photograph © 1985 The Metropolitan Museum of Art. Used by permission.

Plate J. In the course of the fourth century, the domestic architecture of the house church gave way to the monumental architecture of the basilica. The church of Santa Sabina in Rome preserves the basic features of the early basilicas where many Christians would have experienced the drama of the liturgy. Photo credit: Scala / Art Resource, NY.

Fig. 5.5. Font from Sufetula/Sbeitla (basilica I, basilica of Bellator, Chapel of Jucundus), fourth/fifth century. Photo credit: Robin Jensen.

of Tertullian's treatise (*Ep.* 70.2.2–3, 72.1.1). The pollution of such association could be removed only through the complete washing of true baptism, not by a mere laying on of hands, since the convert was essentially coming over from pagan practice.

Thus, in the mid-third century, the church led by Cyprian was defined by its opposition to a new kind of "demonically deceptive imitation" that was identified by its relative leniency toward penitent sinners and the authority granted to martyred saints and confessors. Although the defining issues emerged in the context of the extreme threat posed by the Decian persecution, the outcomes were generated by a clash of competing authorities and either rigorous or lax attitudes toward those who had fallen into the grave sin of idolatry. At first the two competing groups were the confessors and the clergy, but soon the groups comprised at least two different church bodies, each asserting that it was the one and true community and each claiming the exclusive power to condemn or absolve sinners and to transmit the Holy Spirit through its sacraments. Individuals staked their eternal salvation on the hope that they had been baptized by the right bishop and in the right church.

To make matters worse, the kind of ritual that would be imposed on a person moving from one communion to the other became the outward expression of a struggle over power, purity, and identity that brought about a clash between African and Roman bishops. Earlier bishops of Carthage received heretics or schismatics by the simple rite of a laying on of hands. This pattern changed with Agrippinus, a predecessor of Cyprian, for obscure reasons.[9] The bishop of Rome shared the earlier African position, perhaps based on a widespread and ancient practice that had scriptural basis in the book of Acts, which distinguishes between certain Samaritans whose baptisms were in the name of the Lord Jesus only (Acts 8:14-18) and a group of Ephesians who had been baptized by John the Baptist (Acts 19:1-7). While the Samaritans were received by only a laying on of hands, the former disciples of John the Baptist were required to be validly baptized (again).[10] However, both sides could claim these texts in support of their position, depending on whether they viewed heretical or schismatic baptism as invalid or simply incomplete and also on how they assessed the relative significance of the water bath as compared to the imposition of hands that conveyed the gift of the Holy Spirit. Could one part of the rite be efficacious or salvific without the other? Were there, in some sense, two different types of baptism—one a water baptism and the other a Spirit baptism?[11]

The African position, however, as articulated by Cyprian, recognized baptism as valid only if inside a community under the authority of the duly consecrated bishop. By the end of the persecutions of the mid-third century, the power to cleanse a new convert and to confer the Spirit was limited to those who were within a single, unified body established by Christ when he conferred the power to forgive sin upon the apostles (John 20:22-23; *Ep.* 73.7.1-2; *Unity* 4–5). No other community, clergy, or prophetically inspired individuals could claim to have access to this power, since the Holy Spirit did not reside within them. The flock could have only one shepherd. There could be no halfway position. One was either within the ark of salvation (the true church) or on the outside drowning in the flood. For Cyprian, there could be only one fountain of living water, and that was inside an enclosed garden (*Ep.* 69.2.2). Even though the schismatics might recite the same creedal formula, their avowed belief in the forgiveness of sin through the holy church certainly could not possibly refer to *their* church (*Ep.* 69.7.2).

Although Cyprian provides no comprehensive summary of the ritual of baptism in his letters or treatises, he includes enough references to the rite to allow some evaluation of how it may have signified the exclusivist position of his catholic communion and his emphasis on the role of the bishop as guarantor of the validity of baptism. Like Tertullian, Cyprian emphasizes the necessity of the water as the cleansing element in baptism and also insists that it be consecrated by a bishop, a detail not specified by Tertullian (*Ep.* 70.1.3).[12] Moreover, Cyprian maintains, like Tertullian, that the bishop is the appropriate officiant of the ceremony, with presbyters (preferably) and even deacons allowed to impose hands to reconcile penitents or to baptize catechumens in danger of dying. Unlike Tertullian, however, Cyprian omits any mention of a layperson baptizing in emergencies (*Ep.* 18.1.2 and 2.2, addressed to presbyters and deacons). Cyprian also explicitly reserves the laying of hands on the newly baptized for the bishop (except in the already noted emergency cases). Tertullian may simply assume it; alternately, he may have permitted the giving of the Holy Spirit to be made through the laying on of hands of a presbyter or deacon (commissioned by the bishop), or even a layperson in an emergency situation. Cyprian, by reserving this act for the bishop, underscores his claim that only the bishop has the right to bestow the Holy Spirit. Persons who were baptized in an emergency situation by a sprinkling of water (rather than by immersion) and then recovered presumably would seek out the bishop for the necessary ritual completion of the sacrament. However, if they died, they could seek Christ himself to supply the heavenly equivalent of the episcopal supplement, just as he breathed on the apostles after his own resurrection (John 20:22).[13] Cyprian clearly saw the rite as indivisible and (like Tertullian) viewed baptism in water as indispensable. Water and Spirit were both given in the rite, but only water was absolutely required. Baptism of the sick would be valid so long as it was administered by a catholic officiant. Schismatics' water was, however, polluted and invalid for both sickbed and regular baptism (*Ep.* 69.12–16).

> That the Church is one is declared by the Holy Spirit in the Song of Songs, speaking in the person of Christ: *My dove, my perfect one, is but one; she is the only one of her mother, the favourite of her who bore her.* And the Spirit again says of her: *An enclosed garden is my sister, my bride, a sealed fountain, a well of living water.*
>
> Now, if the bride of Christ (that is to say, the Church) is an enclosed garden, then is it just not possible that something which is closed up should lie wide open to outsiders and aliens. And if it is a sealed fountain, then it is just not possible for a man to drink from it or to be sealed at it if, being placed on the outside, he is without access to that fountain. And if it is the one and only well of living water and it, too, is found on the inside, then it is just not possible for a man who is placed on the outside to be given life and sanctification through that water; they and they alone who are on the inside are granted permission to drink of it or to make use of it in any way.
>
> —Cyprian, *Letter* 69.2.1

One rather curious and otherwise unknown ceremonial action associated with the rite of baptism in Cyprian's Carthage is the kissing of the sole of the foot or feet of the newly baptized. This ritual is discussed in a letter from a bishop who asks whether he must baptize as well as kiss the feet of a baby less than eight days old (64.4.1). Apparently this bishop cited the Jewish law regarding withholding of circumcision prior to the eighth day of life. Cyprian's position that, since Jewish law has been superseded, a child may be baptized immediately after birth provides evidence of infant baptism, although possibly only for those children who were mortally ill. Additionally, it appears that the inquiring bishop recoiled from kissing such a child's foot, presumably because he regarded the child as still ritually impure.[14] Kissing the feet of the newly baptized may have been added to the African ceremony of postbaptismal foot washing (a baptismal rite known also in Milan, Gaul, and Spain), perhaps to emphasize the purifying power of the ritual. Cyprian insists that the bishop not only baptize the baby but also kiss the baby's feet, no matter how repugnant the idea might be, since a newly baptized infant could not be in any way impure. Moreover, he continues, since no one is denied access to the grace of baptism—not even old men who have led grievously sinful lives—denying baptism to a newborn who could not have committed any sin of its own is indefensible. The only sin from which such a baby needs cleansing is that sin contracted from his or her ancestor Adam, which transmits the ancient contagion of death (*Ep.* 64.5.2).

AUGUSTINE, INFANT BAPTISM, AND ANCESTRAL SIN

The baptism of infants was a late development in the North African church. Tertullian had advocated baptism for adults and specifically urged that baptism be deferred at least until a child was safely past puberty, married, or "firmly established in continence" and therefore unlikely to incur postbaptismal sin. Baptism, he says, imposes a burden that should bring more anxiety about obtaining it than postponing it. In his mind, children's "natural innocence" makes their coming for baptism unnecessary. Since Jesus said "forbid them not to come to me" (Matt. 19:14), Tertullian would have children educated about the faith but only made Christians when they were competent to "know Christ" and to ask for salvation (Matt. 5:42). To do anything else would put sponsors at risk, as they might fail to fulfill their vows by dying or be imperiled by the child's "subsequent development of an evil disposition" (*Bapt.* 18).

Cyprian's allowing the baptism of a child less than a week old indicates that infant baptism was practiced by his time, at least in cases of mortal danger. The high rate of infant mortality in the ancient world would have made such baptism a fairly regular event, offered not only as assurance of the baby's salvation and resurrection but also as a means of overcoming an essential deficit. Even though, he says, infants cannot have committed any sin of their own volition, they are nevertheless born with the "ancient contagion of death," which must be lifted from them through baptism (*Ep.* 64.5.2).[15] However, the perils faced by a baptized infant could not be discounted, either. Cyprian recalled the case of a wet nurse who implicated a baptized baby in apostasy by feeding her some food sacrificed to idols. Although the child didn't have any conscious idea of what had happened—or any choice in the matter—when she later came to receive the eucharist, she balked and, "by the instinct of the divine majesty," refused to receive the elements. When the deacon forced some of the consecrated food into her mouth, the child vomited it up from her "profane stomach" (*Laps.* 25). This story also shows that baptized babies regularly received the eucharist and would have been both confirmed and communicated as part of their baptismal ceremony.

During the fourth century, Christians no longer feared persecution, and their religion gradually became the dominant faith of the empire. The rapid growth of the church made it less an exclusive community than a more fluid company of insiders and outsiders, seekers as well as the committed. Baptism of infants was still discouraged unless the child was mortally ill, so Christian families enrolled their children (especially males) as catechumens and delayed baptism until the child was safely grown and settled in a stable marriage and acceptable profession. In some cases, baptism would be delayed until life was nearly over. Augustine's family was such a case—his mother, Monica, discouraged the baptism of her son until he was well into adulthood (about age thirty-three) and saw her husband baptized shortly before his death (*Conf.* 9.22). If a child took sick, however, the parents would seek a priest for an emergency baptism, as Monica had, in fact, done when her own son fell ill. In his case, however, he recovered, and baptism was again delayed until he reached an age where he could more easily withstand the temptations of sin (*Conf.* 1.17). The effects of such baptism could be seen if the child survived, as in the

Fig. 5.6. Font from Hippo Regius/Annaba (Basilica Maiorum), late fourth century. Photo credit: Robin Jensen.

case of Augustine's childhood friend who was baptized while unconscious with a life-threatening fever and recovered with a changed personality and attitude toward sin (*Conf.* 4.8). While they waited, catechumens were accepted as members of the community, although not permitted to be present for or receive the eucharist. Since baptism was still asserted as the initial and essential means of obtaining salvation, however, the untimely death of a catechumen or an unbaptized infant was viewed as irredeemable (*Nat. and Grace* 4.4). Baptized penitents, though fallen from grace, might still be reconciled in this life or the next and so had more hope. The practical result of such a system was that lifelong catechumens and noncommunicating penitents were part of a new, more mixed company of Christians that included marginal members, aspiring members, penitent members, and full members. The boundaries of the church's body had become more permeable, its constituency varying according to level of commitment and degree of participation.

Still, infants were often baptized and thus participated in all the rituals of the church. At their baptisms their sponsors would speak for them, both renouncing Satan and professing faith (*Bapt. Donat.* 4.24.32; *Ep.* 98.7). However, as they grew, they could not remain free from sin, as Tertullian would have required. The consequence of more regular infant baptism was a loosening of the expectations of the baptized. No longer could post-baptismal sin be seen as serious as it had been during Tertullian's time, and from the crisis caused by mass apostasy in the mid-third century the church had developed ways for contrite sinners to do effective works of penance and be reconciled and regain their place in the congregation of earthly saints. As postbaptismal sin seemed less dire and exclusivity of member-ship more elusive, the practice of infant baptism undoubtedly became more and more common, in a gradual (and no doubt uneven) evolution of practice.

The acceptance and indeed the familiarity of the practice of infant baptism is clear in the arguments between Augustine and his opponents in the debate over the role of the human free will in salvation, known as the Pelagian controversy. In fact, for Augustine, the practice of infant baptism becomes effectively normative when it is made central to his argument against the followers of Pelagius. In 411 or 412, a certain Caelestius (a dis-ciple of Pelagius) sought ordination from Aurelius, the bishop of Carthage. Known for his teaching that human beings might avoid sin through their own effort, Caelestius was, at his examination, accused by Paulinus of Milan of certain unorthodox teachings, including that the sin of Adam harmed no one but himself and that newly born infants are innocent of sin (that is, that they remain in the same state as Adam and Eve before the fall). Although Caelestius did not actually deny the validity of infant baptism and even acknowledged that the question of original sin was open to debate, his teaching that Adam would have died even if he had not sinned and that children need baptism only for the cleansing of their own sins was con-demned by the next council of bishops convened at Carthage.[16]

Augustine attacked the teachings of the Pelagians vehemently, using the practice of infant baptism as his first line of defense. In his anti-Pelagian treatise, *The Punishment and Forgiveness of Sin and the Baptism of Little Ones,* Augustine insists that infant baptism has scriptural authority and that "little ones" belong to the flock of Christ only by baptism and will perish if they do not receive it (John 10:27-28; *Guilt and Remiss.* 1.18.23). In this, as in his next treatise, *The Spirit and the Letter,* Augustine cites Paul's Epistle to the Romans to argue that sin came into the world through

Adam (Rom. 5:12), that all people are born with the sin of their ancestor, which brings death, and that only baptism can erase the stain of this transgression and its concomitant punishment—even in newly born infants who can have accrued no other sins (*The Spirit and the Letter* 1–11, 21). He asserts baldly that unbaptized infants are condemned, even though they have no personal sins to repent of—a truth demonstrated by the fact that the church baptizes them but based also on the age-old assertion that salvation cannot be obtained outside of the church (and its baptism).

Augustine's opponents, the followers of Pelagius, were equally adamant that unbaptized infants might achieve eternal life and salvation and that God would be unjust to deny them heaven and salvation—a position Augustine actually acknowledges in a letter he wrote to Jerome (*Ep.* 166.10). Admittedly, Paul asserts that Adam "brought sin into the world," but his sin only condemned himself and is not imputed to all his descendants. The supporters of Pelagius believed in the fundamental human potential to overcome sin through ascetic discipline and personal effort—humanity's God-given abilities (*Proceed. Pelag.* 6.16). The attack that Caelestius initially launched on infant baptism, however, challenged not only the necessity but also the unique validity of catholic baptism—a point defended since the time of Cyprian and still at some risk in Augustine's day, due to the ongoing competing claims of the schismatic Donatists.

Augustine's severe position on infant sin and his condemnation of unbaptized babies ironically emerge within a doctrine of grace that presumes human failings after baptism and makes provision for a less than perfect life. Once he or she is inside the church, forgiveness is available to the repentant sinner, and second chances are given freely. Overcoming sin requires humility, which might serve to help equalize the social differences in a flock of imperfect souls. However, the spreading practice of baptizing newly born babies for the remission of ancestral sin not only provided some assurance for their parents (who might well fear letting a child remain at risk) but also led to a gradual yet inevitable transformation of the ritual itself. One practical development seems to be the emerging practice of allowing presbyters to baptize, since the bishop could hardly be near at hand to baptize children individually soon after birth. Augustine himself told the story of a miracle that took place at Uzalis, in the see of his friend Evodius, where a woman's infant child was taken suddenly ill and, even through she hurried to the church, died in her arms as an unbaptized catechumen. Believing him to be condemned without hope of salvation, the mother hurried to the local shrine of Saint Stephen and prayed for her son to be restored to life, at least long enough to be validly baptized. The saint heard her prayer, and the son—at the hands of presbyters (not the bishop)—was baptized, sanctified, anointed, and had hands laid upon him. When all the sacraments were complete, he died again, so that his mother was able to bury him with the knowledge that she was laying her son, not in Hades, but in the lap of the saint (*Serm.* 323, 324). This touching story provides some interesting liturgical details, including a reminder that both exorcism and eucharist were a requirement of a valid baptismal rite, a point that Augustine elaborates elsewhere (see *Guilt and Remiss.* 1.34.63 on exorcism and 1.20.26 on the eucharist). This additional aspect of the rite explains why the mother did not administer—or seek—lay baptism as Tertullian might have urged her to do.

Despite Augustine's arguments that infant baptism was justified and perhaps even necessary, his sermons delivered to the newly baptized at Hippo in the week following Easter were addressed to adults, whom he refers to as metaphorical infants. In these sermons he tells his auditors that they are called infants because they are born again, from the womb of their mother church, with God for their father and the other members their new siblings. Like newly born children they are clothed in white garments (*Serm.* 260A.1, 260C.1, 7). Prior to their baptism, he says, they were called "seekers" (*competentes*) since they were yet agitating in their mother's womb, seeking to be born (*Serm.* 228.1). As if in response to Nicodemus's question of Jesus (John 3:4-5), Augustine tells them that they have had a second birth from a mother's womb, but a birth from above, of water and the Spirit. And then, as a way to remind them what they are in a spiritual sense, he also points out the actual babies among them—infants still nursing and having had grace conferred upon them without their knowing it. Still, he says, all of them, old people, young people, and even teenagers, are infants right after baptism. On the Sunday after Easter, they may lay aside their white robes and "fly out of the nest" to join their older brothers and sisters as full members, whatever their earthly age (*Serm.* 376A.1).

Thus the ritual of baptism had evolved from Tertullian's insistence that the rite should be reserved for responsible adulthood to Augustine's emphasis on the importance of infant baptism for both cleansing and membership in the flock. For Augustine, baptism was not the end of

---

Today is called the octave of the "infants"; they are to unveil their heads, as a sign of freedom. This spiritual birth, you see, means freedom, while birth in the flesh properly speaking means slavery. A person, of course, has two births, being born and being born again. We are born to toil, we are born again to rest; we are born to misery, we are born again to eternal felicity. Take these children, infants, babies, sucklings, clinging to their mothers' breasts—and how much grace has been conferred on them without their knowing it, as you yourselves can see; because they are called infants, they too have their octave today. And these old people, young people, teenagers, they're all infants.

They have one infancy, in fact, that goes with being old, another that goes with being young and new. I mean those whom you see born very recently are born old, and there is in them when they are born, if one may so put it, a young old age. Our old self is called Adam, from whom we are born; our new self is Christ, through whom we are born again. So these here are also new and young, and have been born again to another life.

—Augustine, *Sermon* 376A.1

a time of training and decision making, but the beginning of a life inside a community that offered continuing Christian formation and possessed a means of reincorporating backsliders. Unlike Cyprian, Augustine no longer saw the purity or insider status of the bishop or baptismal administrant as the critical factor, since the ritual itself possessed sanctifying power through the promise and action of Christ. Thus, even sinful or schismatic clergy could offer valid baptism. However, so long as recipients of a schismatic baptism remained outside of the one true church, they were initially cleansed but could not be saved, since they continued in mortal error. Only by repenting their sin of schism and joining the true community would the fruits of baptism be produced in the individual and lead to salvation (*Bapt. Donat.* 1.12.19; 3.13.18).

THE PHYSICAL ENVIRONMENT OF BAPTISM

The unique character and actual experience of Christian baptism cannot be understood through written documents alone. Although we cannot return in time to view (much less to undergo) an actual ritual, we may at least study the physical remains of spaces, fonts, and rooms that housed the rites in antiquity. Each of these spaces or ritual facilities in its own way suggests aspects of the rite and the admittance to paradise it promised. Central was the particular assertion of the candidate's death to an old life and rebirth into a new one. In Africa, as elsewhere, the baptismal font was the fecund womb of mother church, from which her new children emerged naked and wet to begin life within their new family. As Cyprian so expressively enthused: "She [the church] spreads her branches abundantly over the whole earth; she spreads out her flowing rivers even more broadly; yet one is head and one is source and one is a copious mother, of inexhaustible fecundity; of her womb we are born, by her milk we are fed, by her spirit we are animated" (*Unity* 5).

The archaeological evidence for baptism in North Africa cannot, however, be neatly coordinated with the textual evidence, since the material artifacts in many cases must be dated later than surviving written descriptions of—or even references to—the rite. Extant baptismal architecture (baptisteries and fonts) date to the late fourth through seventh centuries, whereas the most detailed textual references to the ritual, as we have seen, derive from the period of the late second to the early fifth century. The only known example in which both significant written and material evidence coincide is the baptistery at Hippo, which scholars presume to belong to Augustine's Basilica Maiorum. The dissonant chronologies of documentary and material evidence raise at least two obvious questions. The first is whether we can presume that later, extant baptismal structures were essentially similar to earlier models that no longer exist. The second is whether we can presume that later rituals were similar to the earlier ones for which we have some evidence. The history of the region makes resolution of these problems even more difficult, since the early fifth-century Vandal invasion transformed the ecclesial landscape of North Africa by introducing a different group of Arian Christians, who took over many of the existing churches, whether formerly catholic or schismatic (Donatist). In less than a century after the Vandal invasion, the area was claimed for the Orthodox church by Byzantine Christians, who in turn brought their own liturgy and saints' cults and both rededicated existing structures and built new churches and baptisteries.

Further complicating the situation and its interpretation is the multiplication of baptisteries in a single urban area. According to tradition, the existence of a baptistery should indicate that the church attached was the seat of the bishop, and thus a community with a single bishop should have only one cathedral church and baptismal font. However, fonts have been found in more than one church in rather close proximity to one another. The city of Carthage, for example, had as many as three baptisteries within its walls and as many as four baptisteries outside the city walls. Duplication of baptistries might be explained by the abandonment of some spaces when new ones were built, the division of a large city like Carthage into distinct regions or parishes (perhaps to accommodate different linguistic groups), or the established practice of allowing presbyters the authority to baptize, as is apparent in the writings of Augustine. These multiple baptisteries, however, could also signal the existence of competing Christian communities with their own bishops. Smaller cities sometimes had two apparently contemporary baptisteries and seem to have had two cathedral churches and probably two competing bishops to administer the rites that each deemed particularly valid and effective.[17]

In addition to being attentive to the chronological divergence between artifacts and documents, scholars have difficulty identifying particular archaeological remains as belonging to specific Christian communities such as the Catholics, Donatists, or Arian Vandals. Apart from occasional inscriptions found in situ or decorative mosaics or other details with a distinctive artistic style, either the evidence has been lost to history, or these groups had no typical art or architecture that would help identify them or distinguish them from other Christian groups. The lack of a characteristic architecture probably indicates a similar lack of sufficient liturgical particularities to require that the design of worship space be altered in easily recognizable ways. The theological and polemical issues that separated various groups are well documented, but such matters do not always find their way into concrete and visible forms. Donatist churches, which claimed to be the true heirs of Cyprian, asserted that they had the only true baptism, since their clergy were unpolluted by apostasy and so required the rebaptism of converts to their communion. By contrast, catholic churches since the Council of Arles in 314 had accepted the position of the Roman church and received those who had been baptized in schism with only a laying on of hands to give the Holy Spirit. However, we have no extant description of Donatist rituals and no reason to presume that theological differences had significant consequences for the architecture or interior design of the church. Furthermore, the power of common tradition, mutual influence, and (probably) shared resources and artisans' workshops would have contributed to the blurring of any distinctions that might have been apparent in the liturgy—in the content of preaching, prayers, or hymnody.

VARIETIES OF BAPTISMAL SPACES

Despite a lack of distinctions between catholic and schismatic architecture, African baptisteries and fonts are often quite different from their counter-parts in Italy or Gaul. They furthermore show a wide variety among themselves, diverging in shape, size, depth, and placement in relationship to the main church. Few freestanding buildings used for baptism can be found in Africa, compared with other Christian regions, although some churches, like those at Carthage (Dermech I), Hippo, Tipasa, and Sufetula, had annexed rooms that were part of a larger cathedral complex. Most African baptisteries were attached to the main church hall, generally either to one side of the apse or just to the right or left of the main entrance at the rear of the nave. These spaces thus open directly into the side aisles of the central nave by means of communicating rooms and doors. In one exceptional case, the baptistery at Bulla Regia, the font is placed in the center of the narthex or entrance space, which would have made it a publicly visible facility, in comparison with other spaces, which could have been more private and hidden from general view (fig. 5.2).

Another exception, the earliest dated baptistery in Sufetula (identified by inscriptional evidence as belonging to a possible Donatist church), seems to have been placed in the converted cella of a former pagan temple (fig. 5.3). When the building was reoriented, the baptistery was thus located off the right aisle. The idea of being baptized in the inner sanctum may have appealed to a community that placed a particularly high value on the purity of the rite. Another converted and reoriented pagan temple, the basilica at

Fig. 5.7. Font from Mustis/Le Krib, date uncertain, probably late fourth, early fifth century. Photo credit: Robin Jensen.

Thuburbo Maius, has its baptistery attached to its narthex (fig. 5.4). The reuse of a pagan temple cella might have been highly symbolic or simply a practical conversion of a small enclosed space.

The small private rooms that accommodated the baptismal pool or font often had an apse at one end (fig. 5.5). Many of the church buildings, however, also provided ancillary chambers that could have housed other parts of the ritual, including the preparation of the catechumens (education, scrutinies, exorcism), preliminary rites (disrobing, renunciation of Satan, profession of faith, or possible prebaptismal anointing), or the rites associated with the giving of the Holy Spirit (chrismation and the laying on of hands). These adjoining rooms often had apses, and separate entrances leading directly into the main church hall. The layout of the baptistery attached to the main basilica at Hippo, the baptistery at Dermech, and the baptistery of Vitalis at Sufetula show this arrangement fairly clearly.

The baptismal pools found within these set-apart spaces are the most interesting aspects of the baptismal architecture of Christian North Africa. Usually set into the floor at the center of the room, they are noted for their wide variety of shapes, some of them unique. They run the gamut from simple squares or circles to octagonal, polylobed, cruciform, and labial-shaped. Although generally it seems that the simpler shapes are earlier—that Vandal-built fonts were quadrilateral, while the later Byzantine fonts tended to be polylobed—proposing any clear evolution of design or shape is hampered by the problems of dating (the lack of examples from the third or early fourth centuries), and a tendency to reuse a traditional shape in a new church building as in Sufetula, where the Byzantine building repeated the earlier fourth-century font design.

Many of the shapes, of course, symbolize one or another of the meanings or aspects of Christian baptism, in particular the death and resurrection of the candidates. A rectangular font might suggest the tomb in which the neophyte underwent a symbolic death to the old life and self. Circular fonts (fig. 5.7) and those recalling the shape of a woman's vulva (color gallery, plate E) all symbolize the neophytes' birth from the fertile womb of the mother church and their status as infants entering a new family. Octagonal shapes refer to the eighth day—the day of Christ's resurrection and the first day of the new creation (fig. 5.8). Cruciform shapes (figs. 5.2 and 5.4) allude to the candidate's participation in the death (and resurrection) of Christ as described by Paul (Rom. 6:3-8). The more complex polylobed shapes (fig. 5.9), which look much like the plunge pools in Roman baths, were often elaborately covered with mosaic designs that refer to the joys of paradise, especially when lavishly decorated with fruit, flowers, paschal candles, trees, fish, and so on.

Fig. 5.8. Font from Carthage (basilica I, Dermech), sixth century. Photo credit: Robin Jensen.

Those fonts that are extant are below floor level (which may explain their survival). All of them have access in and out by steps or descending bench-like structures in their interiors. Two or three steps are most common, but, depending on the depth of the central well, the fonts may have as many as five (cf. fig. 5.2). Some of the fonts are quite small, barely accommodating a single individual, while others may have had space for assisting deacons as well. Water was provided either by means of a cistern nearby or in some cases by a piping system that brought water from a nearby bath facility or well. Fonts were supplied with drains that may have been left open to provide for continuous water flow, that is, "living" water. The depth of the water is unknown, of course, but many of these fonts seem too small or shallow to have accommodated immersion, except, perhaps, of infants. On the other hand, the building of fonts that could have accommodated adult immersion well into the seventh century (for example, the large font at Bir Ftouha) argues against the idea that adult baptism had gone out of use, even at this relatively late date.

Many of the fonts were constructed of marble, while others were merely lined with marble or other fine stone. Some were set into pavements that had complex mosaic decoration, and in certain cases the fonts themselves were covered with decorative mosaic, portions of which have been extensively restored by archaeologists (color gallery, plates E and F). The iconography that we see in these examples has a high level of consistency and, although we no longer have the walls or ceilings of these spaces for comparison, they may well have rivaled the richly decorated fonts in other parts of the Christian world. In addition to geometric patterns, baptisteries and fonts were also beautified with floral motifs (grapevines, acanthus, roses, lilies, and fruit trees), various birds and animals (doves, quails, deer, fish, and dolphins), and liturgical objects or Christian symbols (paschal candles, chalices, Christograms, and the Ark of the Covenant). Deer coming to drink at streams of living water (see Psalm 42) enhanced the pavement of the baptistery discovered at Bir Ftouha outside of Carthage, as in other places in North Africa (color gallery, plate F).[18]

Inscriptions are also found on or near the fonts, sometimes mentioning the donor (as in color gallery, plate E, dedicated to Vitalis and Cardela) or providing an inspirational text. The lavishly decorated font from Bekalta bears the legend "Glory to God in the highest, and in earth peace to all people of good will." This legend surrounds a beautiful pavement and font

Fig. 5.9. Baptismal font from Kelibia, ancient Clypea, Cape Bon, Tunisia (now in the Bardo Museum, Tunis), sixth century. Photo credit: Robin Jensen.

interior covered with acanthus plants, birds, and flowers and displaying a cross at its bottom, adorned with an alpha and omega. The font discovered at Kelibia on Cape Bon combines both text and decoration (fig. 5.9). All around the outside (floor) and the inside (well) of the font are images with a paradisiacal association, including four trees bearing fruit (fig, date, olive, and pear) and references to the baptismal rite itself (paschal candles, a descending dove, and a chalice) as well as a Chi-Rho (Greek letters standing for the name "Christ") with the letters *alpha* and *omega* at the center of the font's well. Around the outside of the font are the words *fides, pax,* and *caritas* ("faith, peace, and love," from 1 Cor. 13:13) as well as an inscription that identifies the donors as Aquinias and Juliana and the persons to whom they dedicated the font as Cyprian and Adelphius, a priest in communion with Cyprian.

BAPTISMAL FONTS AND THE CULT OF THE SAINTS

Many of the fonts themselves had attached columns to support a canopy *(ciborium),* a structure often found over a reliquary or altar in later Roman churches. This arrangement is clear in the font at Hippo, with its still-standing columns (fig. 5.6). Such a structure suggests an implied connection between the rituals of baptism and eucharist and the cult of the saints. Relics had been deposited beneath altars from the beginning of the fourth century, and the extension of the association with the cult of the saints to baptism would have seemed natural. According to tradition, a martyr had received a baptism in blood, and likewise the newly baptized were, at least for a while, saints worthy of victory crowns.[19] Augustine even recounts a miraculous healing performed by a newly baptized woman as she emerged from the women's side of the baptistery and made the sign of the cross upon another woman suffering from breast cancer (*The City of God* 22.8). This connection is strengthened by the architectural similarities between *martyria* (or mausolea) and baptisteries in almost all places in the Christian world. In Sufetula, when a new basilica and baptistery were built adjacent to the fourth-century buildings, the earlier font was probably transformed into a martyrial chapel, because in it were buried the remains of Bishop Jucundus, who was likely killed during the Vandal invasion. At some point, possibly in the early sixth century, at the time when the new basilica was built, relics were placed inside a column within the font itself, and an altar was installed above (fig. 5.5).[20]

Augustine's account of a mother running with her dead child to the shrine of a saint, hoping for his miraculous resurrection and subsequent baptism, suggests the benefits of close proximity between shrine and font (*Serm.* 324, 325). Although examples of burials in baptisteries are known, one would not expect to find baptisteries in *martyria*.[21] Such shrines, after all, were chapels rather than churches, and so not a location for a ritual over which a bishop, or at least a priest, ought to preside in optimal circumstances. Nevertheless, several very large and important North African pilgrimage churches, probably built first as martyrs' shrines and often set into or surrounded by a cemetery, were also provided with baptismal chambers and fonts. For example, the large fifth- or sixth-century Christian complex at Bir Ftouha on the outskirts of Carthage seems to have encompassed a martyrs' shrine, basilica hall, and baptistery annex.[22] Other North African examples of this connection between saints' shrines and baptisteries include the large Christian complexes at Damous el Karita just outside the walls of Carthage; Skhira, south of Sfax; and Djemila in modern-day Algeria.[23] Although any of these churches may have been parish churches at one time or another (explaining their provision of a baptistery), their existence suggests the popularity of baptism *ad sanctos*. The patronage of a saint at baptism clearly added to the drama and power of the rite. A fourth-century Donatist bishop Macrobius elaborated on this point in a sermon preached on the passion of Saints Donatus and Advocatus, in which he directly addresses the catechumens awaiting their baptism and, making the connections between baptism and saints' cult explicit, describes the two martyrs as "holding their arms out to you from heaven, waiting for the time they will run to meet you." Macrobius then urges the candidates to come forward to the font: "Come on, do it, sisters and brothers. Hurry, the sooner the better, so that we may rejoice in the same way over you."[24]

CONCLUSIONS

The ritual of baptism follows no single pattern, since it only exists in specific instances of practice, enacted in particular times and spaces and in relation to actual physical structures. From the late second through the sixth centuries, the ritual forms, theological understandings, and architectural spaces of baptism clearly evolved according to changing external circumstances, internal polemics, pastoral concerns, foreign invasions (and reconquest), and simply a natural and constant impulse to respond to the needs of individuals and communities without seeming to abandon essential aspects of religious identity and personal sanctity. Those thousands of African Christians, of whatever sect, who experienced baptism assuredly believed that they were participating in ritual that was fundamentally unchanged from apostolic times, and in some sense they were right. However, a ritual lives only so long as it can adapt to the exigencies of context. Just as the participants are transformed, reborn, or converted by the ritual, so too the ritual is transformed and renewed by succeeding generations who will claim its power and efficacy, perhaps without consciously recognizing that the flexibility to respond and change in the face of challenges that emerge in the course of history is ultimately essential. A community's long-term survival requires that it continually redefine its own identity as it resists, absorbs, or is rejected by others who have different perceptions of how and where the boundaries must be drawn. Baptism, perhaps more than any other rite, reveals these evolutionary changes. Even as the ritual emphasizes the distinctness of Christian identity, it also highlights the necessary negotiation and redefinition of identity—marks the shifting and porous character of boundaries—through the performance of a passage *across* boundaries. As communal lines are redrawn to incorporate new members into the body of the church, the church itself is continuously transformed.

FOR FURTHER READING

Bedard, W. M. *The Symbolism of the Baptismal Font in Early Christian Thought.* Washington, D.C.: Catholic University of America Press, 1951.

Davies, J. G. *The Architectural Setting of Baptism.* London: Barrie and Rockliff, 1962.

Finn, Thomas M. *Early Christian Baptism and the Catechumenate: Italy, North Africa, and Egypt.* Collegeville, Minn.: Liturgical, 1992.

———. *From Death to Rebirth: Ritual and Conversion in Antiquity.* Mahwah, N.J.: Paulist, 1997.

Johnson, Maxwell E. *The Rites of Christian Initiation: Their Evolution and Interpretation.* Collegeville, Minn.: Liturgical, 1999.

Kavanagh, Aidan. *The Shape of Baptism: The Rite of Christian Initiation.* Collegeville, Minn.: Liturgical, 1991.

FOOD, RITUAL, AND POWER

ANDREW MCGOWAN

CHAPTER SIX

> A woman . . . went up to the priest after Mass and said . . . "Father, I went
> to communion without going to confession first." "How come, my
> daughter?" asked the priest. "Father," she replied, "I arrived rather late,
> after you had begun the offertory. For three days I have had only water
> and nothing to eat. . . . When I saw you handing out the hosts, those little
> pieces of white bread, I went to communion just out of hunger for that
> little bit of bread."[1]

It takes some effort to perceive the eucharist of later Christian tradition
as food, let alone as a meal. Contemporary Westerners may certainly
find it hard to imagine that rudimentary meals centered on bread could
ever have been of any interest or importance beyond some supposed spiritual or sacramental benefit. Yet Christian liturgical tradition has eating
and drinking at its origin, not merely as incidental actions in religious ritual, but as actual food. The power of the story from contemporary Latin
America told above lies in the fact that, in most societies, the pursuit of
staple food such as bread has been a central part of daily living, with hunger
a constant threat. Establishing the meaning of any meal for most of its
participants involves considering food and its value in the most prosaic of
terms.

The physical necessity of food does not, however, exhaust the significance of meals. Food itself is not merely fodder, and meals are complex rituals that involve many elements beyond food—participants, places, times,
words, and rituals—as means of expressing, forming, and transforming
religious, social, and other commitments, as well as of meeting physical
necessity. All these seemingly prosaic elements have the capacity to convey
and construct meaning.[2]

Meals were at the heart of ancient Greco-Roman household life. They
not only served as occasions for physical sustenance, but were the venue

for basic values to be expressed, confirmed, or critiqued, and the power and status of different diners (or nondiners) displayed or developed. Meals were also central to groups or associations formed for purposes we might describe as religious, political, vocational, and social. Such dining clubs, often referred to as *collegia*,[3] might be the most recognizable social formation through which we may understand the life of the first Christian communities and the centrality of meals within them.[4]

Meals of particular festivity and formality—banquets, we might say—had a prominence in the culture somewhat disproportionate to their literal place in the feeding process. Relatively few people dined often with the niceties depicted on painted vases and in philosophical dialogues, or with the types and quantities of food portrayed in such artistic or literary works. Yet the models of procedure and behavior that center on these prominent banquets—"meal ideology," as it has been called—had an influence that extended even to those who could participate in them only rarely.[5] If few banqueted often, many dined in some semblance of formality and festivity at least sometimes.

Ancient images and debates about issues like types of food, portions, and placement of diners are thus potentially relevant to the variety of ways in which Christians participated in the ancient meal tradition, even in less exalted settings. These elements will all be given at least some attention in this chapter, since diversity must be taken into account if we are to re-envision ancient eucharistic meals from the eaters' perspectives. As in wider banqueting practice, the specifics of food and ritual and other aspects of the Christian meal tradition varied across time and space. And the potential value of belonging to Christian communities will have included the enhanced dietary and social opportunities involved in access to an important practice. Even the same meal could be experienced quite differently. The meals of the first Christians did often bring together women and men of different social class and ethnicity, transcending expected boundaries and offering experiences to benefit and empower participants beyond their normal expectations.[6] Yet many aspects of eating, from the food available to the company kept and roles taken, reflected or created distinctions among eaters, as well as between those present and those absent or excluded. The eucharistic gatherings of the early Christians could thus reinforce or reconfigure power relations, existing or new.

So, too, the theologies that informed and arose from the meal were varied. Christian banquets were not just a universal imitation of one particular model such as the Last Supper. Various groups seem to have had different explicit understandings and purposes in mind and to have used eating and drinking together in a variety of ritual forms. Meals were a way of addressing bodily needs and of expressing and constructing community, but also of remembering Jesus in various ways, experiencing the Holy Spirit, sharing traditional and inspired forms of wisdom, and more besides.

Although there were different Christian meals, supposed essential distinctions based on later nomenclature—opposing eucharist to *agape* ("love feast"), for instance—do little to help interpret these varied gatherings. Different terms were certainly used, and various meanings were attached to the events themselves and to the food elements, but a supposed duality between a more sacred token meal (eucharist) and a more everyday substantial community meal *(agape)* does not really help make sense of the evidence for Christian eating in the first two hundred years.[7]

Of course, the diverse meals of the first few centuries of Christian history were eventually to give rise to the event—less obviously a meal in the usual sense—that is known as eucharist in subsequent tradition. That process of attenuation or abbreviation of the meal into a food ritual— still retaining certain trappings of ancient banqueting practice—was related to the emergence of the church as an imperial religion. Yet processes of change were well under way before Emperor Constantine's conversion and the consequent appearance of the eucharistic meal in a form fully suited for civic ritual. The development was not one of transition from real meal to mere ritual or from open community to structured liturgy; from the earliest point, the Christian meal gatherings were about both ritual and feeding, and they involved the subtleties of symbol as well as the clear trappings of power. Even in its eventual state as a token food ritual, characteristics of a meal were and are still sometimes visible at the eucharist.

FOOD AND FOODS

Bread and Wine

Bread and wine were the staple foods of the ancient world, and the most obvious thing about finding and eating them in a communal context would have been how ordinary they were.[8] Stories of Jesus sharing food and drink of this kind, whether in the wilderness or in an upper room, certainly influenced the sacralization and consumption of bread and wine in early Christian settings, but would not have been necessary to explain their use.

The best-known rationale for a Christian meal of bread and wine is the story of Jesus' Last Supper, presented in three of the canonical Gospels and the writings of the apostle Paul. Jesus, taking bread and cup, presents them to his companions as his own body and blood (1 Cor. 11:23-25). These startling word-images, with sacrificial connotations as well as new overtones of cannibalism that still puzzle scholars, seemed to mean that the simplest food elements could bear within themselves a power otherwise associated with the more expensive and exclusive food offerings of animal sacrifice.[9] Thus the actual food content of the best-known Christian meal tradition may not have been especially appealing, except to those who were literally hungry; yet the capacity of the simplest meal to become a vehicle for power and forms of divine presence otherwise associated with civic ritual and elite dining is significant.

Not by Bread Alone

Bread and wine were not, however, the only foods that might have appeared at all Christian banquets. Typical meals in Greco-Roman households might have centered on bread and been accompanied by wine, but included smaller amounts of other valued and flavorful foods such as cheese, olives, meat, or fish. So too some eucharistic meals seem to have involved a more expansive menu.

In Christian communities where bread and wine were the core of the meal, the complexity or variety of the foods may well have depended on the importance of the occasion, as in many other cultures. In the second and third centuries, milk and honey might be added when baptisms were held in conjunction with the meal. These foods carried with them various symbolic associations of plenty and peace, but they were prized and somewhat luxurious items regardless.[10] Even in the fourth century, when the eucharistic meal had become largely token or symbolic in scale, one liturgical document not only prescribes milk and honey in addition to bread, wine, and water for a baptismal eucharist but also gives blessings for cheese and olives at the ordination of a bishop, another dietary expression of festivity (*Ap. Trad.* 6, 21.27–28).[11]

Ironic as it may seem, much of the early evidence for Christian meals involving foods other than bread and wine actually comes from strict ascetic traditions and communities, who might otherwise have been assumed to eat fewer foods, and less of them. Novelistic literature from the ancient Christian milieu makes these concerns and choices especially prominent. The Pseudo-Clementine *Homilies,* from the second or early third century, reject meat eating and wine drinking but depict a sacred meal of bread and salt for the newly initiated recipient of sacred books (*Letter of Peter to James* 4:3; *Letter of Clement to James* 9:1-2). The apocryphal *Acts of Paul and Thecla* present simple meals of, for example, bread, vegetables, and water (not wine) as the substance of the communal meal known as an *agape* (25). Another early Christian novel, the *Acts of Thomas,* depicts its apostolic hero presiding at a sacred meal with surprising ingredients: he took "bread, oil, vegetables and salt, blessed them and gave them to them"

(29). Both these sets of *Acts* also oppose the use of meat and wine altogether. Although these cases are idealized within fictional narratives, they probably reflect real practices. Their extra elements actually reflect a common concern to avoid certain other foods, that is, meat and wine, both connected with pagan meal and sacrificial custom and entirely avoided in these documents and communities.

There are more direct witnesses to this type of avoidance and its tendency to produce meals with other elements: for instance, a group of Christians in Asia Minor connected with the charismatic New Prophecy movement (also known as Montanism) were nicknamed the *Artotyritai* ("bread-and-cheesers") because of the form their eucharistic meal took (Epiphanius, *Panarion* 49.1); again wine was absent, but cheese or perhaps coagulated milk was used, as in the more festive cases already noted. Here the ascetic impulse that rejected impure or idolatrous foods seems to have led to a different pattern of relating eucharistic to everyday meals. In this understanding, all food had to be pure or even sacred, and the distinction between specific community meals with ritual elements and other forms of eating was relativized.

Meat and Fish

Fish and meat raise quite different questions. In the Greco-Roman world meat was generally expensive and desirable, and a prominent feature at banquets in wealthier circles as well as on festive civic or domestic occasions. Central in the sacrificial rituals of Judaism and in the many other temples surrounding the newly emergent Christian movement, eating meat was often a form of sociability with the god to whom it had been offered. As Paul's First Letter to the Corinthians indicates, the production and distribution of meat could thus be fraught with the connotations of pagan religion, since even meat in the market had often been sacrificed in the temples. Paul's own approach was a "don't ask, don't tell" policy, where only meat explicitly known to have been offered to a deity was to be refused.

There is no particular evidence for meat eating at specifically Christian meals, although an argument from silence cannot be definitive. The increasing sense in some communities of Jesus' body and blood in or as other foods at eucharistic meals may have made the actual use of meat, a different sacrificial element, awkward. At least two

> Eat whatever is sold in the meat market without raising any question on the ground of conscience, for "the earth and its fullness are the Lord's." If an unbeliever invites you to a meal and you are disposed to go, eat whatever is set before you without raising any question on the ground of conscience. But if someone says to you, "This has been offered in sacrifice," then do not eat it, out of consideration for the one who informed you, and for the sake of conscience—I mean the other's conscience, not your own.
>
> —1 Cor. 10:25-29

specific attitudes to meat eating in addition to Paul's pragmatism emerged early and were also influential among Christians. As we have already seen, some took a more radical stance and refused all meat eating as well as wine drinking in whatever setting, both elements seen as tainted with idolatry because of their prominence in sacrifice. At the other extreme, some diners relied on a superior understanding whereby faith or knowledge *(gnosis)* allowed them to partake of any food, regardless of origin (1 Cor. 8:1-7). If the pagan gods were not real, what harm was there in eating their offerings? This sort of attempt to reinterpret or ignore qualms about idolatry on the basis of theological sophistication may have opened the social as well as dietary benefits of relatively prestigious banquets to high-status converts for whom they were an important part of life.[12]

The significance of these alternative approaches was sharpened as persecution of Christians grew, and sacrifice—including the eating of meat offerings—became a key element in testing faith and apostasy. Those Christians for whom *gnosis* allowed greater freedom found that their position allowed not just social advantage but literal survival, since they could eat sacrificial meat with impunity, not merely when it was desired, but when demanded. A century or more after Paul's encounter with this suggestion, it was still powerful enough to influence many. A Jewish critic could then be imagined as pointing out that there were many "Christians [who] eat meats offered to idols, and declare that they are by no means injured in consequence" (Justin Martyr, *Dialogue with Trypho* 35.1). A bishop in late second-century Gaul, Irenaeus of Lyons, attributes meat eating and a range of other socially accommodating behaviors specifically to such so-called gnostic Christians (*Her.* 1.6.3, 1.24.5, 1.26.3).

On the other hand, the more ascetic alternative of refusing meat altogether likewise became rather more than a lifestyle matter or expression of dietary dissent when sacrifice became a matter of compulsion rather than of choice. Vegetarian Christians, who included groups labeled Montanists, Marcionites, and Encratites, were often prominent among martyrs, expecting a heavenly banquet as reward for their earthly abstemiousness.[13]

Despite intriguing literary references in the Gospels (for example, John 21:13) and early Christian artistic depictions (fig. 6.1), there is no clear evidence for Christian use of fish as a specifically sacral food. Fish probably was a more acceptable luxury food for Christians than meat. This may again be related to sacrifice and idolatry; although there are various symbolic as well as aesthetic reasons fish might have been prized, the fact that it was not regularly sacrificed was probably crucial to its use, real or artistic. Intriguingly, what may be the oldest surviving depiction of the Last Supper, from the sixth-century decoration of S. Apollinare Nuovo in Ravenna, depicts Jesus reclining with the twelve at the proper *sigma*-shaped

Fig. 6.1. This third-century fresco depicts a fish and a basket of bread that bears the image of a glass of wine, thereby linking meal traditions involving bread and wine with the story of the miracle of the loaves and fishes. Catacomb of S. Callisto, Rome, Italy. Photo credit: Scala / Art Resource, NY.

table, but with two fish rather than the expected paschal lamb before the diners (fig. 6.2). Conflation of the scene with another Gospel story, a miraculous feeding (Mark 6:30-44), avoids the potential difficulty of depicting both the animal and the human victims in one setting.

My Flesh Is Real Food

Bread was the element most often emphasized in Christian meal traditions. Although it was of course used in Jewish temple offerings (for example, Exod. 25:30) and in the ritual meals of Passover, the symbolic usefulness of bread for the early Christians may have been precisely its ordinariness. The ubiquity of bread gave it a capacity to carry a whole variety of associations, rather than just one.

If bread was as common and as necessary in the ancient Mediterranean as such staples are in subsistence-level societies, then the economic value of participating in meals based on bread may have been greater than often assumed, at least for the poorest. Yet one of the most distinctive elements of many Christian meals was the tendency for bread to be treated as central, honored, and sacralized. Those who ate this sacred bread received implied benefits like those otherwise accessible only to meat eaters; thus a characteristic of some eucharistic gatherings was a sort of dietary expression of social reversal.

The most distinctive and powerful understandings of the sacralization of bread invoke the body or flesh of Jesus, which was often understood to be literally present in or as the food (see Ignatius, *Smyrneans* 7.1). This imagery drew upon the words of Jesus in the Last Supper stories and John's Gospel interpretation of the miraculous feeding of five thousand, where Jesus insists on his followers eating his flesh and drinking his blood (John 6:53-56).[14] Paul's Corinthian correspondence also made a number of

Fig. 6.2. Jesus and his disciples dine on fish at the Last Supper. S. Apollinare Nuovo, Ravenna, Italy. Photo credit: Erich Lessing / Art Resource, NY.

comparisons between the meal of the Christians and the carnivorous banquets of their neighbors and associates. Although it is hard to know exactly what Paul himself understood the bread of the meal to be or become, eating the bread and drinking the cup amounted to a participation in the body and blood of Christ (1 Cor. 10:16), and he understood these to be objectively powerful and potentially beneficial or dangerous (1 Cor. 11:30). Ignatius, a Christian leader in Antioch just after the end of the first century, reflects a similar seriousness about the significance of the eucharistic food. He calls on his correspondents in Ephesus to go on "breaking one bread, which is the medicine of immortality, the antidote preventing us from dying, so that we might live for ever in Jesus Christ" (Ignatius, *Ephesians* 20).

These letters also imply that alternative views and practices existed. Paul complains that some eat and drink "not discerning the body," which seems to be a concern both about behavior at the meal and about the under-standing of the meal elements (1 Cor. 11:26-30). Ignatius also bemoans the fact that some do not participate in the preferred form of meal precisely because of difficulty with the belief that the elements are the body and blood of Jesus, the objection apparently tied to an understanding of him as a spiritual rather than a material being (*Smyrneans* 7).

Yet these Christians who were less comfort-able with a literal consumption of eucharistic foods as the remnants of Jesus' sacrificial immo-lation do seem to have had their own versions of a common meal. The slightly later apocryphal *Acts of John* give some idea of the understanding and practice of communities who approached the meal, and Jesus himself, differently (see side-bar). That narrative of deeds attributed to the apostle John reflects the ascetic sort of meal prac-tice already discussed, now with an accompany-ing eucharistic theology replete with symbolism, but not with the specific and difficult imagery of Jesus' body and blood. This different way of sacralizing food is based as much on a different sense of community as on a particular Christol-ogy; rather than singling out bread and wine alone among the elements of a sacred meal, these practices attribute a generally sacred character to all acceptable food and to its eaters. The theo-logical emphasis comes not on the distinction between the bread and wine of the eucharistic meal and normal food, but on that between the pure food of the community and the tainted food of idolaters outside.

Where the more focused understanding on the eucharistic foods as Jesus' body and blood held sway, the fearful and fascinating properties of bread-become-flesh could overshadow the importance of the meal setting itself. Although Ignatius had urged common meals with the presence of the local leader or bishop in Asia Minor, not long afterward Roman Christians were carrying fragments of the eucharistic bread away from the community meal to the sick and others unable to attend the banquet (Justin Martyr, 1 *Apol.* 67). By 200 CE, fragments of the blessed bread were being distributed quite independently of the banquet in North Africa, and carried home for later

And when he had said this John prayed, and taking bread brought it into the sepulcher to break and said:

We glorify your name that converts us from error and pitiless deceit;

We glorify you who have shown before our eyes what we have seen;

We testify to your goodness, in various ways appearing;

We praise your gracious name, O Lord, [which] has convicted those that are con-victed by you;

We thank you, Lord Jesus Christ, that we confide in [...], which is unchanging;

We thank you who have separated the nature that is being saved from that which is per-ishing;

We thank you that you have given us this unwavering [faith] that you alone are [God] both now and for ever;

We your servants, that are assembled and gathered with [good] cause, give thanks to you, O holy one.

And when he had made this prayer and glorified [God] he gave to all the brethren the Lord's Eucharist, and went out of the sepul-cher.

—*Acts of John* 85–86[15]

consumption, especially for breaking fasts (Tertullian, *On Prayer* 19.1–4). Around 250 the Carthaginian bishop Cyprian depicts devotees wearing lockets with the eucharistic bread around their necks as talismans, and these receptacles bursting into flames or their contents turning to ashes in the hands of the unworthy (*Laps.* 25–26). These practices were signs of a shift that would fundamentally change the nature and place of the banquet.

FROM FOOD TO MEAL

Ancient sensibilities could distinguish between mere eating—meeting the needs of hunger—and the more powerful and socially enriching process that makes a meal. Then, as more recently, factors including the identity of the diners, their places at table, the order of proceedings, and the forms of discourse or entertainment would all have to be taken into consideration, along with the food itself, to construct a meal.

Order at the Meal

The typical banquet consisted first of a meal where diners reclined at a U-shaped *(sigma)* table, thus facing one another to some extent (fig. 6.3). After various food courses, tables were removed, and the second part, the *symposium* or drinking party, ensued. During this time conversation and entertainment were expected, as a number of bowls of wine were mixed, with prayers and libations, for the company. The story of Jesus' Last Supper as given in most of the New Testament accounts fits this expected order of meal followed by drinking party. A description of a Christian meal gathering or *agape* from North Africa around 200 CE reflects an adaptation of this structure and process to reflect the specific interests and concerns of one community (see sidebar).

Other versions of the Christian meal tradition were less immediately comparable to the typical Greco-Roman banquet of a meal followed by drinking. Sometimes ritual cups were blessed and drunk at the outset of the eucharistic meal, and not just at the end. This pattern appears in

> Our feast explains itself by its name. The Greeks call it *agape*, i.e., affection. Whatever it costs, our outlay in the name of piety is gain, since with the good things of the feast we benefit the needy.... If the object of our feast is good, consider its further regulations in the light of that. As it is an act of religious service, it permits no vileness or immodesty. The participants, before reclining, taste first of prayer to God. As much is eaten as satisfies the cravings of hunger; as much is drunk as befits the chaste. They say it is enough, as those who remember that even during the night they have to worship God; they talk as those who know that the Lord is one of their auditors. After washing of hands, and the bringing in of lights, each is asked to stand forth and sing, as he can, a hymn to God, either one from the holy Scriptures or one of his own composing—a proof of the measure of our drinking. As the feast commenced with prayer, so with prayer it is closed.
>
> —Tertullian, *Apol.* 39

Fig. 6.3. A Christian funeral banquet is boisterously under way, as represented on this third-century Christian sarcophagus. Museo Nazionale Romano (Terme di Diocleziano), Rome, Italy. Photo credit: Scala / Art Resource, NY.

the earliest known outline of prayers for a Christian meal ritual (called "*Eucharistia*" or "thanksgiving"), presented in the *Didache* or *Teaching of the Twelve Apostles,* perhaps from Syria in the late first century. The same order of cup and bread is also found in the *Mishnah* as well as in meals prescribed in the Dead Sea Scrolls, suggesting this pattern may have been a distinctly Jewish tradition.[16] These cases should still be understood as part of the wider banqueting culture of the Greco-Roman world, since it is clear that Jewish meal traditions, including the Passover seder itself, were influenced by the rest of the banqueting genre, even if there were distinctive formal elements (in addition to well-known Jewish dietary rules). In context, this reversed order of proceedings may have reflected the same concern for moderation and proper behavior evident in Tertullian's North African *agape* account; taking the cup at the beginning seems to have avoided the dubious *symposium* and the connotations of raucous behavior connected with it.

The *Didache* also has no knowledge of, or no interest in, either the Last Supper itself or Jesus' death as the basis for its procedure of thanksgiving. This has led some to suggest that the *Didache* meal has a different character than what Paul refers to as the Lord's Supper. Up to a point this may be true, but it is misleading to suggest that there were two specific forms of meal (least of all eucharist and *agape*) with essentially different meanings, foods, and procedures and that the diversity of early Christian evidence should be allocated to one category or the other. Rather, these different terms, models, and understandings constituted a variety of ways in which the Jesus tradition and other elements of early Christian theology

And concerning the Eucharist, hold Eucharist thus: First concerning the Cup, "We give thanks to you, our Father, for the Holy Vine of David your child, which you made known to us through Jesus your child; to you be glory for ever." And concerning the broken Bread: "We give you thanks, our Father, for the life and knowledge which you made known to us through Jesus your child. To you be glory for ever. As this broken bread was scattered upon the mountains, but was brought together and became one, so let your Church be gathered together from the ends of the earth into your Kingdom, for yours is the glory and the power through Jesus Christ for ever." But let none eat or drink of your Eucharist except those who have been baptized in the Lord's Name. For concerning this also did the Lord say, "Give not that which is holy to the dogs."

—Didache 9[17]

and belief interacted with ancient meal customs, giving rise to a variety of forms and understandings of the banquet.

By the later third or early fourth century, this local diversity would yield to processes of influence and standardization. The outcome was not single or simple, but rather a normative tokenized eucharist with a variety of continuing meal and food practices in its orbit. The preeminent offering remained in some relation not only to a somewhat secularized banquet known as *agape* but to a variety of other rituals connected with consumption of the eucharistic food, meals celebrated in tombs and in honor of saints, and more. At earlier points, however, both eucharist and *agape* had been terms by which particular communities referred to their whole meal tradition, rather than to specific and clearly defined alternative procedures.

Prayers and Discourse

Appropriate talk could be one of the most important elements of a meal, as the literary tradition about banquets reveals. This is not to say that the philosophical dialogues of Plato represent real expectations for discourse at most ancient banquets. Yet for Christians as for others, meal gatherings may often have been the settings at which teaching, argument, or other forms of formal and serious conversation and debate took place. Many of the written works that have survived from the early centuries of the Christian movement may actually have been formed or used in such traditional *symposia,* whether or not they make any reference to it. For instance, Paul in writing to the Corinthians refers to various forms of utterance at the meal gathering (1 Cor. 12:8-10), and Tertullian's *Apology* depicts individual diners as singing when called upon at their pleasant Carthaginian evening, but their own works may also have been read in these settings.

The prayers and blessings used in the actual meal ritual have been the major focus of much study of the eucharistic tradition and can receive less treatment here accordingly.[18] At the outset it can probably be assumed that they were relatively brief utterances—the meal prayers of the *Didache* are the earliest example and are somewhat comparable to contemporary Jewish blessings (for example, *Mishnah* Berakoth). The *Acts of John* provide quite different forms of prayer, connected only by the sense of thanksgiving with those of the *Didache*, but whose list of epithets for Christ still only amounts to a short discourse.

Neither of these makes any reference to the actual story of Jesus' Last Supper, later regarded as the core of prayer appropriate to the eucharistic meal, but at this point somewhat marginal to the actual performance of its ritual. In some cases, that story may have functioned as a rationale for the meal—told and retold, perhaps, in the course of the Christianized *symposium*, but not originally used as a blessing for food. In others, that story was probably simply unknown or irrelevant, with other stories or images of Jesus serving to inform and ground the proceedings.

The development already traced, from substantial meal gathering to an assembly focused on the distribution of token amounts of bread and wine, had its impact on the words spoken also. The link with Jesus' death so central in later, and particularly Western, understandings of the eucharist was to be accentuated in the same developments that brought the eucharistic elements to their eventual place on altars in basilicas rather than at domestic tables.[19] And as the reception of the sacral food was separated from banquets and became a more self-contained process undertaken not at meals but at morning liturgical assemblies, the expectation of extended discourse shifted somewhat. While there were still elements of instruction, the communal *symposium* was no longer part of the process. Sermons and catecheses, on the other hand, continued or expanded, as did the actual prayers and blessings, almost in inverse proportion to the size and scope of the meal itself. As less was eaten, more and more seems to have been said over the sacral foods.

Equality, Inclusion, Diversity

The Greco-Roman meal tradition was a vehicle for competing understandings of its own character and purpose. That is to say, banquets were the place where proper meal conduct was debated—at least in the literary tradition. This was no less the case in Christian circles than otherwise. Luke's Gospel, for instance, depicts teaching by Jesus concerning meal behavior taking place at actual meals (Luke 11, 14). The communities in which this and other Gospels were formed had to confront these same basic questions such as appropriate washing, foods, and seating order when they ate together.

The question of who might even properly be present at Christian meals is an important and difficult one. Although New Testament stories about Jesus at table reflect an early tradition of open commensality, Christians retold these in a somewhat different context, where community formation and boundary maintenance had typically become important. Diners did sometimes move between different groups and their meals, and people who were not identifiably or clearly members of the Christian community may perhaps have taken part in eucharistic meals at times. Generally, however, the Christian meal seems to have drawn and created a distinctive group of participants, usually defined further in terms of baptismal initiation (*Did.* 9.5). As elsewhere, inclusion in the group that celebrated regular meals meant participation in a specific network of support and friendship, at times the creation of a sort of constructed familial structure. The Christian meal was certainly perceived as an exclusive event and often viewed by outsiders with corresponding suspicion and concern.

These meals may nonetheless be described as inclusive, in the sense that those who did dine together were somewhat diverse in terms of class or status, gender, and ethnic or religious background. Although the range of such participants may have signaled transcendence of such distinctions, the proceedings may have reinforced or reflected some new and some existing differences. Diners sometimes found their status outside the meal reflected in their treatment at it, and, in addition, the new social formation of the church created its own specific structures related to the conduct of the meal.

> Now in the following instructions I do not commend you, because when you come together it is not for the better but for the worse. For, to begin with, when you come together as a church, I hear that there are divisions among you; and to some extent I believe it. Indeed, there have to be factions among you, for only so will it become clear who among you are genuine. When you come together, it is not really to eat the Lord's supper. For when the time comes to eat, each of you goes ahead with your own supper, and one goes hungry and another becomes drunk. What! Do you not have homes to eat and drink in? Or do you show contempt for the church of God and humiliate those who have nothing? What should I say to you? Should I commend you? In this matter I do not commend you!
>
> —1 Cor. 11:17-22

The question of equality and hierarchy at table was a vexed one in antiquity. Gender was not always marked or treated in the same way, with local and cultural variations determining the participation of women as diners as well as in the expected roles of food preparation and service.[20] This was, of course, a highly stratified society otherwise, and serious critics of that reality were relatively few. Meals were often an expression of that class structure in a variety of ways: at a given banquet, the seating and even the foods given to different guests might be an unapologetic depiction of wider social realities.[21] Yet there was also a different and prominent tradition that diners were equals and that sharing meals created forms of sociability in some degree of tension with the wider structures and understandings of hierarchy.

Again, Paul's correspondence with the Corinthian Christians reflects these debates. For some of those more elite diners, separate meals in a common venue was already condescension enough toward their lower-status colleagues, and those of lower status need not have expected anything different. Paul, however, argues strongly that the sharing of self shown by Jesus at his Last Supper demanded a more equitable approach. The Letter of James also reflects a concern that the order of seating at the meal not reflect class distinctions (James 2:1-7), but the necessity of making the point shows that this was not always clearly accepted.

Scrutiny of Paul's own letters also suggests caution about assuming just what sort of equality was really intended. Just as his own rhetoric of "weakness" serves to establish his authority, Paul seems to have intended the poor at Corinth to experience acceptance and inclusion within the church, but not necessarily any transformation of their relationships with wealthier Christians outside the meal gathering (1 Cor. 7:24). This approach fits with other ancient constructions of equality, where friendship could actually serve to bind diners into the networks of patronage that dominated social relations.

Presiding and Patronage

The physical setting and the roles exercised by individuals at the meal played an important part in the creation of patronage, the fundamental structure of obligation and dependence in ancient Roman society. The most natural patron at a domestic meal was the householder who invited others to dine, but associations also had their own office-bearers who might exercise authority in matters such as seating, recite prayers and blessings, and by implication benefit from the honor attributed to the host's role. The ministerial offices of the early Christian communities were inevitably linked with such ideas of leadership and patronage at banquets. These roles included the ceremonial; Gospel accounts attribute such actions and words to Jesus in certain cases (see, for example, Mark 6:41), and apostles likewise preside in the accounts of canonical and apocryphal *Acts*. The *Didache* specifies that prophets are to use whatever form of words they are inspired to utter when they pray over cup and bread, implying that set prayers are for the bishop (10.7); in other words, either of these persons might have led the meal.

A tension between the roles of actual householders and church office-bearers could emerge. Ignatius of Antioch, writing early in the second century, insisted that the presence of the bishop was necessary for the *agape* to take place (*Smyrneans* 8). Others clearly thought differently and either persisted in a different form of household leadership or even had a flexibility of leadership roles akin to rotation (see Tertullian, *Prescrip.* 41).

Women may have taken leadership roles at eucharistic meals; as householders they could serve as patrons or hosts and also sometimes as appointed clerics, although these cases were often resisted in emergent catholic structures. In second-century Asia Minor the new Prophecy movement later known as Montanism certainly included women who were leaders and eucharistic hosts. Irenaeus, in Gaul at the same time, gives a rather pejorative description of the eucharistic blessings associated with one community (perhaps comparable with that behind the *Acts of John*). The leadership of this group seems to have included not only a prominent male leader, Marcus, but a number of women (see sidebar).

Irenaeus undercuts his own picture of that "Marcosian" church as just a group of gullible women bewitched by a mountebank when he also indicates that they practiced a sort of liturgical lottery to allocate roles in the expected discourse following the meal. Tertullian, writing just a little later, speaks of another Valentinian group who also had a sort of rotational system for the meal presiders, with the full participation of women (*Prescrip.* 41). Yet the assumption that women's leadership and Gnosticism or other heresies were always and everywhere connected is undermined by evidence that ancient Christian women in the catholic part of the church did sometimes hold offices relevant to the meal celebration, such as deacon, presbyter, and perhaps also bishop.[22]

Third- and fourth-century evidence also reflects a shift away from evening banquets as the primary focus of ritual eating and drinking toward gatherings focused more narrowly on the distribution of sacramental food elements by the bishops. By this time Christian groups were often meeting in adapted or purpose-built spaces rather than private homes, and the changes of space and of meal procedure reflect not just the growth of the church but also the consolidation of the role of clerics as the exclusive hosts and patrons in terms of the sacred food of the eucharist.[23]

By the fourth century, substantial meals in households and in other small gathered settings were also distinguished clearly from the eucharistic gatherings of whole Christian communities. Various subgroups of what was now a much larger church might still be invited for specific suppers by private hosts, and these might include some specific rituals and prayers, indicating a religious purpose (fig. 6.4). These domestic gatherings of selected Christian

Pretending to eucharistize cups prepared with mixed wine, and extending greatly the word of invocation, he contrives to give them a purple and red color, so that Grace, who is one of those that are superior to all things, should be thought to drop her own blood into his cup through means of his invocation, so that those who are present should be led to rejoice to taste of that cup, in order that by doing so, Grace, who is set forth by this magician, may also flow into them. Again, handing mixed cups to women, he tells them to eucharistize these in his presence. When this has been done, he himself produces another cup of much larger size than that which the deluded woman has eucharistized, and pouring from the smaller one eucharistized by the woman into the one brought forward by himself, he at the same time pronounces these words: "May she who is before all things, Grace who transcends all knowledge and speech, fill your inner human, and multiply in you her own knowledge, sowing the grain of mustard seed in good soil." Having uttered such words, and thus goading on the wretched woman, he then appears a wonder-worker when the large cup is seen to have been filled out of the small one, so as even to overflow from out of it. By accomplishing several other similar things, he has completely deceived many, and drawn them away after him.

—Irenaeus, *Against the Heresies* 1.13.2
(adapted from *ANF*)

Fig. 6.4. What kind of meal is depicted on this third-century Christian fresco? Given the variety of existing practices as well as the diversity of possible meanings attributed to eating and drinking, it is not always easy to categorize Christian meals. Catacomb of S. Callisto, Rome, Italy. Photo credit: Scala / Art Resource, NY.

invitees often carried with them the term *agape* that had previously been applied to eucharistic banquets of the wider Christian community. The meal gatherings of the emergent monastic movement were another selective—and often very ascetic—form of banquet that continued alongside the identifiable eucharistic celebration. Interestingly, the dietary concerns of these ascetic specialists continued the exclusion of meat and wine that had earlier distinguished a highly sectarian strand among the diversity of Christian groups.

In other and especially later forms of Christian meal, the fictive equality of the ancient banquet seems to have given way to more explicitly hierarchical expressions of the community's self-understanding. In the fourth-century Syrian *Apostolic Constitutions*, the bishop is encouraged to arrange the church according to a nautical metaphor: "When you call an assembly of the Church as though you are the commander of a great ship, ensure the assemblies are made with all possible skill, charging the deacons as sailors to prepare places for the brothers and sisters as for passengers, with all due care and decency." The possibility of rocking the ecclesiastical boat now invokes a sensibility almost opposite to that of the Letter of James: "if any one be found sitting out of place, let them be rebuked by the deacon, as a manager of the foredeck, and be removed into the place proper for them; for the Church is not only like a ship, but also like a sheepfold" (*Ap. Const.* 2.57).

The detailed instructions for this eucharistic voyage (see sidebar) give a particularly strong emphasis to gender. This is not an entirely new concern, given Paul's awkward instructions about

> Let the young persons sit by themselves, if there be a place for them; if not, let them stand upright. But let those that are already stricken in years sit in order. For the children which stand, let their fathers and mothers take them to them. Let the younger women also sit by themselves, if there be a place for them; but if there be not, let them stand behind the women. Let those women which are married, and have children, be placed by themselves; but let the virgins, and the widows, and the elder women, stand or sit before all the rest; and let the deacon be the disposer of the places, that every one of those that comes in may go to his proper place, and may not sit at the entrance.
>
> —*Ap. Const.* 2.57

women's participation (1 Cor. 14:13), but the elaborated concern may also reflect that the cultic element of the meal—never entirely absent from formal dining, in any case, it must be admitted—has all but overwhelmed the conventions of banqueting. The arrangement of persons in space now seems to owe more to sacrificial ritual and its characteristic impact on the use of space as hierarchical, and especially gendered.[24] The character of the Christian assembly as the meal of a specific association within society, marked by its own limited equality among diners, has given way to the notion of the church as a kind of polis with internal distinctions of many kinds.

Other forms of power and patronage had also emerged during the age of the martyrs, with their own dietary expressions. Food gifts were already a means of extending the significance of common eating beyond the group physically able to be present. Justin Martyr's eucharistic meal in second-century Rome had already invoked this sort of practice in the custom of sending eucharistic bread home to the sick (1 *Apol.* 67). When Christians were imprisoned during times of persecution, food gifts of a more general kind were a very practical means of connection with those martyrs who might otherwise have starved in inhospitable surroundings before their own scheduled and spectacular immolation (see Tertullian, *Mart.*).

After the conversion of Constantine and the end of institutionalized violence against catholic Christians within the empire, the care of the martyrs tended to become a form of devotion to the dead, evoking existing pagan practices of communing with ancestors as well as continuing the specific expression of interest in Christian heroism through food and meals. Christians had already been dining with the dead, as the decorations of catacombs even in the third century attest; these idealized scenes provide oblique evidence for the physical arrangements and roles at meals in other settings as well.

From the fourth century, martyrs and ancestors merged to form a collection of unseen diners with whom one might eat in one form or another. Sometimes older practices of food offerings at ancestral graves were transferred to the martyrs; North African tombs, Christian and other, even exhibit holes through which liquid offerings could be poured, so the faithful dead could partake in what were sometimes rowdy cemeterial picnics. Attempts to guide these practices toward the more orderly celebration of the eucharist proper had mixed success.[25] Perhaps more startling still is evidence that animal sacrifice was assimilated to the cult of the saints, baptized rather than banned in at least one Italian setting around 400.[26] Thus old patterns of using food and meals for earthly and divine patronage were taken up and transformed in these meal rituals, both at and beyond the primary focus of the eucharistic altar.

CONCLUSIONS

Christian eucharistic gatherings in the early centuries are best understood as meal forms exhibiting features comparable to those of other ancient Greco-Roman banquets. The diversity of forms and meanings makes it difficult to generalize any further about the ways in which various diners—wealthy and poor, female and male, African and Syrian—experienced these events. At times both inclusive and exclusive, egalitarian and hierarchical, festive and ascetic, they nonetheless constituted a near-universal element of early Christian experience.

The growth of the Christian churches through the second and third centuries raised concrete issues or problems such as the size of the community and more symbolic ones such as the appropriate function of a meal ritual. Both contributed to the change in the nature of the eucharist itself from associational meal to quasi-civic ritual, even before the Christianization of the civic rituals of the empire. Other meals and food rituals were still to play various important parts in the life of the Christian community, beyond the time of the apparent submersion of the shape of the ancient Christian banquet beneath the surface of the medieval mass. Versions of the actual evening banquet or *agape* continued for some time after the disappearance of the sacralized eucharistic foods into their separate liturgical context. Such "church suppers" continued to have social and economic significance, although within the empire the realignment of the boundaries of church and Roman society meant that such gatherings no longer constituted and reflected the church as such, but defined smaller networks and subcommunities.

Yet the transformed eucharist itself also retained features indicative of its origin. The sequence of bread and cup still echoes the order of the ancient *symposium*; the mixed chalice, the regular manners of the moderate ancient drinker; and the broken bread, the basic needs and pursuits of thousands.

FOR FURTHER READING

Teresa Berger. *Women's Ways of Worship: Gender Analysis and Liturgical History.* Collegeville, Minn.: Liturgical, 1999.

Paul Bradshaw. *The Search for the Origins of Christian Worship.* Rev ed. New York: Oxford University Press, 2002.

Kathleen E. Corley. *Private Women, Public Meals: Social Conflict in the Synoptic Tradition.* Peabody, Mass.: Hendrickson Publishers, 1993.

Gillian Feeley-Harnik. *The Lord's Table: Eucharist and Passover in Early Christianity.* Philadelphia: University of Pennsylvania Press, 1981.

Peter Garnsey. *Food and Society in Classical Antiquity.* Cambridge: Cambridge University Press, 1999.

Nancy Jay. *Throughout Your Generations Forever: Sacrifice, Religion and Paternity.* Chicago: University of Chicago Press, 1992.

Enrico Mazza. *The Origins of the Eucharistic Prayer.* Collegeville, Minn.: Liturgical Press, 1995.

Andrew McGowan. *Ascetic Eucharists: Food and Drink in Early Christian Ritual Meals.* Oxford Early Christian Studies. Oxford: Clarendon, 1999.

Dennis E. Smith. *From Symposium to Eucharist: The Banquet in the Early Christian World.* Minneapolis: Fortress, 2003.

SAINTS, IDENTITY, AND THE CITY

DENNIS TROUT

Sometime in the seventh century, an unknown artist painted an image of Saint Luke on a pillar adjacent to the tombs where the Roman martyrs Felix and Adauctus had been venerated for at least three hundred years (figs. 7.1 and 7.2). Holding a scroll and a medical bag bristling with surgical instruments, Luke still stares back at viewers through wide and steady eyes. For a century or two after they were painted, before the martyrs' relics were removed and the Catacomb of Commodilla was abandoned, those eyes looked on somberly while pilgrims scratched their brief testimonies into the plaster walls of the ancient shrine. Luke's own panel, with its irresistible red and black border, attracted at least thirty-seven separate graffiti. Most are simply names—Cristoforus, Benefacta, Ioannis, Eadbald (in runic script)—but eleven also announce clerical rank in the manner of "Diorno, deacon and servant of God." Frequently the signatories, three of whom were women, prefaced their names with *ego* ("I"), perhaps verifying personal attendance, like "I, Dominicus, presbyter." A few added pious exclamations such as "Live in God" *(biba in deo)*. Some of those who signed in here also did so at other *martyria* around the city, while several are revealed as long-distance travelers by their Anglo-Saxon or Lombard names. Although some of these pilgrims may have been particularly drawn to the majestic calm of the physician's face, for most Luke's panel must simply have offered a ready surface. After all, Felix and Adauctus, the martyr-saints, were the main attractions here. Their tombs had been tended and adorned by Rome's bishops since the fourth century, their painted images were displayed throughout the catacomb, and they had the power to comfort *(refrigerare)* even the dead, as the crude epitaph scratched during the fourth or fifth century into the mortar sealing Virginia Babosa's nearby grave declared.[1]

I will have more to say below about the Catacomb of Commodilla and its *martyrium* of Felix and Adauctus, but for now we may simply observe

Fig. 7.1. In this catacomb chapel, two martyrs, Saint Felix and Saint Adauctus, are portrayed on the central tomb that once held their relics. On a pillar to the right is a painting of Saint Luke, which ancient pilgrims have covered with graffiti. Catacomb of Commodilla, Rome, Italy. Photo credit: Scala / Art Resource, NY.

that this single shrine's collage of epitaphs, paintings, and graffiti reveals with special vividness just how fully the saints had insinuated themselves into the lives of late ancient and early medieval Christians. As we will see, in the course of the fourth, fifth, and sixth centuries, the phenomenon known as the cult of the saints acquired a central place in the imagination and self-understanding of Christians and Christian communities. With the end of persecution in the early fourth century, the wealthy and the poor, emperors and their subjects, clerics and lay-people, embraced the relics of the early martyrs with an energy that reshaped both the contours of Christian iden-tity and the image of the late ancient city. As the sacred tales of the martyrs, rooted in an increasingly distant age, moved from the margins to become the master scripts of civic history, still more ancient heroes and heroic narra-tives that had once played this role so well were absorbed, erased, or forgotten. At the same time, the monumental-ized tombs of the saints outside the city walls emerged as premier staging grounds for many of Christianity's public spectacles, its rituals, and even the factional competitions that continued to redraw almost every community's internal boundaries. Consequently, the gravity of these suburban shrines and basilicas ineluctably pulled the life of the late ancient city into cemetery zones that had once largely been the preserve of the dead.

Fig. 7.2. Close-up of the seventh-century fresco of Saint Luke with pilgrims' graffiti. Photo credit: Scala / Art Resource, NY.

This constellation of features now seems a distinctly late antique configuration. Eventually the bodies and relics of many of the early saints would be translated through the gates and into the city, intramural burial would become acceptable, and many suburban cemeteries and *martyria* would sink from abandonment to oblivion. But throughout the West dur-ing late antiquity the tombs of the saints anchored an extramural perimeter that marked off and protected many communities from the disorderly and demonic forces still held to be at work in the world. Like sentinels, the churches that arose over the graves of the martyrs announced the presence of the city before its walls. In turn, the miracles accomplished around those tombs guaranteed the direct connection of holy grave with heavenly author-ity. Burial near the saints remained desirable, while images of those same saints, displayed on domestic utensils and luxury goods, infiltrated the homes of the living. Meanwhile, pilgrims continued to tramp the suburbs.

Veneration of the martyrs and confessors of the church's heroic age united Christians of all kinds. The cult of the saints, as Peter Brown has force-fully argued and as many in his debt have continued to show, represented neither the unfortunate victory of "vulgar" over enlightened Christianity nor the regrettable capitulation of the educated elites to the "superstitious" practices of the masses, still irremediably rooted in their pagan ways. Rather, the upsurge of the cult of the saints must be seen as a fundamental expression of late ancient Christian piety that flooded across social, economic, and ecclesiastical boundaries.[2] By invoking a variety of voices, by calling upon graffiti and epitaphs as well as literary texts, and by highlighting a selection of visual evidence, I hope here to capture something of the breadth and depth of the refashioning of identity and of the city that unfolded in tandem with the rise of the cult of the saints in late antiquity. Italy (and especially Rome) will receive a disproportionate amount of attention: the nature of the Roman evidence, with its deep and centuries-long flow, may justify this choice. Similarly (and perhaps inevitably), many of the testimonies heard here remain elite in origin, emanating from educated writers and wealthy patrons, clerics, and aristocrats, though I have tried to isolate the themes and concerns that they would have shared with the broader populace. Indeed, this survey will begin with one such elite figure whose surviving writings, however, offer a surprisingly broad and representative sampling of the matters of life and death that late antique Christians sought to resolve around the tombs of their saints.

A PRIVILEGED VIEW: PAULINUS AT NOLA

In 395 the senator Pontius Meropius Paulinus and his wife, Therasia, scandalized some quarters of Roman society and delighted others by abandoning their ancestral estates in Spain and Gaul, renouncing the world, and beginning a new life of ascetic retreat in a cemetery just outside the Italian town of Nola. There they settled as a small community around a basilica-like structure that sheltered the tomb of a local hero of the age of persecution. Despite the backlash, the family's move had been carefully considered. Since he had first visited the Nolan shrine as a boy, Paulinus later asserted, Saint Felix had been his special patron, more peculiarly his than a "private star" *(privatum astrum) (Poem* 27.146). Accordingly, the former governor of Campania now turned his wealth and social authority toward the enhancement of Felix's cult site and the promotion of the saint's reputation. He built churches and hospices decorated with mosaics and paintings. He encouraged local and long-distance pilgrimage. He staged ever-grander events to celebrate the saint's "birthday" *(dies natalis),* the January 14 anniversary of Felix's ascent to heaven. Paulinus's recitations *(natalicia)* on this festal occasion, his other poetry, and his letters spread the news of the miracles accomplished almost daily at Felix's tomb. Such spectacular intrusions of divine favor into people's mundane lives merited announcement because they were, Paulinus knew, indisputable evidence of the power still enduring in the body of a confessor whose soul enjoyed the heavenly friendship of Christ.[3]

Many of the tones that color our view of the cult of the saints in late antiquity appear with unusual luster in Paulinus's poems and letters. There is, of course, a great deal of self-interest entangled in any impresario's elaboration of events. Yet Paulinus's writings suggest, even if indirectly, many of the aims and expectations of the visitors, petitioners, and fairgoers who came to venerate Felix at his Nolan tomb and, in some cases, to see Paulinus as well. Aristocratic friends and travelers, such as the family of Melania the Elder or Nicetas, bishop of distant Remesiana, might stop for a time at Nola, and Paulinus's public verses often praised their faith and ascetic virtues. Yet the anonymous characters who populate Paulinus's *natalicia* better represent the shrine's role in regional society, just as they also foreshadow later accounts of the activity that swirled around the grave of a renowned saint. For such humbler folk, the holy tomb appears as a place of comfort and protection where holy power becomes manifest in awe-inspiring ways. Here the sick and insane are healed or cleansed of their demons. They return home with holy oil charged with curative power through contact with Felix's coffin. They appeal to Felix for the protection of their fields and herds and the well-being of their families. At the fair associated with Felix's midwinter festival, peasants present the saint with gifts of pigs and cattle. Echoing old patterns of behavior, they fulfill vows by butchering their livestock and, at Paulinus's urging, sharing the meat with the poor who have gathered at the shrine. Such practices Paulinus encouraged, while simultaneously working to reform those "rustics" who came to Nola looking simply to fill their bellies with food and late-night wine.

Fortunately, other voices can be added to Paulinus's, illustrating well the range of interests that converged upon the tomb of Felix in the century after Constantine. An unknown trio, Marcus, Reverius, and Leo, implored Felix's aid and (like those visitors to the Roman *martyrium* of Felix and Adauctus) scratched a record of their visit on a wall near his tomb. The Roman bishop Damasus (366–84), whose far greater resources we will consider further below, also testified in stone to his respect for Nola's confessor. Having successfully appealed to the judgment of this "comrade of Christ" against his "enemies' lies," Damasus repaid his vow with the inscription of an elegant verse epigram *(elogium)* near Felix's tomb. But the fame of Felix rippled out beyond Italy. Well-heeled visitors from the provinces, en route to or from Rome, Milan, or Ravenna and seeking rest, news, or books, passed through Paulinus's Nola. Sulpicius Severus's *Dialogues* recounting the life and miracles of Martin of Tours, which Severus hoped Paulinus would help disseminate, dropped Felix's name (3.17). In the early fifth century, Augustine sent two quarreling monks from Hippo to Nola to take their own lie-detector test at Felix's grave. The merger of an individual saint's reputation, carefully managed, with the general assumptions of an age regarding the sanctity of the revered dead, could turn an out-of-the-way confessor's tomb into a hub of activity as well as "a crossroads of the spirit."[4]

Not surprisingly, burial near Felix, whose miracles seemed assurance of his own victory over death, was also highly prized in these years. In the summer of 431, Paulinus himself found final rest beside Felix. Nearby, the recently composed verse epitaph of a certain Cynegius left little doubt about the grave matters at stake in such burial *ad sanctum* (see sidebar). Like the bosom of Abraham, Cynegius's tomb proclaimed, Felix's basilica would shelter the young man in an oasis of peace until the sound of the "terrible trumpet" recalled the souls of men to their bodies *(vasa)*. In that crucial hour, the epitaph assured readers, Felix would stand with Cynegius before Christ's tribunal. It was, at least in part, this belief in Felix's capacity to intercede on behalf of the deceased that prompted Cynegius's mother Flora to request her son's interment within the saint's "holy halls." Here, then, was the ultimate charge laid upon the thresholds of the saints, and surely others among those who attached their prayers to Felix's doorposts or discharged their vows with small gifts were inspired to deeper loyalty by such promises of patronage beyond the grave.[5]

> Cynegius has ended his life in the flower of his years
> and rests now in this holy hall of tranquil peace.
> The bountiful house of blessed Felix now holds him
> and having so received him will possess him through the long years.
> As a patron Felix rejoices in his pleasing guest.
> Thus he will be protected before Christ the judge.
> When the terrible trumpet has shaken the earth with its din
> and the souls of mankind return to their vessels,
> he will justly be joined to Felix before the tribunal.
> Meanwhile he rests peacefully in the bosom of Abraham.
>
> —author's translation with restorations of the Epitaph of Cynegius; *CIL* 10.1370 = *ILCV* 3482 with Walsh, *ACW* 40:345

These images of largely private dependency and care should be set against others that present Felix as guardian of the Nolan community, for the saints and martyrs were now vigorously laying claim to duties long exercised by older civic deities whose favor had once secured the prosperity and safety of the towns of the Mediterranean. In 407, for example, amid squabbles over water rights, Paulinus forcefully asserted Felix's guardianship of Nola and called in the devotion owed to him by the Nolan townsfolk (*Poem* 21.650–858). Three years later, in the late summer of 410 Alaric and his Gothic army, fresh from their sack of Rome, arrived at Nola. Although Paulinus was seized and interrogated during the barbarian attack upon the city, Augustine would later report that Felix himself had aided in the city's defense (*On the Care of the Dead* 19). By the opening decades of the fifth century, local heroes of the age of persecution, like Felix at Nola, were influential participants in civic as well as private affairs. In short, in the world of Paulinus's poems and letters, few areas of private and public life escaped Felix's reach. But elsewhere in Italy other new stars were also well on the rise.

STAR POWER: REFOUNDINGS OF ROME AND MILAN

Seldom are we privy to so poignant a portrait of a saint as that painted by Paulinus, though similar bravura had already been displayed by Damasus at Rome (366–384) and Ambrose at Milan (374–397). These two bishops were pioneers who rode the wave of enthusiasm for the veneration of the martyrs and marshaled the early Christian heroes and heroines of their cities with remarkable panache. Both men had matured under the shadow of Constantine, whose conversion in 312 had created the first real opportunities for the articulation of Christianity in grand, public gestures. Like others of their age across the empire, Damasus and Ambrose seized the moment, enhancing their own authority at the same time as they promoted their particular ideals of Christian doctrine and practice. In the process, they embraced and fostered reverence for the lives, tombs, and relics of the martyrs in ways that would gradually, but fundamentally, alter the image of the city and civic identity.

Constantine had added a new key to the register of imperial benefactions (fig. 7.3). His churches just outside Rome's Aurelian wall were varied in design but their construction established an influential model of patronage and piety. From the large basilica that he erected over Saint Peter's grave to the shrine of Saint Paul on the Ostian Way, Constantine tied his building projects to tombs where heroes of the age of persecution were already honored. The arc of his basilicas sweeps along the cemeteries lining Rome's roads: from the Vatican to the U-shaped funerary halls of Santa Agnese on the Via Nomentana, San Lorenzo on the Via Tiburtina, and the saints Marcellinus and Peter *ad duas Lauros* ("At the two laurel trees") on the Via Labicana, to reach the place called *ad catacumbas* on the Via Appia. There, over an earlier memorial of Peter and Paul, Constantine erected his Basilica Apostolorum, better known since the seventh century as S. Sebastiano. Near these basilicas Constantine and members of his family also prepared their own monumental tombs. The 330s found Helena (died 330), Constantine's mother, at rest in a towering mausoleum adjoining the basilica of Marcellinus and Peter. In the 360s the sarcophagus of Constantina (died 354), the emperor's daughter, was set into the recently finished (and still magnificent) circular mausoleum attached to the Constantinian-age basilica of Santa Agnese (thus the complex is better known as Santa Costanza).[6]

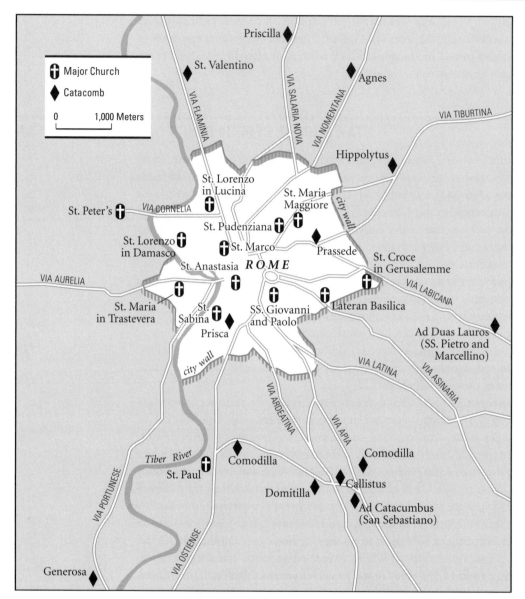

Fig. 7.3. Plan of Rome.
Map by Lucidity Information
Design.

But this was only the beginning, for these Constantinian-age churches and mausoleums initiated a Christian urbanization of Rome's *suburbium* that would substantially alter the image of the city outside the walls *(fuori le mura)*—a pattern that would, moreover, be echoed elsewhere. The results are especially evident in the dense clusters of funerary, ecclesiastical, and monastic buildings that arose across late antiquity around Saint Peter's, Santa Agnese, and San Lorenzo and in the cemetery zones that lined the Via Appia and the Via Ardeatina on the approach to the Basilica Apostolorum *ad catacumbas.* Later in the fourth century the erection of the imperially funded S. Paolo *fuori le mura* would spark a similar construction boom along the Via Ostiensis. Moreover, as these churches, shrines, and mausoleums began to mushroom on the surface, underground the network of catacombs expanded rapidly as new galleries, cubicula, and light wells were excavated. The fourth and early fifth centuries were the heyday of the catacombs as functioning cemeteries. Their total number would reach about sixty; and some, like S. Callisto and Domitilla in the great catacomb zone in the vicinity of the Basilica Apostolorum, would amass twenty or more kilometers of galleries stacked in multiple levels. Within almost all these catacombs special resources—private and ecclesiastical—were devoted to aggrandizing the *memoriae* (memorials) of the saints, for it was especially these that lured the living as well as the dead into the Roman underground.[7]

The well-documented role of Damasus, Rome's bishop from 366 to 384, offers a unique perspective on these developments reshaping the Roman cityscape. Damasus participated energetically in the embellishment of the catacomb *martyria* and composed a remarkable series of epigraphic poems *(elogia)* honoring the Roman martyrs and confessors. Inscribed near the tombs of the saints, these *elogia* provide a crucial link between the topographic changes just outlined and the evolution of public memory and civic identity in late antique Rome. Keyed to the tombs of the Christian community's founders, Damasus's poems encircled Rome with an alternate vision of the city's history. Ranging from eight to twelve lines, elegantly carved in classicizing script, and installed in ornate settings, Damasus's *elogia* epitomized and praised the deeds and rewards of such heroes as Peter, Paul, Lawrence, Agnes, and (in the Catacomb of Commodilla) Felix and Adauctus. In their features and aims, therefore, Damasus's refurbished catacomb shrines bear comparison to earlier Roman "halls of fame." Like the assembly of words and images in the Forum of Augustus, for example, Damasus's monuments to the martyrs proclaimed both a myth of origins and a call to duty. In their intent to preserve the stories of ancestors (in the faith), whose brave displays of *virtus* and self-sacrifice had produced new beginnings and won divine favor, Damasus's poems adhered to the pattern of civic self-fashioning evident earlier, for example, in the Augustan-age writer Livy's still influential *Roman History.* If Livy's early books had spoken about the regal and republican roots of Roman identity to citizens experiencing the dawning of the principate, Damasus's "Roman history" addressed the potential disorientations of Christianizing Romans in the immediately post-Constantinian city.[8]

But Damasus also forcefully proclaimed the apotheosis of the martyr-heroes he celebrated. Though the tombs of the martyrs preserved their still vital bodies, the souls of Damasus's saints resided in heaven, a dual residency with immense consequences for the manner in which many Christians would subsequently conceive of their own afterlives. "The revered tombs [sepulcra] hold the holy bodies; the palace of heaven [regia caeli] has seized their exalted souls," begins an elogium honoring the saints in the Catacomb of S. Callisto (Ferrua 16). Moreover, perched in the "palace of heaven," like the gods and heroes of old, the martyrs would now watch over Rome. At the Basilica Apostolorum, for example, Damasus rehearsed the tale of Peter and Paul's journey from the East to Rome, where they shed their blood to follow Christ "through the stars [per astra]" and reach the "kingdoms of the pious." Thus these premier apostles had claimed their place, Damasus asserted, as Rome's nova sidera, her "new stars." In such conceits were both the seeds of a history worthy of Roma Christiana and a rationale for the veneration of that Rome's early heroes.

> Whoever you are who seeks equally after the names of Peter and Paul,
> you should know that the holy men once dwelt here.
> The East sent its apostles [discipuli], a fact we freely acknowledge.
> By virtue of their martyrdom and having pursued Christ through the stars [per astra],
> they reached the heavenly asylum and the kingdoms of the pious.
> Rome has earned the right to claim them as her own citizens [sui cives].
> These things Damasus wishes to relate in your praise, O new stars [nova sidera].
> —author's translation; Ferrua 20

Rome, thanks to Constantine's jump start, may have held a slight edge in the pace of such developments, but Milan was hardly far behind. Ambrose was a well-born Roman aspiring to a political career when he was elevated to the episcopal cathedra of that city. Milan in 374 was an imperial capital whose Christians were sharply divided over doctrinal issues. Closing the breaches that set factions of the laity, clergy, and the imperial household at odds demanded a tact and bravado of which Ambrose proved capable, and here, as at Rome, episcopal politics also included initiatives in church building and cult management that would tap the stream of popular devotion flowing rich with memories of the martyrs. A new generation of churches was already rising at Milan when, in the 380s, Ambrose turned in earnest to the city's cemeteries. Here, outside the walls, he would build his own Basilica Apostolorum (S. Nazaro) and the Basilica Ambrosiana (S. Ambrogio) and begin the Basilica Virginum (S. Simpliciano). All were fortified with tombs and relics.[9]

The story of the dedication of the Basilica Ambrosiana is especially instructive. Ambrose intended the church both to honor the local martyr Victor, whose tomb was adjacent, and to serve as his own mausoleum, a plan that recalls in an episcopal idiom the imperial projects of Constantinian Rome. But popular agitation for the inclusion of relics within the basilica inspired a prophetic dream that led Ambrose to the graves and wellpreserved bodies of two previously unknown Milanese martyrs, Gervasius and Protasius. Ambrose's transportation to the Basilica Ambrosiana of these bits of "heaven on earth," as he described them to his congregation, was appropriately accompanied by exorcisms and the healing of a blind man, an event that Augustine, then present in Milan, would still relate many years later in the final book of the *City of God*. But well before then, Gervasius and Protasius had become Milan's signature saints—their relics, like burial in their presence, in high demand. So when the quarrels of the fourth century eventually receded, Milan, like Rome, was left with the telltale ring of monumental tombs and extramural churches that was coming to distinguish the image of the city in late antique Italy.

The epitaphs of this age still communicate something of the excitement of this new Roman revolution. In the Basilica Ambrosiana, close by the bodies of Gervasius and Protasius, Manlia Daedalia's verse epitaph, echoing the *elogia* of the saints, proclaimed her return to Christ through the lofty stars *(rettulit ad Christum celsa per astra gradum)* (*CIL* 5.6240 = *ILCV* 1700). That Neoplatonism, then popular with the city's elite and implied here by the notion of the soul's "return," colors Daedalia's epitaph should not surprise us, for Daedalia was the sister (or daughter) of Mallius Theodorus, one of late fourth-century Milan's leading political and intellectual figures. But the fact that Daedalia, like many, now saw burial *martyris ad frontem*, "at the head of the martyr," as the appropriate launching pad for her own celestial flight, highlights the allure for others of the astral life of the saints.

At Rome, too, the rich and powerful were no less eager to secure final resting places *ad sanctos*—and to lay claim to the starry rewards so vividly imagined in the poetry of the martyrs. Ambrose's contemporaries, the eminent nobles Petronius Probus and his wife, Proba, were buried in a large mausoleum set snugly against the apse of Saint Peter's Vatican basilica. Within the tomb long and elegant verses announced Probus's new life in heaven. Dwelling now in the "abode of the saints" *(sedis sanctorum)*, his epitaph read, Probus had exchanged his once-easy familiarity with the emperor for a new intimacy with Christ. His exquisite marble casket, adorned with images of Christ flanked by Peter and Paul and the other apostles two by two, may have received his body, but his soul, "set loose," had run the course to heaven's expanse. Four words in Probus's epitaph neatly sum up the aspirations and self-confidence of this late Roman Christian aristocrat: *vivit et astra tenet*—he lives and holds the stars.[10]

This rush to the stars, initiated by the martyrs, soon swept up others less luminous than Daedalia and Probus. The roughly cut sarcophagus of the otherwise unknown Bassa was discovered in fragments scattered throughout the Catacomb of Praetextatus on the Via Appia and dates to about 400. On its left half it depicts scenes of Christ's miracles. On its right half Bassa's verse epitaph imagines her own reception among the stars of the sky *(sidera caeli)*, where she lived on amid "the kingdoms of the pious" *(regna piorum)*. That phrase, it so happens, echoes a text of Damasus installed elsewhere in this catacomb in honor of the martyrs Felicissimus and Agapitus. But it may be only in the archaeology of the catacombs that we can begin to perceive the scale and depth of the changes implied by these more eloquent epitaphs. The Catacomb of Domitilla, not far from where Bassa's shattered sarcophagus was found, was home to the *memoria* (memorial) of the military martyrs Nereus and Achilles. In the second half of the fourth century, the area around their tombs was reconstructed into a large, semi-subterranean basilica. Their *memoria* was located in this new basilica's apse, where a Damasan *elogium* now related the heroic decision of these two military martyrs to toss aside their bloody weapons and bear instead the "triumphs of Christ." But outside the basilica proper, *retro sanctos,* in galleries behind and around the apse, the graves of the common faithful were now crowding in upon the saints. By the early fifth century the magnetism of the martyrs was well on to realigning crucial elements of Roman identity as those were expressed in burial and commemorative practices.[11]

Finally, this same power of attraction was also drawing the living into the suburbs. Private devotions and funerary anniversaries brought relatives and others to the graves of commoners and martyrs alike. The tables *(mensae)* associated with funerary banquets *(refrigeria)* are well known in North African archaeological contexts, but even in Ambrose's Milan, Augustine's mother, Monica, was not alone in her enthusiasm for taking small meals to the city's cemeteries to dine at the *memoriae sanctorum*. At Rome, likewise, late third- and early fourth-century graffiti scratched on a red wall at the *memoria apostolorum* on the Via Appia (where Constantine would soon erect the Basilica Apostolorum) attest to the custom as well as the hopes and anxieties of those who sought out the saints' shrine. Names and lists of names accompany frequent requests for intercession: "Peter and Paul, keep us in mind" is the constant refrain. Episcopally directed events brought heavier traffic to the suburbs. The great midsummer feast of these same two stars, for example, included a crosstown procession of people and clergy that wound from the Vatican tomb of Peter to Saint Paul's *memoria* south of the city. If we can trust an early fifth-century poet, the pious flocked to the shrine of Hippolytus on the Via Tiburtina, jostling one another just to see the saint's ornately decorated tomb and admire the wall paintings that illustrated his bloody tale of dismemberment.[12]

Fig. 7.4. By the fourth century, images of Christian saints were becoming as familiar and frequently encountered as images of the gods and goddesses had once been. This fifth-century amphora-shaped flask from the house of the Valerii on the Caelian Hill of Rome displays the portraits of the apostle saints Peter and Paul. Photo © Vatican Museums. Used by permission.

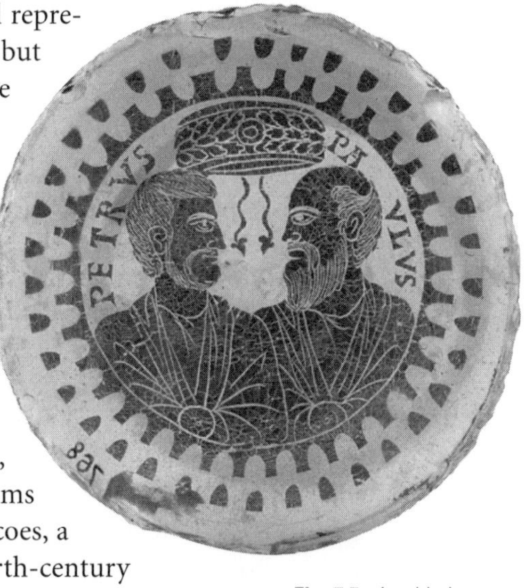

In fact, by the later fourth century such visual representations not only broadcast the martyrs' stories but also gave these heroes vivid form, as statues of the old gods had once provided the templates of dream images. Silver vessels and housewares decorated with busts of Peter and Paul displayed images of the saints (fig. 7.4). Gold-glass bowls (fig. 7.5), their medallion-like bottoms sometimes embedded in the plaster of private graves, represented Lawrence, Agnes, Peter, Paul, and others. Sometimes, however, the juxtaposition of images seems to encourage a broader and deeper imaginative sweep. In the Catacomb of Commodilla, where in the seventh and eighth centuries pilgrims would scrawl their names on the *martyrium*'s frescoes, a rich mural program still decorates the late fourth-century "Cubiculum of Leo." This small triple-niched room in the "cemetery of Adauctus and Felix" takes its name from the man, an official of the city's provisioning system *(officialis annonae)*, who built it to be his tomb (color gallery, plate D). In an *arcosolium* on the cubiculum's back wall, Commodilla's special saints, Felix and Adauctus, stand beside and gesture toward a beardless, young Christ, who holds an open book. As elsewhere in the catacomb, Adauctus appears as a young man while Felix has an older man's whitish hair. Within the *arcosolia* of the two side walls were depicted episodes from the acts of Peter: in one panel he strikes water from a rock; on the other side he denies Christ before cockcrow. Both "historical" scenes allude to the salvation promise that is grandly, if metaphorically, stated on the room's painted ceiling, from which a bearded Christ, flanked by an *alpha* and an *omega*, gazes down amid a canopy of reddish stars. In this single room, the viewer faced (and was invited to take a place within) an imaginative complex that bridged the past and the future, history and eternity, earth and heaven.[13]

Fig. 7.5. A gold-glass bowl bears in its base the images of Peter, Paul, and a martyr's crown. Photo credit: Città de Vaticano, Monumenti Musei e Gallerie Pontificie, Museo Sacro.

We should be careful not to overstate these shifts in self-understanding. The fourth century may have been a period of relatively rapid growth for Christianity, but other practices and beliefs were by no means forgotten. The grand *fora*, temples, and civic buildings of Rome and many other towns of the empire were still important features of both the urban landscape and civic self-consciousness. A plurality of religious affiliations coexisted, licitly or otherwise, and imperial legislation as well as Christian sentiment often worked to preserve, if secularize, the fabric of the pre-Christian city. But the evidence encourages us to believe that by the early fifth century the old trajectories of urban topography and civic identity were being pulled out of orbit by the gravity of the new stars being elevated by popular acclaim as well as episcopal patronage.

RELICS, BISHOPS, AND POPULAR ENTHUSIASM: THE TOMB OF MARTIN AT TOURS

A gift of holy relics might be received, as was a shipment that reached Rouen in the mid-390s, with all the pomp of imperial ceremony. Or the arrival of relics might incite a frenzy of miracles. When the relics of Saint Stephen, discovered in Palestine in 415, traveled through the towns of North Africa over the next few years, even Augustine was moved to report the accompanying rash of incredible victories over disease, blindness, demons, and death. Sight was restored, pain alleviated, conversion wrought. A small boy crushed by a wagon wheel and nearly dead was restored to health at a rural *memoria* of Stephen. Caspaliana, a "woman of God" *(sanctimonialis)*, came back to life when wrapped in a tunic that her parents had taken to the same church. At Hippo, Stephen's relics restored others to life: a daughter of Bassus the Syrian, the son of Irenaeus the money-changer *(collectarius)*, the infant son of an ex-tribune named Eleusinus. Children loom large in these accounts, as do the weeping and lamentation that their sickness and last rites elicited. Highlighting the tragic unpredictability of life in this age, Augustine's field reports are themselves an explanation of the allure of the relics of the saints.[14]

Yet Augustine's cataloging of miracles also reflects a need apparently felt elsewhere to gain control of and give coherent expression to the groundswell of enthusiasm for the cult of the saints. In the panegyric that he wrote to celebrate Rouen's new relics, the city's bishop, Victricius, championed a theological explanation of the power of relics, avowing that God was wholly present in even the smallest bit of the body of a saint. Paulinus, too, would sometimes steer toward a systematic explanation of current phenomena: to bring men from darkness into the light, he once told the Nolan crowd, God had apportioned the tombs of the martyrs throughout the world, like stars in the night sky. The deeper the darkness, the more powerful were the saints assigned to dispel it. No wonder, then, that the "leading physicians," Peter and Paul, were dispatched to Rome (*Poem* 9.16–56). In this vein, Augustine aimed explicitly at producing, and encouraging others to produce, certified miracle narratives *(libelli)* that could be preserved and read out for the edification of the people. If it was impossible to record all of the miracles of the last few years, he realized, at least exemplary and trustworthy accounts could be published, and the confidence created by these would inspire fuller trust in the greater miracle of Christ. Thus, when Augustine heard how a certain Petronia had been healed of a protracted illness at a shrine of Stephen, with the approval of Evodius, the bishop of Uzalis, he exhorted her to prepare a narrative *(libellum)* for public reading *(City of God* 22.8). Characteristically, Augustine's project also bears the earmarks of a pastoral program.

Perhaps nowhere is the overlapping of popular enthusiasm and episcopal initiative better illustrated than at sixth-century Tours, episcopal see of the fourth-century miracle-working ascetic Martin (ca. 372–97). The cult of Martin had international appeal. In the mid-sixth century Agnellus, archbishop of Ravenna (556–69), rededicated to Martin the palace church built earlier in the century by the Ostrogothic king Theodoric (493–526). In Agnellus's church, now S. Apollinare Nuovo, it is Martin who still heads the mosaic procession of crown-bearing saints that advances along the nave's south wall toward an enthroned Christ. In these same years in this city, the rising poet Venantius Fortunatus (ca. 540–600) was cured of an eye ailment as he stood before a portrait of Martin. But Martin's reputation had been made in Gaul, and it was there, now the territory of Merovingian kings, that Fortunatus himself went in 566, drawn by both hopes of patronage and a desire to visit Martin's tomb. At Tours Fortunatus found readymade material for his pen. If Martin was a powerful saint it was not least because he long attracted literary as well as archival specialists, a combination that preserves rare insights into the fortunes of a late antique saint's cult and the motivations of those who kept it alive.[15]

Even before his death, Martin had been the subject of an adulatory biography by the noble but ascetically minded Sulpicius Severus. The miracles of the living Martin and his power to combat demons were central features of Severus's *Vita* and of the *Dialogues* that Severus wrote soon after Martin's death in 397 (and sent to Paulinus at Nola). These works would prove exceptionally durable. They would be recast into hexameter poetry not only by Fortunatus in the sixth century but in the century before him by Paulinus of Petrocorium (Périgueux). Bishops, too, played their part. Martin had been laid to rest in a tomb in the western suburbs of Tours, though largely through popular rather than episcopal initiative, and a modest church was built over his grave only in the 430s. Several decades later, however, Perpetuus, Tours's bishop, fully embraced the political as well as spiritual opportunities made possible by the city's possession of Martin's body. Perpetuus erected a new church over the tomb and translated Martin's sarcophagus to its apse. He commissioned murals as well as inscriptions, several of which were composed by noteworthy Gallo-Roman poets. This new suburban church became the theater for Martin's two annual festivals, other regular vigils, and the miracles that proliferated around the saint's tomb. These wonders Perpetuus would now begin to catalog in a ledger that would find a wide audience as the sixth book of Paulinus of Petrocorium's versified *Vita Martini*. A century later these streams of enthusiasm and initiative would converge upon Gregory of Tours and issue forth in his own church building and archiving of Martin's continuing miracles.

By the time Gregory became bishop in 573, Tours was already well established as "the city of Martin." The paintings near his tomb related Martin's life and miracles. The inscriptions in his funerary church proclaimed both his journey through the stars and his abiding presence in the tomb. That tomb, as well as certain sites hallowed by events of Martin's life, now drew pilgrims from across northern and central Gaul. Gregory himself had once come to Tours as just such a pilgrim. Now, as the city's bishop, Gregory immersed himself in Martin's cult. Episcopal routines and personal piety brought him frequently to Martin's church outside the city walls. And almost immediately he began to compile his own dossier of Martin's contemporary miracles, believing that careful documentation might allay any doubt about the wonders worked by the living Martin two hundred years before.[16]

The four books of Gregory's *Miracles of the Bishop St. Martin* now seem a remarkable portrait of the dilemmas and hopes of his age. Gregory began his second book with an account of his own recovery from near-fatal dysentery, cured by a drink of water laced with dust from Martin's tomb when the wisdom of the doctors had run dry. Thereafter he would continue to record his recourse to the tomb for aid and comfort. But Gregory would seldom, if ever, have been alone there. The *Miracles* portray Martin's church as the refuge of the afflicted. The sick, blind, and possessed crowd in upon the doorways and lie in the courtyard. They represent every level of society. Often they arrive in wagons or carried by friends and family. They stay for days; they return annually. They favor Martin's feast days and other holy days. The fortunate are healed or cleansed, and some stay on to become monks or nuns. Many return home with relics, a bit of dust from the tomb or a candle. Some go away with a lesson learned about Sabbath purity or charity. But few apparently departed unawed by the power of Martin, the "friend of God" (*Miracles* 4.Preface).

One tale suggests how fully Martin's story had become the story of Tours by Gregory's day—closing the gap between civic history and the history of the saints. En route to Martin's church on Christmas Day 575, Gregory's procession was accosted by a madman shouting that it was futile to approach the shrine. Martin, the man ranted, had abandoned Tours for Rome. Dumbfounded, fearful, and weeping, Gregory and the congregation entered the church. Before the tomb they knelt and prayed to be worthy of Martin's presence. The agonized howls of the disabled suppliant Bonulf only increased their alarm. However, as the eucharist was being prepared, Bonulf was suddenly healed. Gregory announced what all so wanted to hear: Martin clearly dwelt among them still. Amid the rejoicing, the once-disabled Bonulf rose to his feet and stood. The demon's lies were revealed. Indeed, they practically had to be, for by the sixth century it had become hard to imagine a Tours without Martin. Martin's past was the city's past, emblazoned in painting, narrated in inscriptions, and reenacted in annual rituals and spectacular miracles. An anonymous sixth-century sermon, though conceding Rome's possession of those "two bright stars," Peter and Paul, nevertheless proclaimed Tours unusually well blessed with Martin. Most fortunate, the unknown preacher asserted, was any region that could boast such an admirable son, respected patron, and worthy intercessor.[17]

ROMAN MEMORIES: RELICS, PILGRIMS, AND THE PRIVATE TOMB

By the sixth century, Rome, of course, was blessed with a galaxy of stars. Two episodes can help us begin to measure their magnitude in the days of Gregory the Great (590–604) and return us to the threshold of the early Middle Ages where this chapter began. Both incidents involve royal women, venerable tombs, and the relic policy of the papacy. The first features Constantina, wife of the emperor Maurice, who wrote to Gregory in the spring or early summer of 594. The empress was building a church in honor of Saint Paul within the palace complex at Constantinople. For its dedication she asked that Gregory send her "the head of this same St. Paul or some other part of his body." Tactfully, the bishop denied her request. The bodies of the apostles, Gregory warned Constantina, "glitter with such great miracles and terrors" that no one even enters their churches to pray without great fear. Recently, a workman, innocently attempting to relocate some bones uncovered near Paul's sepulcher, had died immediately. Not long before that, a group of monks and sacristans who inadvertently looked upon the body of Saint Lawrence were all dead within ten days. As eager as he was to honor her request, Gregory could not. Instead, he offered the empress a piece of cloth sanctified by being placed in a box and set down near the "sacred bodies of the saints." Such *brandea*, Gregory assured Constantina, were as efficacious as the bodies themselves, though, he added, he would also send filings from Paul's chains if these could be obtained. Paul's head and body remained in his tomb along the Ostian Way.[18]

A few years later, another royal lady sought and acquired Roman relics to fortify a palatial church. Sometime during Gregory's episcopacy a certain John arrived at the Lombard court in northern Italy with fourteen oil-filled glass vials. With the exception of the saints John and Paul, whose church was on the Caelian Hill, John's "oils of the saints" had all been collected in Rome's extramural *martyria,* probably drawn from lamps burning near the holy tombs. The vials *(ampullae)* were sealed with wax and individually labeled with small papyrus tags *(pittacia)* that recorded the names of the saints whose oils each contained. A separate bottle preserved the "oil of Peter," as did another that of Paul, but the other twelve *ampullae* each held the oils of numerous saints. The heading of the papyrus catalog of the collection *(notitia)* still reads "a list of oils of the holy martyrs who rest in the body at Rome." Below the heading, two columns tally the names of sixty-five Roman saints, introduced by Peter and Paul and punctuated by references to "many thousands" of others. The catalog ends with the statement "which holy oils in the times of the lord Gregory, Pope, John, unworthy and a sinner, brought to the ruler Theodelinda, queen, from Rome." The whole lot, it seems, was destined for a home in the new church of Saint John the Baptist being built at Monza by Theodelinda, wife of the Lombard king Agilulf (590–615).[19]

Though it is unlikely that Theodelinda's Roman oils were actually a gift from Gregory, their journey to the court of a Lombard queen is another sign of the times. Read alongside a Byzantine empress's power play for the head of Saint Paul and Gregory's careful management of Rome's store-house of corporeal and contact relics, Theodelinda's oils attest not only to the continuing allure and talismanic power of the Roman saints but also to early seventh-century Rome's reputation as the city of the martyrs par excellence. Theodelinda's glass vials from the Roman underground (like the ornate cast metal *ampullae* from the Holy Land that also came to Monza in this period)[20] established a tangible link between her city and a topography hallowed by remarkable displays of faith and fortitude believed to have burst forth at Rome during the Christian heroic age. As the mementos of that Roman history spread out across Europe, they ensured both that Rome would be widely recognized as a city of special stars and that Rome's sacred landscape would profoundly, if immeasurably, leave its imprint upon the sensibilities of Western Christians.

Desire for a more fully realized connection to the past memorialized in the Roman *martyria* inspired not only relic acquisition but also pilgrimage. At least the several remaining contemporary guidebooks to the Roman shrines seem both to indulge and to encourage such longing. One of the earliest of these *itineraria,* the *Notitia ecclesiarum urbis Romae (List of the Churches of the City of Rome)* was composed between 625 and 642, not long after Theodelinda's death.[21] The city it maps is firmly anchored to the tombs of the saints. Its itinerary begins along the Via Flaminia, "where Saint Valentine the martyr rests in his great basilica that [Pope] Honorius [625–38] repaired," and leads the pilgrim (or armchair traveler) clockwise around the city's roads. Like the catalog of Monzan oils, with the sole exception of the Caelian basilica of SS. Giovanni e Paolo, the *Notitia's* sites lie outside the Aurelian walls. Strikingly, the *Notitia* fashions pilgrimage as the personal encounter of visitor and martyr. On the city's south side, for example, "you will afterwards come by the Via Appia to the holy martyr Sebastian, whose body lies in a lower spot. And there are the tombs of the Apostles Peter and Paul, in which they reposed for forty years. And in the western part of the church by steps you descend to where saint Cyrinus, pope and martyr, rests" (20). When the *Notitia* reaches its final destination, a Vatican complex thickly crowded with tombs, relics, and shrines, the saints themselves step forward to guide the pilgrim along a tortuous circuit that culminates at the tomb of Peter:

> And so you will walk along the Via Vaticana until you reach the basilica of blessed Peter—which Constantine, emperor of the whole world, founded—towering over all other churches and beautiful, in whose western part Peter's blessed body rests.... Saint Martin will receive you and he will lead you to Saint Petronella: there the Savior of the World will first receive you ... who sends you by blessed Theodore to Holy Michael the Archangel so that with his support you may be led once more to his most holy Mother... by whose aid you will at last pass through the crypt to the head of the blessed Peter, Prince of the Apostles. (37)

The experience, the *Notitia* assumed, could be overwhelming: "Thereafter you will come to Peter's Greater Altar and Confessio" and pour out your "tears of repentance" (38).

The *Notitia's* Rome is, of course, a contrived *veduta,* a panorama, in part animating the past to recharge the circuits of public memory. But the *Notitia's* quickening of ancient funerary monuments was apparently also intended, in the manner of the best funeral orations, to encourage contemplation of the future. Among the last objects that the *Notitia* isolates for comment are the crib of Holy Mary, a cruciform pattern of purple stones in an oratory pavement, and a "standard of the life-bringing cross" (40–42). With this apparent redirection toward signs of incarnation and resurrection, the *Notitia* trumps its Roman history with both the anticipation of history's ultimate dissolution and the promise of personal salvation. So we return to a fundamental aspect of the cult of the saints that has surfaced so many times already—in the epitaph of Virginia Babosa (noted at the beginning of this chapter), for example, or that of Cynegius at Nola. The history of the saints, friends of God sharing in and advancing Christ's triumph, was inevitably also a prelude to the end of time. Or, more immediately (and as we have already noticed), venerating the martyrs at their tombs often entailed imagining one's own journey beyond life's earthly boundary. And if, indeed, the saints had already blazed trails into that further realm, then the frequently expressed hopes for their support and refreshment of the deceased were hardly unreasonable.

We can sense both the emotional and intellectual bulk of this imaginative complex in a stunning fresco in (once more) the Catacomb of Commodilla. Sometime in the sixth century (or perhaps the early seventh), in the same room where our anonymous artist would eventually paint the image of the physician Luke, the widow Turtura ("Turtle-Dove") was buried near the tombs of Felix and Adauctus. The *martyrium* of these saints, as noted earlier, had been lavishly adorned and heavily trafficked since the fourth century. Damasus had composed an *elogium* to celebrate them and improved the area around their tombs. His successor Siricius (384–99) followed suit. But in the early sixth century John I (523–26) transformed the gallery containing their graves into a "basilichetta" (fig. 7.1). It was on the walls of this enlarged cubiculum that the deceased Turtura was commemorated in a painted panel and verse epitaph. The five elegiac couplets of the inscription are at once a celebration of Turtura's thirty-six years of widowed fidelity and a son's moving, if traditional, lament for a lost mother. Turtura, the poem summarily declared, had faithfully fulfilled her namesake's role: "You have the name Turtura, but you were a true turtle-dove *[turtur]*."[22]

> O Felix, twice fortunate in your true name,
> with pure faith, despising the prince of the world,
> you confessed Christ and sought out the celestial kingdoms *[caelestia regna]*.
> O truly precious faith of a brother—recognize it!—
> by which Adauctus likewise rushed to heaven *[ad caelum]*, a victor.
> On their behalf, in accord with the wishes of Damasus the bishop,
> Verus the presbyter cared for their tomb *[tumulus]*, adorning the dwelling *[limina]* of the saints.
> —author's translation; Ferrua 7

But while the son's verses honored the life Turtura had lived, the painting above them was an image from her present and future (fig. 7.6). While Cynegius's Nolan epitaph had promised that Felix would stand with him before Christ the Judge, Commodilla's Felix and Adauctus present Turtura before a majestic Madonna and Christ. In a large, nearly square panel, bordered in red, Mary holds the Christ child in her lap. She sits on a bright red cushion upon a jewel-encrusted throne, grasping a white cloth in her left hand. The Christ child wears a golden tunic and *pallium* (cloak) and holds a sealed scroll. Mary is flanked by the standing figures of Felix and Adauctus. Felix is once again older and bearded, Adauctus young and beardless, gently resting his right hand upon Turtura's shoulder. Turtura turns slightly toward Mary, her hands covered by a white fringed cloth on which rest two flat white objects, usually identified as scrolls or books. But it is to the viewer as much as to the Madonna that Adauctus presents Turtura and the painting seems less a visualization of the epitaph's verses than a gloss upon its postscript: "Here rests in peace Turtura who lived sixty years, more or less." Certainly, visual correspondences encourage the viewer to link Turtura and Mary, highlighting like the poem an ensemble of ideals that privileges maternal care and chaste fidelity. But Turtura's repose, however earned, her panel reports, was being enjoyed in the heavenly company of the saints. It is in those same "celestial kingdoms" that Damasus's epigram, apparently still on display in the *martyrium* when Turtura was interred,[23] had once located Felix and Adauctus.

In this panel, then, time has already dissolved. Although the representations of the two martyrs and of Turtura, even in their static equilibrium, may hint at their stories, notions of narrative and events are overshadowed by the lustrous and timeless dominance of the centrally placed, forever young, gold-clad Christ child. The witness of the saints, like the long years of Turtura's widowhood, fades to relative insignificance against the promise of eternal rest in the presence of Christ. Yet it is also part of this picture's message that the saints have not forgotten those left behind. Here, as in the *elogia* of Damasus, the mural program of Leo's cubiculum, or the long perspective of the *Notitia ecclesiarum urbis Romae,* the martyr-saints' special role is to bridge two realms. They still inhabit the sacred cityscape; here is where Felix "sleeps," notes one seventh-century *itinerarium* when it reaches the Catacomb of Commodilla. Moreover, their tombs, as Gregory warned Constantina, remain sources of miraculous and unpredictable power. Yet the saints dwelt no less fully in the celestial realm, as the privileged forerunners of all hopeful Christians. Turtura's panel, then, like other records left around the tombs of the martyrs in these centuries, reveals how memories of the saints provided late ancient Christians not only with maps of their communal origins or the means to withstand life's vagaries, but also with ways of conceiving of and anticipating their own eventual passage into that number.

> Take up now the tears, mother, and a surviving son's
> lamentations which, lo, he pours out in your praise.
> After father's death, thus widowed, you chastely preserved
> for thirty-six years your husband's trust in you.
> You performed the duty of father and mother for your son:
> your husband, Obas, lived on for you in your son's face.
> You are named Turtura, but you were a true "turtle-dove,"
> for whom there was no other love after your husband's death.
> There is a single reason why a woman draws praise,
> because you show that you devoted yourself to your marriage.
> Here rests in peace Turtura who lived sixty years, more or less.
>
> —author's translation;
> *ILCV* 2142 = *ICUR* 2.6018

Fig. 7.6. This fresco adorns the tomb of the widow Turtura, or "Turtle-dove," who was buried in the sixth century in the martyrium of Felix and Adauctus. Time collapses, as Turtura is depicted in the company not only of the two saints but also of Mary and the infant Christ. Catacomb of Commodilla, Rome, Italy. Photo credit: Scala / Art Resource, NY.

POSTSCRIPT

In the middle years of the seventh century, Wilfrid of Northumbria (circa 634–709) set out from northern England to visit Rome. When he finally reached the city he had so long desired to see, his biographer reported, he spent months in prayer at the city's *loca sanctorum,* the abodes of the saints. But Wilfrid was only one of many pilgrims who came from afar to see the shrines of the Roman saints. Here they might gain access to a Christian past far deeper than most places outside the East could boast. In some *martyria* they could still read *elogia* of the martyrs installed by Damasus three centuries earlier. Relying upon *itineraria,* they could descend into the catacombs to see the resting places of the bodies of the saints and walk through the churches of the apostles. When they returned home, they often took with them mementos and relics. Only a few decades before Wilfrid, Theodelinda's agents passed through Rome's extramural shrines collecting holy oil. Wilfrid left Rome, his biographer relates, with both the Pope's blessing and a cache of "holy relics" (*Vita* 5). Yet in such respects, Rome was distinct from cites like Nola, Milan, Hippo, and Tours primarily in the vast number and antiquity of its saints, not in the nature of the changes that had transformed its image.[24]

By the seventh century, the Roman catacombs may have provided some Western Christians with a sense of common origins and identity in a fragmented post-Roman world, but here again it is largely scale and depth that set Rome apart. To be sure, the Roman *martyria* had become, in a sense, national cemeteries, and it might even be possible to imagine that Rome was the capital of Anglo-Saxon England,[25] yet elsewhere the local saints and their tombs were hardly less fundamental to the way many Christians understood the world and their place in it. The saints gave hope, aid, and comfort to those who sought them out. Local and regional societies were shaped by the influence of these stars in their midst. Public memory was ever refreshed by the legends of the martyrs and confessors, while the miracles accomplished at their graves were the guarantee of both wonders past and promises for the future. Gradually but steadily the cult of the saints had become part of the lives of late antique men and women, giving late ancient Christianity many of its most striking features.

FOR FURTHER READING

Brown, Peter. *The Cult of the Saints: Its Rise and Function in Latin Christianity.* Chicago: University of Chicago Press, 1981.

Curran, John. *Pagan City and Christian Capital: Rome in the Fourth Century.* Oxford: Oxford University Press, 2000.

Donati, Angela. *Pietro e Paolo: La storia, il culto, la memoria nei primi secoli.* Milan: Electa, 2000.

Howard-Johnston, J., and P. Hayward, eds. *The Cult of the Saints in Late Antiquity and the Early Middle Ages: Essays on the Contribution of Peter Brown.* Oxford: Oxford University Press, 1999.

Krautheimer, Richard. *Rome: Profile of a City, 312–1308.* Princeton, N.J.: Princeton University Press, 2000 [1980].

———. *Three Christian Capitals: Topography and Politics.* Berkeley: University of California Press, 1983.

Rutgers, L. V. *Subterranean Rome: In Search of the Roots of Christianity in the Catacombs of the Eternal City.* Leuven: Peeters, 2000.

Trout, Dennis. *Paulinus of Nola: Life, Letters, and Poems.* Berkeley: University of California Press, 1999.

Van Dam, Raymond. *Saints and Their Miracles in Late Antique Gaul.* Princeton, N.J.: Princeton University Press, 1993.

PERSONAL DEVOTIONS AND PRIVATE CHAPELS

KIMBERLY BOWES

CHAPTER EIGHT

O n a hot August night sometime in the 390s, while Rome's Christians flocked to the tomb of Saint Lawrence for the feast vigil, one young woman did not join the throng. Melania, heiress to the great Valerian fortune and as devout a Christian as her grandmother of the same name, remained in her house on the Caelian Hill and wrestled with her conscience. She was pregnant with her second child, but what should have been a joyous occasion was, for the ascetically minded girl, the greatest of disasters. How could she follow in her grandmother's footsteps and travel to the holy places, casting aside the mantle of worldliness and wealth, if she were to be burdened with children? She had not even wanted marriage and, once married, had tried unsuccessfully to convince her husband to reject the marriage bed and live with her in chastity. Melania longed for divine intervention and aid for her problems, longed, on this most special of nights, to approach the saint's tomb and pray for guidance. But at night, Rome's crowded martyr shrines were no place for a woman mindful of her virtue and reputation, and in any case her pregnancy would have kept her sequestered at home. Unable and unwilling to approach the holy places without, she turned to a holy place within her house, a chapel that she herself had probably constructed after her marriage and move to the mansion on the Caelian Hill.[1] In this chapel, away from the public eye, she spent the whole night at prayer and in the morning went into labor, giving birth to a boy who immediately died (Gerontius, *Life of Melania*, 4–6).

The story of Melania's miscarriage has served as the poster child for modern studies of Christian women, the chilling single-mindedness of its heroine a stark example of the new Christian asceticism that rejected the traditional roles of wife and mother in favor of physical renunciation and spiritual devotion. But scholars' understandable preoccupation with Melania's desire to be rid of her child has obscured the finer points of how the event actually took place. The site of this most pivotal moment in her ascetic career and the site of God's miraculous intervention in her life was explicitly *not* the public martyr shrines or the new public basilicas. The event took place in the home, in a private chapel.

The phenomena of private chapels and private ritual during the late antique period remain as cloaked in shadow as Melania's private midnight vigil. Indeed, the Christianity of the fourth through sixth centuries is typically characterized as rejecting the private for the public, as the church emerged from the homes that had sheltered it during the persecutions to assume the mantel of state-sponsored religion of empire. And yet, by defining the "triumph of the church" as the triumphal procession away from privately based cult to public religion, we have almost wholly overlooked one of late antique Christianity's most important substrands, the continuation and flourishing of private cult and the significant challenge it posed to a nascent institutional church.

This chapter offers a basic sketch of this largely unexplored landscape of private worship. It will describe the pre-Nicene origins of private Christian ritual, particularly the practice of the reserved eucharist and its centrality in pre-Nicene Christian lives. It will then go on to explore the continuation and expansion of private cult after the cessation of persecution, and the reflexive relationship that developed between public ecclesiastical rituals, such as the liturgy of the mass and martyr cult, and private, home-based cult. From the large estate churches that provided Christian services to huge swaths of the western provinces to the tiny basilicas-in-miniature inside urban mansions, from peasants-turned-priests in the service of rural landlords to bizarre private healing rituals using the eucharistic bread, even this briefest trawl through the evidence for private piety reveals the rich Christian world that existed outside the public churches.

Indeed, the very richness of this world and its impact on so many areas of late antique Christian life presented an adolescent church with a series of difficult questions: What defined the Christian community? How had that definition changed with the shift from imperial persecution to imperial patronage of the church? Given these radical changes in community identity, what now constituted "the public" and "the private"? This chapter suggests that many of the great doctrinal controversies of the later fourth through sixth centuries, controversies that were the hallmark of late antique Christian growing pains, had at their heart these problems of privacy and community. In particular, the church's frequent pairing of private worship with heresy documents an institution's attempts to redraw the lines of public and private to align with those of the official church community.

HISTORIOGRAPHY AND DEFINITIONS

Any attempt to illuminate the dark corner of late antique private piety must begin in the well-lit corridors of traditional Christian histories. From the nineteenth century until the late twentieth century, these histories have viewed the ascension of Constantine and the "Peace of the Church" in 313 as a wall, on either side of which existed two radically different Christianities. On one side were the pre-Nicene churches of the second century, small but active communities of highly regional nature, whose small stage was the neighborhood, the home, the family. Their architecture was similarly shaped by the preexisting spaces of the private sphere—the house, the warehouse, the bath—while artistic production was suited to these spaces and to the memorialization of the dead on the walls of catacombs and tombs. On the other side of the divide was the triumphant public church, defined by powerful bishops assuming civic duties, a rising tide of aristocratic converts, and a now-public battle with paganism over the physical and temporal geography of the ancient city. The years after the Peace of the Church were the years of the great basilicas, the martyr shrines, and the urban public liturgy, all representative of the church's quick and apparently seamless absorption of imperial power and classical culture.

The need to see the Peace of the Church as a watershed that separated two radically different worlds was shared by Protestant and Catholic scholars alike. Although they vehemently disagreed as to the nature of pre-Nicene Christianity and the significance of Constantine's conversion, they nonetheless agreed that 313 ushered in a radically new world. They had little sense of any continuity across this imagined divide and thus shared the belief that the private Christian world had, for all intents and purposes, ceased to exist. For Protestant scholars, the history of pre-Nicene Christianity was that of a headlong rush away from a pure church of small communities speaking directly to their God toward an increasingly cumbersome and bumptious hierarchy. The private relationship of an individual with God was the defining casualty of this transformation; thus, the possibility that a private Christianity survived the Peace of the Church was never considered. For Catholic scholars, intent on documenting the rise of institutional structures, expanding concepts of universality and the symbiotic relationships between secular and religious authorities, private piety was a necessary camouflage in times of persecution. With the conversion of Constantine, it was eagerly shed in favor of Christianity's inevitable universal, imperial garb. For both scholarly traditions, the private was the defining feature of pre-Nicene faith, one that had to vanish for the church's triumph, whether positively or negatively defined, to be complete.

Yet the a priori assumptions of scholarly methodology are not the only reasons late antique private piety has been ignored: the problem of evidence is even more daunting. The realm of the home, the family, the private, is thinly documented in the ancient world. Our knowledge of ancient domestic life is paltry compared to the tomes dedicated to the study of political structures, rhetoric, literature, and public cult. This disparity reflects the simple fact that the ancients poured their writing and building talents into the creation and maintenance of status, and status was principally defined through the public sphere. The problem is particularly troublesome for the study of private piety: we should not expect the numerous daily rituals of Christian life to have excited literary description any more than we can expect to excavate the physical detritus of prayers from the ancient house. Those aspects of private life that made it into the textual and material record were those that impinged most closely on public image: a husband's relationship with his wife was described in order to comment on his moral political character; a picture of one's country house was an abstract rendering designed to convey seigniorial power. Thus, what little evidence we do have requires careful sifting and massaging before it can be used to understand a now largely vanished world.

Even more daunting is the very nature of the subject itself. What is the private? Who defines it, and how? Are there not as many definitions of what constitutes the private sphere as there are people who occupy it? Indeed, in the case of private Christian ritual, how can a group whose liturgical activities are defined as a collective sacrifice have any truly private worship? One way around these difficulties is to adopt the institutional church's own perception of what constituted private worship, namely, individuals or groups engaged in ritual outside the direct supervision of the official church or its clergy. This definition embraces an individual's undertaking a solitary healing ritual in his or her bedroom using a privately owned relic, an estate church built and controlled by a landowner and attended by his peasantry, and a family who, in addition to regular Sunday services, attended periodic meetings in their house chapel.

It would seem, however, that even in this definition the hand of the institutional church might be so pervasive as to trump any secondary privateness. The matter of private clergy is the most obvious case, for late antique sources make it clear that private chapels and churches were staffed by ordained clergy, nominated for their posts by the patron in question, but approved and indeed ordained by the episcopate. Thus, such private churches could be seen as simply outposts of the church writ large, supervised by its clergy. However, while they might be episcopal creatures in name, these clerics were undoubtedly the patrons' men in practice, for it was the patrons who held the power of appointment, sustenance, and (frequently) legal power over their clergy, just as they would over a dependent. Far from proving the inherent public nature of the private church, these clergy instead demonstrate how fully intertwined the institutional and private might be and what little hope we should entertain of being able to separate one from the other neatly.

It is this very phenomenon of intertwining, of the overlap between the public church and private practitioners, that raises the all-important question of community. One means of defining Christian community is that propounded by the institutional church—namely, a community of believers in the Christ as Lord, grouped under a recognized hierarchy and sharing in the same liturgical practices and doctrinal beliefs. Yet all Christians, elite and nonelite, clerical and lay, also belong to other communities simultaneously: their family, their class, their gender. While in theory the institutional church might fold all such communities into its own communal umbrella, in actuality these communities existed in a shifting, dynamic state of overlap with the community of the faithful. This fact is so obvious to us today as almost to escape notice: families operate on their own rules, somewhat independent of their Christian identity, just as wealthy Christians sometimes obey the dictates of business at the expense of their Christian beliefs. Depending on time and circumstance, different, non-Christian communal affiliations may influence identity and action more than the rules and expectations of church membership. Thus, a husband's activities may conform to Christian communal expectations in some instances but be more influenced by his membership in a marriage relationship in others.

The triumph of Christianity is traditionally measured by the church's ability to alter the definitions of other communities and communal relationships so that they meshed neatly with the community of the faithful: the senator exchanged his consular toga for bishop's miter; the civic bureaucracy was charged with building churches and hostels instead of amphitheaters and baths; the poor became the emblem of a community's humility and the altar on which it might sacrifice the sin of extra wealth. Even the family was enfolded into the bosom of the church, as the ritual of marriage was made a symbol of Christ's marriage to his church and, by the sixth century, the birth of children was entwined with the baptism of new church members.

This process by which preexistent communities were enmeshed into institutional church communities is, however, rarely contemplated, and, when it is considered at all, it is typically imagined to have been wholly successful and all-embracing: the only group believed to have escaped its affects were pagans who remained entirely outside the Christian faith. Yet the holes in the umbrella of Christian community were more numerous and more subtle than is indicated by a simple gesture toward a dwindling number of recalcitrant pagans. The tenacity of other forms of communal identity and organization meant that, even within the circle of the faithful, other identities might fail to mesh smoothly with the new community of the institutional church. The Roman aristocracy did not immediately or even successfully enter the church hierarchy, families did not necessarily conform their Christian domestic rituals with Sunday mass prayers, landowners did not abandon their century-old religious prerogatives simply because they and their estate populations had converted to Christianity, and even bishops themselves frequently responded to the dictates of friendship and patronage rather than the obligations of episcopal office.

These were the communal interstices untouched (or only lightly touched) by the Christianizing process, the disconnects in which membership in the community of faithful Christians did not necessarily mean membership in the institutional church—that is, where the overlap between the church as an institutional community and other forms of community was imperfect or incomplete. The study of private piety is the study of these disconnects, of the places where worship, particularly liturgy, took place in groups defined first and foremost by nonchurch affiliation: by family ties, by economic ties, by friendship ties. Private piety thus embraced all types of people, clergy and lay, aristocracy and poor, for, unlike these simple categories that describe but one facet of a person's identity, the "private" of private piety was temporal and contextual: depending on time and place, anyone might find their Christian rituals to be private. Bishops worshipping in their palace chapels, clergy performing unauthorized rituals at the request of wealthy patrons, families performing domestic rituals on weekdays—all were engaged in private worship, and all found themselves, for those moments, outside the fold of the institutionally defined Christian community. It is these people, and the problems raised by this realm of practice, that will be the focus of this chapter.

THE LITURGY OF PRIVATE PIETY

Prayer was the simplest form of private ritual in the early church. Tertullian, Hippolytus, and Origen all wrote on the subject, offering advice as to the timing, content, and appropriate locations for private prayer. All recommended a daily prayer regimen punctuating certain hours of the day and night with devotions, to take place in an undisturbed part of the house. The content of the recommended prayer varied, from a simple recitation of the Lord's Prayer to scriptural readings. Indeed, these ritual rhythms of the pious pre-Nicene household would indirectly form the basis of the medieval monastic office.

While private prayer was probably the most common private ritual, another, more physical rite was likewise central to early Christian private devotions: the consumption of the reserved sacrament, a portion of the eucharist, typically the bread only, consecrated at the Sunday service and distributed among the faithful to eat during the week.[2] Tertullian, Hippolytus, Novatian, and others attest to this practice, which seems to have been customary in the North African, Roman, and Egyptian churches, if not universally (Tertullian, *On Prayer* 19.2–4; Hippolytus, *Ap. Trad.* 36; Novatian, *On Spectacles* 5.4–5; Jerome, *Ep.* 48.15). Many liturgists have assumed, based on its later manifestations, that the reserved sacrament was given only to the sick, as described by Justin Martyr (*Apol.* 1.67), or reserved for the last rites, or *viaticum*. However, the numerous descriptions of daily communion, from Tertullian's description of a Christian wife consuming the sacrament before each meal to Hippolytus's inclusion of the reserved eucharist as part of the daily round of prayers, indicate that the role of the reserved sacrament was much broader. Consuming the reserved sacrament as part of the evening meal or during prayer rituals, the average pre-Nicene Christian probably took many more communions from his or her own hand, in the confines of the home, than he or she did from the few eucharistic masses offered during the week.

The practice of the reserved eucharist did not cease with the Peace of the Church but seems to have continued unabated, particularly in the East, where evidence for its use is plentiful. While detailed descriptions of the circumstances and rituals surrounding its consumption are almost nonexistent, we may assume that it continued to be taken as part of meal or prayer rituals. Some sources describe the bread being kept in a special casket or *arca,* and it has been suggested that some of the many preserved fourth-through sixth-century ivory *pyxides,* or round caskets, may have also served as reserved eucharist containers (color gallery, plate I).[3] Many of these caskets are carved with biblical scenes alluding to the eucharistic rite, such as the Multiplication of the Loaves and Fishes, or the Sacrifice of Isaac, believed to be a prefiguration of the eucharistic sacrifice.

The most notable aspect of this later history of the reserved sacrament, particularly during the fifth and sixth centuries, is the increasing divorce between sacrament and the public liturgy. With the rise to fame of great bishops and holy men, a thriving "mail-order" business in the reserved sacrament developed in which laymen and women procured sacramental elements blessed by famous clerics, even if those clerics were in faraway lands. The bishop Severus of Antioch was plagued by such requests and chastised the applicants for assuming his sacrament to be any different from that available locally (*Ep.* 3.1, 3.3, 3.4). Indeed, the Council of Laodicea in the mid-to-late fourth century had prohibited the sacrament from being distributed across diocesan lines, and Severus's and others' capitulation to their fans' requests would probably have been viewed as somewhat irregular, if not outright wrong (Can. 14). The practice was likewise worrisome because such special sacraments seemed to have had significant market value, and some parishioners made a tidy profit selling or trading them.[4] The bread did not simply represent a convenient form of private communion but was also believed to channel divine power in extraordinary ways. Gregory Nazianzen claims that his sister, Gorgonia, once rubbed her entire body with the eucharistic bread soaked in wine, thereby miraculously curing a fever (*Oration* 8.17). In John Moschus's later sixth-century *Spiritual Garden*, the reserved sacrament is described as "defending itself" from corruption or destruction by transforming into sheaves of wheat or disappearing with a clap of thunder (30, 79). What is most striking about these stories is the degree to which the eucharist had become, particularly by the later sixth century, a holy thing, utterly divorced from both its liturgical origins and the community whose sacrifice it was to represent. Thus objectified, it was utterly possessable by the individual—bought, sold, traded, and shipped to and fro.

While practice of the reserved eucharist seems to have been a significant part of private ritual on both sides of the Nicene divide, other private rites are largely post-Nicene developments, inspired by new public liturgies or simply by the expansion of Christian ritual activity generally. The cult of relics is one such practice, the origins of which lay in that "fine and private place," the grave, a space where private memory and public commemoration had always collided.[5] The earliest evidence for the private ownership of relics comes from the turn of the fourth century, when one Lucilla, a wealthy Spaniard living in Carthage, was reprimanded by her bishop for carrying around a martyr's bone of dubious origins and kissing it before taking communion (Optatus, *Don.* 1.16; Augustine, *Ep. Cath.* 25.73). However, the real floodgates of private relic owning were probably opened by Constantine himself; he, his mother, Helena, or the two of them together transported the relics of the true cross to the Sessorian Palace in Rome (now the Church of Santa Croce), and perhaps also to the Great Palace in Constantinople.[6] Their Holy Land activities gave a monumental boost to an already burgeoning cult of the martyrs. In addition, by immediately appropriating a portion of the newly discovered cross for a palace-based cult, they made plain the possibility and desirability of cornering a piece of

the holy for personal use. By the later fourth century, privately held relics abounded. Melania the Elder, for example, procured a piece of the true cross for Paulinus of Nola, who in turn gave it to his friend Sulpicius Severus. Paulinus suggested that Sulpicius might not wish to place it beneath the altar of his new estate chapel as planned, but rather reserve it for "daily protection and healing" (Paulinus, *Ep.* 31). Sulpicius had already amassed quite a collection of relics, including the body of Clarus, confidant of Martin of Tours, and various Holy Land relics obtained through his extensive network of aristocratic connections. The holy woman Macrina wore a piece of the true cross around her neck (*Life of Mac.* 30), while the Georgian prince-turned-holy-man Peter the Iberian possessed not only a piece of the true cross but also relics of Persian martyrs (John Rufus, *Life of Peter the Iberian* 41 [39]). Archaeological evidence for the private ownership and worship of relics confirms this picture: the house chapel in the so-called Palace of the Dux (described below) possessed a large reliquary, and a new interpretation of the so-called *confessio* beneath the church of Ss. Giovanni e Paolo in Rome, previously believed to be a communal *martyrium,* has likewise identified this small, closet-like space, decorated with images of martyrdom, as a private reliquary shrine in a large wealthy home.[7]

While not relics in the strictest definition, *eulogia,* earth or oil blessed through contact with a holy person or site, served many of the same functions as relics and were probably among the most common holy ritual objects.[8] *The Life of Simeon Stylites the Younger* is filled with miraculous tales of such *eulogia,* typically earth taken from the base of the saint's column and used by clerics, travelers, and families. The monk Dorotheus used his, crumbled and thrown into the water, to calm the seas and prevent shipwreck; a praetorian prefect drank his, along with some of the saint's hair, as a cure for diarrhea; an Iberian priest received pieces of the saints hair as a *eulogia,* which he encased in a cross and placed in a chapel (235, 232, 130, respectively). The many pilgrim flasks preserved in modern museums (fig. 8.1) would have served a similar function by holding oil taken from lamps burning at holy sites, such as Simeon the Younger's column outside Antioch, the Church of the Holy Sepulcher in Jerusalem, or the hugely popular shrine to Saint Menas in Egypt.

As Paulinus's and Dorotheus's stories attest, privately owned relics and *eulogia* seem to have been particularly valued for their protective and healing qualities: Theodoret describes how he himself kept a vial of oil "of the martyrs" tacked to his bed for protection and, as a child, wore a belt of the holy man Peter to expel disease, while Augustine tells of one Hesperius of Hippo, who hung a piece of earth from the Holy Sepulcher in his bedroom as protection, which, when transferred to a local shrine, began to effect

Fig. 8.1. Most pilgrim ampullae, or oil flasks, were made of humble clay, crudely impressed with abbreviated images of the saint or shrine. This example from Antioch depicts Saint John the Evangelist, whose shrine at Ephesus was an important stop on the pilgrim tour. Most ampullae have neck ridges and/or holes to hold a chain, indicating that they were frequently worn around the neck where the relic's protective power might be clasped tightly to the body. Photo credit: clay pilgrim ampulla found at Antioch, © Research Photographs, Department of Art & Archaeology, Princeton University.

healing miracles (Theodoret, *Rel. Hist.* 21.15–16, 9.15; Augustine, *City of God* 22.8). *Eulogia* were thus frequently used to effect healing when travel to the holy man or site was not possible. Some combination of prayer, incense, and physical contact with the holy body, earth, or oil brought saint and supplicant together, bridging the gaps of time and space and permitting the saint's healing powers to flow into the object's owner. Private holy items thus offered immediate access to holy power, no matter the time or place, plugging up the keenly felt gaps between holy places, such as churches and martyr shrines, and the exigencies of everyday life.

Pictures of the holy also had this immediate, transportable power to bridge worlds.[9] Images, either in the form of panel paintings of saints or impressed or painted on holy objects, such as *eulogia* or pilgrimage containers, were common accoutrements in private ritual. Constantine's daughter may have asked a disapproving Eusebius to obtain for her an "icon" of Christ for her private devotional use (*Ep. Const.* 1545). According to the *Life of St. Simeon Stylites the Younger*, a Cilician woman placed an image of the saint in her home, where it proceeded to work miracles (118). Also from the life of Simeon is the tale of a priest who brought his son to the saint to cure. The saint gave to him a *eulogia* impressed with his image, saying, "The power of God . . . is efficacious everywhere. Therefore, take this *eulogia* made of my dust, depart and when you look at the imprint of our image, it is us that you will see" (231). The use of images as a means of ushering in divine presence was a commonplace of the ancient world, in both the public and private spheres. The pagan *lararium*, or shrine holding small statues or paintings of the household gods, was a functional antecedent to the Byzantine *iconostási*, the shelf that carried the household's icons. And yet the expectations of intimacy with the divine mediated through the Christian icon seem to have been far greater than those surrounding the pagan *lararium*: not only would the icon permit the viewer to call upon divine power, but, like a visual radio, it would permit an actual conversation between human and divine.

From the transformation of the reserved eucharist into healing salve to the use of *eulogia* to prevent shipwreck, private ritual's greatest power was its ability to mold around temporal and experiential demand. Reflective of this need to respond to circumstance are the several rituals associated with nighttime, a time associated with danger as well as with holy presence, yet one in which clerical guidance or access to holy spaces might be particularly hard to find. The *lucernarium*, the lighting of the lamps at sundown, is probably the oldest of these rituals, one that may have originated in Jewish or even pagan households and was adopted by pre-Nicene Christian homes before being picked up in the public liturgies of the fourth century

Fig. 8.2. This fifth-sixth bronze century lamp from the area of Herculaneum, Italy, includes both traditional apotropaic iconography, such as the griffin's head, as well Christian symbols, here a dove seated on the Chi-Rho initials of Christ. Such lamps may have formed part of the lucernarium, or lamp-lighting ritual that was carried out in the home as well as in the public church, or simply used for everyday lighting needs. Photo credit: Erich Lessing / Art Resource, NY.

(see fig. 8.2).[10] It may have been supervised by women, as mothers supervised the ritual in Jewish homes, and a Spanish church council circa 400 seems to associate the *lucernarium* with "learned women" and "widows" (Toledo, Can. 9). Incubation or sleep in a holy space in order to initiate divine contact through dreams is similarly associated with private contexts. Theodore of Sykeon, when still a boy, forged his close relationship with the martyr George through nights spent in the saint's oratory, during which the saint would regularly appear to him to encourage and edify (*Theod. Syk.* 7–14). Peter the Iberian likewise began his life of prayer and holy works by "sleeping with the martyrs," spending nights on the floor of a chapel in which he had placed his relics of Persian martyrs.

It is important to note that none of the above-described private rituals were exclusive to the private sphere. Specially designed private masses, crafted particularly for domestic use, were centuries away in the West and may never have developed fully in the East. Rather, private rituals in late antiquity seemed to have developed out of or in conjunction with their public cousins, one sphere reflexively informing the other. The use of relics and *eulogia* in the home grew alongside the increasingly popularity of martyr shrines and pilgrimage, while the changing nature of the reserved eucharist may relate to shifting notions of the communion liturgy in the East brought on by the Chalcedonian controversy. What distinguishes these rituals in their private context is the particular nature of community they created there. Each of these rituals—the reserved eucharist, the use of private relics for healing and protection, the practice of incubation—had the result of ritually crafting a smaller Christian subcommunity, sometimes as narrow as simply the petitioner and God himself. These rituals not only forged particularized links between small groups or individuals and the divine, but they also further strengthened the ties within those groups: the father who brought home the Simeon *eulogia* to cure his son reforged the father–son relationship under

Simeon's guidance; Sulpicius's possession of the Holy Land relics increased the status of his own estate-cum-monastery community while also strengthening its bonds to Paulinus, the relic procurer, who was himself portrayed along with the saints on the walls of the estate church. Private rituals were not simply a private version of public ritual: they created and maintained separate subcommunities within the Christian faithful.

THE SPACE OF PRIVATE PIETY: CHAPELS AND CHURCHES

If privacy exists only as a relative category, conditioned by time and place, then what constituted a private space must also be wholly relative to circumstance and context: a city street, a dining room, or a closet might all be construed as private, given the particularities of occasion, function, or even psychology of the individual in question. Thus, the spaces that accommodated the many private rites described above were as varied as the rich landscape of the ancient world: one couple's private eucharistic miracle, inspired by fractures within their marriage, took place in the street outside their home; for another pious layman, the garden seems to have been the site of his eucharistic devotions; a ship, a picnic spot, and a bedroom were all used as sites of private rituals (John Moschus, *Spiritual Garden* 30; John Rufus, *Plerophoria* 77). Indeed, the knowledge that any space could serve as a site of holy ritual caused church officials no small degree of discomfort. One fear was that space itself might accumulate the moral detritus of the activities it witnessed. Origen admonishes that the space selected for prayer must be one unstained by sin, particularly sexual sin: "For it must be considered whether it is a holy and pure thing to intercede with God in the place of intercourse" (*On Prayer* 31.4). Bedrooms, so frequently mentioned as preferred spaces of private ritual, were thus particularly suspect. This fear was heightened when the eucharistic bread was involved, for not only space but holy objects might be rendered impure by surrounding activity of dubious morality. Novatian bewails the fate of the reserved sacrament that was carried through a red-light district by a feckless parishioner: "That faithless man has carried into the midst of the foul bodies of prostitutes the sacred Body of the Lord" (*On Spectacles* 5.4–5). The unclean bodies of such women rendered the very streets thick with sin, sin that was absorbed sponge-like into the holy bread.

It is no wonder, then, that when resources permitted, Christians might build special spaces within the domestic sphere for private worship. A growing number of such chapels or churches have been unearthed in archaeological excavations, although these necessarily represent only those spaces

with permanent, Christian features such as a monumental altar or reliquary. Spaces whose Christian equipment consisted simply of a portable
altar or reliquary, wooden furnishings, or other ephemera do not appear
in the archaeological record but are attested in numerous textual descriptions. From this increasingly large collection of evidence, two fundamentally different categories of such churches may be distinguished on the
basis of context and function: private churches in urban homes and private churches on rural estates. The preserved examples of each type also
demonstrate a significant geographical bias: urban chapels are known
largely from the Eastern empire, while most villa-churches are clustered in
the great estates of the West. While this bias undoubtedly reflects certain
late antique realities, namely, a more vibrant urbanism in the East and a
largely Western rural estate culture, textual sources indicate that both kinds
of private churches existed throughout the empire.

Two examples, both from wealthy houses in cities and both dated ten-
tatively to the sixth century, provide provocative glimpses of the urban
chapel phenomenon. In the North African city of Apollonia (modern Susa),
a large residence known as the Palace of the Dux included an ornate chapel,
complete with a large stone reliquary box (fig. 8.3). The chapel was set on
the far side of the house along the peristyle, and measured about nine
meters by seven meters. Built as a basilica in miniature, the chapel had
three aisles, a relatively large narthex, and an eastern apse flanked by two
side chambers. The large reliquary was probably set in front of the apse
and protected by a series of flanking screens, and its prominence, as well as
the absence of an altar, suggests that the chapel was principally used for
martyrial cult.

Another example, this from the city of Ephesus, was added to a large
house overlooking the city's theater. Set in a remote corner of the rambling
residence, the Ephesus chapel was smaller than its Apollonia cousin and
had only a single nave. Nonetheless, its sanctuary was carefully separated
from the nave by chancel screens and pierced by two deep cupboards,
presumably to store ritual implements. The apse itself contained an elaborate stepped clergy bench *(synthronon)* and was preceded by a small stone
altar. The altar and cupboards both indicate that the chapel may have been
built with eucharistic functions in mind, although, as we shall see, these
accoutrements may have had other uses. In the cases of both Apollonia
and Ephesus, the chapels' location deep within the house and their relatively small size suggest a worshipping community formed principally of
the family.[11]

Despite their relatively protected location and likely familial function,
both examples betray a complex relationship between public and private
holy space. The three-aisled plan with apse and flanking side rooms in the

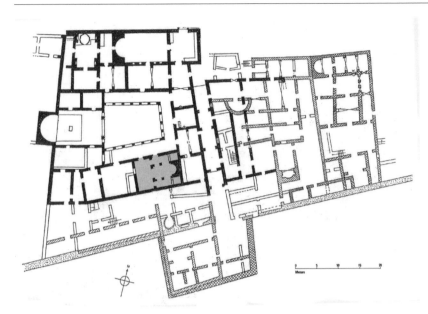

Fig. 8.3. Apollonia (modern Susa), Libya, offers an excellent example of a private chapel in an urban house that may have belonged to the provincial governor or "dux." The small chapel, located along the south wall of the house, was comprised of a nave, two aisles, apse and flanking chambers. A large reliquary box was found in the excavations and probably sat in the chapel's center.

Apollonia example is essentially a miniaturized version of Apollonia's grand central church. At Ephesus, a clergy bench, designed to seat the various clerical orders of a major urban church, has been shrunk and crowded into the tiny chapel apse. Indeed, it is the very miniaturization of these furnishings that provides a glimpse into their meaning. Chancel screens designed to keep crowds at a distance from the sacred, aisled arrangements built for proper liturgical circulation, clergy benches to seat a bevy of clerics—none of these would have been strictly necessary in a private chapel, and indeed, many of these furnishings, such as the *synthonon*, have been miniaturized past actual functionality. Clearly, it was not important that such furnishings be functional, but only that they be present. By the sixth century, when these chapels were likely built, the great martyr shrines and urban basilicas had developed an architectural language of holiness. No longer only functional, the plans and furnishings of urban churches might themselves stand for the liturgies they housed and the holiness they embodied and contained. As with the reserved eucharist, so, too, the church's physical components might be detached from their liturgical origins, miniaturized and transplanted into the home, where simply their presence was sufficient to recall their ritual implications. That is, these elaborate private chapel furnishings were shorthand for the complex liturgies and communities they had short-circuited in their migration into the private sphere.

An equally complex relationship between public and private Christian spaces is evident in the second category of private churches, the rural estate church. Some of these churches, like the urban chapels examined

Fig. 8.4. Lullingstone, England, provides an example of a private chapel in a rural villa. The small chapel (indicated by the shaded areas) was set on the villa's north side and entered from the outside via a series of vestibules.

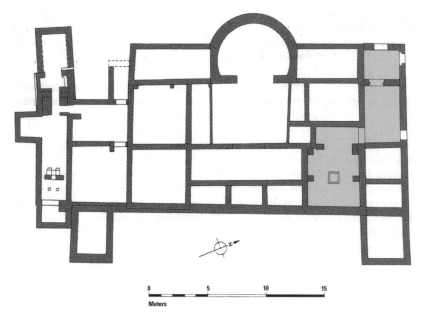

above, were constructed within the villa's residential nucleus. In the villa of Lullingstone in Kent, for instance, the Christian church was set into a far corner of the villa, over a cellar that had previously held a small pagan shrine (fig. 8.4). The main worship space consisted simply of a small (seven meters by four meters) rectangular room equipped with an eastern niche. Its simplicity is belied, however, by a series of annexes, including a large antechamber and side chambers, and its remarkable and complex fresco decoration. Highly fragmentary, these frescoes included a series of unidentified scenes along the long walls, plus three large paintings of the symbol of Christ, the Chi-Rho (fig. 8.5). The placement of these three Chi-Rhos seems to mark a path from the vestibule to the church's eastern focus wall, echoing the procession of the faithful from the entrance into the church. Furthermore, the frescoes depicting six praying figures were arrayed on the church's western wall, mimicking the position and actions of the faithful as they faced the eastern niche (color gallery, plate H). A similarly sized chapel in the villa of Fortunatus, in Huesca, Spain, was more elaborate in design. Dating to the later fourth or early fifth century, it was placed in an earlier, three-aisled dining room, whose basilican plan probably inspired its choice for chapel use. It boasted a sanctuary, two side rooms, and a pseudo-crypt, accessed by three narrow stairs and protected, like the reliquary box at Apollonia, by a series of rough stone screens. Too small to have held an actual burial, the crypt, like Ephesus's too-small *synthronon*, was a miniaturized reference to crypt architecture, which probably simply held a portable reliquary.[12]

Fig. 8.5. At Lullingstone, the path to the chapel was marked by large fresco images of the Chi-Rho, as shown in this reconstruction. Illustration by Mr. Pal Rook, taken from THE LULLING-STONE ROMAN VILLA by Lt. Col. G. W. Meates, FSA, published by William Heinemann. Reprinted by permission of The Random House Group Ltd.

These small integrated villa-churches probably served, like their urban church counterparts, as family chapels. Also constructed primarily for family use were the imposing funerary chapels set near Roman villas. The octagonal mausoleum set next to the villa at Pueblanueva in central Spain was encircled by an ambulatory and may have had a separate, eastern chamber for ritual function. The below-ground crypt held three sarcophagi, one of which was finely carved with images of the Twelve Apostles. Also in Spain, the villa of La Cocosa included a separate tetraconch funerary chapel, oriented east-west and covered with a mosaic-encrusted dome.[13] A single marble sarcophagus, also oriented east-west, was placed in the apse beneath the floor. Textual sources suggest that such funerary chapels might also include relics, such as that built by the aristocrat Rufinus in Chalcedon, intended to hold both his own body and relics of the apostles of Peter and Paul imported specially from Rome (Callinicus, *Life of Hypatius* 66.19). The deaconess Eusebia was similarly buried with her collection of the relics of the Forty Martyrs in her suburban villa outside Constantinople (Sozomon, *Eccl. Hist.* 9.2).

A final category of villa-churches seemed to have embraced a much larger worshipping community. Such churches may have become increasingly common as time went on, and most date to the fifth and sixth centuries. These churches were set apart from the villa as freestanding buildings, and thus careful archaeology is required to ascertain if the churches functioned contemporaneously with the residential use of the villa or were built long after the villa had been abandoned or transformed. The former are true villa-churches, while the latter represent a different, although equally interesting, phenomenon. One example in which church and villa seem to be contemporary is the church of the villa of Loupian, in Languedoc. The villa itself was rebuilt in the late fourth or early fifth century, with new reception rooms and fine mosaic floors. At approximately the same time, a large church was built some eight hundred meters from the villa. A thirty-five meter by ten meter single-aisled building, it included a baptistery on its north flank, while its inscribed, eastern apse was almost an exact replica of the inscribed apses in the new villa. The villa-church at Torre de Palma in central Portugal, while later in date, was similarly large and well furnished. The villa itself was unusually expansive, and by the early sixth century, when the church had been built, its residential sector may have shifted to a large, newly constructed house. The church was built some twenty-five meters away from this house and assumed its same northeast by southwest orientation. A large (thirty meters by ten meters) basilica, the building was fitted with a liturgical walkway *(solea)*, eastern and western apses, and an attached baptistery. Clearly, neither of these churches were just small family chapels; rather, they were mostly likely built to serve rural communities, almost certainly the workers and landlords of the estate itself.[14]

The textual record tends to confirm this quasi-public, estate-wide function. For instance, a series of Gallic church councils of fifth- and sixth-century date prohibited villa owners from celebrating eucharistic masses in their estate churches on Christmas, Easter, Pentecost, and other major feast days, insisting that they present themselves to their bishop in the urban cathedral church (Agde, Can. 21; Orléans 1, Can. 25; Épaone, Can. 3; Orléans 2, Can. 3; Clermont, Can. 15). The prohibition of feast-day services tacitly assumes (and approves) the celebration of ordinary masses in these villa-churches. Furthermore, one council's allowance that these oratories might serve the weekly needs of a "family," interpreted here to mean the larger estate community of blood relations and dependents, as well as several written permissions for "public masses" in estate churches, eloquently support the archaeological picture of quasi-public villa-churches (see Galasius, *Ep.* 32). Landowning aristocrats such as Sidonius Apollinaris and Paulinus of Nola wrote laudatory descriptions of their friends' villa-baptisteries, describing these as demonstrations not simply of piety but of civic generosity, likewise suggesting that such baptisteries served a broader rural population (Paulinus, *Ep.* 32; Sidonius Apollinaris, *Ep.* 4.15).

Given the expansive community and wide variety of liturgical services provided by some estate churches, a clerical staff was clearly requisite. Certainly by the later fifth century and probably earlier, a landlord claimed the right to nominate his own clergy, for ordination if need be, while the final choice of such clerics remained with the local bishop.[15] Nominees were frequently estate tenants or other working dependents. A variety of sources, from a disgruntled holy man-cum-villa-presbyter who lost his job, to disciplinary cases against dissolute estate clerics, make it likely that the clergy staffing these churches were permanent staff, rather than occasional visitors.

We have only just begun to appreciate the impact that these estate churches, particularly those of quasi-public function, would have had not only on the character of the late antique estate but also on the Western countryside more broadly. The repeated discussions of such churches by episcopal authorities, together with their increasing prominence in the archaeological record, describe a deeply complex world in which the rural parish church may not have been the sole or even primary space of Christian worship and community. Christianity not only seeped slowly from the urban episcopal centers into a resilient pagan countryside but also emerged in the distinct islands of the rural estate, where its impresarios were not bishops or other representatives of the institutional church but the same persons who had always ruled the rural world, namely, the landowners themselves. In many areas of the West, particularly in Hispania, where cities were few and bishops even fewer, these landowners and their estates may have been the real engine of Christianization. Thus, the Christian communities of these rural provinces would likewise have been shaped by the age-old institutions of land tenure, and their internal hierarchies built less around lay/clerical distinctions than around the dependent relationships of landowner and tenant.

COMMUNITIES OF RESISTANCE: PRIVATE PIETY IN THE EYES OF THE INSTITUTIONAL CHURCH

From daily communion at home to estate churches under the thumb of powerful landowners, the above survey of private liturgy and private churches presents a landscape of alternative Christian communities. Christian experience shaped through the mold of the rural economy, the rhythms of daily home life, and the exigencies of travel or sickness was experience shaped outside the liturgy of the public churches, outside the rhythms of the Christian calendar, and thus in ambiguous relationship to institutional structures supervised by Christian bishops. How did the episcopate regard acts of private worship and the existence of these subcommunities within the Christian faithful? How did these subcommunities regard the episcopate, or did they even recognize themselves to be communities outside that of the institutional church? These questions address the more basic issue of how the public and the private, the individual and the collective came to define themselves in the centuries after the Peace of the Church, when the nature of one type of Christian community, the institutional episcopate, changed radically, while other kinds of community swirled in a state of both flux and continuity around it.

A large chunk of evidence describes a world in conflict, one in which the episcopate regarded private worship with suspicion and sought (with uneven success) to control private communities through clerical oversight and restriction on the kinds of worship permitted in the private sphere. Even the most cursory trawl through the sea of church and imperial law reveals an episcopate profoundly troubled by private worship, particularly private churches. Some of the very first church councils held after the Peace of the Church took up the problem. At the council of Laodicea in Phrygia, held sometime during the late fourth century, the assembled bishops prohibited eucharistic services from being held in private houses, even with an attending bishop or presbyter (58). The prohibition was repeated at the council of Gangra in Galatia, although here, as we shall see, the prohibition is likely related to doctrinal disputes (Can. 6). While these proscriptions were among the harshest and, if later legislation is any indication, probably widely ignored, the same kinds of concerns appear regularly throughout conciliar legislation of the fourth through sixth centuries and beyond. Typically, such legislation focused on clergy serving in private homes as well as private churches, insisting that both be approved by the local bishop. Thus, contrary to the mandates of Laodicea and Gangra, it seems that private masses were eventually tolerated as long as they took place under the watchful eye of the episcopate. Imperial law codes also included regulations on private churches but tended to focus their attention on the founders rather than the clergy. As described above, private church founders were permitted to nominate clergy of their choice to serve in their private churches, but their choices had to be approved by the local bishop.

While private church concerns sounded a periodic refrain throughout the period's regulatory documentation, crescendos of concern punctuated certain times and places. One such time and place was the later fifth and sixth century in the western provinces, where particular concerns about estate churches seem to have troubled the churches of Gaul, Hispania, and Italy.[16] Rural landowners had seemingly carved out a highly self-sufficient Christian experience for themselves and their dependents through their estate churches, which provided all manner of services throughout the liturgical year. A worried episcopate insisted that the landowners and their immediate family make periodic appearances in the urban episcopal church, particularly on important feast days such as Easter and Epiphany. It similarly sought to wrest the sacraments of baptism, ordination, and consecration out of the hands of estate clergy, who had seemingly appropriated them, and to place them back under exclusive episcopal control.

In northwestern Hispania, bishops fought repeatedly against landowners who built estate churches or monasteries for profit, presumably pocketing the proceeds of the collection plate. Similar monetary concerns troubled the Italian episcopate, who finally began to wrest from donors' control any financial rights over donations, including lands meant to support their estate churches. What began as a series of gentle reproofs may have grown somewhat sharper in later sixth-century Italy, as the papacy cracked down on private church owners, requiring them to obtain permission to build any private church directly from the bishop of Rome and seriously restricting their activities by prohibiting public masses, baptisteries, burial, and permanent clergy. Since much of this legislation was again directed against the rural estate church, the increasing hostility may have been born of the institutional church's own growing presence in the countryside through the expansion of the parish system. That is, the growing hostility of the Italian legislation may have been brought about as two kinds of Christian community organization, the rural estate and the parish church, came into increasingly close and thus potentially volatile contact.

Irascible bishops struggling to control independent-minded church patrons was one issue, but heresy was quite another. Woven into many descriptions of private churches and ritual, particularly those of the fourth and early fifth centuries, was the insidious taint of heretical accusation. This subject is discussed at length in the next chapter, so only a brief sketch will be presented here. For the heresiologist, rooting out heretics meant rooting out their meeting places, and these meeting places were presumed to consist, at least in part, of private homes. The Theodosian Code repeats in edict after edict the same assumption, namely, that heretical gatherings took place in private houses, just as it repeats the same punishments, namely, confiscation of said properties (see, for example, *CTh*. 16.5.3 [372], 16.5.9.1 [382], 16.5.11 [383], 16.5.40 [407], 16.5.65.3 [435], 16.7.3 [383]). While Manichees are sometimes singled out, heresies are frequently lumped together in grocery lists of heretical "isms," whose "nefarious retreats and wicked seclusion," "secret and hidden assemblies" are repeatedly constituted as part and parcel of their incorrect belief (*CTh*. 16.7.3 praef. [383], 16.5.9.1 [382], among many). The tone of the whole corpus can be summarized in one edict issued in Constantinople in 383:

> All persons whatever who are tossed about by the false doctrine of divers heresies, namely the Eunomians, the Arians, the Macedonians, the Pneumatomachi, the Manichaeans, the Encratites, the Apotactites, the Saccophori and the Hydroparastatae shall not show any walls of private houses after the likeness of churches, and shall practice nothing publicly or privately which may be detrimental to the Catholic sanctity. (*CTh*. 16.5.11)[17]

Indeed, there is scarcely a heresy that the late fourth-century edicts and councils do not damn with allegations of private worship. The format of the edicts varies little from the example cited in full above, including the name of the heresy or heresies, their condemnation for false belief, the prohibition of domestic assemblies, and a warning to would-be sympathizers of the consequences of using their homes for such purposes.

It is important to note that the above-listed examples, plus the dozens more that might be cited, make up the vast majority of all fourth- and early fifth-century textual evidence on private cult. That is to say, when private worship appears in the textual record, it most often appears in the company of heretical discussions. What are we to make of this phenomenon and how are we to interpret these dozens of descriptions of "secret gatherings" and "houses in the likeness of churches"? As Maier describes in this volume, the domestic sphere was clearly favored by schismatic or persecuted groups as spaces to air new ideas, harangue potential members, and gather for meetings and worship.[18] And yet, in the sameness of the allegations, the doggedly repetitious language of the Theodosian Code, and the constancy of language employed by early Christian bishops, we may perceive indications of even deeper stirrings. Twenty years ago Alain Le Boulluec persuaded us not only that heresies were carefully constructed by knowing heresiologists, but that categories of heresy and orthodoxy were yin and yang, the negative image of "other" created to derive a correspondingly positive image of self. That constructive process required building blocks, relatively simple concepts whose moral implications were readily understood and shared by all. Modern historians of religion have become adept at identifying these heresiological building blocks, such as gender and magic, and disentangling them from the polemical structures in which they were so successfully placed.[19] It may be that the allegations of private cult lies are precisely this type of powerful and flexible trope.

That this evidence should be viewed as polemical, as well as or in addition to reflective of actual circumstance, is suggested from the character of the evidence itself. We have already mentioned the repetitive, list-like quality of so many of the Theodosian Code edicts that included prohibitions of private cult. We have the sense that we are far from the world of observed reality and that we are caught between legalistic thoroughness, manifested through the careful removal of all worship venues and a ponderous enumeration of heresies, and stock formulas of heretical behavior. The same may also be said of the flip side, the oft-repeated insistence that one's home rituals were simply a return to an apostolic purity. The use of the obvious biblical precedent only emphasizes the polemical nature of both accusation and defense, and tells us little about real houses used as sites of doctrinal resistance. Even more persuasive is the very antiquity of the trope itself. It would seem that as soon as the exodus from the *domus ecclesiae* (house church) to the basilica was initiated after the Peace of the Church, the increasingly deserted concept of "the private" was taken over by heresiologists and refitted as a "den," "a lair," "a nefarious retreat." Already in the 320s Alexander of Alexandria included among his list of Arian sins private cult meetings (*Ep. Alex.* 1.1). The concept can be pushed back further still, for Alexander's "secret meetings" were a later, Christian echo of centuries of pagan accusations. Minucius Felix's record of pagan opinion included jeers about private Christian worship: "a people skulking and shunning the light, silent in public, but garrulous in corners.... Why do they never speak openly, never congregate freely, unless for the reason that what they adore and conceal is either worthy of punishment, or something to be ashamed of...?" (Minucius Felix, *Octavius* 8, 10).

Thus, the topos or theme of the private generally and of private worship specifically as the inverse of corporate consent had a long and weighty pedigree. Most importantly, its longtime presence in the debate over correctness of belief and deed had permitted it to evolve from fact into symbol. Like the emblem of the uppity woman or the sorcerer, the topos of domestic worship had a shopworn place among both the heresiologist's and the downtrodden's polemical tools of trade. The tired, repetitive quality of the Theodosian Code edicts now becomes understandable. The abrupt prohibition of private services by the councils of Gangra likewise becomes clear. In addition to their vivid descriptions of the home as an alternative venue of community identity or resistance, these prohibitions describe the struggle to redefine the private and the domestic in a world in which the very definitions of community were being redrawn.

CONCLUSIONS

This use of the private as shorthand for heretical practice reveals the yawning gap between institutional church communities and other kinds of communities that opened up after the Peace of the Church. The rich variety of extra-church rituals, and the growth of private churches to serve family and dependents, presented the institutional church with a fundamental challenge, in which nothing less than the future form of Christian experience was at stake. Around what community model would a burgeoning Christian population live their Christian lives? Would it be a constellation of private homes, each a "holy household" whose members' pious daily lives were the touchstone of Christian identity?[20] Or would it be a civic principate, a Christian citizen body, hierarchically organized and led from the top by a bishop? To what degree might these models be made to overlap, and in what ways did they resist collusion? The family and the aristocratic friendship network, the bedroom and the estate chapel all lay in the tectonic zone where different ways of organizing Christian experience collided. The centrality of such private worship in the construction of heretical identities was symptomatic of growing pains of the new church and its bishops and the concomitant urgency to find the correct place, at least conceptually, for the private in a newly public world.

FOR FURTHER READING

Brenk, Beat. *Die Christianisierung der spätrömischen Welt: Stadt, Land, Haus und Kloster in frühchristlicher Zeit.* Weisbaden: Reichert, 2003.

Percival, John. "Villas and Monasteries in Late Roman Gaul." *Journal of Ecclesiastical History* 48/1 (1987): 1–21.

Pietri, Charles. "Chiesa e communitá locali nell' occidente cristiano (IV–VI d.c.): L'esempio della Gallia." In *Societá Romana e Imperio Tardoantico, 3: Le merci gli insediamenti,* 761–95. Rome: Laterza, 1986.

Thomas, John Philip. *Private Religious Foundations in the Byzantine Empire.* Dumbarton Oaks Studies 24. Washington, D.C.: Dumbarton Oaks Research Library and Collection, 1987.

Violante, Cinzio. "Le strutture organizzative della cura d'anime nelle campagne dell'Italia centrosettentrionale." In *Cristianizzazione ed organizzazione ecclesiastica delle campagne nell'alto medioevo: espansione e resistenze,* vol. 2, 963–1158. Spoleto: Il Centro, 1980.

IDENTITY AT
THE BOUNDARIES

Part 3

Late Ancient Christianity

HERESY, HOUSEHOLDS, AND THE DISCIPLINING OF DIVERSITY

HARRY O. MAIER

Church historians have often touted antiquity as the seminal epoch of Christian doctrinal formulation and development. Theological controversies, councils, and creeds take center stage in descriptions of the complex constellation of ideas, social forces, and historical contingencies that conspired to transform a diverse Christianity of humble origins into the powerful, unified religion eventually endorsed and promoted by the Roman Empire. Indeed, many accounts of the Roman period may leave the misleading impression that early Christianity was a movement of armchair theologians, far removed from the practicalities of daily life, strictly devoted to the pure formulation of orthodox Christian teaching. The reader first stumbling upon this scholarship and the ancient writings and figures it rests upon may be forgiven if she comes away thinking that early Christians—exemplified by the figures of male bishops—spent the majority of their days either secluded in their studies or journeying from city to city, reeling from one council to the next to debate points of philosophically dizzying doctrine, offering here their imprimatur, there their anathema over ideas as exotically named as the people thinking them: Valentinians, Montanists, Arians, Eunomians, Origenists, Nestorians, and their like. To imagine early Christianity not as the movement of a theological elite confidently combating heresy but instead as a complex network of diverse communities representing competing perspectives is to return the period's creeds, councils, and controversies to the flesh and blood of daily life—to return history to the people.

Or at least it will return history to some of them: famously, history is written by the winners. This chapter, however, seeks a people's history of the infamous, the losers—those condemned (sometimes repeatedly) as heretics in the official pronouncements of church and empire. Our interest here does not lie primarily in the ideas and teachings that the dominant tradition came to label heretical. It lies rather in exploring how orthodoxy and heresy took place quite concretely in early Christianity, as we turn our attention to the spaces and gathering places of early Christians and the ways in which place—in particular, the physical and social space of the private household—contributed to the self-definition of ancient Christians confronted with the challenge of their own differences and diversity. Attention to *place* invites us to imagine spaces filled with people whose competing moral and religious values and practices arise out of the complex social negotiations typical of the culturally pluralistic cities and towns of late antiquity. It helps us to pin down and also to put flesh and blood on those peripatetic theologian-bishops, as well as their disparaged rivals, by locating them spatially as well as culturally amid the complex historical forces that shaped the communities of early Christianity and eventually relegated heresy to the margins of the church. What we may call a "topography of heresy" was formed by groups meeting privately, often clandestinely, in household conventicles.

In order more fully to understand the role of households in the survival and promotion of officially rejected expressions of Christian faith, and thus their place in a topography of heresy, it is necessary briefly to sketch the household patterns of gathering in the pre-Constantinian period, especially as these relate to struggles by leaders to control the teachings and assemblies of Christians. This will allow us subsequently to see more clearly the role of household gatherings in the life of groups meeting in the post-Constantinian era. Alongside an increasingly monumental Christianity endorsed by Christian emperors and the bishops they promoted existed a heterodox Christianity that continued an ancient pattern of household assembly. Households furnished suppressed movements with a means of survival, recruitment, and even self-definition.

EARLY CHRISTIAN DIVERSITY

Christianity was from the start a household movement. The New Testament Gospel representations of Jesus circulating in and among households, eating with his followers and offering his teachings in the homes of various hosts, attest to the importance of the domestic setting of early Christian faith. Early Christian memory located Jesus in household settings to help believers elucidate and interpret their own household patterns of assembly and the rituals and teachings that went along with them. Turning to the period immediately following Jesus' death, the canonical book of Acts similarly depicts the earliest Christians meeting in households to break bread together (Acts 2:44-47). The household setting was also crucial to the spread of the new faith. Luke, the author of Acts, situates the apostles' missionary enterprise in social networks that embraced the hierarchical order of the traditional Greco-Roman and Jewish household. His account of Paul's baptism of Lydia "with her household" offers a good example of an early Christian teacher winning the patronage of a convert—in this case, a well-to-do merchant of luxury purple goods—who readily makes her home available for religious gatherings (Acts 16:14-15, 40). But it is not only hospitality that a well-placed convert like Lydia provides; we may also imagine Paul gaining access to the typical network of social relationships associated with the household of someone of her socioeconomic location—namely, her slaves, freedpersons, and clients. Winning an adherent of Lydia's social stature meant gaining entry to a range of hierarchically ordered social relationships constellated around the patron's household and thus securing a hearing from a potentially wide audience. When New Testament authors send greetings, such as the salutation to Nympha "and the church in her house" (Col. 4:15), to Prisca and Aquila and "the church in their house" (Rom. 16:5), or from "Gaius, host to me and the whole church" (Rom. 16:8), it is this hierarchically ordered social world of the household that we are to imagine.

Luke offers us a view of early Christianity from the top down, as it were—a movement situated among the relatively well-placed, expanding along a divinely appointed way, through the roads, trade routes, and household networks of the Roman Empire. Pagan detractors and satirists viewed the same phenomenon from the bottom up and discovered a less salubrious path. Celsus, a second-century opponent of Christianity, depicts early Christians as "workers in wool and leather, and fullers, and persons of the most uninstructed and rustic characters"—in other words, the urban poor—who circulate "in private houses" of more well-to-do pagans, quietly recruiting new adherents from their masters' family members, slaves, and clients and inviting them to their shops and apartment rooms for further instruction in the faith (Origen, *Celsus* 3.55). For Celsus, these apartment meetings—taking place in the flats of tenement buildings or *insulae,* where the vast majority of ancient urban populations lived—promote a socially corrosive religion that undermines the good order of families and cities. This fascinating snapshot of early Christian evangelism by the rank and file presumes as its backdrop the complex spatiality and intersecting sociality of the Greco-Roman household. Celsus has us imagine a Christianity of the *Lumpenproletariat* (degraded members of the masses) traded along with goods in the workshops and slaves' quarters that typically comprised the forecourt of the well-to-do household. As this Christianity moved from the master's forecourt—and hence from the ordered discipline of ancient domestic culture—to the grotty apartment workshops of the urban poor, it and its adherents removed themselves ever further away from the time-honored and civilization-preserving religion of the master's hearth and the status and respectability associated with it, unleashing upon the world reckless innovation in ethics and teaching.

An antisocial Christianity concocted behind closed doors becomes the object of a polemical imagination in the attack of another second-century pagan critic, Marcus Cornelius Fronto.

> Is it not scandalous that the gods should be mobbed by a gang of outlawed and reckless desperadoes? They have collected from the lowest possible dregs of society the more ignorant fools together with gullible women (readily persuaded, as the weaker sex); they have thus formed a rabble of blasphemous conspirators, who with nocturnal assemblies, periodic fasts, and inhuman feasts seal their pact not with some religious ritual but with desecrating profanation; they are a crowd that furtively lurks in hiding places, shunning the light; they are speechless in pubic but gabble away in corners.

Fronto goes on to imagine the worst when he describes how these Christians "gather for a feast with all their children, sisters, mothers—all sexes and all ages" and "flushed with the banquet after such feasting... begin to burn with incestuous passions" and engage in orgies (Minucius Felix, *Octavius* 8–9).[1] He reveals his social class in these charges. It is a snob's critique that pillories Christianity as an upstart religion of the masses drawing women away from their traditional place at the hearth; mixing genders, ages, and social classes; undermining traditional religion; and destroying the ideals of manly virtue, social stratification, and self-governance on which social order is based. Here the basic building block of Christian assembly—domestic hospitality—is turned into the object of pagan scorn as an occasion for the rabble and women to practice a religion that erodes the very foundations of society.

The domestic free-trade zone of religious ideas created by Christian hospitality likewise becomes the brunt of pagan scorn in the second-century writings of Lucian. He pillories early Christians and their house church assemblies in a satirical portrait of a self-proclaimed prophet ironically named Peregrinus ("Stranger"), who capitalizes on early Christian domestic gatherings. Peregrinus, studiously cultivating a disheveled ascetic appearance, invades Christian assemblies and milks naive believers of financial and material resources while promoting his dubious ideas. Lucian's critique finds some resonance in the roughly contemporary Christian writing known as the *Didache*. The author warns its audience to stay on the lookout for false prophets and apostles who overstay their welcome and take advantage of the material resources of their hosts: "Let every apostle who comes to you be received as the Lord, but let him not stay more than one day...; if he stay three days, he is a false prophet.... If he ask for money, he is a false prophet" (11.5, 6). These references arise out of an ancient Christianity at home in ancient Greco-Roman and Jewish households, where teachings and teachers circulate and are received (or, in some cases, rejected).

Such patterns of hospitality and the social associations arising as a consequence of them gave rise to ancient Christian communities as diverse as they were impossible to regulate. "Whosoever then comes and teaches you all these things I have written," concludes the Didachist at the end of his instruction to his community, outlining rules for extending hospitality, "receive him. But if the teacher himself be perverted and teach another doctrine to destroy these things, do not listen to him" (11.1). The offering and withholding of hospitality and the willingness to associate with one another in household assembly was the ancient Christian means of promoting and screening teachers and their teachings. Paul's letters are filled with descriptions attesting to the importance of hospitality and household assembly in the regulation of Christian ideas. His complaint of schismatic Corinthians, for example, who boast of belonging to Paul, Apollos, or Cephas is best accounted for by reference to competing house churches tracing their pedigree back to apostolic missionaries (1 Cor. 1:12), each one of which preserves its founder's preaching. Later, Paul anathematizes competing "super apostles" (2 Cor. 12:11), Jewish missionaries he claims have invaded the city he has staked out as his own apostolic territory. He charges them with capitalizing on whatever successes his preaching has won in establishing house churches, by seeking the hospitality of house-church hosts and questioning Paul's authority in his absence (2 Cor. 10:13-18). In language anticipating themes that will recur regularly in subsequent decades and centuries, Paul attempts to delimit the activities of competitors through invective: "such boasters are false apostles, deceitful workers, disguising themselves as apostles of Christ" (2 Cor. 11:13).

A later inheritor of Paul's theology, probably writing early in the second century, faces similar diversity in house churches, complaining of competing teachers who "are upsetting whole families by teaching for sordid gain what it is not right to teach" (Titus 1:11). More particularly, they "make their way into households and captivate silly women, overwhelmed by their sins and swayed by all kinds of desires, who are always being instructed and can never arrive at a knowledge of truth" (2 Tim. 3:6-7). They undermine conduct befitting "the household of God" (1 Tim. 3:15) by forbidding marriage (4:3). Women coming under their sway are observed "gadding about from house to house . . . saying what they should not say" (1 Tim. 5:13). Upon the heads of these home-invaders the author heaps scorn: they are "factious" *(hairetikoi)* (Titus 3:10), "liars" *(pseudologoi)* (1 Tim. 4:1); they seek "to teach different doctrine" *(heterodidaskalein)* (1 Tim. 1:3).

This writer turns the female members of his community into the dupes of false male teachers. But a closer reading of the ancient evidence indicates a far less passive role on the part of early Christian women in the promotion and spread of Christian teaching in domestic networks and beyond. Intriguingly, a body of extracanonical evidence survives from the period when these letters were probably written—the first half of the second century—that narrates stories about well-to-do young women, either married or betrothed in marriage, who, upon welcoming into their homes apostolic teachers urging sexual abstinence from marriage, break off their marriages or engagements, thereby throwing their husbands or fiancés and families into turmoil. Some have argued that this literature circulated in networks of women seeking freedom from social and cultural values that prescribed gender-specific roles and norms.[2] Our interest here is in the role of Christian hospitality in the promotion and extension of diverse teachings. The *Acts of Paul and Thecla* intersects remarkably with what is described in 1 and 2 Timothy and Titus, associating Paul with the same people named in canonical letters, who enjoyed hospitality from the same host, Onesiphorus (2 Tim. 1:16). But unlike the New Testament account of an apostle Paul polemically exhorting his audience—especially women—to refuse to offer hospitality to those who come teaching a gospel of sexual abstinence and to place themselves firmly under the leadership of married male house-church hosts (1 Tim. 3:1-13; Titus 1:5-6; 2:1-10), the extracanonical Paul champions freedom from marriage and sexual abstinence.

The extracanonical tradition thus positions Paul in the role the canonical letters condemn: the apostle goes into homes and preaches his message of continence, resulting in no small consternation among those who—like Thecla's fiancé, Thamyrus—reject his ascetic gospel. Placing the canonical letters alongside the extracanonical *Acts,* it is at least possible, as Dennis MacDonald has argued, to discern in the latter an account of history's "losing side," subsequently marginalized by the canonical polemic against those who promote "the godless chatter and contradictions of what is falsely called knowledge [*gnosis*]" (1 Tim. 6:20).[3] If this is the case, then we glimpse profiles of competing house-church assemblies, each invoking the authority of Paul for their practices and teachings.

Absent from the extracanonical *Acts* is the invective of the canonical letters. Such polemical rhetoric can be accounted for socially as the attempt to tighten control of reception of teachers and to urge upon households the teachings the letter outlines, placing both under the strict control of (married!) bishops, elders, and deacons. The shrill tone of these letters' denunciations is evidence of their author's impossible cause: in a poignant moment in the *Acts of Paul and Thecla,* Theocleia, Thecla's mother, tells the about-to-be-jilted Thamyrus that her daughter has been listening to

Paul night and day, neither eating nor drinking, transfixed by his gospel of abstinence. There is little Theocleia can do but stand helplessly by as she watches her daughter sit by the window, listening to the words of Paul, who is hosted by his patron, Onesiphorous, along with others gathering in his house church who are similarly won over to the apostle's exhortations to sexual renunciation. Finally, Thamyrus reaches for weapons more powerful than words in opposing Paul and his supporters: he reports Onesiphorous's house-church gathering to the authorities, who promptly shut it down and throw the apostle in jail.

The willingness of Christians to extend hospitality to one another could result in complex permutations of belief and practice and the production of ambiguity discomfiting to bishops seeking firm boundaries that divide true believers from heretics. An early second-century bishop, Ignatius of Antioch, en route to martyrdom in Rome, was faced with a distressing variety of religious meetings. In a series of letters composed to churches of western Asia Minor that he visits on his journey, he complains of traveling teachers who use hospitality to promote teachings about Jesus that question his physical suffering and death (*Ephesians* 9.1; *Trallians* 9.1—10.1). In response, Ignatius urges the bishops, who are probably also house-church hosts, to "let the meetings be more numerous" (*Polycarp* 4.2; *Ephesians* 13.1)—a ploy designed to drown out the opposition. In a further attempt to limit the diversity of meetings, he instructs the churches that the only eucharists and *agape* meals to be considered valid are those celebrated or endorsed by the bishop; the church is only to gather where he does (*Smyrnaeans* 8.2; *Magnesians* 4.1; *Ephesians* 5.3). Ignatius's letters hint that the Christians of Asia Minor were less stringent than he in distinguishing differing christological teachings and in withholding their hospitality. He accuses some of hypocrisy in apparently showing obedience to the bishop while at the same time deceiving him (*Magnesians* 3.2—4.1; *Philadelphians* 7.1–2)—very possibly by attending a common house-church assembly as well as either welcoming allegedly false teachers or organizing meetings around them.

Irenaeus, late second-century bishop of Lyons, echoes many of Ignatius's concerns. He complains of believers who attend the assemblies conducted by him and his fellow leaders but also welcome teachers whom he deems heretics into their homes for other assemblies. One of them, the gnostic teacher Marcus, circulates in the homes of the community's more well-to-do women (again, we find the recurring theme of female patronage), where he conducts worship (*Her.* 1.13.3). To Irenaeus's outrage, even one of his own deacons and his wife have welcomed Marcus into their home to teach and worship (1.13.5). By such extensions of hospitality, Irenaeus pronounces, these members show themselves to be "neither inside nor outside the church." Such judgments might equally indicate, however, that, while bishops may have wanted to draw hard-and-fast distinctions, the people under their charge had more relaxed standards of faith and practice and opened their doors to a variety of teachers. In a slightly later period, a wealthy Christian woman was host to both the Alexandrian theologian Origen and a gnostic teacher named Paul of Antioch, who, the ancient church historian Eusebius reports, was visited by "a great multitude...not only of heretics but also our people" (*Ecclesiastical History* 6.2.13–14). For some bishops such openness was intolerable. (Eusebius is careful to note that while some of "our people" prayed with Paul, Origen kept himself separate.) Irenaeus does not hide his impatience when he observes that "the more simple" people question their bishop's wisdom in urging them to refuse hospitality to gnostic teachers. How is it, they are prompted from their associations with Gnostic teachers to ask, "when they [the gnostics] say the same things as us, and hold the same doctrine, that we call them heretics and that we, without cause, are to keep ourselves aloof from their company?" (3.15.2). As in Ignatius's Asia Minor, so in Irenaeus's Lyons the house churches made possible a spectrum of religious teachings and rituals that offered a daunting challenge for any bishop who would limit and control them. Irenaeus, like Ignatius, attempted to regulate Christian communities by cementing them more firmly to their bishops.

The North African antiheretical writer Tertullian, writing slightly later than Irenaeus, preserves in his polemic references to early believers very much opposed to these kinds of restrictions and regulations. In his *Prescription of the Heretics* he vilifies "the heretics' way of life" by railing against their lack of discipline with respect to communal governance. His case against heretical belief offers a cross section of practices that some early Christian leaders—such as Ignatius and Irenaeus—found unacceptable, giving us a hint of the kinds of diversity bishops sought to bring under their control.

> I must not leave out a description of the heretics' way of life—futility, earthly, all too human, lacking in gravity, in authority, in discipline, as suits their faith. To begin with, one cannot tell who is a catechumen and who is baptized. They come together, listen together, pray together. Even if any of the heathen arrive, they are quite willing to cast that which is holy to the dogs and their pearls (false ones!) before swine. The destruction of discipline is to them simplicity, and our attention to it they call affectation. They are in communion with everyone everywhere. Differences of theology are of no concern to them as long as they are agreed in attacking the truth. They are all puffed up, they all promise knowledge. As for the women of the heretics, how forward they are! They have the impudence to teach, to argue, to perform exorcisms, to promise cures, perhaps even to baptize. Their ordinations are hasty, irresponsible, and unstable. Sometimes they appoint novices, sometimes people tied to secular office, sometimes renegades from us, hoping to bind them by ambition as they cannot bind them by truth. Nowhere can you get quicker promotion than in the camp of the rebels, where your mere presence is a merit. So one man is bishop today, another tomorrow. The deacon of today is tomorrow's reader, the priest of today is tomorrow's layman. For they impose priestly function even upon laymen.
>
> —Tertullian, *Prescription against Heretics* 41[4]

A writing of roughly the same period offers a depiction of proper Christian assembly that contrasts strikingly with the assemblies described in Tertullian's polemical work. Tertullian portrays early heterodox Christianity in a kind of domestic free fall where social order is thrown out the window. *The Apostolic Tradition,* a liturgical writing associated with the third-century bishop of Rome Hippolytus, in turn offers directions for Christian worship and assembly expressly designed to ward off this kind of democratic chaos. He is careful to prescribe strict rules for the conduct of household eucharistic gatherings made possible by the hospitality of Christian patrons. Whereas in Tertullian's heretical assemblies, anything goes, Hippolytus keeps a tight rein on domestic religion. Witnessing to the ancient pattern of Christian assembly, patrons continue to invite guests to their homes for worship, but it falls to the bishop alone, or, if he is absent, to a presbyter or deacon, to bless the gifts and distribute them. "If only lay-people meet, let them not act presumptuously, for a layperson cannot bless the blessed bread" (*Ap. Trad.* 26.12). Those who gather for meals are to "eat silently, not arguing, giving their attention to such things as the bishop may teach" (26.10). "And even if the bishop should be absent when the faithful meet for supper, if a presbyter or a deacon is present they shall eat in a similar orderly fashion, and each shall be careful to take the blessed bread from the presbyter's or deacon's hand" (26.11). Hippolytus's liturgical rubrics are a means of ordering tendencies toward diversity arising naturally from early Christian domestic religion and hospitality.

FROM DIVERSITY TO HERESY

As Christianity moved in the fourth century from the margins to the position of a tolerated religion endorsed by the emperor Constantine (who reigned 312–37 CE) and then became the empire's official and solely sanctioned cult under Theodosius (379–95 CE), attempts to regulate religious diversity took on a new form in laws limiting household Christian assembly. Where once bishops struggled to limit assemblies, now emperors stepped in and published laws forbidding the meetings of heretics. Legislation banning heresy outlawed those Christian groups considered deviant and threatened their patrons with corporal punishment, fines, and—most notably for our purposes—confiscation of property. Dozens of decrees condemning household gatherings of heretics were published over the course of a century and a half, as emperors and bishops sought to define catholic Christian faith and to limit the activities of those who fell outside its pale.[5] The more or less formulaic nature of these laws proscribing long lists of heretical movements, repeatedly banned—sometimes within a relatively

Fig. 9.1. Emperor Theodosius I is credited with making Christianity the state religion of the Roman Empire as well as sponsoring antiheretical legislation. Theodosius sits enthroned in a portrait on a votive platter from Thessalonika, made in 388 CE to commemorate the tenth anniversary of the accession of the emperor. Academia de la Historia, Madrid, Spain. Photo credit: Werner Forman / Art Resource, NY.

short time span—leads one to wonder to what extent this legislation was actually enforced and thus also to question its function. These laws point to the relative ineffectiveness of cumbersome imperial bureaucracies in executing the legislative will of emperors; as one historian succinctly puts it, "emperors had to shout to be heard—and were still ignored."[6] Antiheretical legislation, nevertheless, had an important propagandistic function in erecting and preserving the conceit of a Christian empire and the status of its governing household as guardians of a divinely appointed religio-political order.

An early and representative example of this legislation comes to us from the emperor Constantine sometime in the 320s, during a period when the imperial regime was seeking to unite its empire under the banner of universal creedal affirmation (see sidebar). Here the emperor forbids heretics from meeting publicly and outlaws meetings in private households, threatening their patrons with confiscation of property.

In rhetorically charged language, the decree studiously avoids using the word "church" to describe the outlawed assemblies, assigning them instead the label "superstition"—a technical term used from the early days of the Roman Empire onward to describe any illegitimate, socially corrosive religion. By contrast, it celebrates "the catholic Church" as the edifice upon which is built a prosperous imperial peace, where one finds housed the guaranteed truth of salvation. The several laws published by Constantine and his successors seeking to curtail household meetings of heretics attest to the wide variety of early Christian communities worshipping in private spaces alongside or outside the boundaries of officially endorsed imperial Christianity.

A close reading of these laws and the literary sources and archaeological evidence associated with them reveals the outline of a heterodox landscape—a topography that has its origins in the domestic patterns of meeting and organization of earliest Christianity already discussed. The topography of heresy this evidence points toward allows us to imagine that the ancient worshipper wishing to go to church on Sunday morning was sometimes met with a variety of options that officials sought aggressively to limit. For example, Cyril, the bishop of Jerusalem (died 386 CE), instructs those preparing for baptism that when arriving in a city they should not ask where "the house of the Lord is" but rather where they might find "the catholic church," thereby warning them of the diversity of meetings available to them while also strictly circumscribing those gatherings that could rightly be named "church" (*Catechetical Orations* 18.26). We can infer, however, that those who gathered in their "houses of the Lord" were able safely to promote their own characteristic teachings and practices even in an imperial environment hostile to nonsanctioned Christian movements. For some, the necessity of gathering in domestic meeting places, outside the walls of officially approved spaces, became an important source of self-definition and, as we shall see, an incentive for pillorying officially endorsed champions of saving Christian faith.

The fourth- and fifth-century mapping of heresy emerged alongside and as a consequence of the creation of a sacred topography oriented around holy sites and public worship spaces that was the hallmark of a new Christian empire. Such an orthodox landscape was legitimated by the kind of imperial legislation cited above and regulated by officially endorsed bishops. The elaboration and sacralization of a network of Christian places and spaces associated with the saints and martyrs of the pre-Constantinian period redefined the pagan city of late antiquity. It guaranteed a permanent monumental character for catholic Christianity, one that had already been developing in the pre-Constantinian period, when—as in the decree from Constantine cited above—Christians increasingly associated the term *ecclesia* ("church") with both physical meeting places and a sanctified geography. An official, public, imperially recognized network of holy places was, beginning in the fourth century, consciously constructed as an orthodox topography. Emperors, bishops, and Christian aristocrats alike ambitiously promoted their own positions as well as the cause of the new Christian empire

Forasmuch, then, as it is no longer possible to bear with your pernicious errors, we give warning by this present statute that none of you henceforth presume to assemble yourselves together. We have directed, accordingly, that you be deprived of all the houses in which you are accustomed to hold your assemblies: and our care in this respect extends so far as to forbid the holding of your superstitious and senseless meetings, not in public merely, but in any private house or place whatsoever. Let those of you, therefore, who are desirous of embracing the true and pure religion, take the far better course of entering the catholic Church, and uniting with it in holy fellowship, whereby you will be enabled to arrive at the knowledge of the truth. In any case, the delusions of your perverted understandings must entirely cease to mingle with and mar the felicity of our present times: I mean the impious and wretched double-mindedness of heretics and schismatics. For it is an object worthy of that prosperity which we enjoy through the favor of God, to endeavor to bring back those who in time past were living in the hope of future blessing, from all irregularity and error to the right path, from darkness to light, from vanity to truth, from death to salvation. And in order that this remedy may be applied with effectual power, we have commanded, as before said, that you be positively deprived of every gathering point for your superstitious meetings, I mean all the houses of prayer, if such be worthy of the name, which belong to heretics, and that these be made over without delay to the catholic Church; that any other places be confiscated to the public service, and no facility whatever be left for any future gathering; in order that from this day forward none of your unlawful assemblies may presume to appear in any public or private place. Let this edict be made public.

—Eusebius, *Life of Constantine* 3.65

by furnishing ancient and newly founded cities with basilicas and other monuments honoring both the heroes of a sacred Christian past and the places associated with them. An enterprisingly monumental Christianity transformed ancient civic culture by offering elites, who included not only the traditional aristocracy but also bishops and others rising through the ranks of an emergent Christian establishment, new opportunities for benefaction and the winning of social status in the honorific culture of late antiquity.[7]

Nevertheless, alongside this new monumental Christianity, an older and more private Christian religion survived. As late as 410 CE, at the Syrian Council of Ctesiphon, for example, in an area bordering the Roman Empire, where imperial Christian control of territory came relatively late, the assembly attempted to regulate ecclesiastical diversity by declaring that in each town only one eucharistic sacrifice was to be offered and that the practice of celebrating several eucharists in various local private households was to be stopped.[8] If the Christian city of late antiquity represents an end to one socially diversified version of a once persecuted ancient Christianity, the continuing gatherings of proscribed groups in households is testimony to enduring patterns of variegated social assembly.

Archaeological evidence for Christian use and adaptation of private space for communal purposes from the third century until well beyond the Constantinian period is suggestive for imagining the heterodox topography of the fourth and fifth centuries. Well into the fifth century, Christian groups—alongside other religions and social movements of the period, including Jews, mystery religions, philosophical movements, and associations—continued to use or adapt private dwellings and estates as worship spaces and assembly places. The third-century house church unearthed virtually intact from the Syrian Roman outpost of Dura-Europos offers vivid archaeological testimony to an early Christian custom of converting private dwellings into churches and furnishing them for religious purposes. In this case, the household was entirely devoted to religious purposes: the dining room was enlarged to facilitate assembly and liturgical functions; another room was transformed into a baptistery; the walls were painted with Christian frescoes. The Dura-Europos house church represents a hybrid case of a household adapted and dedicated to cultic use (figs. 9.2 and 9.3). Elsewhere there is evidence of patrons renovating portions of their homes for Christian assembly. At Lullingstone, England, a wealthy fourth-century Christian benefactor welcomed worshippers onto a large estate where an entire wing of a villa was refurbished for religious assembly (fig. 8.4). Adaptation of such space for heretical purposes is attested to in both ancient Christian writings and imperial legislation. Augustine describes the spread of fourth-century Donatism from North Africa to Spain through the promotion of one of its patrons, Lucilla, who welcomed local Donatists to meet on her estate.[9]

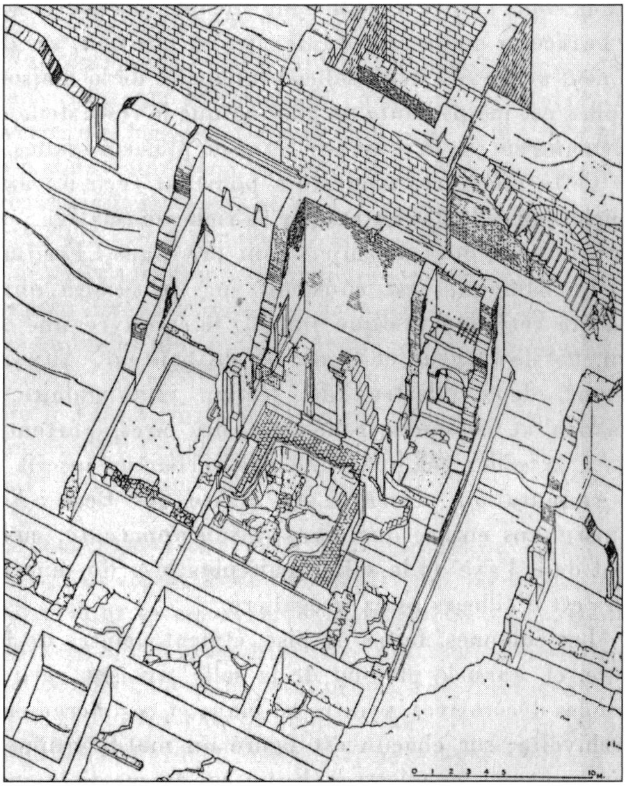

It is precisely this kind of renovation of households and villas into churches that ancient Christian anti-heretical legislation forbids when it prohibits a variety of heretical groups from gathering and furnishing "any walls of private houses after the likeness of churches" as well as doing anything "publicly or privately which may be detrimental to Catholic sanctity" (*CTh.* 16.5.11 [383 CE]). It also outlaws establishing churches "either by public or private undertakings, within the localities of cities and of the fields and of the villas" and threatens the owners who permit or promote such meetings on their estates with confiscation of their property

Fig. 9.2. Prior to the fourth century, Christians met in homes, such as the third-century house discovered at Dura-Europos, a Roman frontier town on the Euphrates, the only distinctly Christian feature of which is the small room equipped as a baptistery. In the post-Constantinian era, private residences like this one continued to provide meeting space for those Christians deemed "heretical."

(for example, *CTh.* 16.5.12 [383 CE]; 16.5.58.5 [415 CE]). These examples of the adaptation of private space for public worship, together with the attempts of officials to control it, are representative of tensions and struggles to control the diversity of meetings and teachings that attended the growth and development of early Christianity.

As official Christianity became increasingly associated with its public monuments and gathering places, some gained from household gatherings a source of communal self-definition and even resistance to an imperially sanctioned and episcopally regulated Christendom. A good example of this is preserved from the late fourth-century episcopate of the Roman bishop Damasus, an ambitious patron who nearly single-handedly transformed Rome into a Christian monument through an aggressive program of church construction, including the furnishing of holy sites such as *martyria* with inscriptions and buildings. A fledgling circle of Christians, critical of Damasus's luxurious expressions of Christianity, expressed their protest by gathering in households. One of their leaders, Faustinus, complaining of Damasus's attempts to suppress these meetings, contrasts the ostentation of the bishop's basilicas with the simplicity of his own people's house church:

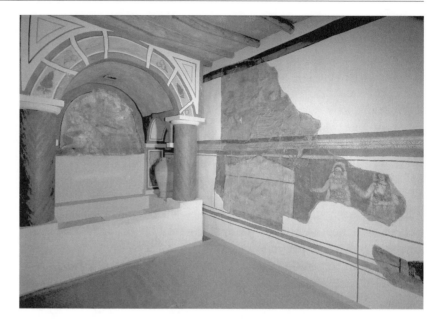

> Let them have their basilicas glittering with gold and ornamented with the osten-tation of expensive marble, held up by the splendour of columns; let them also have extensive property, from which one runs the risk of losing the true faith.... As for us, the true salt, it is enough piously to worship and adore Christ our God in the meanest and most abject of hovels—the kind of place where once Christ... found good enough to sleep as a baby. (*Libellus precum* 34.121 [*CCSL* 69.390])

Household space here embodies a theological identity of protest: on Fausti-nus's account, the very monumentality of Catholic orthodoxy counts against its being representative of theological truth. Damasus responded by seizing the house church and arresting its leaders.

Another example of domestic space contributing to communal self-definition comes from late fourth- or early fifth-century northern Italy, where an underground apocalyptic Arian movement survived in house-holds. A series of sermons on the Gospel of Matthew have been preserved, preached by itinerant Arian leaders to comfort and instruct circles of house churches forbidden by anti-Arian heretical legislation from gathering pub-licly. The Arian leaders likened themselves to the disciples described by Matthew 10, suffering persecution from enemies and instructed by Jesus to travel from household to household relying on the generosity of their hosts. The preacher portrays Arian leaders as seeking reception in the homes of hosts and offering their blessing on those who welcome them. In a fasci-nating turning of the tables on imperially endorsed Christian theology, the homilist takes comfort from the fact of his people's suppression and the necessity of his audience to meet in secret. This is proof positive that the heretical promoters of Nicaea are the representatives of the Antichrist and that the emperor Theodosius is the Beast of Revelation (11:13-18), while persecution and the necessity of meeting secretly in households are the hallmark of true orthodoxy.[10] Here necessity has become the mother of ideological invention; again, space and Christian self-definition are closely linked.

Elsewhere we find leaders exhorting people to boycott officially endorsed gatherings and to signal their rejection of imperially sponsored bishops and their teachings by gathering outside basilicas. Hilary, bishop of Poitiers, writing in the 360s, at a time when the Arians controlled the basilicas and the supporters of Nicaea were out of imperial favor, chides Milanese Christians for their "love of walls" and their venerating "the church of God in shelters and buildings" controlled by the Arian bishop Auxentius. He exhorts them to follow the example of the early Christians who resisted the decrees and edicts of governors and gathered secretly in households.[11] There is evidence that Hilary's exhortations did not entirely fall on deaf ears. In a sermon commemorating the life of Philaster, bishop of Brescia, his successor, Gaudentius, recalls how, during the 360s, Philaster exercised leadership of pro-Nicene Christians as a kind of circuit preacher, traveling about the countryside and meeting with the faithful in villages and villas, even convincing some Arians "by public and private disputation" to embrace Nicene faith.[12] Later, in the fifth century, this time in Constantinople, a local priest, Philip, rejecting the teaching of his bishop, Nestorius, broke off communion with the patriarch and began to celebrate the eucharist in private where he had gathered a church.[13]

Most were not so bold. It is likely that gathering in households furnished those ostracized by imperial legislation from public churches more with a means of survival than with a way to engage in explicit social and theological critique. For example, throughout the checkered history of the Arian controversy, we see bishops who have been deposed from their thrones in periods of imperial disfavor gathering their faithful in house churches, waiting in the wings for a shift in political fortunes and the opportunity to seize the official basilicas, the possession of which would guarantee them legitimacy. Late fourth-century Alexandria and Constantinople offer an instructive series of snapshots of conflicting communities moving with their leaders from households to basilicas and back again as they fall in and out of imperial favor. Charting the rise and fall of Arian fortunes from the 360s, the fifth-century church historian Sozomen on several occasions describes the exclusion of Arians from official basilicas and their retreat to domestic assembly places. In Alexandria in 361, upon Athanasius's regaining control of the city's churches after a period of exile, the Arian community was expelled from the city's basilicas and was forced to gather around its bishop Lucius in private homes (*Eccl. Hist.* 5.7.1). This same Lucius led the opposition against Athanasius in the years that followed, surfacing briefly, upon Athanasius's death, from Arian households to regain control of the city's basilicas (6.19.1–6).

We next meet Lucius in Constantinople, where he migrated after being expelled from Alexandria by a pro-Nicene populace (7.5.6). It is here that he joined forces with the Arian bishop Demophilus. In Constantinople there was also a tradition of meeting in households when met with persecution. In 360 the Arian bishop Macedonius held church in private when supplanted by the Nicene Paul (3.24.4). Later, in 375, when Demophilus controlled the basilicas, a fledgling pro-Nicene community was able to survive and flourish under the leadership of Gregory Nazianzus, who gathered the community in the Anastasis, a relative's private residence converted into an assembly place (7.5.1). The fortunes of Arians and Nicenes were reversed when Demophilus and his flock were forced to leave Constantinople after the accession of the pro-Nicene emperor, Theodosius, in 379 CE. Demophilus, given the option of subscription to Nicene faith or exile, chose the latter, invoking Jesus' words in Matt. 10:23 that a disciple when persecuted in one city is to flee to another. His flight was to the Constantinopolitan suburbs where, judging from the anti-Arian legislation that followed, forbidding the renovation of private houses into churches (*CTh.* 16.5.11 and 12, both published in 383 CE), he gathered his followers in house churches, even as Gregory had before him. In the meantime, even as Demophilus gathered faithful Arians in house churches, another Arian teacher, Eunomius, similarly banished to the suburbs of Constantinople in 381, held "frequent churches in private houses" (7.17.1); the church historian Socrates (*Eccl. Hist.* 5.20) describes Eunomius welcoming disciples into his own home and reading his theological treatises to them. Contemporary legislation commands that he and his followers "be driven from all the hiding places of this City" (*CTh.* 16.5.13). Later Constantinopolitan legislation forbids Eunomian clergy from using private assemblies for baptisms and instruction (*CTh.* 16.5.58 [415 CE]). The complicated careers of these leaders and the histories of the communities they led offer a view onto the complex chessboard of competing Christian orthodoxies in late antiquity and demonstrate how theological fortunes were insolubly linked with space.

Eunomius is a good example of the use of private space not only to promote a distinctive teaching or secure the survival of a persecuted doctrinal party but also to pursue a particular discipline. There are numerous references in the decrees of early Christian synods and councils condemning heretical teachers for retreating with their devotees to private conventicles, where they supplement or innovate accepted ritual and practices.

These references often target ascetical disciplines and as such point to a popular ascetic Christianity of late antiquity existing sometimes alongside and at other times outside the officially endorsed (and housed) faith. The fourth-century Spanish layperson and ascetic Priscillian, for example, was condemned by the Synod of Saragossa for withdrawing with his disciples to mountain retreats to pursue ascetic disciplines and for encouraging women to visit men's homes for Bible reading.[14] Priscillian urged times for periodic retreat and Bible study as disciplines to help Christians lead the lives of rigorous discipleship that he believed Christ demanded. Another synod convened in circa 344 at Gangra in northern Asia Minor condemned militantly ascetic teachers for boycotting official eucharistic assemblies celebrated by married clergy. The canons anathematize these leaders for "teaching that the house of God is to be despised, as well as the services held there" (Can. 5) and for causing people "to forsake public assemblies for divine service, and to organize private conventicles" (Can. 5).[15]

DOMESTIC FRONTIERS

The fourth-century ascetic movement returns us to the fluid sociality of the ancient household already observed in the domestic networks in the pre-Constantinian period. As we saw above with reference to Celsus's complaint of Christians peddling their faith in the households of masters and then exporting it to their own apartment workshops, ancient domestic space was a complex social arena of intersecting public and private domains. There masters of more well-to-do households enjoyed the intimacy of their family members and closest associates and also met with clients, received visitors, commissioned slaves, and conducted daily business. To speak of the household of late antiquity, a world defined by hierarchical relationships and extensive social networks interconnected by complex ritualized activities of patronage and obligation, is to invoke the realm of relationality as well as of social institutions. It was perhaps as a nexus of dynamic relationships that household movements presented the most profound challenge to a sacred, catholic topography increasingly defined by its official monumentality.

This is nowhere more evident than in the diversity associated with ancient Christian asceticism. Repeatedly we see the ascetic's household as a kind of a wild ecclesiastical frontier keeping the careers of outlawed theologians alive and allowing for the survival of diverse Christian practices frowned upon by officials. At the start of the Arian controversy, for example, Alexander, the Nicene bishop of Alexandria, complained that Arius survived in Alexandria through the support of Arian female ascetics, in whose domestic cells he circulated and from which he mounted attacks against the bishop.[16] Nicenes equally cultivated and exploited their own ascetic networks. Athanasius survived one of his many exiles by retreating to a virgin's home during his fourth exile from the episcopate in 361 (Socrates, *Eccl. Hist.* 5.7.1). He himself reports that four years prior to this, the Arian bishop, George, attempted to eliminate Nicene opposition to his episcopate in an attack that included arresting domestic ascetics, plundering "the homes of orphans and widows," and "attacking houses" (Athanasius, *Defense of Flight* 6). George was very probably attempting to neutralize the danger of the pro-Nicene domestic front formed by Athanasius's supporters, especially household monastics. During the same period, Sulpitius Severus recounts in his biography of the ascetic Martin, later bishop of Tours, how Martin conducted a kind of guerrilla warfare against Arians from his hut in Milan, when, during the Golden Age of mid-fourth-century Western Arianism, the city was controlled by an Arian bishop protected by a pro-Arian emperor (*Life of Martin* 6). He was engaged in a form of domestic resistance similar to that of his contemporaries. These are examples of some of the more noticeable flash points of conflict associated with the homes of ascetic Christians.

The households of ascetics and the social networks associated with them created opportunities for diverse practices and teachings extremely difficult for officials to regulate. Diversity was a by-product of an age when small circles of associates, such as the one that pre-Christian Augustine considered forming with his friends (*Conf.* 6.12,14), banded together in domestic cells to form like-minded devotion to philosophical and religious ideals. The fourth-century Roman writer Jerome—who was himself a teacher and client of an aristocratic circle of domestic women ascetics led by his patron, Marcella—rails against these kinds of domestic ascetic experiments. He attacks the ascetic practices of those he named "Remoboth"—small cells of Roman domestic ascetic Christians who gathered to pursue a common life of religious devotion.

> These live together in twos and threes, but seldom in larger numbers, and are bound by no rule; but do exactly as they choose. A portion of their earnings they contribute to a common fund, out of which food is provided for all. In most cases they reside in cities and strongholds; and, as though it were their workmanship which is holy, and not their life, all that they sell is extremely dear. They often quarrel because they are unwilling, while supplying their own food, to be subordinate to others. It is true that they compete with each other in fasting; they make what should be a private concern an occasion for a triumph. In everything they study effect: their sleeves are loose, their boots bulge, their garb is of the coarsest. They are always sighing, or visiting virgins, or sneering at the clergy; yet when a holiday comes, they make themselves sick—they eat so much. (*Ep.* 22.34)

The complaint belongs to a long letter outlining abuses of ascetic practices Jerome seeks to correct. Earlier in the same letter (22.14) he complains of female domestics who live with male ascetics, thus becoming "one-man whores" as they seek a common life of continent devotion. At the same time, John Chrysostom, describing similar practices in the Eastern empire, criticizes male and female ascetics who practice "spiritual marriage" in domestic cells. He complains that these couples seek celebrity by appearing at official eucharistic assemblies only to parade themselves and to show off their perfect control of sexual desire.[17] It is clear that Chrysostom, like Jerome, can do little more to control these domestic practices than to rail against them.

While the lives of domestic ascetics, especially virgins, were celebrated as ideals from the fourth century onward, they were, from the perspective of the official ecclesial establishment, maddeningly uncontrollable. In the case of the Remoboth, for example, the fact that Jerome can only speculate about what goes on behind closed doors illustrates the challenge ascetic experiments represented to a church trying to control the actions and beliefs of the faithful. In another letter (*Ep.* 50), again describing ascetic practices in Rome, Jerome pillories an unnamed opponent for "frequenting no society but that of weak women" (50.1), among whom he finds a sympathetic audience.

> He likes, I am told, to visit the cells of widows and virgins, and to lecture them with his brows knit on sacred literature. What is it that he teaches these poor women in the privacy of their own chambers? ... He is a young man—a monk, and in his own eyes an eloquent one (do not pearls fall from his lips, and are not his elegant phrases sprinkled with comic salt and humor?)—I am surprised, therefore, that he can without a blush frequent noblemen's houses, pay constant visits to married ladies, make our religion a subject of contention, distort the faith of Christ by misapplying words. (50.3)

Jerome wonders, "What is it that he teaches these poor women in the privacy of their own chambers?" That there is no way for him to know points to the unpredictability and uncontrollability of domestic ascetic Christianity in this period. "Let him admit publicly what he says privately. Or, if his private teaching is the same as his public, he should keep aloof from the society of girls."

Jerome liked to imagine the worst. In a treatise against a rival Roman ascetic theologian, he rails against Jovinian, a Roman ascetic who circulated in the homes of well-to-do Roman matrons preaching against Jerome's militant brand of Christian continence and defending marriage and sexual intercourse as sound biblical values. In perhaps some of the most purple prose written by a rhetorician too inclined to let passion get the better of his reason, Jerome rages against Jovinian and his house visits of wealthy Roman women:

> The noble make way for you, the wealthy print kisses on your face. For unless you had come, the drunkard and the glutton could not have entered paradise. All honor to your virtue, or rather to your vices! You have in your camp, even amazons with uncovered breasts, bare arms and knees, who challenge the men who come against them to a battle of lust. Your household is a large one, and so in your aviaries not only turtle-doves, but hoopoes are fed, which may wing their flight over the whole field of rank debauchery. (*Jov.* 2.37)

This description represents a fascinating adaptation of a long rhetorical tradition of invective against suspect religious faith and practice—upstart religion as the secret and domestic domain of sexually predatory males and weak-minded women, erosive of the public good. We have already seen it in the anti-Christian polemic of second-century pagan critics, as well as the New Testament Pastoral Epistles.

Jerome's rhetoric is less florid when he is writing to his own household network of female supporters, among whom, like Jovinian, he circulated, trading exegetical insights on biblical passages and offering theological instruction on ascetic ideals. One of the more remarkable letters sent to him by his patron, Marcella, asks him to comment upon the ideas of a Montanist heretical teacher who had paid her a household visit to engage in theological conversation. What this letter indicates is the messiness of ancient domestic Christianity and the continuing blurring of lines between orthodoxy and heresy that imperial antiheretical legislation tried to keep clear. From the perspective of Marcella's Montanist visitor, such a visit could be profoundly strategic: to win the sympathies of an aristocratic matron was not only to win religious legitimacy in a complexly coded honorific culture but also to gain access to a network of social equals and their subordinates, not to mention its wealth.

Such tactically targeted visits by ascetics to the homes of the wealthy surely form the backdrop of Theodosian legislation (*CTh.* 16.2.20, 27) that forbids "continents" from receiving legacies from widows. The tending, as well as the policing, of such relationships was of great importance. Paulinus, in his biography of the fourth-century aristocratic bishop of Milan, Ambrose, comments how as a child the bishop-to-be foreshadowed ecclesiastical glory when he played at being bishop and imitated clerics who visited in his home (*Life of Ambrose* 2.4). Later, as a full-grown bishop, Ambrose himself paid household visits to wealthy Roman Christian families (3.10). Such visits easily became the brunt of satirical attack by Christianity's detractors. The pagan historian Ammianus Marcellinus pillories Ambrose's contemporary, Bishop Damasus of Rome, as an "ear-tickler" of women who is suspiciously fond of his connections with the Roman elite (*Res Gestae* 27.3.11–14). These references alert us to the importance of household patrons and their social networks in the cementing of allegiances and the flow of ideas in early Christianity. They reveal a world in which orthodoxy and heresy were dynamic phenomena, as much spatial and social as they were doctrinal, evolving and changing as alliances shifted and teachers competed for followers. On this account, early Christian orthodoxy and heresy were less discrete and defined than textbook discussions of early Christian theologies would lead one to suppose.

From the accession of Constantine onward, when the Roman Empire was increasingly defined by adherence to a particular orthodoxy, households offered proscribed movements an alternative landscape. Marginalized or disenfranchised by imperial legislation, heterodox groups found in this landscape a means of surviving, defining themselves, and promoting their interests. The fact of their suppression and the studied efforts of the antiheretical Theodosian legislation to avoid reference to their meeting places as churches is evidence of the emergence of competing religious topographies in late antiquity. If sometimes only anecdotally, ancient references to domestic meeting places help us to envision how heterodox groups met and even thrived in the often-hostile religious climate of the post-Constantinian era.

FOR FURTHER READING

Bauer, Walter. *Orthodoxy and Heresy in Earliest Christianity*. Trans. Robert A. Kraft and Gerhard Krodel. London: SCM, 1972.

Clark, Elizabeth A. *The Origenist Controversy: The Cultural Construction of an Early Christian Debate*. Princeton, N.J.: Princeton University Press, 1992.

Davies, Stevan L. *The Revolt of the Widows: The Social World of the Apocryphal Acts*. Carbondale: Southern Illinois University Press, 1980.

Krautheimer, Richard. *Three Christian Capitals: Topography and Politics*. Berkeley: University of California Press, 1983.

Markus, Robert. *The End of Ancient Christianity*. Cambridge: Cambridge University Press, 1990.

Osiek, Carolyn, and David L. Balch. *Families in the New Testament World: Households and House Churches*. Louisville, Ky.: Westminster John Knox, 1997.

Snyder, Graydon F. *Ante Pacem: Archaeological Evidence of Church Life before Constantine*. Macon, Ga.: Mercer University Press, 1985.

White, L. Michael. *The Social Origins of Christian Architecture*. Volume 1: *Building God's House in the Roman World*. Volume 2: *Texts and Monuments for the Christian Domus Ecclesiae in Its Environment*. Harvard Theological Studies 42. Valley Forge, Pa.: Trinity Press International, 1996–97.

JEWISH CHRISTIANS, JUDAIZERS, AND CHRISTIAN ANTI-JUDAISM

CHARLOTTE ELISHEVA FONROBERT

CHAPTER TEN

In recent years studying the history of the separation of Christianity and Judaism has taken dramatic turns, opening up new vistas on the complex relations and overlapped identities of Christians and Jews in antiquity. Older accounts of this process had by and large assumed that the separation between the two religions was completed by the end of the first century CE, when, in the aftermath of the destruction of the Second Temple, the rabbinic movement emerged as the sole religious authority on the Jewish side (an event typically associated with the legendary Council of Yavneh), while a more and more Gentile church evolved on the Christian side in the wake of Paul's rejection of the Law. According to that traditional narrative, the rabbis subsequently rarely felt compelled to engage their Christian rivals. They simply ignored the Christian rise to imperial power and devoted themselves to the task at hand, namely, the interpretation of the biblical laws and the development of the legal trajectory from Moses to Hillel and beyond. Christian writers, on the other hand, often did engage Judaism, considered to be their mother religion, later morphed into a competitive sibling.[1] When they did so, the terms were typically supersessionist, spiteful, or otherwise derogatory: Judaism was viewed by ancient Christians as an antiquated religion at best, one whose true promise had been fulfilled in Christianity.

By and large, this traditional narrative presented its two protagonists, Judaism and Christianity, as coherent characters with complete and separate identities from the beginning of the story—that is, by the end of the first century, if not even earlier. Within that narrative, certain groups of people typically labeled "Jewish Christians" or "Judaizers" came to play an important supportive role. They, too, were thought to have exhibited a more or less coherent character as a movement, whose history could be told from the beginnings in the New Testament—Paul's Judaizers in his Epistle to the Galatians—till their eventual demise sometime in the fourth or possibly the fifth century. Importantly, these Jewish Christians were positioned so as not to disturb the overall plot resting on the assumption of clear boundaries between Judaism and Christianity. Jewish Christianity was represented as a distinct and therefore marginal movement, restricted to Christians who happened to be ethnic Jews or observant of Jewish practices—who were, in other words, heretics and schismatics, as the church fathers regarded them.

As historians have begun to read the late ancient sources in more sophisticated, critical, and less partisan ways, this traditional narrative has been challenged: the "parting of the ways" between Judaism and Christianity is now viewed as having taken place much later and through a more gradual and varied process. Accordingly, the self-representation of a writer or a group of writers as already inhabiting a position of authority or as representing the only true, and therefore orthodox or catholic, form of Judaism or Christianity can no longer be taken at face value but must rather be considered as a strategy for claiming an authoritative voice, in a context in which such claims would have frequently been disputed or even ignored. Similarly, the so-called Jewish Christians can no longer simply be viewed as heretics because church fathers or rabbis categorize them as such. Indeed, sometimes it is orthodoxy that turns out to be sectarian, as has, for instance, been argued for the case of rabbinic Judaism, which may have remained a marginal and minority movement for most of the period of late antiquity.[2]

This change of perspective has endowed those formerly dubbed heretics with new significance in their own right. While the ancient heresy-hunters, whether rabbinic or patristic, no doubt want us to believe that Christians who engage in Jewish ritual practice or Jews who are attracted to Christian doctrine are religious deviants, such people may in fact have their own, potentially no less legitimate, idea about the nature of Christianity or Judaism. Further, they may not at all understand themselves to establish a third religious option but rather perceive themselves to embody an authentic Christianity or Judaism. It is therefore our task as historians to listen much more attentively to these voices, where possible, so that they may be more adequately represented in our historical accounts. This entails abandoning the presumption of a coherent, more or less uniform movement of Jewish Christianity and instead assuming a number of locally determined struggles over legitimate versions of Christianity that may not be directly connected with each other at all.

The consideration of the self-perception of those who are called Jewish Christians or Judaizers poses, of course, a significant challenge, since our sources are rather limited. In fact, most of the time the evidence at our disposal consists of texts that argue against them, and even such texts are few and far between. In this chapter we will focus on two works that provide us with some significant evidence of ancient Christians who for different reasons engaged in Jewish ritual practices, provoking the ire of the respective authorities polemicizing against them. The analysis does not follow a chronological order but will first turn to the later text or group of texts—John Chrysostom's collection of anti-Jewish homilies—because of its prominence in early Christian literature and the fact that we are able to date and locate the writing with relative precision. Subsequently we will consider the anonymously authored work known as the *Teaching of the Twelve Apostles,* or *Didascalia Apostolorum,* which likewise polemicizes against certain Judaizing practices. Consideration of the two cases will allow us to propose some conclusions regarding the phenomenon of Jewish Christianity and its significance for our understanding of Christianity, Judaism, and their interrelationship.

JOHN CHRYSOSTOM AND HIS JUDAIZING OPPONENTS

Beginning in the fall of 386 CE John Chrysostom delivered eight sermons over a period of slightly more than a year that were later collated as his homilies *Adversus Judaeos,* or *Against the Jews.* Chrysostom had by then already acquired fame for his oratorical skills and was one of the principal preachers in Antioch.[3] This series of sermons has become infamous for the vicious anti-Jewish rhetoric it espouses. Even within the genre of early Christian *Adversus Judaeos* literature[4] Chrysostom's texts stand out with their passionate invective. For this reason they have played a prominent role in the numerous studies of the root causes of anti-Semitism. As early as 1934 James Parkes, a remarkable intellectual figure in British Christianity of the early twentieth century, published *The Conflict of the Church and Synagogue: A Study in the Origins of Anti-Semitism.*[5] Written a few decades earlier than the American theologians of the post-Holocaust era and anticipating their concerns about the rise of anti-Semitism in Europe and Christian responsibility for these developments, the book attempts to account for the history of Christian anti-Judaism. John Chrysostom's homilies have a prominent place in Parkes's study, as they do in almost every study of Christian anti-Judaism since. Marcel Simon, who published his justly famous monograph *Verus Israel* originally in 1948 in France and then again in an expanded version in 1964, calls Chrysostom "the master of anti-Jewish invective."[6] In her 1974 study of the theological roots of anti-Semitism, better known to U.S. readers because of the amount of responses it generated among theologians, Rosemary Radford Ruether draws on similar sources, coming to a similar but more theological conclusion.[7] All these studies underline the uniqueness of John Chrysostom's sermons, as far as their violent rhetoric is concerned, while they also point out that he is scarcely the only ancient Christian to engage in anti-Jewish rhetoric and actions, as John Gager has pointed out quite poignantly:

> Clearly this is an extreme case. And yet, how far removed are we from Cyril, bishop of Alexandria in 412, or Ambrose, bishop of Milan from 374? Cyril, shortly after having ascended his Episcopal throne, expelled the large Jewish community from the city of Alexandria. As for Ambrose, in 388 he countermanded an edict of the emperor Theodosius concerning the destruction of a synagogue in Callinicum (Asia Minor). . . . In justifying his opposition to the emperor's edict, the bishop denies that the incident amounted to a crime and adds that it was only his own laziness that had prevented him from burning down the synagogue of Milan![8]

However, in addition to offering important evidence for the history of Christian anti-Judaism, Chrysostom's sermons can serve as a valuable resource for our study of Jewish Christianity. For underneath John's "rhetoric of abuse"[9] we can discern that his interlocutors, people from his own community, engage in what appears as boundary-crossing behavior. Already Parkes suggested that "the only explanation of his bitterness contained in the sermons themselves is the too close fellowship between Jews and Christians in Antioch."[10]

Fig. 10.1. Forbidden territory? John Chrysostom warned the Christians of Antioch not to enter the local synagogue, advice they apparently frequently ignored. Antioch's ancient synagogue no longer stands, but this entrance to the ancient synagogue of Sardis, Turkey, might give us some sense of the architectural and religious boundaries so often transgressed by the footloose Antiochene Christians. Photo credit: Vanni / Art Resource, NY.

However, perhaps this explanation does not explain all that much. For why would a fellowship between Jews and Christians cause such offense? Further, Parkes's theory rests on the assumption that there were already definitive and separate identities in place, which we cannot and should not take for granted. Perhaps for John the problem is not that his people socialize with the Jews per se but that the very boundaries between Jewish and Christian practice remain blurred and porous, at least in the eyes of his flock. We may suspect that he has to convince even himself of the absolute difference between Jewish and Christian practice, if we recall the old principle that the person who screams the loudest is often guilty of (or insecure about) the very thing he or she does not like. Exclaims the orator, famously: "This is the reason I hate the Jews, because they have the law and the prophets: indeed I hate them more because of this than if they did not have them" (*Against the Jews* 6:6, 913).[11] A shared biblical heritage, in other words, blurs the boundaries between Christianity and Judaism, boundaries that Chrysostom attempts to strengthen by the very force of his hatred.

> The majority of the city is Christian, and still some suffer the Judaizing disease. How would those of us who are healthy defend ourselves on this point?
>
> —John Chrysostom, *Against the Jews* 1

If we look at the sermons, John Chrysostom cites only one concrete example of Judaizing practice, while otherwise he talks in more general terms about what he regards to be the offending attitude of certain community members. But from some of his remarks we can easily deduce what was transpiring in his community. Let us begin with the example, as Chrysostom does himself in the first sermon. He claims to have witnessed the incident himself:

> Three days ago—believe me, I am not lying—I saw a noble and free woman, who is modest and faithful, being forced by a coarse and senseless person who *appeared to be a Christian* (for *I would not call a person who would dare to do such a thing a sincere Christian*) to enter the shrine of the Hebrews and to swear there an oath about certain business matters that were under dispute. She came up to me and asked for help; she begged me to prevent this lawless violence—for it was forbidden to her, who had shared in the divine mysteries, to enter that place. I was inflamed with indignation and enraged; I was galvanized into action and refused to allow her to be dragged any further into that transgression. . . . I snatched her from the hands of her abductor. *I asked him if he were a Christian, and he said he was.* Then I set upon him vigorously, charging him with lack of feeling and the worst stupidity; I told him he was no better off than a mule if he, who professed to worship Christ, would drag someone off to the dens of the Jews who had crucified him. (1:3, 847–48; emphasis added)

Chrysostom further reports to his listeners that he interrogated the "transgressor" as to the motives for his behavior: "I asked him why he rejected the Church and dragged the woman to the place where the Hebrews assembled. He answered that many people had told him that oaths sworn there were more to be feared" (1:3, 848).

Read with a dose of hermeneutical suspicion, the story does not necessarily reflect an actual historical incident, as many scholars simply assume. It is just as possible that Chrysostom constructed the incident as an example serving his rhetorical purposes. The description of the scene in terms that suggest an impending rape happily averted by the bishop who happens to have witnessed it seems to suggest as much. Even if the incident is a rhetorical invention, we can safely assume that Chrysostom expected his cautionary anecdote to be an effective means of persuasion. Indeed, what seems to be the most reliable historical aspect of the story is the evidence it provides of the public reputation of the synagogue and the fear and respect it induced in people, as invoked by the villain of the story. Whether this particular man actually acted in such a manner is, again, not of crucial importance to our historical assessment of the story. What *is* crucial is Chrysostom's near-obsessive attempt to derail the high regard in which the synagogue is held by members of his community.

The logic of the story seems to imply that the synagogue ("shrine of the Hebrews") commanded public respect even among non-Jews, to such a degree that it would prevent a person from swearing falsely. "Many people" had told the man about this aura of the synagogue. Chrysostom neglects to tell his audience what the actual disagreement between the woman and the man might have been (perhaps involving a property dispute, for example), but it is obvious that the synagogue seemed the appropriate place to resolve it. This incident is clearly not out of the ordinary, since Chrysostom returns to the topic of the veneration of the synagogue as a holy space throughout his sermons: "Since there are some who think of the synagogue as a holy place, I must say a few words to them. Why do you venerate that place? Must you not despise it, hold it in abomination, run away from it? They answer that the Law and the books of the prophets are kept there. What is this? Will any place where these books are be a holy place? By no means!" (1:5, 850). And again: "Even if there is no idol there, still demons do inhabit the place. And I say this not only about the synagogue here in town but about the one in Daphne as well; for at Daphne you have a more wicked place of perdition which they call the Matrona's. I have heard that many of the faithful go up there and sleep beside the place" (1:6, 852).[12] But "the spot where the synagogue is, is less worthy of honor than any inn. For it's not only a resting-place for robbers and cheats, but also for demons" (1:3, 848–49). We cannot know whether Chrysostom's strategy of calling the synagogue "no better than a brothel or the theater" (1:2, 847) was successful in responding to the general veneration he was combating.

But we can surmise that at least some, if not many, Christians in Antioch regarded the synagogue as a holy place, partially because of the scriptural texts housed therein, aided by the lack of idols in the synagogue. Indeed, this veneration appears as a widely accepted attitude in his audience.[13]

> I know that many people respect the Jews and think that their present way of life is honorable. That is why it is urgent for me to tear out this deadly notion by the root. I said that the synagogue is no better than the theater.
>
> —John Chrysostom, *Against the Jews* 1

Scholars have sometimes attributed the kind of attitude and behavior espoused by the villain of Chrysostom's narrative to the simple and uneducated in the community, for whom "the books had magical powers and were capable of working wonders and miracles."[14] However, not only does such an account take

Chrysostom's rhetoric at face value,[15] but it also obscures the likelihood that the villain who identifies as a Christian simply does not consider using the synagogue in this manner an un-Christian act, nor would the other members in the community who venerate the institution of the synagogue. Indeed, it appears that they had no reason to consider his behavior to be other than Christian.

It is Chrysostom who insists that the act of entering the synagogue is problematic and attempts to turn it into transgressive behavior. Accordingly, he designs the narrative in such a way that everyone will understand that it is Christian identity that is at stake: the villain "appears to be a Christian," while Chrysostom "would not call a person who would do such a thing a sincere Christian," implying that he is not really a Christian at all. At the same time Chrysostom appears to be fighting an uphill battle, so much so that his narrative of the abduction of the noble woman into the synagogue ends up running into contradictions and incoherencies. For instance, the woman about to be victimized asks the priest for help, "for it was forbidden to her, who had shared in the divine mysteries, to enter that place." Why is it forbidden to her? By whom? If it is indeed forbidden, why then is it not sufficient for our orator simply to remind the villain of this during his interrogation, without needing to go on to accuse him of "lack of feeling and the worst stupidity"? Why does the woman, "a believer," know that entering the synagogue is purportedly forbidden to her, while the man, obviously also a believer (since even Chrysostom grants that he professes to worship Christ), does not and instead relies on the public veneration of the synagogue? It appears that Chrysostom feels compelled to fire all his rhetorical canons to convince his audience—and perhaps also himself— that entering a synagogue or venerating it is a boundary violation. Either you are a Christian, or you enter a synagogue. Christians cannot enter a synagogue, let alone consider it a holy place. At the same time, the more rhetorical guns he fires, the clearer it becomes how deeply ingrained the veneration of the synagogue was in his audience.

The same is true for the other, related practices that Chrysostom brands as un-Christian, such as watching the celebration of the Jewish holidays of the fall season—the Feast of Trumpets (*Rosh ha-Shanah,* the Jewish New Year), the Day of Atonement, and the Feast of Tabernacles (1:1, 844)—and even joining in the festivities, including perhaps observing the fast on the Day of Atonement. Indeed, he invokes the same equation previously established: those who revere the Jewish rituals declare "ours to be false" (1:6; 852). You cannot participate in both rituals, in other words. Chrysostom offers his audience a few ideas about how to affirm their Christian identity. He demands complete shunning of any involvement with Jewish practices and even with Jews, making the infamous suggestion that a Christian should avoid sharing even a greeting with them and turn away, "since they are the common disgrace and infection of the whole world" (1:6, 852). Husbands should restrain their wives from going to the synagogue on the Feast of the Trumpets (2:2, 860). Finally, he demands that each member of the community watch out for the behavior of their fellows, drawing on the graphic metaphor of the hunt: "Straight after you leave here rouse yourselves to undertake this hunt, and let each of you bring me one of those who are sick in this way.... Let the women chase after women, the men after men, and the slaves after slaves, and the freemen after freemen, and the children after children, and in general let everyone be very scrupulous in chasing after people who are suffering from this kind of illness" (1:8, 856). Investigate scrupulously (1:4, 849), denounce them (1:8, 856), accuse them (1:8, 856), show them up (1:8, 856), he insists. Chrysostom's vision of combating what he has declared to be un-Christian is one in which the church acts as a House un-Christian Activities Committee.

John Chrysostom's sermons therefore expose the gap that often separates the laity or the general practitioners from the leadership of the church. Or, as Parkes put it, "The canons of the councils and the violence of such as Chrysostom both have their origin in the friendly relations between local Jewish and Christian communities. Trouble, when it comes, comes clearly from the ecclesiastical or imperial authorities, and not from the populace."[16] Even though this view surely does not encompass the whole picture, some truth may adhere to it. If we put this again in terms of how identity is constructed, we may suggest that some (many?) members of the community do not consider being a believer and a member of Chrysostom's church while also watching or attending the synagogue for various reasons of piety to be contradictory, problematic, or threatening. For all we know, this might have been a case of comparing apples and oranges to them, where the one (being a believer) and the other (fasting on the Day of Atonement, for example) simply did not operate on the same plane. Or perhaps they did not consider Jewish rituals to be the building blocks of a different religion: after all, these derive from biblical law. Alternately, even if the two sets of practices were considered to imply affiliation with different religions, worshipping Christ may not have implied an exclusionary commitment for all Christians. Unfortunately, we cannot reconstruct the consciousness of those people, since we catch a glimpse of them only through Chrysostom's hostile lens. All we know is that Christians at the end of the fourth century in Antioch could easily shuttle between synagogue and

> What's this disease? The festivals of the wretched and miserable Jews are about to approach thick and fast: the Trumpets, the Tabernacles, the Fasts. Of the many in our ranks who go to watch the festivals, who say they think as we do, some will both join in the festivities and take part in the Fasts. This bad habit I want to drive out of the church right now.
>
> —John Chrysostom, *Against the Jews* 1

Fig. 10.2. This bronze stamp from the third or fourth century CE depicts a seven-branched candlestick, a palm frond, a small cluster of fruits, and the inscription "the property of Leontios." Palm frond and fruit are used in the rites of Sukkot, or Tabernacles, a festival that some Christians of Antioch appear to have enjoyed. British Museum, London, Great Britain. Photo credit: Werner Forman / Art Resource, NY.

church and could participate in local cults such as that at the Matrona synagogue in Daphne. To them, and to us, it is Chrysostom's attempt to construct impervious boundaries that requires explanation.

The question that remains to be considered, then, is why Chrysostom is so nervous about attraction to Jewish rituals in Antioch. We may easily agree with Robert Wilken when he argues that "the threat in Antioch does not seem to be actual conversion to Judaism, though this must have taken place on occasion."[17] What seems to be at stake in this conflict is the issue of authority. Just as the rabbis' project in the Talmud is to gather all forms of religious knowledge under the mantle of Torah, so too Chrysostom aims to assemble all forms of pious veneration in the bishop's church. There were not to be forms of piety outside of the church or separate from one's identity as a Christian believer. Attending other people's rituals for whatever reason was not to be understood as a neutral act that took place on a different plane from one's life as a Christian believer. The presence of the divine was to manifest itself solely in places authorized by the church: "the Jews scare the more simple-minded Christians, for how could [their synagogues] be frightening, when they're full of great shame and ridicule . . . ? Our [churches] are not like that, but are truly frightening and filled with awe. For the place where God is present, possessing power over life and death, is a frightening place—where homilies are delivered on everlasting punishments, on rivers of fire, the poisonous worm, chains that can't be broken, external darkness" (1:4, 848).

Before we speculate further about the relationship between popular boundary-crossing behavior and the boundary-making, anti-Jewish rhetoric of Christian leaders, we should consider one additional, but slightly different and more complicated case. This case focuses on ritual behavior as well, even though here the behavior in question is less public and perhaps less publicly exposed. It further introduces the dimension of gender into the discussion, since in this case the transgressors addressed by the author of the text are primarily women.

THE *DIDASCALIA APOSTOLORUM* AND ITS JEWISH CHRISTIAN OPPONENTS

The text in question is the *Didascalia Apostolorum*, most likely composed some time during the third century CE by an anonymous author or authors. This text contains a significant amount of legal material and relatively less overt theological material. For this reason scholars classify the *Didascalia* as a church order or early Christian canon law. Furthermore, the *Didascalia* is not a univocal text, but rather a composite text that includes later additions to the original version. As a narrative framing device, the authors choose the so-called Apostolic Council of the mid-first century CE, described in Acts 15 and referred to by Paul in his Epistle to the Galatians. This choice gives the document its name, even as the authors adopt the narrative, pseudepigraphic voice of the twelve apostles: "We the twelve apostles of the only Son, the eternal Word of God, our Lord and our God and our Savior Jesus Christ, as we were assembled with one accord in Jerusalem, the city of the great king, and with us our brother Paul, the apostle of the Gentiles, and James the bishop of the above-mentioned city, have ratified this *Didascalia*, in which are included the confession and the creed, and we have named all the ordinances, as the ordinances of the celestial (orders), and thus again the ordinances of the holy church" (CSCO 402, 7–8).[18]

For these reasons the *Didascalia* provides us with a very different type of literary evidence from John Chrysostom's sermons. In the latter case, it is relatively easy to situate the single-authored texts in a specific historical situation, especially since we are able to date and locate them rather precisely. The *Didascalia*, however, disguises not only its own authorial voice but also its own historical situation. Furthermore, while John Chrysostom's interlocutors are identifiable at least in general terms, namely, his flock in Antioch at the end of the fourth century, the audience of the *Didascalia* is not easily identifiable even in those general terms, since we do not know the specific community it addresses. The authors themselves claim that they have written this book to enlighten the "inhabitable world," to be read and taught in the churches—presumably of Syria. But we do not know how the text in its form of church order or legislation was implemented. What we do know is that the *Didascalia*, originally a Greek text of which only fragments are left, was popular enough to be translated into numerous languages, first into Syriac in the fourth century, and subsequently into Latin, Ethiopian, and Arabic.

Despite our virtual ignorance of its precise historical context, we can learn something significant about the conflict with which the authors of the *Didascalia* are dealing. Like John Chrysostom's sermons, the *Didascalia* is at least in parts a polemical text that denounces and argues against what it considers to be deviant behavior by people in its audience. It devotes its last few chapters to raising concerns about schisms within the church. Initially, the authors situate their polemic against schismatics within the first century CE by retelling the story of Simon the Magician from the Acts of the Apostles (Acts 8:9-13) and adding a group of undefined false apostles to the New Testament account. In the course of retelling this story the *Didascalia* repeatedly lists the types of behavior that the authors mark as heretical:

> They were teaching and troubling [the people] with many opinions. Indeed, many of them were teaching that a man should not take a wife, and were saying that if a man did not take a wife, this was holiness. And through holiness they glorified opinions of their heresies. Again others of them taught that a man should not eat flesh, and said that a man must not eat anything that has a soul in it. Others, however, said that one was bound to withhold from swine only, but might eat those things which the Law pronounces clean, and that he should be circumcised according to the Law. (CSCO 408, 123)

Another list also mentions that "some abstained from flesh and from wine" (CSCO 408, 214). As a whole, these lists do not seem to form any coherent ideology or theology as we know it, various scholarly attempts to distinguish coherent groups notwithstanding.[19] Some of these practices are of course familiar from the conflicts between Paul and the other apostles during the first century CE, especially circumcision and forms of *kashrut* (Jewish dietary laws). But other practices, such as vegetarianism and celibacy, go beyond the ones that were at the center of those earlier conflicts. It is here that the historical situation of conflict for the authors of the *Didascalia* begins to shine through its various tactics of disguise.

The main conflict centers on the observation of the "bonds which are in the second legislation" (CSCO 408, 214, and 223ff.). Indeed, the *Didascalia*'s authors do not seriously engage the vegetarians or even the celibates in any argumentation. Fully engaged are only those who, according to the authors, observe the laws of the "second legislation" (Greek: *deuterosis*, Syriac: *tinyan nimosa*, Latin: *secundatio*), a prominent term in the *Didascalia*. This language emerged as a technical term among fourth-century patristic writers who clearly applied it to rabbinic exegesis and more specifically to the Mishnah, the earliest anthology of rabbinic law (dating from the late second or early third century CE) with canonical status in rabbinic Judaism.[20] In the *Didascalia* it has not yet definitively obtained a technical sense but does at the very least mark contemporary ritual practices that have a basis in biblical law and are at the same time obviously recognizable as Jewish. Practices that exemplify what the authors of the *Didascalia* classify as "second legislation" include the preference of the Sabbath instead of Sunday and, even more important, the immersion in water by women for purposes of menstrual purification. Further, the "distinction of meats" is mentioned as one of the "bonds of the second legislation" (CSCO 408, 223).

The discussion concerning the women who immerse themselves monthly is the most extensive and merits some analysis here, since it adds a unique perspective to our understanding of the early Christian debates about the boundaries between Judaism and Christianity. This is the only text where *women's* ritual practice plays a central role in such debates, albeit reflected through a (presumably) male-authored text. Normally, it is the biblically ordained practice of circumcision that is in question, as it is already in the debates between Paul and the apostles. Alternately, the Sabbath or the Jewish holidays take on the role as boundary markers between Jews and others or between Jews and Christians. Indeed, as early as the traditions reflected in the Synoptic Gospels, the Sabbath laws turn into an issue of controversy between the Pharisees and the disciples of Jesus (Matt. 12:1-14; Mark 2:23—3:6; Luke 6:1-11) and from then on recur in almost every text that deals with Jewish and Christian relations.[21] Thus, the fact that the Sabbath is at issue between the authors of the *Didascalia* and their audience, once Jewish ritual practices are in question, is not entirely surprising.

What is more surprising is the effort the authors exert to debate with the women in the community. In the course of this debate, we learn not

Fig. 10.3. The lines between Jews and Christians were frequently blurred. Some Christian women, for example, appear to have observed menstrual purity laws, including use of a ritual bath, or *miqveh*. This late Roman *miqveh* is located in a private domicile on the western summit of Sepphoris. Note the well-preserved plastered edges along the stairway leading down to the immersion area. Photo credit: Eric M. Meyers, courtesy of the Sepphoris Regional Project.

only what the women do but also what they argue in explanation and defense of their practice. The former is relatively easy to reconstruct: the *Didascalia* cites their practice as consisting in refraining "from prayer, and from the Scripture and from the Eucharist" during "the seven days of their flux" (CSCO 408, 239). In other words, they keep a distance from the *sancta* or holy things of Christian life during their menstrual periods. After the seven days ordained by Levitical law for the period of menstrual impurity (Lev. 15:19-25), the women immerse themselves in order to purify themselves (CSCO 408, 241). Further, they do not have sex while menstruating (Lev. 18:20; 20:19).

The writers of the *Didascalia* classify these practices as heretical and seek to put an end to them. In fact, this work goes farther than any other early Christian text in rejecting the Levitical purity laws by demanding explicitly that husbands should have sex with their menstruating wives: "And when your wives have those issues which are according to nature, take care, as is right that you cleave to them, for you know they are your members, and love them as your soul" (CSCO 408, 244).[22]

> But if there are any who are concerned and desire, according to the "second legislation" to observe the [purity] laws concerning the rhythms of nature, of bodily fluids and sexual intercourse, first let them know that together with the second legislation they affirm the curse against our Savior and condemn themselves vainly.
>
> —*Didascalia Apostolorum* 26

To persuade the women in particular and their audience in general to end their observance of biblical law, the writers use insults and threats, not entirely unlike those of Chrysostom, but also not quite as colorful. The women are addressed as foolish (CSCO 408, 241), and the observances are "foolish and harmful" (CSCO 408, 245). They are threatened with various forms of spiritual condemnation—with abandonment by the Holy Spirit, with possession by impure spirits, and finally, employing Jesus' eschatological words from the Gospel of Matthew (25:41) as polemical weapons, with fire everlasting (CSCO 408, 241). The writers self-consciously excuse their rhetorical choices by drawing on the widespread metaphor of the physician:

> And now, in the same manner [as Jesus' eschatological threats] this our writing appears to [some] people in such a way that it speaks roughly and severely because of its truth. Indeed, as a physician, when he has not been able to conquer and heal a sore with drugs and compresses, comes to severity in treatment and to surgery of medicine, that is to iron and branding irons, by which alone the physician is able to overcome and conquer [the sore] and heal quickly the one suffering— thus of the same type is the word to those who hear and do it. (CSCO 408, 247)

However, this line of reasoning does not seem sufficient in the writers' own minds, and thus they draw on a tactics of persuasion and engage the women in a protracted argument. Within this discussion the authors, much like Paul in his first Epistle to the Corinthians, cite the women's explanations for their own ritual behavior. Thus the *Didascalia* accords us another unique perspective on Jewish–Christian relations in late antiquity, since it is perhaps the only text in which we learn something about the perspective of those who transgress the boundaries created and invoked by the authors of the texts we have at our disposal. Of course, there is no way of being certain whether the women really advanced the arguments that the authors of the *Didascalia* strive to dismantle: what the *Didascalia* presents as the women's arguments may in fact be colored by its own theological interests.

Keeping this cautionary remark in mind, we can nonetheless distill two main arguments purportedly advanced by the women: (1) they observe a form of menstrual abstinence simply because this is anchored in biblical law; (2) their specific understandings of the Holy Spirit require such observances. The former argument has its own inherent persuasiveness, which is why the author goes to such great lengths to categorize most of biblical law as "second legislation," or more precisely as secondary and therefore no longer valid. In fact, invoking an argument that was already established in Christian anti-Jewish polemics, the *Didascalia* regards the entire corpus of biblical law following the sin of the golden calf as merely punitive, a punishment imposed by God in return for the collective transgression.[23] Subsequently, Jesus comes to lift the punishment or the burden of the "bonds of the law," ordaining only a "simple law of life" (CSCO 408, 223), namely, the Ten Commandments.

The second argument that the women advance concerns their understanding of the Holy Spirit as a mediator between the believer and the Christian *sancta*.[24] They separate themselves from the *sancta* because they consider themselves to be void of the Holy Spirit while menstruating, an absence they can only reverse with immersion.[25] However, this belief and the practices it mandates fly in the face of the *Didascalia*'s teaching of baptism, according to which baptism is the rite of entry into what the writers call the "catholic church which is the receptacle of the Holy Spirit" (CSCO 408, 221). Baptism signifies filiation with God and the bishop as God's servant and mediator: "[The bishop] is a servant of the word and mediator, but to you a teacher and your father after God, who has begotten you through water" (CSCO 402, 100). But above and beyond everything else, the "unbreakable seal of baptism" (CSCO 402, 113; 408, 157) signifies the gift of the Holy Spirit: "A believer is filled with the Holy Spirit, and he [*sic*] who does not believe, with an unclean spirit. . . . He therefore who has departed and abides afar from the unclean spirit by baptism, he is filled with the Holy Spirit" (CSCO 408, 241). Thus it becomes clear what disturbs the writers of the *Didascalia* about the women's practice of monthly immersion: that practice looks very much like repeated baptisms and as such challenges the centrality of the initial baptism in its function of making a person a believer once and for all (as signified in the language of the "unbreakable seal"). Indeed, it challenges not only the centrality of the baptismal ritual as a transformative act but also, at least indirectly, the central authority of the bishop through whom baptism gains its legitimacy. The women, then, would seem to have adapted what they learned about the Holy Spirit upon being baptized to the particularity of their gender, insofar as they consider the Holy Spirit to be subjected to the cyclical habits of their physical bodies. As their bodies bleed periodically, the Holy Spirit leaves and reenters their wombs, and does so, moreover, without the mediation of the bishop.

We might, however, also interpret the women's practice with specific reference to Jewish custom, if we take into consideration that the authors of the *Didascalia* address them as converts from Judaism, along with the collective group of converts addressed by the last polemical chapter of the text, devoted to the second legislation: "You, however, who have been converted from the people to believe in God our Savior Jesus Christ, do not henceforth remain in your former manner of life, brethren, that you should keep vain bonds, purifications and sprinklings and baptisms and distinction of meats, for the Lord has said to you: 'Remember not the former things' and 'Behold, I make all things new, these which I now declare, that you may know them; and I will make in the desert a way' [Isa. 43:18-19]" (CSCO 408, 223). Similarly, when the *Didascalia*'s authors begin their discussion of Sunday versus the Sabbath, they address their audience as "beloved brethren, you who from among the people have believed, and [yet] wish to be bound with the bonds" (CSCO 408, 232). The concept of "the people" here operates as a quasi-ethnic term. It is used throughout the *Didascalia*'s retelling of Israelite history in the argumentation against the second legislation. Let us leave aside for a moment the question of whether it is specifically Jewish Christians — that is, Christians who were once Jews — who generate problems of heteropraxis in the community by importing Jewish rituals. For now, suffice it to note that we are led to believe that the women who observe the Levitical laws of menstrual impurity are Jewish converts who are beholden to the previous way of life that they bring with them into their new community of believers. In other words, the authors suggest that they may not be compelled so much by the persuasiveness of the authority of biblical law per se as by the force of tradition.

> For if you think, o woman, that in the seven days of your menstrual period you are void of the Holy Spirit, if you die in those days, you will depart empty handed and without hope. But if the Holy Spirit is always in you, without any real hindrance you keep yourself from prayer and from Scriptures and the eucharist.
> — *Didascalia Apostolorum* 26

This is entirely possible. However, the question that such a suggestion raises is which kind of Judaism they converted from, for in the rabbinic corpus, namely, the *Tosefta,* an approximately contemporaneous text of the mid-third century CE, we find the following ruling: "Men and women with irregular genital emissions, women who menstruate and parturients [all of whom are in a status of ritual impurity according to Levitical law] are permitted to read in the Torah, and to study *Mishnah,* midrash, religious law and legend, but men who had a regular ejaculation are prohibited to do so" (*Tosefta Berakhot* 2:13). Rabbinic law here explicitly permits menstruating women to approach what might be considered the *sancta* in rabbinic Judaism. This raises a number of possibilities: Did our purported Jewish women converts come from a community that was not yet ruled by rabbinic law, in which case the *Didascalia* would provide evidence for extra-rabbinic Jewish communities? Or did they come from a community that was ruled by rabbinic law but developed their own ritual interpretations, in response to what they learned at baptism? Obviously, these fragments of male-authored prescriptive texts provide only minimal information with which to respond to such questions. Yet we can learn something important from the fact that both boundary-making authorities, the legislators of the *Tosefta* and of the *Didascalia,* discuss the same issue, a rare enough occurrence. Furthermore, both authorities rule that menstruating women can, and in the case of the *Didascalia* even should, study scripture, albeit for different reasons. The rabbinic text allows menstruating women to study scripture in spite of their ritual status of impurity, since according to rabbinic law the physical text of the Torah as ritual sacred object cannot be rendered impure. But it certainly does not want women to otherwise abandon biblical regulations concerning menstruation, especially not the prohibition of sex during menstruation. The *Didascalia,* on the other hand, attempts to persuade women to continue studying during their menstrual period in order to transcend their Jewish past. It regards the women's practice as a sign of an inappropriate attachment to their former community and practices and as an indicator of their insufficient identification with the new community. This convergence between the rabbinic and the Christian texts is evidence for the fact that both communities struggled, sharing the same textual and authoritative reference in scripture, to define the role and identity of women as part of establishing their own collective identity.

This discussion of the textual evidence for boundary crossing leaves us with the question of what type of boundary crossing we are dealing with, especially if we compare the women addressed by the *Didascalia* with John Chrysostom's "transgressors." In John's case, the boundaries seem to be more clearly established, at least on the surface, since he clearly juxtaposes Jews and Christians, us and them, the institution of the church and the synagogue as demarcated by two different places of worship. The people targeted by John's wrath act as if they consider both places to be compatible in their power to invoke a presence of the divine, and hence they shuttle back and forth between the two. To them, a practice of piety seeking the presence of the divine, whether that is in the form of an ancient book said to contain the divine voice (the Torah in the synagogue) or in the form of worshipping Jesus, can embrace what already appear as different religious formations. John Chrysostom, on the other hand, considers both places of worship and their respective ritual practices to be competing for the power to invoke the divine presence and authority. One should worship either here or there, but not in both places: "If the ceremonies of the Jews move you to admiration, what do you have in common with us? If the Jewish ceremonies are venerable and great, ours are lies" (*Against the Jews* 1:6, 852). Those who shuttle between both are mere pretenders, in his view.

The heretics of the *Didascalia,* on the other hand, would appear to be only half-Christian rather than pretenders. If we extend the metaphor of boundary crossing, from the perspective of the *Didascalia* these heretics either did not make it completely across the border, being stuck somewhere in the liminal space of the borderlands, or they brought too much baggage with them, baggage that should have been left behind to allow them sufficient assimilation. Either way, the logic of the boundary-making authority is one of supersessionism rather than of straightforward competition: leave behind what is old, and enjoy the new. Our migrants, however, refuse to obey that logic, and in their view a form of piety that venerates the authority of biblical law embraces the old as well as the new. Hence both groups of opponents offer powerful models of religious identity making that integrate Jewish and Christian elements with each other and refuse to validate the ideological boundaries of their authorities.

JEWISH CHRISTIANS, JUDAIZERS, AND OTHER HYBRIDS

We have encountered two different types of Christians who observed Jewish rituals in some form or other and were denounced—but also thereby brought to the light of history—by two different types of heresiologies. We have followed scholarly convention in labeling them "Judaizers" in one case and "Jewish Christians" in the other, both highly problematic terms that deserve some special attention in the last section of this chapter. This will allow us to return to and conclude with the discussion of the so-called parting of the ways between Judaism and Christianity with which we began.

As far as the first term is concerned, John Chrysostom himself uses it as a label for the primary targets of his venom, namely, those Christians who venerate the synagogue or celebrate the Jewish holidays, rather than Jews per se. He claims that "the majority of the city is Christian, and still some suffer the *Judaizing* disease!" (*Against the Jews* 1:3, 849; emphasis added) and encourages his listeners to "practice this scrutiny in the case of the *Judaizers* as well. When you recognise a *Judaizer*, take hold of them, make the situation plain to them, so that you too don't become party to the danger" (*Against the Jews* 1:4, 849; emphasis added). In Chrysostom's case, the referent for the term is rather obvious, despite the fact that some scholars raise the further question of whether these believers who observe some Jewish rituals are in fact ethnic Jews or Gentiles. Not only can that question not be answered, it also clearly did not matter to Chrysostom whether the Judaizers were ethnic Jews or Gentiles. What mattered to him were their transgressions of boundaries, and to him those were enough to label them as something other than truly Christian.

> Don't you see how the deacon entrusts you with the careful scrutiny of your brothers and sisters? Practice this scrutiny in the case of the Judaizers as well. When you recognise a Judaizer, take hold of them, make the situation plain to them, so that you too don't become party to the danger.
> —John Chrysostom, *Against the Jews* 1

The term "Judaizer" itself has a fraught history in early Christian literature. The Greek verb for "Judaizing" (*ioudaizein*; Latin: *iudaizare*) has its origin in Paul's Letter to the Galatians (2:14) and does not occur elsewhere in the New Testament. Paul employs the term when he accuses Peter of forcing non-Jewish believers "to live Jewishly," while Peter himself, a Jewish man, lives "like a Gentile and not like a Jew." The issue of controversy in this case was the observance of dietary laws, which Peter supposedly encouraged Gentile believers to follow, although—so Paul charges—he had previously not done so himself. Both Paul's and Josephus's use of the term (Josephus, *Jewish War* 2, 17:10 and 18:2) is more descriptive than polemical, referring to non-Jews who live like Jews, that is, according to Jewish customs.

This usage, however, changes in early patristic literature, especially and prominently in Chrysostom's sermons. Here the term takes on an increasingly polemical ring, heightened by the metaphors of disease (as we have seen above) and collaboration with the enemy: "When you recognize a Judaizer, take hold of them. . . . I say this because also in the case of army camps outside the country, if someone from the ranks of the soldiers is caught favouring barbarians, that is, being well-disposed towards Persians, not only is he in danger, but so also is everyone who knew his inclinations and failed to point him out to the general" (*Against the Jews* 1:4, 849). Indeed, the term comes to play a prominent role in Christian heresiology,[26] frequently referring to those who do not merely (continue to) live according to Jewish customs but actively threaten the integrity, and hence the orthodoxy, of Christianity. Thus "Judaizers" comes to designate that distinct group of people who try to lure others into their misconceptions. Not only do they live like Jews, in accordance with Jewish customs, but they also try to convince others to do so.

Finally, the term acquires a polemical life of its own, dislodged from any concrete context of Jewish practice, as early Christian authors brand assorted theologians and their followers as Jews and Judaizers if their Christologies or hermeneutics are deemed even slightly unorthodox. As a scholar remarking on Jerome's use of the term put it recently, "Sabellians, Arians, Photinians, Nestorians, and others could all become Jewish with a few strokes of the pen."[27] Indeed, so luminous and orthodox a figure as Jerome himself could be exposed to a charge of latent Judaizing because he fraternized with Jews for the express purpose of learning Hebrew and, for his scriptural translations, privileged the Jewish canon and Hebrew Bible over the Greek Septuagint version traditionally used by Christians.[28]

Matters become even more complicated when we turn to the concept of "Jewish Christianity." In contrast with language of "Judaizing" or "Judaizers," this is not a term that appears in the ancient sources themselves, although scholars have confidently categorized various sects listed in both Christian and rabbinic heresiologies as "Jewish Christian"—as, for example, the Ebionites, the Nazorites, the Symmachites, and the Elkanites. Even the *Didascalia* does not use the label "Jewish Christians" but addresses the heretics as "you who have been converted from among the people." "Jewish Christianity" is, then, a term invoked by modern scholarship to refer to and describe the phenomenon discussed in this chapter, namely, Christian believers who observe Jewish rituals. Beyond that, it is also used to designate a type of theology or thought.[29] Despite its apparent neutrality, "Jewish Christian" is no more a simple, descriptive term than is "Judaizer"—as is evidenced by the definitional chaos that confronts any reader of the enormous body of scholarly literature on Jewish Christianity. Some scholars have drawn on an ethnic definition. Accordingly, the term refers to the Christianity of born Jews, whether that applies to the earliest Christian community in Jerusalem or to such people as are addressed by the *Didascalia*. Others have gone so far as to make a distinction between "Judaeo-Christians"—Gentiles who for whatever reasons observe certain biblical commandments—and "Jewish Christians"—Jews who become Christians yet do not totally abandon their observance of certain biblical commandments.[30] This approach has by necessity run into trouble. Not all born Jews or Jewish converts to Christianity necessarily continue in their observance of Jewish ritual or Law after baptism. Nor is there any reason why some Gentile Christians should not have remained unconvinced by Paul's rejection of the Law. In other words, ethnic identity does not and cannot predict or determine theology or ideology. Indeed, it scarcely seems to matter at all to Jerome or Chrysostom whether the Judaizers they oppose are born Jews or Gentiles. Even in the case of the *Didascalia,* which addresses its heretics as Jewish converts, the problem is not restricted to that particular subgroup. The authoritative nature of biblical law seems to be attractive to the community or the audience as a whole. In the chapter "Concerning Husbands," the *Didascalia* warns the general audience of lay members, "When you read in the Law, be watchful regarding [the second legislation] that you do but read it simply *[pshita'it]*. But extremely abstain from the commands and prohibitions that are therein so that you may not lead yourself astray and bind yourself with the bonds of heavy burdens which may not be loosed.... And this shall be set before your eyes that you may discern and know what in the Law is the Law, and what are the bonds that are in the second legislation" (CSCO 402, 15).

Other scholars have taken theology in the broadest sense to be the determining factor of Jewish Christian identity. Accordingly, the demonstrated presence of any concept or idea that can be related to Judaism turns its adherents into Jewish Christians. However, such an approach ends up colluding with the early Christian polemicists, who seem prepared to detect Judaizing anywhere and everywhere. At the same time, it promotes its own form of boundary making by assuming a particular definition of pure Christianity, or, for that matter, pure Judaism. Hence Daniel Boyarin has suggested recently that what requires explanation is not the existence of Jewish Christianity as a supposed historical phenomenon but the fact that early Christian writers invested so much rhetorical effort to expose and at the same time denounce and declare heretical those who engaged in supposed Jewish practices or adopted Jewish teachings. Both Christian writers, Boyarin argues, and their rabbinic counterparts who similarly hereticized Christianizing Jews deployed the hybrid category of Jewish Christian or Judaizer/Christianizer not only to reinforce their respective orthodoxies but also to assure the very categorical purity of orthodoxy itself: "The ascription of existence to the 'hybrids' assumes (and thus assures) the existence of nonhybrid, 'pure' religions."[31]

Boyarin's rhetorical analysis provides an important account of the interests of those early Christians and Jews who were in pursuit of fixing and guarding the borders against illegal immigrants, so to speak. However, we should not throw out the baby with the bathwater and reduce the phenomenon of Jewish Christianity to a mere rhetorical construction or figment of the orthodox imagination. Sometimes, even if only rarely, the people who did in fact cross the boundaries of religious identity come to light through the very polemics that seek to obscure them, as we have explored in this chapter. It is the existence of these actual border-crossers that keeps challenging and undermining the fantasies of orthodox purity. In fact, we may posit that the Christian commitment to the Hebrew Bible as part of its canon itself kept the two religions bound to each other. Attempts for hermeneutical control over the text on behalf of the bishops and rabbis notwithstanding, the fact that both shared the same text created a borderland that remained difficult to control.

It is perhaps this inability to control the borderland that finally accounts for the anti-Jewish rhetoric in early Christianity. A number of scholars have attributed the anti-Judaism of early Christian literature to the (presumably widespread) phenomenon of Christian Judaizing, a theory articulated most forcefully by Marcel Simon.[32] However, although this suggestion laudably attempts to divert the blame from Jews and Judaism, it still ends up blaming the wrong people and removing the burden from those who produced and promoted the hate speech evidenced in Chrysostom's rhetoric. It is, rather, the fact that clear boundaries separating Christianity from Judaism were frequently impossible to establish, together with the anxiety that resulted from this fact, that gave rise to the anti-Jewish rhetoric in early Christian texts. In a certain sense, then, the parting of the ways never really did take place decisively in late antiquity, or it only did so by political fiat when one religion gained imperial power.

FOR FURTHER READING

Boyarin, Daniel. *Border Lines: The Partition of Judaeo-Christianity.* Divinations: Rereading Late Ancient Religion. Philadelphia: University of Pennsylvania Press, 2004.

Cohen, Shaye J. D. *The Beginnings of Jewishness: Boundaries, Varieties, Uncertainties.* Hellenistic Culture and Society 31. Berkeley: University of California Press, 1998.

Dunn, James D. G. *The Parting of the Ways between Christianity and Judaism and Their Significance for the Character of Christianity.* Harrisburg, Pa.: Trinity Press International, 1991.

Fonrobert, Charlotte Elisheva. *Menstrual Purity: Rabbinic and Christian Reconstructions of Biblical Gender.* Stanford, Calif.: Stanford University Press, 2000. Chapter 6.

Lieu, Judith. *Image and Reality: The Jews in the World of the Christians in the Second Century.* Edinburgh: T. & T. Clark, 1996.

Simon, Marcel. *Verus Israel: A Study of the Relations between Christians and Jews in the Roman Empire, 135–425.* Trans. H. McKeating. Littman Library of Jewish Civilization. London: Oxford University Press, 1986 [1948].

Strecker, Georg. "On the Problem of Jewish Christianity." In Walter Bauer, ed., *Orthodoxy and Heresy in Earliest Christianity,* 241–85. Philadelphia: Fortress, 1971.

Taylor, Joan E. *Christians and the Holy Places: The Myth of Jewish-Christian Origins.* Oxford: Clarendon, 1993.

Taylor, Miriam S. *Anti-Judaism and Early Christian Identity: A Critique of the Scholarly Consensus.* Leiden: Brill, 1995.

BEYOND MAGIC AND SUPERSTITION

DAVID FRANKFURTER

I t is always exciting to discover, out in some rural village, an erotic masque at the Easter festival long folded into the year's liturgical life, a sacred pool associated with Diana and proven to expand one's herd, or a saint's image brimming with stories of exorcism and direct intervention in the lives of those who light candles by her. We find ourselves struck by the appearance—ostensible, to be sure—of some authenticity and originality in these regional practices that are muted, if not outright prohibited, in the official liturgy of the church. Perhaps we intuit a deeper, more ancient religious meaning in such activities, over which Christianization has provided but a thin veneer. Or perhaps we find ourselves impressed with the creativity, the agency, and the self-determination of people who assert local traditions *within* a religious world established as Christian.

If our own encounters with such incidences of a "popular religion" may inspire exhilaration and respect, church historians of the last century, like their patristic forebears, looked upon the religious expressions of *hoi polloi*—rural villagers, lower classes, indeed the mass of the postapostolic devout—as decadent, untaught, and even heathen. For the Reverend Blomfield Jackson, the signs of decline from a pure, apostolic faith appear "just at this period when the Pagan idols were destroyed, [when] faint traces of image worship begin to appear in the Church. In another two centuries and a half it was becoming common, and in this particular point, Christianity relapsed into paganism." More recently the Jesuit scholar George Dennis explained the profusion of unorthodox expressions among the masses as symptomatic of a lapse in doctrinal instruction: "It is not uncommon, even in the highly structured Christian church, for beliefs and practices to develop among ordinary people without the guidance of their ordained leaders or teachers and gradually to assume such importance that they become accepted as part of the faith."[1]

For both Jackson and Dennis, the amalgamation of pieties that emerges in popular Christianity represents a departure, even a fall, from a pure, apostolic, and properly guided orthodoxy. For others, as I have already hinted, the definition of popular religion as somehow distinct from an elite or ecclesiastical—"learned"—religion may carry a more positive connotation, gesturing toward a sphere of devotion more spontaneous and culturally authentic than the alien salvation systems and rarefied mysteries that the official church and its clergy were promoting. Class factors invariably play into all these constructions of popular religion. That is, the devotions of the poor and uneducated typically come off as a soup of magic, crisis rites, image worship, festival hilarity, and superstition in contrast to the staid and rational religion ascribed to the upper classes.

Yet it is precisely this picture of a lower tier of religiosity, distinct from the devotions of the elite, that Arnaldo Momigliano criticized already in 1971 as completely inapplicable to late antique Christian culture, in which the same ritual forms took place across social classes, in both cities and countryside. Peter Brown regarded the two-tier model of religion as the legacy of an eighteenth-century rationalism that could not comprehend the fact that the cult of the saints was a central religious form for bishops, emperors, and peasants alike. Jonathan Z. Smith critiqued in even stronger terms the Protestant anti-Catholic polemic that has long underlain scholarly attempts to distinguish some lower grade of Christianity as syncretistic, ritual-bound, and decadent—epitomized in Jackson's remarks above. Similar constructions of popular religion in the study of early modern Europe, the historian Natalie Zemon Davis observes, have allowed scholars first to trot out random incidences of unorthodox folk practices with no context but their cumulative oddity, and then—she laments—to "sort religious behavior into approved and disapproved categories."[2]

Today the notion of a popular religion has come under even broader criticism, as many scholars grow increasingly conscious of the political legacy of Western intellectual discourse. What categories are operating in our Christian sources to represent a religious practice in such and such a way? And what categories—explicit and implicit—do *we* use to represent our subjects, to determine what we study and how? When we write appreciatively about saint cults, shrines, iconography, or magic, are we merely carrying on those elitist, early Protestant prejudices in different guise—as historical voyeurism or nostalgic inversion, championing the popular as authentic and shunning the elite as—well, elitist?

We can only profit from these several decades' worth of critiques of popular religion as a distinct lower tier of piety. And yet, despite the undeniable challenges entailed, many of us still try to pursue the historical study of the very forms of Christianity classically relegated to this lower tier of religion. This chapter seeks to contribute to the clarity of this important enterprise by proposing two ways of thinking about popular religion: first, to interrogate the very biases of those ancient testimonies from which scholars have constructed a popular religion in late antiquity, and second, to reconstruct the religious worlds behind these testimonies in a more holistic and less polarized way.

The first mode of thinking about popular religion in this essay involves analyzing the actual *rhetoric of dichotomy and denigration* in antiquity—the voices of church fathers, synods, narratives, and purist movements that construct various boundaries to edit out the magical, the heathen, the heretical, the confused, as inauthentic and thus to invent some (admittedly shifting) notion of orthodoxy and orthopraxy. This rhetoric tends to address itself to a consistent range of phenomena, from festivals to mortuary practices, and yet the criticisms themselves arise inconsistently and usually in charged political situations. The second mode entails studying the actual *historical dynamics* of Christianization in the local culture and landscape, the ways that people integrate tradition with new schemes of authority, and the terms or categories that *we* use to describe those dynamics. That is, what are people doing in that village, by that shrine, before that tree, in that church?

ORIGINS AND SPECTRUM OF THE CENSURING OF RITUAL

Let us first consider the historical rhetoric of religious dichotomy and authenticity. In this case, church fathers' appraisals of certain religious forms—rituals, images, texts—as idolatrous or crude or childish or superstitious or heathen become part of a bandolier of polemical categories that include "magic," "heathen," "devil worship," "heretic," "Manichaean," and "barbarian." These were supremely flexible and ever-mutating categories, often applied ad hoc in situations to envelop and marginalize any sort of religious practice (sometimes even images or texts). Such polemical tactics comprise what we might call a *discourse of ritual censure,* insofar as the proscribed phenomena invariably consist of inappropriate behavior or gesture in a sanctioned context (like a saint's festival, a liturgy, or a cemetery); inappropriate ritual exploitation of sanctioned materials, like gospels or shrine materials; or ceremonial acts in proscribed—demonized—places in the landscape, like temples or springs. Thus, for example, in the first sidebar, an anonymous fifth-century Coptic preacher rails against a variety of ritual practices (and their ingredients) conducted by people in his vicinity for the

sake of protection and healing. The discourse of censure here is demono-
logical; the author seeks to edit out of proper religious conduct this range
of gestures and materials by associating them with the realm of the demonic.

The roots of the late antique Christian discourse of ritual censure go
back to early Roman imperial ideology. Roman notions of a cosmic and
civic order maintained through public ritual had
their antithesis in another ritual category that
denoted secrecy and disruption of the social
order: *magia* ("wizardry") and its corollary,
superstitio ("immoral devotion"). Both terms
were ambiguous and could be applied to different individuals and groups at the whim of the
accusers. For this reason it is preferable to keep
the terms untranslated: "magic" and "superstition," heirs to centuries of post-Reformation and
post-Enlightenment thought, do not reflect the
distinctive ways that Roman and late antique
writers used these terms. In the imperial period,
for example, *magia* and *superstitio* were epitomized in techniques of divination that lay outside the official work of the Roman *haruspices*
and *augures* (the traditional divination priestly
ranks), associated instead with prophets and foreign technologies. Thus the discourse of ritual
censure revolved around foreignness, subversion,
manipulation, social breakdown, and fantasies
about the wizards and witches who gleefully engaged in such deviance,
often in the context of monstrous sacrifices. Articulating cultural difference and its ambiguity in terms of ritual practice became central to the
Roman imperial worldview. Were foreign rites and their often itinerant
experts a threat or a resource? This ambiguity preoccupied Roman thought
on religious practice.[4]

Christianization maintained this focus on ritual difference, polarizing
it further as devil worship, a far more insidious notion of subversion. The
inverted, cannibalistic sacrifices of the witch or barbarian now became all
the more horrific, for they recalled the sacrificial performances that in
Christian memory led to martyrdoms. Hence the chief atrocity of the heathen—the imagined non-Christian—is blood sacrifice of any kind. In some
writers like Augustine of Hippo, heathen devotions in home or square are
cumulatively labeled *magia*, "sorcery," assimilated to the old category of
disruptive foreign ritual, while in the Theodosian Code *magia* is only one
of the various outside practices that amount to *superstitio*—that is, in this

> There are among us today those who worship
> the "poetic" forms of demons—(forms) con-
> trived from the beginning in their deceitfulness
> and deluding people as healing cults. . . .
>
> Some of them practice abominations in
> city and village. For it is said that some of them
> ablute their children in polluted water and water
> from the arena, from the theater, and moreover
> they pour all over themselves water with incan-
> tations [spoken over it], and they break their
> clay pots claiming it repels the evil eye. Some
> tie amulets on their children, hand-crafted by
> men—those [men] who provide a place for the
> dwelling of demons—while others anoint them-
> selves with oil that is evil and incantations and
> such things that they tie on their heads and
> necks.
>
> —Pseudo-Athanasius,
> *Hom. on Virginity*, 92, 95[3]

case, heathenism. Traditional civic and domestic rites are thus thrown together with such nefarious categories of specialist as *haruspices, mathematici* ("calculators"), *harioli* ("soothsayers"), *vates* ("prophets"), *chaldaei* ("Chaldaeans"), *magi* ("wizards"), *malefici* ("sorcerers"), and *venefici* ("poison-mongers")—all types of diviners and freelance ritual specialists long deemed suspect in Roman imperial ideology (*CTh.* 9.16, 16.10).[5]

As in the early empire, when the monstrosity of *superstitio* could be captured in fantastic pornographic tableaux of reprehensible rituals (and so imputed to Bacchic devotees and Christians), so religious otherness in late antiquity was often epitomized in spectacles of human sacrifice, infant cannibalism, orgy, and mock sacraments, applied not only to heterodox enclaves like "Gnostics" but also the distinctively "fallen" and heretical folk religion of whole regions of the empire, like Phrygia in Asia Minor. Much as it associated discomfiting "folk" ritual forms with notions of *magia* or *superstitio*, the discourse of ritual censure had the capacity to collapse such forms with heretical labels. Athanasius of Alexandria, for example, labeled certain Egyptian Christian mortuary practices "Meletian"—associating them with a particularly divisive fourth-century "heresy." For the sixth-century Coptic monk John of Paralos, the primary complaint about apocryphal texts circulating in the vicinity of Scetis is the "simple folks'" proclivity to "pay attention [to the books], and [that] the zealous ones who hear them ... think that the words of these books ... are truthful things."[6]

The discourse of ritual censure, with all its multiple terms for demarcating and demonizing Christians' manifold ritual practices, nonetheless encountered limits in its capacity to grasp the various religious worlds to which Christianization gave rise and in which various expressive forms made sense. John of Ephesus, for example, recounts the holy man Simeon the Mountaineer's encounter with a mountain village in Syria that, as far as he can figure out, is *neither* Christian *nor* heathen. They know no liturgy nor basic doctrine, nor have they ever seen scriptures; yet they call themselves Christian and do have a church. "What pagan is there," declares Simeon in amazement, "or what other worshippers of creation, who for so long a period of time would neglect to pay honour to the object of his worship, and would not always worship that which is reckoned by him as God? These men neither worship God like Christians, nor honour something else like pagans; and they are apostates against the one and against the other." Ultimately, Simeon (in the memory of John of Ephesus) can only compare these people to animals.[7]

This story of Simeon the Mountaineer highlights our sources' problems of recognition and classification in the area of variant ritual practice. How familiar does some practice strike a Christian author—in its similarity either to Christianity or to some notion of heathenism? How can he render it comprehensible by reference to known Christian practices (for example, the martyr cult) or to classic stereotypes of heathenism or barbarian sacrifice? While Simeon cannot find anything recognizable in the Syrian villages except for the church building, other holy men and church leaders return again and again to certain basic themes in their efforts to demarcate acceptable Christian expression and also to construct a category of improper ritual behavior related to heathenism, demon worship, magic, or other terms. Let us examine what the church leaders tended to pick out as heathen, demonic, or worse, in their view, sorcery.

Festival Behavior

One of the chief objects of ritual censure was festival behavior. In festivals, of course, a public church ceremonial could invite a range of local festival significances and customs, along with enthusiastic public participation. Rarely could it remain an exclusively ecclesiastical theater. Yet, as we see in witnesses of the fourth and fifth centuries, festivals also represented the resilience of traditional calendars, persisting within or alongside ecclesiastical calendars. Epiphanius laments "the orgies of Memphis and Heliopolis, where the tambourine and the flute capture hearts, and the dancing girls, and the triennial festivals of Batheia and Menouthis where women abandon their modesty and their customary state" (*De fides* 12.1). His attention to sexual excess anticipates church leaders' criticisms of festivals well into the eleventh century. An eroticized "anti-structure" in the local festival triggers in the ecclesiastical observer a discourse of ritual censure couched specifically in terms of heathenism, excluding such performance from the purview of Christianity and labeling it as a noxious holdover of the rejected religion. The association with heathenism does not in any way represent local participants' perspectives on the nature of these festivals; rather, it demonstrates how the discourse of ritual censure might draw its own associations in order to repudiate certain practices.

Christian leaders also pick out festival practices of a less hilarious sort, conducted at home with ceremonial implements or in specially designated places: "Woe to any man or woman who gives thanks to demons," Abbot Shenoute of Atripe proclaims to an audience presumably invested in their church affiliation, "saying that 'Today is the worship of *Shai* [Fortune], or *Shai* of the village or *Shai* of the house,' while burning lamps for empty things and offering incense in the name of phantoms" (*The Lord Thundered*, p. 45). Bishop Martin of Braga, also speaking to initiated Christians, rebukes them for "observing days for idols, . . . for observing Vulcan's day and the Kalends, for setting out tables and putting up laurel wreaths, . . . for observing Venus's day at weddings, . . . what else is this but devil-worship?" (*On the Correction of the Rustics* 16). A late seventh-century church council repudiates "the rituals known as the 'Calends,' the 'Bota,' the 'Broumalia,'. . . as well as the dances and rites performed by men or women in the name of those falsely called gods of the Greeks, according to an ancient custom foreign to the life of Christians." Nor may people "invoke the name of the abhorrent Dionysus while crushing grapes in wine presses"; indeed, the canon demands strict punishment for the *clerics* who participate! (Council of Trullo, Can. 62). While we may prize such testimony for illuminating the range of local Christian practice, we must also recognize that the authors seek to disengage such practices from Christianity through a discourse of ritual censure that emphasizes both heathenism and demonolatry.

Misuses of Church Property and Places

A different kind of ritual censure governs the range of perceived practices that we might label the misuse of ecclesiastical property. Church leaders alternate between expressions of curiosity at the diverse ways people might exploit church materials and often flustered attempts to relate them to heresy, heathenism, or demons. John Chrysostom several times remarks on a practice among Antiochene women and children of wearing Gospels around their necks "as a powerful amulet." At one point the amulet serves as a favorable analogy to Jewish tefillin; at another point it serves as an exterior form of what should instead be "inscribed on" the mind (*Hom. on Matthew* 72 [about Matt. 23:5]; *Hom. on Statues* 19.14). The practice stands out for its concrete use, rather than reading, of Christian scripture. Yet Chrysostom perceives it not in relationship to "magic" but to Jewish sacred scripture, in his terms a mark of ambivalence. For John of Paralos, however, it is the so-called simple folks' *informative*—that is, intellectual—use of marginalized Christian books that impels him to censure: because they are simple-minded, they "think that the words of these books . . . are truthful things."[8]

Holy oils too become commodities with proper and condemnable uses. Administered in a saints' shrine or church liturgy, carried in one of the numerous souvenir ampullae sold at pilgrimage centers, oil was universally regarded as one of the chief vehicles of the holy and so could not properly be relegated to some putative sphere of lower-class piety.[9] Yet, as Abbot Shenoute complains in one of his most important polemics against ritual practices, oil could be blessed and administered in diverse ritual contexts—by monks and elders, and for protective or healing purposes as well as ecclesiastical sealing (line 259; see sidebar).

Shenoute, like the author of the Coptic homily quoted above (see first sidebar), clearly views this extramural use of oil to convey healing power

(255) But at the time of suffering, those fallen into poverty or in sickness or indeed some other trial abandon God and run after enchanters or diviners or indeed seek other acts of deception, (256) just as I myself have seen: the snake's head tied on someone's hand, another one with the crocodile's tooth tied to his arm, and another with fox claws tied to his legs—(257) especially since it was an official who told him that it was wise to do so! Indeed, when I demanded whether the fox claws would heal him, he answered, "It was a great monk who gave them to me, saying 'Tie them on you (and) you will find relief.'"

(258) Listen to this impiety! Fox claws! Snakes' heads! Crocodiles' teeth! And many other vanities that men put on themselves for their own relief, while others deceive them.

(259) Moreover, this is the manner that they anoint themselves with oil or that they pour over themselves water while receiving [ministrations] from enchanters or drug-makers, with every deceptive kind of relief.... Still again, they pour water over themselves or anoint themselves with oil from elders of the church, or even from monks!

(260) It is about them that the Prophet Elijah blamed Israel in that time, saying "How long will you limp on two legs? If the Lord is God, follow him, but if Baal, then follow him!" [see 1 Kings 18:21]

(261) Thus also, those [of you] who do these things or who put these things on themselves, how long will you "limp on two legs"? If the oracle sanctuary of demons is useful to you—and enchanters and drug-makers and all the other things that thus work for lawlessness—then go to them, so that you will receive their curse on earth and eternal punishment on the day of judgment!

(262) But if it is the house of God, the Church, that is useful to you, go to it.

—Shenoute, *Acephalous Work* A14[10]

as beyond the pale of Christian practice, yet, as we noted with regard to festivals, the audience certainly did understand this use of oil, and the freelance ritual experts (monks and elders) who administered it, within a coherent spectrum of Christian practice. Shenoute describes this wider spectrum of sensible ritual practices and consultations in the beginning of this polemic, referring disparagingly to a local official who considered his healing amulet of fox claws entirely legitimate, insofar as it had been delivered by a "great monk" (lines 255–58). In a world of diverse blessings—*eulogia*—in circulation from church and shrine for popular protection, Shenoute here seeks to discriminate acceptable from unacceptable sorts, and animal parts are doubtless meant to strike the audience as unacceptable, even if many did make use of such amulets. Shenoute does not, to be sure, relate these practices to demon worship or magic, drawing instead on labels like "vanity," "deception," and "impiety." Yet by the end of the passage he has inserted a wedge between these "works of lawlessness" and the works of Christ. Quoting the biblical Elijah, he accuses the amulet-wearers and their purveyors as "limping on two legs": if this (altogether vague) range of marginal ritual practices is useful to you, go to it and suffer God's curse, "but if it is the house of God, the Church, that is useful to you, go to it."

Local practices at saints' shrines provoke the full range of ecclesiastical responses. Theodoret celebrates such shrines' expropriation of sites, building materials, and even festival forms from heathen temples: "so, now that you see the advantage of the cult of martyrs, friends, flee the error of the demons" (*Therapeutikē* 8.68–70). In this context the rich ceremonial life of the saint shrine is entirely within the purview of official Christian practice. Some church leaders might nonetheless find themselves amazed at the peculiarity of local practices at such shrines. Evagrius, visiting the shrine of Saint Simeon the Stylite's pillar on a mountaintop east of Antioch, reports with some curiosity the "country people dancing around the pillar" and even "circumambulating the column repeatedly with their beasts of burden." Here the discourse of ritual censure assumes an elitist air, casting the local practices as *agroikos* ("backwoods, boorish") (*Eccl. Hist.* 1.14).

In fourth- and fifth-century Egypt, however, local practices around saints' shrines could inspire much more bitter censure. Athanasius complains that people who sleep in martyr-shrines to rid themselves of demons, far from crediting Christ with the exorcism, go on to question the demons as oracular spirits. If for Athanasius the trafficking in martyrs' relics to produce such shrines indicates "Meletian" heresy, these spirit-consultations amount to nothing less than demon worship (*Festal Letter* 42). And several decades later, Shenoute shows equal familiarity with these ritual practices and equal condemnation. People are claiming visitations by dead martyrs, he charges, who instruct them where to exhume relics and build *martyria*. People are bringing these relics into churches to have them enshrined there. People are visiting shrines to gain oracular dreams and healing. And Shenoute declares that

Fig. 11.1. The shrine of Simeon the Stylite, built around his pillar on a Syrian mountaintop east of Antioch, attracted pilgrims from around the Mediterranean world in the fifth and sixth centuries. The rotunda surrounding the pillar, photographed here (with the pillar-base to the right), also became the focus of regional ritual traditions, observed by Evagrius of Pontus in the 590s. Photo credit: © Elizabeth Bolman. Used by permission.

> Those who adore [martyrs] in some shrine built in their name worship demons, not God. Those who trust that healings come to them, or goods, in a place that they built over some skeletons without knowing whose they are, are no different from those who worshipped the calves that Jeroboam set up in Samaria....
>
> Who among those who fear God will not say, "Woe to those who say, 'I saw a light in the shrine that they built over some bones of a skeleton in the church, and I was eased of my illness after I slept there'"?

As for those who would introduce martyrs' bones to a church, he declares, they simply "do not understand what is proper to do in a church" (*Those Who Work Evil*). Shenoute, like Athanasius, applies a range of terms and ideas to reject these martyr-cult traditions as beyond the pale of Christian practice, not only detailing certain customs as blatantly inappropriate but insisting on their demonic, polluting nature. His testimony here is valuable not because it highlights a "popular" practice or "pagan survival" but because it rejects a religious complex that in fact became quite central to Christianity in Egypt (and elsewhere), even in its extensions to divination.[11]

Private or Idiosyncratic Ritual Practices

Local mortuary practices in late antiquity have long impressed archaeologists and historians for their minimal evolution over time despite new religious identities, and yet these practices seem rarely to have attracted church leaders' discourse of ritual censure.[12] On the other hand, a great range of regular ritual customs were plucked from their contexts, in home or festival, and held up precisely as examples of heathenism, devil worship, or sorcery. The sixth-century Portuguese bishop Martin of Braga expresses shock that people who had declared themselves Christian might continue to practice devotions at old sacred places and to maintain various domestic and life-crisis or life-passage rites. These practices, as Martin describes them, have nothing to do with each other, and indeed their coherence remains difficult to discern. They range from private to collective acts and from occasional to regular in performance. They express, not untypically for late antique religion, the actors' sense of landscape, holy media, the power of the spoken word, and a concern to address the exigencies of life. Yet we are given no sense of what they mean or how their performance fits into local culture. Martin seeks to divorce them from context and to relate them to the world of the devil and idolatry, outside and prior to Christendom—that is, a constructed heathenism.

> How is it possible that some of you who have renounced the devil and his messengers and his worship and his evil ways turn again to the worship of the devil! To light candles beside rocks and beside trees and beside fountains and at crossroads, what else is this but worship of the devil? To observe divination and auguries and days for idols, ... to pour fruit and wine on a log in the hearth, to throw bread into a fountain, what else is this but worship of the devil? For women at their weaving to call on the name of Minerva and to observe the day of Venus at weddings and to be careful about the day on which one commences a journey, what else is this but worship of the devil? And many other things which it would take too long to mention here. Lo, you do all these things after renunciation of the devil, after baptism, and by returning to the worship of demons and to the evil works of idols you have transgressed your faith and have broken the pact which you made with God.
>
> —Martin of Braga,
> *On the Correction of the Rustics* 16[13]

A similar strategy of decontextualizing practices that were obviously enmeshed with civic and domestic life characterizes the legal declarations of synods and, above all, of the Theodosian Code. In one such pronouncement from 391 CE, grand festival acts like blood sacrifice are combined with more basic and personal gestures within the potent landscape of east Roman cities and villages, and all are proscribed as contrary to the cosmos: "No person shall pollute himself with sacrificial animals; no person shall slaughter an innocent victim; no person shall approach the shrines, shall wander through the temples, or revere the images formed by mortal labor, lest he become guilty by divine and human laws" (*CTh*. 16.10.10).[14]

Another edict, from 392 CE, enumerates ritual practices in the domestic sphere as well as those devoted to public images, and even some to holy trees—again without regard to the circumstances and habits by which people might engage in such practices (see sidebar). These expressions are finally labeled as "heathen superstition [*gentilicia superstitione*]"—implying that they are both non-Christian holdovers and illegitimate, barbarian rites.

In reflecting on the effectiveness of these edicts in a sermon of circa 404 CE, Augustine draws on a similarly Roman imperial discourse of ritual censure: just as the temple cults had been shut down "as public magic rites . . . , so too these things are still being done secretly, after their public practice has been forbidden." He refers here to the continuity of rites that have shifted from the public to the domestic domain, but by describing such rites as "magic" (and, earlier, as the work of the devil), he signals their intrinsically reprehensible nature.[15]

Conclusions regarding the Censuring of Ritual

Across this selection of late antique witnesses to the persistence of an illegitimate and somewhat curious type of ritual behavior within Christianity, we see a general discourse of ritual censure capable of picking out certain practices—private devotions, attention to sacred sites, festivals—and associating them with anything from vulgar rural culture to magic, heresy, and heathenism. When we speak of a popular religion, it is important to be aware how much our own sense of the contours of this type of piety depends on this ancient discourse, insofar as our sources emerge within this discourse. At the same time, if we try to avoid the term "popular religion," we must still reckon with a general inclination among such church leaders themselves to discriminate areas of religious practice, even if the discourse they employed to make such discriminations tended not to distinguish religious practices by economic class. That is, the church leaders we read as sources for popular piety and pagan survival were, in fact, actively trying to construct an area of marginal or illegitimate Christian practice, partly in continuity with Roman imperial notions of *superstitio* and *magia*—subversive ritual—and partly out of a distinctive Christian ideology of the demonic. It was a discourse committed to editing in and

> No person at all, . . . shall sacrifice an innocent victim to senseless images in any place at all or in any city. He shall not, by more secret wickedness, venerate his *lar* with fire, his *genius* with wine, his *penates* with fragrant odors; he shall not burn lights to them, place incense before them, or suspend wreaths for them. . . .
>
> But if any person should venerate, by placing incense before them, images made by the work of mortals and destined to suffer the ravages of time, and if, in a ridiculous manner, he should suddenly fear effigies which he himself has formed, or should bind a tree with fillets, or should erect an altar of turf that he has dug up, or should attempt to honor vain images with the offering of a gift, . . . [he] shall be punished by the forfeiture of that house or landholding in which it is proved that he served a pagan superstition.
>
> —*Theodosian Code* 16.10.12[16]

editing out certain ritual acts in order to construct—in quite diverse and regionally and personally specific ways—a sphere of Christian behavior entirely separate from another behavior considered to be of the devil, associated with heresy and with a general, negative, and quite unperceptive notion of traditional, ancestral religion.

In many cases (like the Theodosian Code and the writings of Martin of Braga) we do get the sense that the practices listed have been maintained since before people identified themselves as Christian, even if they now continue—we must assume—as complements, not challenges, to Christian identity. In other cases, such as Shenoute's story of the monk dispensing fox-claw amulets, the Coptic homily about healing and protective gestures, and many other attacks on *magia,* we discern a range of acts carried on between families and ritual experts, peripheral to broader cultic or religious systems and to some degree spontaneous and perennial in their genesis. And in still other cases, such as Shenoute's and Athanasius's complaints about the forms in which the Egyptian martyr cult was developing, we see practices (with somewhat more vivid life contexts) thoroughly informed by Christian notions of sainthood and power.

We must recognize that all three of these types of censured ritual practice have been used to substantiate a model of popular religion in modern scholarship. And more critically, all three have been interpreted as "pagan survivals," that is, holdovers from the old religion maintained alongside Christianity out of ignorance, an untaught inclination to see theologically incompatible practices as complementary. Whether by their festival practices, sacred trees, or age-old notions of the holy dead (to which the Egyptian martyr cult has often been traced), these villagers' religious inertia seems to beg the appropriateness of the label "Christian."

THE REDISCOVERY OF LOCAL RELIGIOUS WORLDS

Is there a way of reading through these testimonies and their censorious decontextualizing of ritual practices? Can we reconstruct social, ecological, or broader religious contexts in which these practices would make sense as distinct expressions of community and tradition? Is there any sense to the proposition, oft-assumed in the history of the study of popular religion, that such village-based or culturally rooted traditions might predate the process of Christianization or persist as "syncretisms"?

The terms that surround this proposition, of course, come heavily loaded with bias, both theological and cultural. "Syncretism" implies mixture in contrast to purity, a mixture occasioned by insufficient instruction (as Dennis suggests in the passage above), geographical remoteness, cultural crudeness or aloofness to history, or even church leaders' cynical acculturation of great theological ideas (as Jackson suggests in the first quotation). "Pagan survival" associates a people with a sort of timeless primitivity. Indeed, the discovery of pagan survivals has often carried an imperialist or missionary program, establishing the archaic nature of some culture in order to sanction forced change—or, conversely, a nationalist program, rooting the heritage of a people in some mythical prehistory. At the same time, paradoxically, the term questions a practice's resilience in the face of Christianity: "one of the interesting characteristics of the temporal mirage of pagan survivals," the anthropologist João de Pina-Cabral points out, "is that they are seen as constantly on the verge of disappearing."[17]

And yet, as Pina-Cabral and others have argued, it would be a mistake to deny that religious practices and attitudes do continue over great periods of history. The challenge for the observer, whether anthropologist or historian, is to conceptualize the continuities in more subtle terms than did those ancient and modern "survival" collectors. Anthropologists of popular religion and ritual continuities have drawn, for example, on Maurice Bloch's principle of "ritual fixity" and Rodney Needham's distillation of "primary factors" in cultural imagination. One might also invoke notions of habitus or "habit-memory," developed by Pierre Bourdieu and Paul Connerton with reference to the gestural code by which members of a culture perform and repeat socially meaningful acts, from table manners to games to ceremonies. Through habit-memories actions gain meaning, group activities are coordinated, and collective memories are actualized. Habit-memories serve as the links between action and past and social context, even grounding perception itself, in innumerable areas of life but most vividly in the negotiation of the holy—both its contours and the practices through which it is recognized. How does someone know what to do at a sacred tree or a healing shrine, how to approach a saint, how to react to a neighbor's unsafe word, or how to dance at a festival?[18]

But the dynamics of habit-memories should not be taken to imply a stilted or rigid adherence to tradition. As we delve more deeply into the "work" of popular religion and the ritual bricolages, or constructions using the materials at hand, whether at trees or at domestic altars, that have subsequently been taken as pagan survivals and syncretisms, we do not find either an ignorant bondage to archaic ideas or resistance to notions of purity and authority. Rather, we find local communities' active engagement with new, hegemonic religious forms and ideas and their attendant notions of authority, power, and text. We find cultures appropriating and articulating these religious forms and ideas within the primary religious contexts of the regional and local environments: the landscape, the home, the economy, the social structure and its tensions, the calendar, and all the fortunes and misfortunes that challenge these contexts. Understanding the elements of popular religion and the continuities in religious practice that it necessarily involves requires the recognition of indigenous *agency* in accepting some religious forms and rejecting others, asserting the preeminence of local spirits in one domain and the hegemony of Christ or a saint in another.[19]

Understanding popular religion also requires an engagement with the variety of ways that traditions are maintained or revitalized: some are recast in Christian terms, such that Christian discourse provides a means for a ritual's revitalization, for example, while others are preserved within older systems of expression, like the names of local gods, traditional masks, or ancient shrines. In this sense a local spring converted to celebrate a Christian saint and baptismal waters must be viewed both as a potent element of the landscape celebrated within a Christian ideology of power and as that same Christian ideology of power mapped onto the local topography and its central points. It does not represent the simple survival of a pagan belief or practice nor the struggle (even victory) of one religion against another.

In some cases Christian demonology itself becomes a means for maintaining older gods' presence and power while holding them at a distance, juxtaposing them to Christ and Christian saints. Demonizing traditional gods and spirits is a way of keeping them alive, accessible, and still embedded in a region's landscape. The demons that greet Theodore of Sykeon in Gordine (Asia Minor) claim to be "much tougher and not milder" than those in Galatia, underlining (even in hagiographical fantasy) the topographical nature of demons (*Life of Theodore of Sykeon* 43).

But as we return, newly informed, to the data for late antique popular religion, we inevitably find that those who have culled these data—both in antiquity and in modern scholarship—have plucked phenomena out of all religious context. It is against this tendency toward the *anecdotal* construction of popular religion—abbreviated and decontextualized mentions of sacred springs, domestic gestures, protective rites—that one scholar has recommended a richer account of the religious worlds in which the phenomena take place, arguing that we should

> examine the range of people's relations with the sacred and the supernatural, so as not to fragment those rites, practices, symbols, beliefs and institutions which to villagers or citydwellers constitute a whole. We consider how all of these may provide groups and individuals some sense of the ordering of their world, some explanation for baffling events or injustice, and some notion of who and where they are. We ask what feelings, moods and motives they encourage or try to repress. We

look to see what means are offered to move people through the stages of their lives, to prepare for their future, and to cope with suffering or catastrophe.[20]

Each report of incubation at martyr shrines, prenuptial visits to sacred rocks, festival dances, the manufacture of amulets, or a mule at Saint Simeon's pillar must be assumed to be embedded in a social context, in a web of meanings and associated acts, and in ongoing conversations about authenticity and propriety. To understand popular religion is to comprehend how devotional and festal acts are embedded in the immediate social and physical environment. For this reason it seems useful to begin to speak more of a *local religion,* embracing the concentric worlds of village, region, and district, than a popular religion, dependent on notions of "elite" or "educated" religion that tend to say more about the prejudices of the observer than the phenomenon observed. The local religion model, which has been applied effectively in studies of the modern Yucatán, the modern Andes, modern Greece, and early modern and modern Spain, assumes neither that religion is static nor that it is immune to continuities.[21] Religion takes place not according to a series of levels of sophistication but rather within the context of the village, the city, the district, in dialectic with broader frames of reference, like regional cults, national cults, and textual traditions and their interpreters. The result is not "folk Christianity" but various contextualized Christianities: the Christianity of the Thebaid or Gaza or Minorca, and even the local variations within these regions.

The local religion model is particularly effective in comprehending the forms that conversion can take in a culture, recognizing as it does the relationship of religious adaptation to traditions enmeshed with local ecology—the pools and trees and valleys brimming with associations. The local religion model also admits the distinctive constructions of power, mediation, and language that individual missionaries might present to communities, as well as the varieties of ways in which communities might respond. A Gospel text might be accepted as a talisman rather than an intellectual resource, as John Chrysostom observed in Antioch. A formal blessing might be regarded as potent word magic. The missionary (or scribe or holy man) might be actively reconfigured in his duties, not as teacher of salvation, but as one with the capacity to address the exigencies of local experience with his crafts and powers—blessing donkeys, cursing bandits, writing amulets for healthy pregnancies, assembling charms from local fauna, even composing spells to bind disruptive people.[22]

Indeed, we come to appreciate the very range of exigencies and crises in local culture that impel people to develop ritual practices or demand ritual resolutions of local professionals. A woman fearful of her husband's infidelity, especially for economic reasons, for example, might well seek an impotence spell against him. A shopkeeper anxious for success might seek to "bind" his competitors. If we focus merely on the theological impropriety or curiosity of such acts, classifying them as "magic," for example, we miss the extent to which they are embedded in real social worlds and tensions and their demonstration of individuals' agency in resolving crises through various ideologies of power.

Late antique cultures in particular involved supernatural worlds far more complex than can be accommodated by the figures of Christ and the saints, evil demons, and shadowy old gods with classical names. Despite the attempts by church leaders to cast the world in the simplest, most dualist schemes, people everywhere and at all social levels encountered a diverse range of spirits, some repeatedly predatory, some dependably beneficial, and the vast majority ambiguous—harmful unless invoked properly. The Christian term *daimon* was entirely inadequate to capture the ambivalent and fluctuating nature of this world. The landscape pulsated with spirits; homes, families, and communities maintained ancestral relationships with some of these spirits, often through local and regional shrines. So, many centuries before the Protestant "disenchantment of the world," no context existed for the elimination of such relationships. Thus, for example, what Athanasius and Shenoute described of Egyptians' active involvement in developing martyr shrines and contacting these martyrs certainly represented a shift in the location and definition of ancestral spirits from prior Egyptian local religion. Yet the basic expectations for a relationship with spirits remained fairly constant—a phenomenon in no way unique to Egypt.[23] Cross-culturally, the need to maintain such contact may assume forms that embrace and assert novel religious forms like the martyr cult; it may take rebellious forms, as in the case of the possessed, oracles, or spirit mediums who speak against the new religion (as has often happened in colonial situations); or it may simply involve everyday or festal devotions, whose practitioners could not conceive of a discrepancy between their ritual acts and their identity as Christians—witness, for example, the modern Mexican *Día de los Muertos* (Day of the Dead) festivities. Most of the specific "heathen" acts brought up in imperial codes, Martin of Braga, Shenoute, and other texts involve this basic endeavor to maintain connections with ancestral spirits in the landscape—not in any way a "paganism." Indeed, Augustine mentions that some articulate conservatives in his region cannot believe that Christ himself "would have had a hostile sentiment towards their gods, but rather would have [himself] revered them with magic rites" (*Harmony of the Gospels* 1.34.52). Would not people assume that a new religion would maintain contact with the spirits, even if it proposed to reorder the cosmos in which those spirits function?

WORLDS OF LOCAL RELIGION:
EGYPT, PALESTINE, ASIA MINOR, GAUL

The concept of local religion serves primarily as a series of presuppositions about the way religious practices are embedded in a social world and a local ecology. It is not a partner to dichotomies—for example, contrasted to a putative world religion or official religion—even if we can speak, in Robert Redfield's heuristic sense, of a "great tradition" representing that sense of authority, hierarchy, and learned tradition with which local communities claim participation.[24] In practice, even the great tradition that local communities encounter and indigenize through texts and doctrines exists only in local or regional forms: witness the apocryphal texts that, John of Paralos complained, fascinated people near Scetis, the orthodoxy that Simeon the Stylite manifested to the Arab tribes that visited him (Theodoret, *Hist. of the Monks of Syria* 26.13–16), or the contrasting ideologies of holiness presented by the sixth-century Gallic stylite Saint Vulfolaic and the bishops who arrived to force him off his pillar (Gregory of Tours, *Hist. of the Franks* 8.15). In examining local religion we seek a kind of "thick description" of scenarios of religious expression that have invariably come to us embedded in that discourse of ritual censure described above.[25] I will here offer five types of evidence for which the use of a local religion paradigm produces a more textured and meaningful glimpse of religious life than prior scholarship on pagan survivals or folk religion allowed.

Atripe (Egypt), Late Fourth to Mid-Fifth Century CE

Our primary evidence for religious culture in late antique Atripe, near Panopolis in Upper Egypt, derives from the extensive sermons of Abbot Shenoute, which have been only partially collated and edited. In these texts we see the abbot furiously excoriating the abiding Egyptian cults and their patrons, even attacking some cults physically. Out of these testimonies, bolstered by a posthumous *vita* ("life," or biography) attributed to Shenoute's successor Besa (as well as by a considerable corpus of third-century CE documentation for temple religion in the area), we encounter as rich a picture of local religion as one could expect in late antiquity. Egyptian divine images persist in some villages. People fear Christian demolition of their sanctuaries, in one case trying to repel Shenoute with binding spells, in another ritually sprinkling a demolished temple. One major patron of traditional cult even tries to hide the divine images from Shenoute after the temple is destroyed. People—perhaps churchgoers, perhaps not—celebrate the local fortune-god *Shai* with lamps in their homes. Decades later, an

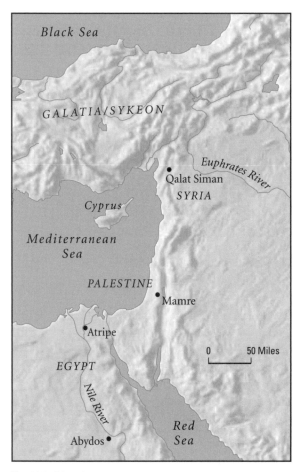

Fig. 11.2. Map of eastern Mediterranean regions. Map by Lucidity Information Design.

increasingly dominant and probably youthful population of Christians attacks those who still maintain an Egyptian divine image, "fighting for nothing over a piece of wood," as Besa denounces the act. A considerably later hagiography recalls a village somewhat north of Atripe, populated both by Christians and by devotees of a temple to the god *Shai-Agathodaimon,* offering details of domestic veneration of the temple deity and, again, of the terror and anger with which the temple devotees perceive the monks who come to invade the temple.[26]

Alongside these nuanced and quite credible glimpses of an abiding temple religion bound up with home, community, and landscape that evidently continued to attract many churchgoers, too, we also see in Shenoute's polemics against the cult of martyrs the endeavors of those who may have abandoned the temples to create and energize new centers, a new sacred landscape, from which a new class of ancestral spirits might now speak and heal. In seeking to put relics in the church itself—appalling to Shenoute—these people are exercising agency, drawing the church into that sacred landscape, while at the same time seeking a greater legitimacy for the relics.

And, of course, there is the monk who dispenses amulets of animal parts (see sidebar above, *Acephalous Work* A14). Shenoute shows us a world of diverse ritual bricolages, manifested at temples and shrines, and in the works of holy men, any one of which involves both a sense of necessity—driven in part by the force of habit-memories—and a complex and creative engagement with authority. Shenoute reveals a religious world lived between Christianity and so-called heathenism, in which tradition and local social identities dominate ritual practice.

Abydos (Egypt), circa Second to Eighth Century CE

A pilgrimage center had existed at Abydos, some fifty kilometers (about thirty-one miles) south of Atripe, since Pharaonic times, when the chief

Fig. 11.3. Near this spot at the temple of Abydos in upper Egypt, the popular god Bes was said to give oracles from the third through fourth centuries CE. The fifth-century Christian holy man Moses of Abydos is said to have exorcised the temple, following which a convent was installed nearby. Photo credit: © Françoise Dunand. Used by permission.

deity was Osiris, and continued through the early Roman period, when Serapis ruled there (and offered oracles as well), up through 359 CE, when Constantius II closed it down for entertaining politically subversive oracle inquiries. At that time the chief god was Bes, a dream, protection, and fertility god with few other known temples, and pilgrims would apparently be allowed into some chambers of the Memnonion to incubate for dreams, later acclaiming Bes in graffiti inscribed on the walls just outside the speaking part of the temple. Portable dream-seeking rituals were also developed under the aegis of Bes, suggesting that this familiar domestic figure had been effectively elevated by scribes and folklore to an authority over divination by the early Roman period. This development in itself tells us much about the dynamic relationship of domestic and pilgrimage-cult spheres in late antique temple religion: this was no "paganism in decline" but a dynamic center of religious creativity.[27]

Indeed, Constantius's repression of the cult does not seem to have obliterated it, for a century or so later—we learn from an admittedly lacunose and nostalgic hagiography—one Apa Moses arrives to exorcise the temple of "an evil *demon* named Bes . . . [who] would come out and *afflict* those passing by" (emphasis added). The extant text does not explain what took place after a successful, if terrifying, night of exorcistic chanting, but archaeology and a collection of letters show that, around this time,

Moses installed a convent in the Osireion shrine just north of the oracle temple, which he continued to advise.[28]

Assuming a minimum of historicity in the hagiographic sources, we have then to reckon with this transformation of Bes. How did his association with the temple continue through the Christianization of the region, and how demonic was the god really envisioned by the people in the area? Much depends on our models of Christianization and of afflicting spirits in late antiquity. Bes's associations with the temple would have continued in the course of communities' preservation of the sacred topographies basic to local religion: what places to avoid, what places to visit if pregnant, what places to go to contact oracular spirits, and so forth. Cross-culturally, empty temples and other abandoned structures have invariably been conceptualized as powerfully ambivalent in their liminality, and a temple active through the fourth century was obviously hotter than one abandoned in the second century.[29] But for a place to be haunted in this local sense does not mean that it was viewed as evil or utterly destructive in the way that the hagiographer recounts. Our model of local religion should allow a multiplicity of local responses to Bes in his temple, from terror and avoidance to occasional supplication, and perhaps even to the active solicitation of oracles, for it is doubtful that the practice would simply have ceased with Constantius's edict. Bes, that is, remained an ancestral spirit in the landscape, and while his deeds might be variously evaluated, his place remained fixed.

Mamre (Palestine), Fourth to Fifth Century CE

In local religion, the resolution of crises and the allure of entertainment both crystallize in the shrine festival. Processions and public readings, religious theater and storytelling, the concentration of devotional acts, festival foods and blessings, and all the collective effervescence that arises when people come together at sacred places in sacred time invite a diversity of ritual expressions and—more important—a diversity of visitors. At Mamre in Palestine, so the fifth-century church historian Sozomen reports, such a festival continued in his time, shared among groups he identifies variously as Christians, Jews, and heathens. Eusebius and Jerome allude to the pilgrimage with less detail but some curiosity at such quaint, persistent heathenism: the tree is "worshipped openly" (Eusebius) or even "superstitiously" (Jerome) by the "Gentiles" (*Onomasticon: Liber Locorum*, s.v. *Arbo*[s]).

A shrine that attracts so many religious groups from such a broad catchment area cannot, of course, be called an example of local religion; it is, rather, a "regional cult," as Aryeh Kofsky has described, inviting occasional and festal pilgrimages and complementing rather than opposing local shrines from its geographically peripheral location.[30] And yet such ecumenical regional cults, properly called "shared shrines," do teach us much about how local religion functions. Regional ritual customs, such as (Sozomen notes) festival celibacy, unite participants in one sphere, while prayers, invocations, and devotional gestures may be peculiar to individual groups and their local traditions. Religion is here a function of group expression and of expressive act, not creed. Recent work on the Christianization of Palestine in the fourth and fifth centuries suggests that this kind of movement from village out to Christian shrine may indeed have characterized people's interaction with the new religion. Christianity took place on the peripheries of settlements and by the investment of those committed to traveling to those peripheries, rather than in the invading and reordering of village life (as, for example, Bishop Porphyry did in Gaza).[31] Acceptance of Christian identity through attendance at such shrines was a function of local and personal agency: making the trip, participating in the total theater of the shrine, reaffirming regional traditions with others, even donating shrines.

Galatia and Gaul, Sixth Century CE

Local religion is personified in a variety of ritual experts, individuals in whom the community invests some degree of authority over ritual bricolage, intimacy with spirits, or efficacious technologies like writing. The range of ritual experts extends from one's own grandmother to the local priest and includes all manner of individuals, skilled or gifted, any of whom might be credited with certain kinds of skills or powers—aiding in childbirth, protecting sheep or travelers, binding rivals. Often drawn into this complex of local ritual experts are figures somewhat peripheral to the community: holy men or prophets viewed with some ambivalence for their liminal relationship to local social networks. Such figures are often

Here the inhabitants of the country and of the regions round Palestine, the Phoenicians, and the Arabians, assemble annually during the summer season to keep a brilliant feast; and many others, both buyers and sellers, resort thither on account of the fair. Indeed, this feast is diligently frequented by all nations: by the Jews, because they boast of their descent from the patriarch Abraham; by the Pagans, because angels there appeared to men; and by Christians, because He who for the salvation of mankind was born of a virgin, afterwards manifested Himself there to a godly man. This place was moreover honored fittingly with religious exercises. Here some prayed to the God of all; some called upon the angels, poured out wine, burnt incense, or offered an ox, or he-goat, a sheep, or a cock. Each one made some beautiful product of his labor, and after carefully husbanding it through the entire year, he offered it according to promise as provision for that feast, both for himself and his dependents. And either from honor to the place, or from fear of Divine wrath, they all abstained from coming near their wives, although during the feast these were more than ordinarily studious of their beauty and adornment. Nor, if they chanced to appear and to take part in the public processions, did they act at all licentiously. Nor did they behave imprudently in any other respect, although the tents were contiguous to each other, and they all lay promiscuously together. The place is open country, and arable, and without houses, with the exception of the buildings around Abraham's old oak and the well he prepared. No one during the time of the feast drew water from that well; for according to Pagan usage, some placed burning lamps near it; some poured out wine, or cast in cakes; and others, coins, myrrh, or incense.

—Sozomen, *Eccl. Hist.* 2.4; *NPNF* 2:261

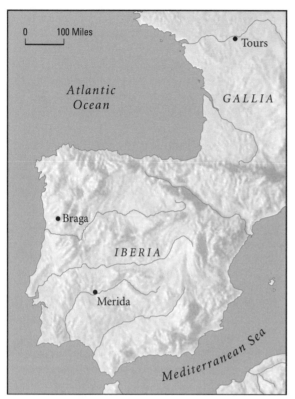

regarded as ultimate resources in cases of disaster, or they may be viewed with the capability to express particularly harmful intentions against one's neighbors. In this way such peripheral experts stand in a complementary rather than antagonistic relationship with local experts. However, there are sometimes cases in which a rivalry will develop between these peripheral or regional ritual experts and those established in the local sphere. In these cases, the regional prophet might try to consolidate his authority and assert the all-encompassing reach of his ideology by demanding, as part of his new movement, the elimination of local experts.

Christianization contributed both peripheral and local ritual experts to this scenario, and in both complementary and competitive relationships: the local priests or scribes who provided sacred oil or written charms for amulets, the monks who dispensed crocodile teeth, as well as regional holy men who, according to their hagiographers, encouraged clients to shift religious allegiance away from community ritual experts and entirely to the holy man's mediation. It is these dynamics that we see in two sixth-century accounts, the *Life of Theodore of Sykeon* (western Galatia) and Gregory of Tours's description of the cult of Saint Martin.

It is said that one "Theodotus dwelt in the same village as the Saint [Theodore] and was a skilled sorcerer, thoroughly versed in wickedness." This Theodotus tried various means to kill Theodore out of envy for his powers. After failing twice to accomplish this, he converted to Theodore's religion, loosed the binding spells he had thrown on various people, and burned his books of magic (*Life of Theodore of Sykeon* 37–38). The presentation of Theodotus's status as sorcerer emerges clearly from a discourse of ritual censure that sought rhetorically to draw the clearest possible distinctions between Theodore of Sykeon, regional expert in efficacious blessings, and Theodotus, who seems to have played a similar role. But the legend of their rivalry should not be read simply in terms of the hagiographic construction of sorcery (or the literary distinctiveness of Theodore's miracle working). Our study of local religion suggests also that the story should be read in terms of competing ritual experts, each with broad authority in the region. The text recalls one's triumph over the other, much as other legends cross-culturally have imagined wizards pitted against each other and their fantastic victories. The triumphant ritual expert, already carrying strongly local associations as "our saint," gains all the more charisma for having defeated a dangerous sorcerer.

In sixth-century Tours the competition is posed not by a renowned ritual expert like Theodore but by a regional healing cult, that of the martyr Saint Martin. Typically, cult literature like Bishop Gregory's extols the power of the deceased saint for every conceivable purpose, transmittable in every conceivable medium, from dust to curtain scraps. One might almost imagine that villages in the region had no other resources for healing and protection before the installation of Martin's relics. And yet Gregory does make a brief reference to the local *sortilegi* ("diviners") and *harioli* ("soothsayers") from whom the parents of an afflicted child tried to gain a cure. By his use of these words, Gregory means to associate these shadowy local healers with divination, a perennially suspect and subversive craft in Roman tradition. Thus he censures the entire spectrum of these healers' local roles. This denigration of local healers as nefarious fortune-tellers seems to mask a historical rivalry between the regional shrine of the deceased saint and ritual experts of the local milieu: "Therefore," Gregory declares, "I urge that no one be tempted by *harioli*, because they will never benefit ill people. A bit of dust from the church [of Saint Martin] is more powerful than those men with their foolish medicines" (*Life of St. Martin* 1, 26–27).

In some respects, and certainly in many regions, Christianization amounted to little more than a differentiation of ritual practices and their experts. This is not a question of popular religion per se but of the location of specialized authority in society. Nor is this social mapping of ritual expertise a matter of belief or affiliation so much as utility: who can best resolve danger, illness, social tension, and afflicting spirits. Like Shenoute in the *Acephalous Work*, Augustine of Hippo lays out a scenario in which crisis, rather than ideological affiliation, dictates which experts one consults, and those known locally for efficacious words and amulets are always close at hand (see sidebar).

For Augustine, however, it is better to die than to succumb to such rites, which "are unlawful, diabolical, to be detested and cursed." They are the work of sorcerers and wizards—*magi*—figures

> Someone comes along as you're lying there in a fever and in danger of death, and assures you that he can rid you of your fever with certain spells and charms.... And then the man who's trying to persuade you to this course mentions instances of people who have been cured in this way, and says to you, "When that person had this fever, I did this to him, I recited a spell over him, I purified him, I attended him, and he got better. Ask him, question him, listen to him." The others also say, "It really happened, we were at death's door, and we were delivered in this manner; and you can be quite sure that if you allow that charm to be recited over you, you will be delivered in that very moment from this disease."
>
> —Augustine, *Serm.* 306E [32]

of long-standing negative caricature in Roman culture, associated with secret rites and horrible sacrifices, cemeteries and dark crossroads, witches and subversion. By invoking *magia,* the discourse of ritual censure immediately removes the subject from his or her local function and social nexus, assimilating her to a grotesque and dangerous underworld that was largely cultural fantasy while obscuring the more plausible historical scenario of local religion, its multiple ritual experts, and the regional cults that often try to draw clients from those local milieus.

Egypt (Second to Tenth Century CE) and England (Tenth to Eleventh Century CE)

The Roman imperial ideology that Christianization carried throughout the Mediterranean world had long embraced the term *magia* [Greek: *mageia*] to make sense of the diversity of private, extra-cultic, and sometimes foreign ritual practices that people everywhere employed to resolve tensions and crises in life. As we have seen, this term, which is better translated "sorcery" or "wizardry" than "magic" for its exotic and dangerous connotations, served to define and alienate an enormous range of rituals by associating them with the foreign, the subversive, the sexually and politically disruptive. Archaeological evidence for private rituals does show that many people in the ancient Mediterranean world used binding spells and sought supernatural clairvoyance into political events. Yet the term *magia* (and such cognate labels as *sortilegi*) could as easily be applied to traditional divination procedures in Egypt or traditional healers in Gaul. Persecutions and inquisitions of sorcery might occur anywhere at the whim of an anxious emperor or governor.[33]

But as much as the term was flexibly applied and anxiety-driven and brought grave penalties to whoever was charged with it, *magia* came particularly to denote some realm of ritual fundamentally separate from the central cult—civic or Christian. And this link between *magia* and social (or performative) marginality has lasted even in translation—"magic"— down to the present. Whatever is regarded as basically peripheral or subversive in practice is labeled as "magic," "sorcery," or "witchcraft," while those rites we regard as customary and appropriate we classify by their purpose: "healing," "protection," "curse," or "binding."

In scholarship on late antiquity, evidence for the continuity of a *magia* in whatever form that church fathers collected and defined it has been interpreted as prima facie testimony to a popular religion of incomplete Christian instruction, neglect of church sacraments, and general superstition.[34] Such anecdotal collections of magic, as we have seen, provide a field for hunting so-called pagan survivals, for demonstrating the supposedly primitive worldviews of certain communities, and for legitimating a category of superstition or popular religion fundamentally separate from official or mainstream Christianity.

But how are private or extra-cultic ritual practices—those designed for protection, healing, or resolving social tensions—understood on their own terms by their clients and practitioners? It is one of the principles of the study of local religion to presume that practices are embedded in social experience. And indeed, looking beyond the images of *magia* held up for censure in early sermons, edicts, and church councils, we can gather a sense of rituals' meanings by studying the actual ritual manuals from the late antique and early medieval world. These manuals comprise often elaborate written instructions for preparing and conducting specific spells, invoking whole pantheons of heavenly and ambiguous spirits both. One important corpus comes from Coptic Egypt and includes caches and individual writings from about the fifth through the tenth centuries, preserved on clay ostraca, parchment, leather, papyrus, and bone. The spells range in goal from protection, healing, and successful fishing to those that shrivel penises, withhold customers from stores, and call destruction down on neighbors. Another corpus comes from tenth- and eleventh-century England and combines protective charms against malicious beings ("elves") with various healing recipes. In both corpora the supernatural pantheon invoked to protect, curse, and prosper belongs fundamentally to Christian tradition, and the spectrum of efficacious ingredients draws on those provided by the church (scripture, salt, oil). Most important, the collectors, scribes, and experts in the use of the spells in both corpora had some status—even authority—in the church, as monks or priests. That is, Christian spells truly represent an extension of the center—the church—not the ignorant syncretisms concocted by the untaught.[36]

Taking these features of magical corpora in combination with their sheer range of spells, we see that the spells themselves cannot be understood separately from a Christianity that, as "great tradition," endows materials, words, and gestures with efficacy. Nor can the spells be understood separately from Christian officials—monks, scribes, priests—and the mediation and expertise they offered in communities. Like the local monks and elders that Shenoute criticizes, the local representatives of Christianity are expected to address local tensions and anxieties—to mediate Christianity's

> I beg, I invoke, I pray to you, holy martyrs, I, Theodora, the injured party. I lodge this suit against Joor and his wife, throwing myself on your goodness, so that you may do as I would with Joor and his wife. Beat them and bring them to naught. [Let] the curse, the worm, and scattering overtake them. [Let] the wrath of God overtake Joor and his wife and all that is his. [Let there] be a great distress and outcry on his house and wife. [May] you lay your hands on [him]; may the strong hand and the exalted arm come upon them quickly, [upon both] him and his wife. Holy martyrs, may you speedily decide in my favor against them. [Send] your powers and miracles. Holy [martyrs], may you decide in my favor [. . .] Koloje.
>
> —Michigan 1523[35]

pantheon and powers to real-world purposes in ways not unlike the concrete blessings of saints one received at shrines. Sometimes this mediation involves the expert's development of new substances (perhaps fox claws or human bones) and sometimes the reassignment of older substances (like oil or Gospel texts), sometimes the invocation of well-known beings, like Christ or Mary, and sometimes the verbal binding of obscure, even demonic, powers. Indeed, special words spoken or written carry particular potency in resolving problems, and those in positions of ecclesiastical or monastic authority were generally understood to have unique powers to convey the efficacy of such words.

The soliciting or engaging of spells, whether to protect a child or to bind the rival to one's husband, is also a process embedded in the social milieu, where tensions are rife and little privacy surrounds crises and desire. Thus Sura, daughter of Pelca, carries an amulet for the protection of her unborn child from disease and demons. Maria commissions an amulet to heal her son Phoibammon of a fever. A father, it seems likely, seeks to bind the penis of Shinte, son of Tanheu, lest he deflower Seine, daughter of Moune. And a mother "call[s] upon the Lord God Almighty" to curse "Tnoute [who has] separated my son from me so that he scorns me. You must not listen to her, O [God . . .] if she calls up to you. . . . You must strike her womb and make her barren." In the two texts from Theodora and Severus (see sidebars) we find a man desperately seeking revenge against a couple that has somehow afflicted him and another ensuring the success of his fishing enterprise. Such spells serve fundamentally to articulate crises and desires in focused action—an utterance over a cup, the burning of some hair, the drawing of a character—that can be carried out in the local environment: the cemetery, a competitor's house, a crossroads, a storefront. Such ritual actions, as the anthropologist Bronislaw Malinowski observed almost a century ago, never replace instrumental, rational action but complement it: they are gestures one ought to do in order to be complete in a pursuit, and sometimes the only expressive means of resolving a crisis.[38]

These corpora of spell manuals, amulets, and curses show the diversity of ritual practices that are embedded in various local contexts: the church

---

Greetings, Father!
Greetings, Son!
Greetings, Holy Spirit! . . .

O you who came to his apostles upon the sea! [Peter] said to him, "Lord, we have labored a lot, yet nothing has shown up." The Lord said to him, "Cast your nets to the right side of the boat and you will find something." They cast them and discovered one hundred fifty-three.

You are the one whom I invoke today, I, Severus son of Joanna.

So you must ordain Raphael the archangel for me, and he must collect every species of fish for me [to the place] where your figure and your amulet will [be], just as a shepherd collects his sheep [in] their sheepfold and blesses them, so they neither become foul nor get lost, and grants favor to them before the entire race of Adam and all the children of Zoe. And strengthen the net, so it will not receive, it will not [catch], until it delivers all of them to my hands.

—London Or. 6795[37]

and its liturgy, the shrine and its active saints and potent materials, the family and its social world, the marketplace, and the local topography of houses, arenas, grave sites, and fields. The collections show that in their local milieus these spells were not considered to belong to an utterly separate domain of religious thought, a magic or superstition, but rather to be part of a spectrum of efficacious speech and action—a spectrum that extended from church liturgy and festival panegyric to the personal protective gesture. As with other categories that have been used to demarcate a popular religion, "magic" and "superstition" isolate gestures and ritual practices from their social contexts, shifting them from "ritual practices" in a spectrum of local expressive gestures to "that-which-is-not-religion."

While it is certainly incorrect to regard ritual practices for healing, binding, and protection as witnesses to a distinct popular religion rife with *magia* and heathenism, the actual primary evidence for these practices—the magical corpora—do teach us much about religion in the microcosm of local society and environment. Behind these spells we glimpse real people contending with real neighbors, real noonday demons, and real obstetrical crises, and doing so creatively with the holy names, materials, and experts that Christianity sanctioned.

CONCLUSIONS

Discourses that censure ritual practice, whether in antiquity (revolving around charges of demon worship, heathenism, and sorcery) or today (invoking pagan survivals, superstition, and the ignorant rustic), stem from more basic cultural attempts to distinguish between "us" and "them" in terms of religious custom. While "our" customs make sense, contain holiness and efficacy, and ground morality and social stability, "theirs" are chaotic, mysterious, violent, false, and disruptive of moral and social orders. Cross-culturally one finds the perennial accusation that "those people" practice sorcery and cannibalistic rites—that their rituals are fundamentally monstrous. Roman imperial culture rationalized this xenophobic response to ritual with a nomenclature meant to clarify what, in a society increasingly beset by foreign influences, might count as proper, integral religious custom and what, on the other hand, should be proscribed: *magia, superstitio,* as well as the still more denigrating *hariolatio* and *maleficia.* Each word conjured a stereotypical practitioner—wizard, witch, huckster, sorcerer— and a rich scenario of otherness: nighttime, graveyards, barbaric incantations, child sacrifice, sexual perversion, exploitation of the unwary, and political subversion. In Christian antiquity these scenarios took on a more insidious character, denoting the worship of demons, even of Satan

Fig. 11.5. Composed and utilized by monks and shrine scribes, Coptic magical texts like this one demonstrate the continuity between folk and liturgical practice and between worlds of magic and of official religion. While meant to protect, heal, or even curse, the incantations invoke Christ, Mary, and angels in the language of prayer and hymn. London Hay 10434 recto and verso. Photos © The Trustees of The British Museum. Used by permission.

 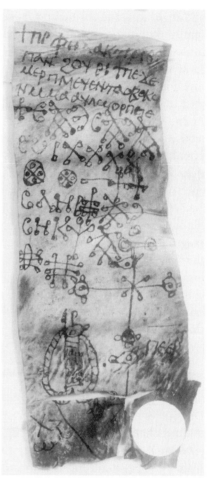

himself, while the specific activities deemed "other" also began to reflect some familiarity with rituals actually practiced in the local environment, like devotions before divine statues or trees, domestic festivals, incubation at shrines, and the preparation of amulets. Occasionally a Christian leader would censure practices conducted explicitly within Christianity. If he could not repudiate them as demonic (as Shenoute does, for example), he might draw on discourses of authenticity (false martyr bones), heresy ("Meletian" mortuary practices), or purity (true Christians don't participate in *that* festival).

Ultimately, this discourse of ritual censure would assume an extreme form in the time of the Reformation, as radical theologians promulgated aniconicism (banning religious images) and the disenchantment of the landscape in attempting to purify the faith. Now the efficacious gesture, the holy spring, the amulet, and the saint's medal became at best distractions from interior reflection and at worst heathen deceptions. Hence arises the ambivalent heritage of ritual and even the subtle equation in modern history of religions of Christian empire with decay and heathen influence. Hence arises also the construction of a popular religion oblivious to the niceties of Christian doctrine and prone to idolatry and superstition. Indeed, if one examines late antique church leaders' discourses of ritual censure without these traditional ideological preconceptions, one is hard-pressed to find an actual popular religion to which they might be referring. In their various pictures of *magia* and *superstitio,* these leaders are not simply reflecting a real phenomenon, that is, popular piety, but are rather attempting in idiosyncratic ways to define a suspect or illegitimate sphere of religious practice, one that should be reformed or forcibly cleansed.

However, if we clear away the polemical distortions of many centuries, it is possible to perceive certain patterns in the way ritual practices take form in regional and local worlds, invariably in dialectic with what we might call the great tradition—that is, the representation of a central, literate authority and orthodoxy that is often as much a product of local perceptions as it is a historical effort by urban elites. "Local religion," as the term has been used in this chapter, refers to the particular, geographically situated syntheses of central and peripheral traditions, practices, and notions of power that villages and towns mediate through their landscapes and folklore. Understanding a ritual practice as part of local religion requires the recognition of its enmeshment with a particular social world and a particular geography: healing gestures and curse spells, festival lamps and shrine incubation, sacred trees and charms for vineyard fertility all make sense only as expressions of social interaction and performance in a real landscape, with real neighbors.

FOR FURTHER READING

Brown, Peter. *Authority and the Sacred: Aspects of the Christianisation of the Roman World.* Cambridge: Cambridge University Press, 1995.

Christian, William A., Jr. *Local Religion in Sixteenth-Century Spain.* Princeton, N.J.: Princeton University Press, 1981.

———. "Introduction: Approaches to Coptic Pilgrimage." In *Pilgrimage and Holy Space in Late Antique Egypt,* 3–48. Ed. David Frankfurter. Leiden: Brill, 1998.

———. "The Perils of Love: Magic and Counter-Magic in Coptic Egypt." *Journal of the History of Sexuality* 10 (2001): 480–500.

Frankfurter, David. *Religion in Roman Egypt: Assimilation and Resistance.* Princeton, N.J.: Princeton University Press, 1998.

————. "Syncretism and the Holy Man in Late Antique Egypt." *Journal of Early Christian Studies* 11/3 (2003): 339–85.

Hertz, Robert. "St. Besse: A Study of an Alpine Cult." In *Saints and Their Cults: Studies in Religious Sociology, Folklore, and History,* 55–100. Ed. and trans. Stephen Wilson. Cambridge: Cambridge University Press, 1983.

Leemans, Johan, Wendy Mayer, Pauline Allen, and Boudewijn Dehandschutter. *"Let Us Die That We May Live": Greek Homilies on Christian Martyrs from Asia Minor, Palestine, and Syria (ca. AD 350–AD 450).* London: Routledge, 2003.

Stewart, Charles. *Demons and the Devil: Moral Imagination in Modern Greek Culture.* Princeton, N.J.: Princeton University Press, 1991.

Van Dam, Raymond. *Leadership and Community in Late Antique Gaul.* Transformation of the Classical Heritage 8. Berkeley: University of California Press, 1985.

ABBREVIATIONS

ACW	*Ancient Christian Writers*
Ag. Jews	John Chrysostom, *Against the Jews*
ANF	*Ante-Nicene Fathers*
Ap. Const.	*Apostolic Constitutions*
Apol.	*Apology*
Ap. Trad.	Hippolytus, *The Apostolic Tradition*
Bapt.	Tertullian, *On Baptism*
Bapt. Donat.	Augustine, *On Baptism against the Donatists*
Can.	Canon
Catech.	Cyril of Jerusalem, *Catecheses*
CCSL	*Corpus Christianorum Series Latina*
Celsus	Origen, *Against Celsus*
CIL	*Corpus Inscriptionum Latinarum*
CLE	*Carmina Latina Epigraphica*
Conf.	Augustine, *Confessions*
Crown.	Tertullian, *On the Soldier's Crown*
CSCO	Corpus Scriptorum Christianorum Orientalium
CSEL	*Corpus Scriptorum Ecclesiasticorum Latinorum*
CTh.	*Codex Theodosianus (Theodosian Code)*
Div. Inst.	Lactantius, *Divine Institutes*
Don.	Optatus, *On the Donatist Schism*
Eccl. Hist.	*Ecclesiastical History*
Ep.	*Epistle*
Ep. Alex.	Alexander of Alexandria, *Letter to Alexander*
Ep. Cath.	Augustine, *Letter to Catholics of the Donatist Sect*

Ep. Const.	Eusebius, *Letter to Constantina*
Exhortation	Clement of Alexandria, *Exhortation to the Greeks*
Ferrua	Antonio Ferrua, *Epigrammata Damasiana* (Rome: Pontificio Istituto di Archeologia Cristiana, 1942)
Guilt and Remiss.	Augustine, *Guilt and Remission of Sins*
Her.	Irenaeus, *Against the Heresies*
Hist.	*History*
Hom.	*Homily/Homilies*
ICUR	*Inscriptiones Christianae Urbis Romae*
ILCV	*Inscriptiones Latinae Christianae Veteres*
Jov.	Jerome, *Against Jovinian*
Laps.	Cyprian, *Treastise on the Lapsed*
Laus. Hist.	Palladius, *Lausiac History*
Life of Ant.	Athanasius, *Life of Antony*
Life of Aug.	Possidius, *Life of Augustine*
Life of Const.	Eusebius, *Life of Constantine*
Life of Mac.	Gregory of Nyssa, *Life of Macrina, Life of Martin Severus, Life of Martin*
Life of Mel.	Gerontius, *Life of Melania the Younger*
Life of Pach.	*Life of Pachomius*
Magn.	Ignatius, *Epistle to the Magnesians*
Mart.	Tertullian, *To the Martyrs*
MGH SRL	*Monumenta Germaniae Historica, Scriptores Rerum Langobardicarum et Italicarum*
MGH SRM	*Monumenta Germaniae Historica, Scriptores Rerum Merovingicarum*
Misc.	Clement of Alexandria, *Miscellanies*
Mod.	Tertullian, *On Modesty*
Nat. and Grace	Augustine, *Nature and Grace*
NPNF	*Nicene and Post-Nicene Fathers*
On the Governance	Salvian of Marseilles, *On the Governance of God*
On Love	Gregory of Nazianzus, *On the Love of the Poor*

On Works	Cyprian, *On Works and Almsgiving*
Oration	Gregory of Nazianzus, *Oration in Praise of Basil*
Pan.	Epiphanius, *Panarion* (Medicine Box)
Passion of Perp.	*Passion of Ss. Perpetua and Felicity*
PG	Patrologia graeca. Edited by J.-P. Migne. 162 vols. Paris, 1857–86.
PL	Patrologia latina. Edited by J.-P. Migne. 217 vols. Paris, 1844–64.
Prax.	Tertullian, *Against Praxeas*
Prescrip.	Tertullian, *Prescription against Heretics*
Proceed. Pelag.	*Proceedings against Pelagius*
Rebapt.	Pseudo-Cyprian, *Treatise on Rebaptism*
Ref.	Hippolytus, *Refutation of All Heresies*
Ref. Her.	Theodoret, *Refutation of the Heretics*
Rel. Hist.	Theodoret, *Religious History*
Res. Flesh	Tertullian, *On the Resurrection of the Flesh*
Sacr.	Ambrose, *The Sacraments*
Sayings	*Sayings of the Desert Fathers*
Sayings Alph.	*Sayings of the Desert Fathers, Alphabetical List*
Scorp.	Tertullian, *Antidote for the Scorpion's Sting*
Serm.	Augustine, *Sermon*
Sim.	Shepherd of Hermas, *Similitudes*
Strom.	Clement of Alexandria, *Stromata*
Theod. Syk.	*Life of Theodore of Sykeon*
To the People	John Chrysostom, *To the People of Antioch*
Unity	Cyprian, *On the Unity of the Church*
Val.	Tertullian, *Against Valentinus*
Who Is the Rich Man?	Clement of Alexandria, *Who Is the Rich Man Who Is to Be Saved?*

NOTES

Chapter One. Asceticism, Class, and Gender

1. Ramsay MacMullen, *Roman Social Relations, 50 B.C. to A.D. 284* (New Haven: Yale University Press, 1974), 122.

2. See the summary discussion in L. William Countryman, *The Rich Christian in the Church of the Early Empire: Contradictions and Accommodations*, Texts and Studies in Religion 7 (New York: Mellen, 1980), 22–26.

3. G. E. M. de Ste. Croix, "Karl Marx and the History of Classical Antiquity," *Arethusa* 8 (1975): 26. See also Padelis Lekas, *Marx on Classical Antiquity: Problems of Historical Methodology* (New York: St. Martin's, 1988), 133–34, 180, 201, discussing passages from Marx's *Capital* I and III. As Lekas warns, we should not misunderstand the word "unproductive": for the ancients, the display of wealth served a "productive" purpose in reproducing the political relations that "alone gave access to economic appropriation" (140). Marx wrote that if labor power had become (as it did not) an exchangeable commodity in antiquity, Rome and Byzantium would have "begun a new history" (Karl Marx, *Grundrisse*, 506, 605, discussed in Lekas, *Marx on Classical Antiquity*, 97).

4. E.g., Hermas, *Sim.* 2.5–8; Clement of Alexandria, *Who Is the Rich Man?* 34–35. See Countryman, *The Rich Christian*, 81–88.

5. Countryman, *The Rich Christian*, chap. 3. See, e.g., Acts 10 (Cornelius); 13:7 (Sergius Paulus); 18:12-16 (Gallio). The Apologists Justin Martyr (*Apol.* 1.1) and Athenagoras (*Apol.*, preface) claim to write to emperors, while hagiographies can represent their subjects as consorting with emperors and empresses (*Life of Mel.* 11–12).

6. See Victor Saxer, *Bible et hagiographie: Textes et thèmes bibliques dans les Actes des martyrs authentiques des premiers siècles* (Berne: Peter Lang, 1986), 162; Brian Stock, *Listening for the Text: On the Uses of the Past*, Parallax: Re-visions of Culture and Society (Baltimore: Johns Hopkins University Press, 1990), 100–101, 125, 150.

7. Averil Cameron, *Christianity and the Rhetoric of Empire: The Development of Christian Discourse*, Sather Classical Lectures 55 (Berkeley: University of California Press, 1991), 138–41, 143, 147; Evelyne Patlagean, "Ancienne hagiographie byzantine et histoire sociale," *Annales: Économies, Sociétés, Civilisations* 23 (1968): 108–9.

8. See James Goehring, "Asceticism," in *Encyclopedia of Early Christianity*, ed. Everett Ferguson, 2d ed. (New York: Garland, 1997), 127–30. For a longer discussion of

early Christian asceticism, see Elizabeth A. Clark, *Reading Renunciation: Asceticism and Scripture in Early Christianity* (Princeton, N.J.: Princeton University Press, 1999), 14–42; and James E. Goehring, "The Origins of Monasticism," in Goehring, *Ascetics, Society, and the Desert: Studies in Early Egyptian Monasticism* (Harrisburg, Pa.: Trinity Press International, 1999), 13–35.

9. See Theodoret, *Hist. of the Monks of Syria* 26 (Simeon Stylites). For discussion of the practices of Syrian asceticism, see Sidney H. Griffith, "Asceticism in the Church of Syria: The Hermeneutics of Early Syrian Monasticism," in *Asceticism*, ed. Vincent L. Wimbush and Richard Valantasis (New York: Oxford University Press, 1995), 220–45. For Egypt, Sozomen, *Church Hist.* 6.33. On the practice of homelessness, see Hans von Campenhausen, *Die asketische Heimatlosigkeit im altkirchlichen und frühmittelalterischen Mönchtums* (Tübingen: Mohr/Siebeck, 1930). For critiques of some practices, see, e.g., *Hist. of the Monks of Egypt* 8 (Apollo 59); Augustine, *Ep.* 262.5, *On the Work of Monks* 28.36; *Rule of Benedict* 1.10–11.

10. For a brief overview, see Clark, *Reading Renunciation*, 27–38.

11. Émile Durkheim, *The Elementary Forms of the Religious Life: A Study in Religious Sociology*, trans. J. W. Swain (London: Allen & Unwin, 1915), 309–16, citation at 316.

12. Geoffrey Galt Harpham, *The Ascetic Imperative in Culture and Criticism* (Chicago: University of Chicago Press, 1987), 61. For the fungibility of various kinds of capital, see John B. Thompson's introduction to Pierre Bourdieu, *Language and Symbolic Power*, trans. Gino Raymond and Matthew Adamson (Cambridge: Harvard University Press, 1991), 14, explaining Bourdieu's concept.

13. As Peter Brown observes, some thought that the requirement of clerical celibacy might open higher office to the wrong class of people (*The Body and Society: Men, Women, and Sexual Renunciation*, Lectures on the History of Religions n.s. 13 [New York: Columbia University Press, 1988], 138).

14. Palladius, *Laus. Hist.* 22.1; 35.1; 49.1; 8.3; 19.1. On the simple backgrounds of many of the Egyptian monks, see Peter Nagel, *Die Motivierung der Askese in der alten Kirche und der Ursprung des Mönchtums*, Texte und Untersuchungen zur Geschichte der altchristlichen Literatur 95 (Berlin: Akademie, 1966), 89.

15. Hugh E. Evelyn White, *The Monasteries of the Wâdi 'N Natrûn, Part II: The History of the Monasteries of Nitria and Scete*, ed. Walter Hauser (New York: Metropolitan Museum of Art, 1932), 190. The desert father Megethios, for example, is said to be "very humble" because he had been raised by Egyptians (*Sayings Alph.*, Megethios 2).

16. On Paulinus's background, and the sources, see Dennis E. Trout, *Paulinus of Nola: Life, Letters, and Poems*, Transformation of the Classical Heritage 27 (Berkeley: University of California Press, 1999).

17. On the backgrounds of Basil and Macrina, see Thomas A. Kopecek, "The Cappadocian Fathers and Civic Patriotism," *Church History* 43 (1974): 293–303; Raymond Van Dam, *Families and Friends in Late Roman Cappadocia* (Philadelphia: University of Pennsylvania Press, 2003), esp. chaps. 1 and 6.

18. See Samuel Rubenson, *The Letters of St. Antony: Monasticism and the Making of a Saint*, Studies in Antiquity and Christianity (Minneapolis: Fortress, 1995).

19. See Athanasius's efforts to make God, not Antony himself, responsible for extraordinary deeds: *Life of Antony* 7; 10; 44; 56; and commentary by Robert C. Gregg

and Dennis E. Groh, *Early Arianism: A View of Salvation* (Philadelphia: Fortress, 1981), chap. 4 ("Claims on the Life of St. Antony").

20. Melania the Younger visits Lausus while in Constantinople (*Life of Mel.* 53). Palladius knew Melania the Elder from the Mount of Olives monastery (*Laus. Hist.* 55) and was shown hospitality by Melania the Younger in Rome (61).

21. The exceptions include two accounts of fallen virgins—one of a martyr who had been a slave, one described as a "maidservant"—and one account concerning two women with Egyptian names in a monastery in Antinoë (*Laus. Hist.* 28; 69; 3; 5; 59). Palladius also includes a tale of a rich but stingy virgin (apparently not a dedicated or consecrated virgin [6]).

22. Palladius, *Dialogue concerning the Life of John Chrysostom* 17. For other women in Chrysostom's circle and what can be ascertained about their pedigrees, see Elizabeth A. Clark, "Friendship between the Sexes: Classical Theory and Christian Practice," in Clark, *Jerome, Chrysostom, and Friends: Essays and Translations*, Studies in Women and Religion 1 (New York: Mellen, 1979), 68–70.

23. Basil, *Longer Rules* 3. For discussion of Basil's approach to asceticism, see Philip Rousseau, *Basil of Caesarea*, Transformation of the Classical Heritage 20 (Berkeley: University of California Press, 1994), chap. 6. For various types of ascetic practice in Cappadocia, see Susanna Elm, *"Virgins of God": The Making of Asceticism in Late Antiquity*, Oxford Classical Monographs (Oxford: Clarendon, 1994), chaps. 1–6.

24. Augustine, *Regulations for a Monastery (Ordo monasterii)* 4. On Augustine's *Rules*, with text and translation, see George A. Lawless, *Augustine of Hippo and His Monastic Rule* (Oxford: Clarendon, 1987).

25. For a discussion of attitudes toward work in early monasticism, see Antoine Guillaumont, "Le Travail manuel dans le monachisme ancien: Contestation et valorisation," in Guillaumont, *Aux Origines du monachisme chrétien: Pour une phénoménologie du monachisme*, Spiritualité orientale 30 (Bégrolles en Mauges: Abbaye de Bellefontaine, 1979), 117–26; and Adalbert de Vogüé, *Histoire littéraire du mouvement monastique dans l'antiquité* (Paris: Cerf, 1991), 1:305–6.

26. See James E. Goehring, "The World Engaged: The Social and Economic World of Early Egyptian Monasticism," in Goehring, *Ascetics, Society, and the Desert*, 39–52.

27. Jerome, *Jov.* 3. For a discussion of Jovinian's position, see David G. Hunter, "Resistance to the Virginal Ideal in Fourth-Century Rome: The Case of Jovinian," *Theological Studies* 48 (1987): 45–64.

28. See Augustine, *On the Good of Marriage* and *On Holy Virginity;* and Robert Markus, *The End of Ancient Christianity* (Cambridge: Cambridge University Press, 1990), chap. 4 ("Augustine: A Defense of Christian Mediocrity"). As Peter Brown phrases it, the North African clergy had avoided a "'High Church' asceticism" (*The Body and Society*, 396).

29. Julian of Eclanum, "To Florus" (in Augustine, *The Unfinished Work against Julian*), trans. Elizabeth A. Clark, in *Ascetic Behavior in Greco-Roman Antiquity: A Sourcebook*, ed. Vincent L. Wimbush (Minneapolis: Fortress, 1990), 156–68; see also discussion in Elizabeth A. Clark, "Vitiated Seeds and Holy Vessels: Augustine's Manichean Past," in Clark, *Ascetic Piety and Women's Faith: Essays on Late Ancient Christianity*, Studies in Women and Religion 20 (Lewiston, N.Y.: Mellen, 1986), 291–349.

Chapter Two. Fictional Narratives and Social Critique

1. Some of the material in this chapter is drawn from my earlier work on the Acts, where more documentation can be found. "Resurrection in the Acts of John and Peter," in Jo-Ann Brant, Charles Hedrick, and Christine Shea, eds., *Ancient Fiction: The Matrix of Early Christian and Jewish Narrative*, SBL Symposium Series 32 (Atlanta: Scholars, 2005); "Social Geography in the Apocryphal Acts," *Ancient Fiction*, Supplement 1, Space in the Ancient Novel (2002): 118–31; and *The Suffering Self: Pain and Narrative Representation in Early Christian Era* (London: Routledge, 1995).

2. The text of this passage, *Baptism* 17, is in dispute, but most commentators accept its reference to the *Acts of Paul*. Some, however, challenge that Tertullian's comments necessarily support actual women using the model of Thecla as a warrant for teaching and baptizing. For a recent discussion, see Esther Yue L. Ng, "*Acts of Paul and Thecla:* Women's Stories and Precedent?" *Journal of Theological Studies* 55 (2004): 1–29.

3. François Bovon, "Canonical and Apocryphal Acts of the Apostles," *Journal of Early Christian Studies* 11 (2003): 194.

4. Christine M. Thomas, *The Acts of Peter, Gospel Literature, and the Ancient Novel: Rewriting the Past* (New York: Oxford University Press, 2003), 104. Thomas's work is important for its discussion of the genre and the role of works like the *Acts* in the negotiations around identity during the period.

5. Translations are from J. K. Elliott and M. R. James, *The Apocryphal New Testament: A Collection of Apocryphal Christian Literature in an English Translation* (New York: Clarendon, 1993), with some changes. Texts used are R. A. Lipsius and M. Bonnet, eds., *Acta Apostolorum Apocrypha*, vol. 2 (Darmstadt: George Olms, 1959 [1891–98]); Eric Junod and Jean Daniel Kaestli, *Acta Iohannis*, 2 vols., Corpus Christianorum Series Apocryphorum (Turnhout: Brehols, 1983); Dennis Ronald MacDonald, *The Acts of Andrew and the Acts of Andrew and Matthias in the City of the Cannibals,* Texts and Translations: Christian Apocrypha Series 1 (Atlanta: Scholars, 1990).

6. Peter Brown, *The Body and Society: Men, Women, and Sexual Renunciation in Early Christianity* (New York: Columbia University Press, 1988), 17.

7. In earlier work, I read the Greek romance primarily as an affirmation of Greek culture, but subsequent work on Heliodorus has persuaded me that a more nuanced attention should be given to the various ethnicities and subcultures encoded in the romance plots. Helen Morales has cautioned in her introduction to Tim Whitmarsh's *Achilles Tatius* (New York: Oxford University Press, 2001), "'Greek' and 'Roman' were by no means always exclusive categories" (xvii). With reference to Achilles Tatius's romance, where the protagonists are Phoenicians, Morales suggests, "Focusing on 'Greek' and 'Roman' has tended to occlude other more local cultural affiliations, such as 'Phoenician.'"

8. Andrew S. Jacobs, "A Family Affair: Marriage, Class and Ethics in the *Apocryphal Acts of the Apostles,*" *Journal of Early Christian Studies* 7 (1999): 125.

9. Nicholas P. Constas, "The Last Temptation of Satan: Divine Deception in Greek Patristic Interpretations of the Passion Narrative," *Harvard Theological Review* 97 (2004): 139–63. Constas surveys the development of this notion that Jesus used the incarnation to deceive Satan as part of the plan of salvation.

10. Paul Veyne, *From Pagan Rome to Byzantium,* trans. Arthur Goldhammer, ed. Philippe Ariès and George Duby, vol. 1 of *A History of Private Life* (Cambridge: Belknap, 1987): 186.

11. Dimitris Kyrtatas, *The Social Structure of Early Christian Communities* (London: Verso, 1987), 66.

12. This discussion of talking animals depends on Christopher R. Matthews, "Articulate Animals: A Multivalent Motif in the Apocryphal Acts of the Apostles," 205–32, in *The Apocryphal Acts of the Apostles: Harvard Divinity School Studies,* ed. François Bovon, Ann Brock, and Christopher R. Matthews (Cambridge: Harvard University Center for the Study of World Religions, 1999): 231. Matthews also examines the case for animal rationality put forward in Greek philosophy (213–16).

13. R. Kasser's translation of this still-unpublished Coptic papyrus is included in Wilhelm Schneemelcher and R. M. Wilson, *New Testament Apocrypha,* rev. ed. (Louisville, Ky.: Westminster/John Knox, 1991), 263.

14. Text: François Bovon, Bertrand Bouvier, and Frédéric Amsler, *Acta Philippi* (Turnhout: Brepols, 1999). Matthews notes how often the talking animal sections were later omitted in the texts. One cannot help wondering what would have been the ecological effects if these sections had been allowed to play more of a role in the Christian tradition.

15. Dale Martin, *The Corinthian Body* (New Haven: Yale University Press, 1995), 30.

16. This section shows similarities with attested gnostic themes, especially Valentinianism. See Junod and Kaestli, *Acta Iohannis,* 581–632 and 660–68, but a spiritual understanding of Jesus' body and of human resurrection appears throughout the narrative.

17. Janos Bolyki, "Miracle Stories in the Acts of John," in *Apocryphal Acts of John,* ed. Jan N. Bremmer (Kampen: Kok Pharos, 1995), 32.

Chapter Three. Martyrdom as Exaltation

1. For the hymn in praise of Eulalia, see the convenient edition and translation by H. J. Thomson in *Prudentius,* Loeb Classical Library (Cambridge: Harvard University Press, 1979), 2:142–57. For commentary and translation, see Anne-Marie Palmer, *Prudentius on the Martyrs* (Oxford: Clarendon, 1989). See also John Petruccione, "The Portrait of St. Eulalia of Mérida in Prudentius' Peristephanon," *Analecta Bollandiana* 108 (1990): 81–104.

2. For sources on martyrdom in early Christianity, see "For Further Reading" at the end of this chapter and also Donald Riddle, *The Martyrs: A Study in Social Control* (Chicago: University of Chicago Press, 1931).

3. For an extensive treatment of this theme, see Margaret Barker, *The Great High Priest: The Temple Roots of Christian Liturgy* (London: T. & T. Clark, 2003); for its connection with an early "high" Christology, see Larry Hurtado, *Lord Jesus Christ: Devotion to Jesus in Earliest Christianity* (Grand Rapids: Eerdmans, 2004).

4. See David Flusser's essays on the relevance of the Qumran community for this reconstrual of the Temple, especially in *Judaism and the Origins of Christianity* (Jerusalem: Magnes, 1988).

5. For a recent discussion of the controversies over authority, see J. Patout Burns, *Cyprian the Bishop* (London: Routledge, 2002), especially chap. 2, "Christians of Carthage under Persecution," 12–24.

6. See "The Martyrdom of Perpetua and Felicity 13," 120–22 in Herbert Musurillo, ed. and trans., *The Acts of the Christian Martyrs* (Oxford: Oxford University Press, 1972). See also Jacqueline Amat, ed., *Passion de Perpétue et de Félicité suivie des Actes: Introduction, texte critique, traduction, commentaire et index,* Sources chrétiennes 417 (Paris: Cerf, 1996), 239–42.

7. See Annewies van den Hoek, "Clement of Alexandria on Martyrdom," *Studia Patristica* 26 (1993): 324–41.

8. The fullest discussions of Ignatius and martyrdom are found in William R. Schoedel, *Ignatius of Antioch: A Commentary on the Letters of Ignatius of Antioch,* Hermeneia (Philadelphia: Fortress, 1985), and idem, "Polycarp of Smyrna and Ignatius," in *Aufstieg und Niedergang des römischen Welt* 2.27/1 (Berlin: de Gruyter, 1992), 272–358.

9. See Musurillo, *Acts of the Christian Martyrs,* xlii–xliii, for discussion of the edition, and pp. 282–93 for text and translation.

Chapter Four. Children's Play as Social Ritual

1. On rebirth in baptism, see John 3:3-10; see also Titus 3:5, Rom. 6:4; 1 Peter 1:3, 23; 2:2, and the discussion in Hugh M. Riley, *Christian Initiation: A Comparative Study of the Interpretation of the Baptismal Liturgy in the Mystagogical Writings of Cyril of Jerusalem, John Chrysostom, Theodore of Mopsuestia, and Ambrose of Milan,* Catholic University of America Studies in Christian Antiquity 17 (Washington, D.C.: Catholic University of America Press, 1974), 298–348. For the identity of the Christian as a child of God throughout his or her life, see 1 John 2:1. Also note that the "Our Father," from the beginning one of the central Christian prayers, daily confirmed for the believer that identity of being a child in relationship to God the Father; see, for example, *Didache* 8.3. For references to God as father or as mother, see, for example, Matt. 23:37; Luke 13:34; *Odes of Solomon* 19.2–5 and 35.4–5.

2. See Hugo Rahner, *Man at Play or Did You Ever Practise Eutrapelia?,* trans. Brian Battershaw and Edward Quinn (London: Burns & Oats, 1965).

3. This reading of Prov. 8:21-31 hinges on the problematic *hapax* "'*amôn.*" Interpreters and translators have been quite divided as to how to translate this word. Aquila decided it meant "nurseling," therefore "child," and was followed by some Jewish commentators. R. N. Whybray, *Proverbs,* The New Century Bible Commentary (Grand Rapids: Eerdmans, 1994), 136–37, has demonstrated that this reading is speculative. Jerome's translation of Proverbs in the Vulgate promoted the reading of "playing" *(ludens)* in this context.

4. Keith Hopkins, "The Age of Roman Girls at Marriage," *Population Studies* 18 (1965): 309–27; Charles Pietri, "Le mariage chrétien à Rome," in Jean Delumeau, ed., *Histoire vécue du peuple chrétien* (Toulouse: Privat, 1979), 105–31; and Brent Shaw, "The Age of Roman Girls at Marriage: Some Reconsiderations," *Journal of Roman Studies* 77 (1987): 30–46.

5. On Cicero and Epictetus, see Leslie Joan Shumka, "Children and Toys in the Roman World: A Contribution to the History of the Roman Family," PhD diss. (University of Victoria, Canada, 1993), 22–41.

6. For example, in the studies of the classicists Thomas Wiedemann, *Adults and Children in the Roman Empire* (New Haven: Yale University Press, 1989); and Shumka, "Children and Toys in the Roman World"; as well as the exhibition catalog *Jouer dans l'Antiquité,* Musée d'Archéologie Méditerranéenne, Centre de la Vieille Charité, catalog of exhibition held from November 22, 1991, to February 16, 1992 (Marseilles, France: Musées de Marseille—Réunion des Musées Nationaux, 1992).

7. Plautus, *Rudens,* IV.IV.1151–59, provides literary witness to such a usage. See also Jean-Pierre Néraudau, "Les jeux de l'enfance en Grèce et à Rome," in *Jouer dans l'Antiquité,* 44; and Marie-Odille Kastner, "L'enfant et les jeux dans les documents d'époque romaine," *Bulletin de l'Association Guillaume Budé* (1995): 86.

8. See the object exhibited in the Museum of Cycladic Art, Athens, K. Politis Collection, no. 124; pictured in Marina Plati, *Playing in Ancient Greece* (Athens: N. P. Goulandris Foundation, 1999), 26.

9. For the classification of the different types of balls, see Kastner, "L'enfant et les jeux," 94. For gift giving in the service of advancing the early educational efforts of children, see also Jerome, *Letter* 128.1: "Meanwhile let her learn the alphabet, spelling, grammar, and syntax. To induce her to repeat her lessons with her little shrill voice, hold out to her as rewards cakes and mead and sweetmeat."

10. Karl R. Mühlbauer and Theresa Miller, "Spielzeug und Kult: Zur religiösen und kultischen Bedeutung von Kinderspielzeug in der griechischen Antike," *American Journal of Ancient History* 13.2 (1997): 156–57.

11. Ibid., 158.

12. See especially Kate McKnight Elderkin, "Jointed Dolls in Antiquity," *American Journal of Archaeology* 34/2 (1930): 455–79; Michel Manson, "Les Poupées Antiques," in *Jeux et Jouets dans l'Antiquité et au Moyen Âge, Dossiers de l'Archéologie* 168 (1992): 48–57; and Georges Lafaye, "Pupa," in *Dictionnaire des antiquités grecques et romaines,* vol. 4.1, eds. C. Daremberg and E. Saglio (Paris: Hachette, 1905), 768–69.

13. Suzanne Dixon, *The Roman Mother* (Norman: University of Oklahoma Press, 1988); Beryl Rawson, "Adult–Child Relationships in Roman Society," in Beryl Rawson, ed., *Marriage, Divorce, and Children in Ancient Rome* (Oxford: Clarendon, 1991), 19–20.

14. The other one was Hermes. See *Anthologia Palatina* IV.309: "his favorite ball, and his noisy wooden rattle, and the knucklebones that he so wanted, and the top that he used to whip—all these Philokles offered to Hermes [when he grew up]."

15. Mühlbauer and Miller, "Spielzeug und Kult," 161.

16. Manson, "Les Poupées Antiques," 56; Kastner, "L'enfant et les jeux," 90; Eugenia S. P. Ricotti, *Giochi e giocattoli,* Vita e costumi dei romani antichi 18 (Rome: Quasar, 1995), 57–58; M. R. Rinaldi, "Ricerche sui giocattoli nell'antichità a proposito di un'iscrizione di Brescello," *Epigraphica* 18 (1956): 118–19.

17. Elderkin, "Jointed Dolls," 471–72; Rinaldi, "Ricerche sui giocattoli nell'antichità," 116–17; A. Reith, "Die Puppe im Grab der Crepereia," *Atlantis* 33 (1961): 367–69; Jutta Väterlein, *Roma ludens: Kinder und Erwachsene beim Spiel im antiken Rom* (Amsterdam: B. R. Grüner, 1976), 29–30; Anna Mura Somella, *Crepereia Tryphaena: Le scoperte*

archeologiche nell'area del Palazzo di Guistizia (Venice: Marsilio Editori, 1983); Ricotti, *Giochi e giocattoli,* 54–56; and Wiedemann, *Adults and Children,* 150.

18. See Elderkin, "Jointed Dolls," 475; Ricotti, *Giochi e giocattoli,* 58–59; Wiedemann, *Adults and Children,* 149–50.

19. Wiedemann, *Adults and Children,* 149.

20. Quoted from the Greek Anthology, an ancient collection of Greek lyric and epigrammatic poems, in ibid., 153.

21. Wiedemann, *Adults and Children,* plate 22.

22. For respective depictions of these two artifacts see ibid. and Rawson, *Marriage, Divorce, and Children,* plate 3.

23. Cassius Dio, while commenting on Livia, speaks of "one of the prattling boys, such as the women keep about them for their amusement, naked as a rule"; elsewhere he refers to "one of the naked 'whispering' boys" who filched away a two-leaved tablet of linden wood from under Domitian's pillow (*Roman History* 48.44, 67.15). Herodian reports that "[Commodus] forgot about the little boy, who was one of those that fashionable Roman fops are pleased to keep in their households running around without any clothes on, decked out in gold and fine jewels. Commodus had such a favourite, whom he often used to sleep with. He used to call him Philocommodus, a name to show his fondness for the boy" (*History* 1.17.3). See also Wiedemann, *Adults and Children,* 26 and 45.

24. Rawson, *Marriage, Divorce, and Children,* plate preceding title page.

25. Ibid., plate 4b.

26. See François Poplin, "Les jeux d'osselets antiques," in *Jeux et Jouets dans l'Antiquité et au Moyen Âge,* 46–47; and Mühlbauer and Miller, "Spielzeug und Kult," 159–60.

27. Paul Veyne, "The Roman Empire," in Paul Veyne, ed., *From Pagan Rome to Byzantium,* vol. 1 of *A History of Private Life* (Cambridge: Belknap, 1987), 16.

28. See the depiction in Poplin, "Les jeux d'osselets antiques," 46.

29. See also Kastner, "L'enfant et les jeux," 92. Depictions can be found in Veyne, "The Roman Empire," 15–16 and 18; Poplin, "Les jeux d'osselets antiques," 47, showing two young women playing knucklebones; and Wiedemann, *Adults and Children,* plate 20.

30. See Wiedemann, *Adults and Children,* plate 20.

31. Walter S. Hett, "The Games of the Greek Boy," *Greece and Rome* 1 (1931): 26.

32. Joseph Amar and Edward Mathews, *St. Ephrem the Syrian: Selected Prose Works,* Fathers of the Church 91 (Washington, D.C.: Catholic University of America Press, 1994), 41.

33. Ephraem the Syrian, *Armenian Hymns* 16 in *Hymnes de Saint Ephrem conservées en version arménienne,* ed. and trans. L. Mariés and C. Mercier, Patrologia Orientalis 30/1 (Paris: Firmin-Didot, 1961), 105–9. For an English translation with notes, see Robert Murray, "'A Marriage for All Eternity': The Consecration of a Syrian Bride of Christ," *Sobornost* 11 (1989): 65–68.

34. For paintings of the scene in the Roman catacombs, see Josef Wilpert, *Die Malereien der Katakomben Roms* (Freiburg: Herdersche, 1903), plates 13, 78.1, and 172.2. For a relief on a Christian sarcophagus, see S. R. F. Price, *Rituals and Power: The Roman*

Imperial Cult in Asia Minor (Cambridge: Cambridge University Press, 1984), plate 1c. See also Price, *Rituals and Power,* 199 n. 156.

35. Veyne, "The Roman Empire," 14, and probably also the picture of the section of the Tomb of the Haterii, depicted there on page 24; see also Wiedemann, *Adults and Children,* plate 18.

36. Wiedemann, *Adults and Children,* 150–51.

37. Ibid., plate 21.

38. Ibid., 150, see also 60.

Chapter Five. Baptismal Rites and Architecture

1. Renunciation, not specifically alluded to here, is mentioned in *Crown.* 3 and *Mart.* 2.

2. Actually, the triple immersion is not mentioned in *Bapt.,* but is in *Crown.* 3 and *Prax.* 26.

3. No explicit mention of the sign of the cross occurs here, although it is mentioned in *Res. Flesh* 8, but it may be implied by the reference to Jacob's cross-handed blessing of Ephraim and Manasseh (Gen. 48:14) in *Bapt.* 8.

4. Both ancient and modern authors have associated the Cainites with other groups, including the Orphites, Noachites, and Nicolaitans. Cainites are frequently mentioned by other early antiheresy writers, including Clement of Alexandria, *Misc.* 8.17; Hippolytus, *Ref.* 8; Origen, *Celsus* 3.13, and Irenaeus, *Her.* 2.5. Later writers who mention the Cainites include Epiphanius, *Pan.* 38; Theodoret, *Ref. Her.* 1.15; and Augustine, *Heresies* 18. See Kurt Rudolph, *Gnosis: The Nature and History of Gnosticism,* ed. Robert McLachlan Wilson (San Francisco: Harper & Row, 1985), 256–57.

5. Birger Pearson, "Cain and the Cainites," in *Gnosticism, Judaism, and Egyptian Christianity* (Minneapolis: Fortress, 1990), 107.

6. On Valentinians in Carthage, see Tertullian, *Val.* 1.1 and *Scorp.* 1 (where he describes them as preaching against martyrdom and winning over many in times of persecution). Valentinian baptism is mentioned by Irenaeus in *Her.* 1.21.3–4, and see *The Gospel of Philip* (from the Nag Hammadi) 67, for example. Marcionite baptism is described in Tertullian, *Against Marcion* 1.14; 3.22.

7. *The Testimony of Truth* (from the Nag Hammadi) 69, for example, rejects baptism because Jesus did not baptize anyone, including his apostles—an argument very close to the one that Tertullian refutes in *Bapt.* 11.

8. Baptism in blood is also referred to in Hippolytus, *Ap. Trad.* 19; *Passion of Perp.* 18.3, 21.2; Cyprian, *Ep.* 73.22.2 and *The Lord's Prayer* 24; and Cyril of Jerusalem, *Catech.* 3.10.

9. Cyprian admitted that the policy of rebaptism was an innovation of his predecessor (*Ep.* 75.19.1–4).

10. Cyprian also cites this text on his own behalf (*Ep.* 73.9.1). Compare the baptism of the Ephesians in Acts 19:1-7, which describes a "rebaptism" for those who lacked the Holy Spirit because of their baptism by John. This line is also taken by the anonymous author of *Rebapt.* 4. See also Tertullian's use of these texts in *Bapt.* 10.

11. The author of *Rebapt.* seems to make this argument. In *Rebapt.* 5, the same author cites Peter's baptism of the Gentiles (Acts 10:44-48), in which the Spirit was given first and the water added afterwards, and even says "there will be no doubt that persons may be baptized with the Holy Spirit without water," since "these were baptized before they were baptized with water." In *Rebapt.* 10–11, the author explicitly speaks of a baptism of water and a baptism of the Spirit.

12. Compare Tertullian, *Bapt.* 6, in which he speaks of the action of the angel in the water as making the candidates clean and ready for the laying on of hands, which welcome the Holy Spirit (*Bapt.* 8).

13. This supplement is not in Cyprian but rather described by the author of *Rebapt.,* who raises the problem in chap. 4 and resolves it in chap. 10: "if, by necessity of the case, [water baptism] should be administered by an inferior cleric, let us wait for the result, that it may either be supplied by [the bishop] or reserved to be supplied by the Lord."

14. In addition to the reference to circumcision, in regard to the force of Jewish purity law, See G. Clarke, "Cyprian's Epistle 64 and the Kissing of Feet in Baptism," *Harvard Theological Review* 66 (1973): 147–52, for a persuasive argument to this end.

15. As discussed above. Origen also urges infant baptism but notes that it must be for the remission of their own sin (*Hom. on Leviticus* 8.3).

16. A summary of Caelestius's teachings is included in Augustine's first anti-Pelagian treatise, *Guilt and Remiss.* (passim). A list of the statements of Caelestius condemned at Carthage is contained in *Proceed. Pelag.* 11.23–24.

17. A good example of a smaller city with two such baptisteries is Belalis Minor, although Sufetula also had two distinct churches with separate baptisteries and historical record of a Donatist as well as Catholic bishop. Maktar seems to have had an Arian basilica as well as a Catholic and perhaps Donatist church. The Arian identity of one of its basilicas is based on a tomb inscription that bears the Vandal name "Hildegun" near its entrance.

18. Deer and streams also appear in the baptisteries of Skhira, near Sfax, and at Oued Ramel. Similar mosaics were found at Salona in Dalmatia (with the inscription "*sicut cervus desiderat ad fontes aquarum ita desiderat anima mea ad te Deus,*" or "Just as a deer longs for springs of water, so my soul longs for you, O God" [Psalm 42]), in the baptistery of the Cathedral in Naples, in the Orthodox Baptistery of Ravenna, and in the baptistery at Ras Siaga (Nebo).

19. One can see the procession of saints in the baptisteries of Ravenna, for instance, or the hand of God offering a crown of victory directly above the fourth-century font in Naples.

20. This is based on the reconstruction of N. Duval and F. Baratte, *Les ruines de Sufetula: Sbeitla* (Tunis, 1973), 46–47. In some places it is difficult to tell a baptistery from a *martryrium* or mausoleum based on their architectural structures. For example, the mausoleum of Constantina in Rome was long thought to have served as a baptistery, while the baptistery at Iulia Concordia Sagittaria in northern Italy was probably first a *martyrium*. See P. L. Zovatto, "Une nouvelle aire sépulchral paléochrétienne à Julia Concordia Sagittaria," *Cahiers Archéologiques* 6 (1952): 147–55.

21. There is some evidence of burials in the Arian baptistery of Ravenna and at Albenga in Italy. The council of Auxerre in 578 prohibited the practice.

22. See S. T. Stevens, "A New Christian Structure on the Outskirts of Carthage: A Preliminary Report on the 1994 Excavations at Bir Ftouha," *Dumbarton Oaks Papers* 50 (1996): 369–78; and S. T. Stevens, A. V. Kalinowski, and H. vanderLeest, *Bir Ftouha: A Byzantine Pilgrimage Church Complex at Carthage*, Journal of Roman Archaeology Supplement Series 58 (December 2004).

23. The coincidence of baptistery and shrine is not uniquely North African by any means. Other examples include the shrine of Symeon Stylites at Qal'at Siman in Syria, with its imposing baptistery. See P.-A. Février, "Baptistères, martyrs, et reliques," *Reallexikon für Antik und Christentum* 62 (1986): 109–38.

24. Text and trans. from M. Tilley, *Donatist Martyr Stories* (Liverpool: Liverpool University Press, 1996), 74–75.

Chapter Six. Food, Ritual, and Power

1. Leonardo Boff and Clodovis Boff, *Introducing Liberation Theology* (Maryknoll, N.Y.: Orbis, 1987), 1.

2. See Mary Douglas, "Food as a System of Communication," in *In the Active Voice* (London: Routledge, 1982), 82–124.

3. The ancient terminology was more varied, and these groups included the Jewish meal clubs known as *haburoth*. See further Jacob Neusner, "Two Pictures of the Pharisees: Philosophical Circle or Eating Club," *Anglican Theological Review* 64 (1982): 525–38.

4. See Dennis E. Smith, *From Symposium to Eucharist: The Banquet in the Early Christian World* (Minneapolis: Fortress, 2003).

5. Ibid., 47–65.

6. See Dale Martin, "Tongues of Angels and Other Status Indicators," *Journal of the American Academy of Religion* 59 (1991): 547–89.

7. Michael Townsend, "Exit the *Agape?*" *Expository Times* 90 (1979): 356–61.

8. See Peter Garnsey, *Food and Society in Classical Antiquity* (Cambridge: Cambridge University Press, 1999), 12–21.

9. See Jonathan Klawans, "Interpreting the Last Supper: Sacrifice, Spiritualization, and Anti-Sacrifice," *New Testament Studies* 48/1 (2002): 1–17.

10. This sort of elaboration of the meal is well attested in North Africa around the year 200; see, for instance, Tertullian, *Against Marcion* 1.14.1, and also the *Martyrdom of Perpetua and Felicitas* 4.9–10. On these cases, see Andrew McGowan, *Ascetic Eucharists: Food and Drink in Early Christian Ritual Meals* (Oxford: Clarendon, 1999), 95–115.

11. The early third-century date, authorship, and even title of the supposed *Apostolic Tradition* by Hippolytus of Rome, assumed through much of the twentieth century, must now be scrutinized and almost certainly rejected; see Paul F. Bradshaw, Maxwell E. Johnson, and L. Edward Philips, *The Apostolic Tradition: A Commentary*, Hermeneia (Minneapolis: Fortress, 2002), 1–17.

12. On these issues, see the essays in Gerd Theissen, *The Social Setting of Pauline Christianity: Essays on Corinth* (Philadelphia: Fortress, 1982).

13. McGowan, *Ascetic Eucharists,* 143–74.

14. The original story need not be understood as a direct reference to the eucharistic meal, but it should be understood as making use of images also applied to it for a more general christological purpose.

15. Translation adapted from *New Testament Apocrypha,* 2 vols., ed. Wilhelm Schneemelcher (Louisville, Ky.: Westminster/John Knox, 1992), 200–201.

16. See Andrew McGowan, "The Inordinate Cup: Issues of Order in Early Eucharistic Drinking," *Studia Patristica* 35 (2001): 283–91.

17. Adapted from the translation of Kirsopp Lake, *The Apostolic Fathers,* Loeb Classical Library (Cambridge: Harvard University Press, 1965).

18. See Enrico Mazza, *The Origins of the Eucharistic Prayer* (Collegeville, Minn.: Liturgical, 1995).

19. Andrew McGowan, "'Is There a Liturgical Text in This Gospel?' The Institution Narratives and Their Early Interpretive Communities," *Journal of Biblical Literature* 118 (1999): 77–89.

20. On these issues, see Kathleen E. Corley, *Private Women, Public Meals: Social Conflict in the Synoptic Tradition* (Peabody, Mass.: Hendrickson, 1993).

21. See John D'Arms, "The Roman *Convivium* and the Idea of Equality," in *Sympotica: A Symposium on the 'Symposium',* ed. Oswyn Murray (Oxford: Clarendon, 1990), 308–20.

22. The study by Ute Eisen is useful: *Women Officeholders in Early Christianity: Epigraphical and Literary Studies* (Collegeville, Minn.: Liturgical, 2000).

23. The treatment by Charles A. Bobertz ("The Role of the Patron in the *Cena Dominica* of Hippolytus' *Apostolic Tradition,*" *Journal of Theological Studies* n.s. 44 [1993]: 170–84) is helpful. The present chapter assumes a different chronology and character for that work, but the issues raised are still relevant.

24. See Joan R. Branham, "Women as *Objets de Sacrifice?* An Early Christian 'Chancel of the Virgins,'" in *De la cuisine à l'autel. Les sacrifices en question dans les sociétés de la méditerranée ancienne,* ed. S. Georgoudi, R. Koch Piettre, and F. Schmidt, Bibliothèque de l'École des Hautes Études, Sciences religieuses (Paris: Brepols, forthcoming).

25. Augustine provides evidence for North African practice around 400 and how it differed from Italian; *On the Morals of the Catholic Church* 34.75 and *Conf.* 8.27.

26. The shrine of Felix at Nola, accepted and even advocated as a legitimate site of sacrificial practice by Paulinus; see Dennis Trout, "Christianizing the Nolan Countryside: Animal Sacrifice at the Tomb of St Felix," *Journal of Early Christian Studies* 3 (1995): 281–98.

Chapter Seven. Saints, Identity, and the City

1. C. Carletti, "I graffiti sull'affresco di S. Luca nel cimitero di Commodilla: Addenda et corrigenda," *Atti della Pontificia Accademia Romana di Archeologia. Rendiconti* 57 (1984–85): 129–43; J. Osborne, "The Roman Catacombs in the Middle Ages," *Papers of the British School at Rome* 53 (1985): esp. 299–305; J. Deckers, G. Mietke, and

A. Weiland, *Die Katakombe "Commodilla": Repertorium der Malereien*, 3 vols. (Vatican City: Pontificio Istituto di Archeologia Cristiana, 1994), Textband 83–85; and P. Pergola, *Le catacombe romane: storia e topografia* (Rome: Carocci, 1998), 218–21. The epitaph of Virgynia Babosa is *ICUR* 2.6152.

2. Peter Brown, *The Cult of the Saints: Its Rise and Function in Latin Christianity* (Chicago: University of Chicago Press, 1981); and, for example, the essays in J. Howard-Johnston and P. Hayward, *The Cult of the Saints in Late Antiquity and the Early Middle Ages: Essays on the Contribution of Peter Brown* (Oxford: Oxford University Press, 1999).

3. For more on Paulinus, see Brown, *The Cult of the Saints;* Dennis Trout, *Paulinus of Nola: Life, Letters, and Poems* (Berkeley: University of California Press, 1999); and Catherine Conybeare, *Paulinus Noster: Self and Symbols in the Letters of Paulinus of Nola* (Oxford: Oxford University Press, 2000). Paulinus's letters and poems have been translated by P. G. Walsh in *ACW* vols. 35, 36, and 40. The standard Latin editions are *CSEL* vols. 29 and 30, revised by M. Kampter (1999).

4. Antonio Ferrua, "Graffiti di pellegrini alla tomba di San Felice," *Palladio* n.s. 13 (1963): 17–19; Damasus *carmen* 59 in A. Ferrua, *Epigrammata Damasiana* (Rome: Pontificio Istituto di Archeologia Cristiana, 1942).

5. *CIL* 10.1370 = *ILCV* 3482 with Walsh *ACW* 40:345 and Trout, *Paulinus,* 244–46, with Paulinus as the likely author.

6. Richard Krautheimer, *Three Christian Capitals: Topography and Politics* (Berkeley: University of California Press, 1983); Richard Krautheimer, *Rome: Profile of a City, 312–1308* (Princeton, N.J.: Princeton University Press, 2000 [1980]); John Curran, *Pagan City and Christian Capital: Rome in the Fourth Century* (Oxford: Oxford University Press, 2000). But note the caution summarized by D. Kinney, "Krautheimer's Constantine," in *Ecclesiae Urbis: Atti del congresso internazionale di studi sulle chiese di Roma (IV–X secolo), Roma, 4–10 settembre 2000,* ed. F. Guidobaldi and A. Guidobaldi (Vatican City: Pontificio Istituto di Archeologia Cristiana, 2002).

7. L. Reekman "L'implantation monumentale chrétienne dans le paysage urbain de Rome de 300 à 850," in *Actes du XIe congrès international d'archéologie chrétienne,* vol. 2 (Rome: École française de Rome, 1989), 861–915; L. Pani Ermini, "Roma da Alarico a Teodorico," in *The Transformations of Urbs Roma in Late Antiquity,* ed. W. V. Harris, Journal of Roman Archaeology Supplementary Series 33 (Portsmouth, R.I.: Journal of Roman Archaeology, 1999), 35–52; Pergola, *Le catacombe romane;* L. V. Rutgers, *Subterranean Rome: In Search of the Roots of Christianity in the Catacombs of the Eternal City* (Leuven: Peeters, 2000); and M. Webb, *The Churches and Catacombs of Early Christian Rome* (Brighton: Sussex Academic, 2001).

8. Ferrua's *Epigrammata Damasiana* is still the standard edition of the poems. Fuller bibliography at Dennis Trout, "Damasus and the Invention of Early Christian Rome," in *The Cultural Turn in Late Ancient Studies: Gender, Asceticism, and Historiography,* ed. P. Cox Miller and D. Martin (Durham, N.C.: Duke University Press, 2005).

9. Krautheimer, *Three Christian Capitals;* Neil McLynn, *Ambrose of Milan: Church and Court in a Christian Capital* (Berkeley: University of California Press, 1994). On the invention of Gervasius and Protasius (next paragraph), see Ambrose, *Letter 77* (*CSEL* 82 = PL *Letter* 22) with Augustine, *Conf.* 9.7.16 and *City of God* 22.8.

10. *CIL* 6.1, p. 389 = *ILCV* 63 = *ICUR* 2. 4219; Friedrich Deichmann, *Repertorium der christlich-antiken Sarkophage,* 2 vols. (Wiesbaden: Franz Steiner, 1967), no. 678. More on this theme at Dennis Trout, "The Verse Epitaph(s) of Petronius Probus: Competitive Commemoration in Late-Fourth-Century Rome," *New England Classical Journal* 28 (2001): 157–76.

11. Bassa: *ICUR* 5.14076 with photograph at Tab. 34.1; Deichmann, *Repertorium,* no. 556. Felicissimus and Agapitus: Ferrua 25. Nereus and Achilleus: Ferrua 8.

12. Monica: *Conf.* 6.2.2. Graffiti at San Sebastiano: *ICUR* 5.12907–13096 with the *refrigerium* at, e.g., 12932, 12974, and 12981; see also photo at Angela Donati, ed., *Pietro e Paolo: La storia, il culto, la memoria nei primi secoli* (Milan: Electa, 2000), nos. 107–8. Hippolytus: Prudentius, *Peristephanon* 11.

13. Silverware and gold glass: see, e.g., *Pietro e Paolo,* nos. 65–66 and 84–91; Kurt Weitzmann, ed., *Age of Spirituality* (New York: Metropolitan Museum of Art, 1979), nos. 506–8, 510–11. Cubiculum Leonis at J. Deckers et al., *Die Katakombe "Commodilla,"* Texteband 89–104. Leo's identifying inscription is *ICUR* 2.6152.

14. Victricius of Rouen, *On the Praise of the Saints,* with translation and commentary by G. Clark at *Journal of Early Christian Studies* 7 (1999): 365–99. Augustine, *City of God* 22.8.

15. Agnellus and Martin: *Liber Pontificalis Ecclesiae Ravennatis* 86, ed. O. Holder-Egger *MGH SRL* (1878, 1964), 265–391. Fortunatus and Martin: Fortunatus, *Vita Martini* 4.686–701; Gregory of Tours, *The Miracles of the Bishop St. Martin* 1.15; Paul the Deacon, *History of the Lombards* 2.13. For this and what follows, see especially Luce Pietri, *La ville de Tours du IVe au VIe siècle: Naissance d'une cité chrétienne* (Rome: École française de Rome, 1983); and Raymond Van Dam, *Saints and Their Miracles in Late Antique Gaul* (Princeton, N.J.: Princeton University Press, 1993), which includes (198–303) a translation of Gregory's *Miracles of the Bishop St. Martin* (from B. Krusch, ed., *De virtutibus sancti Martini episcopi, MGH SRM* 1.2 [1969]).

16. "City of Martin": Paulinus of Périgueux, *Vita* 5.295. Inscriptions: Pietri, *La ville,* nos. 5 and 13, with Van Dam, *Saints and Their Miracles,* 312–15.

17. The madman and Bonulf: Gregory of Tours, *Miracles of Martin* 2.25. For the sermon, see Van Dam, *Saints and Their Miracles,* 304–7.

18. Gregory, *Letter* 4.30, to Constantina. See further John McCulloh, "The Cult of Relics in the Letters and 'Dialogues' of Pope Gregory the Great: A Lexicographical Study," *Traditio* 32 (1976): 145–84.

19. Following here the text and reconstruction offered by Jan-Olof Tjäder, *Die nichtliterarischen lateinischen Papyri italiens,* vol. 2 (Stockholm: Paul Åströms, 1982), 205–22. On Theodelinda at Monza, see Paul the Deacon, *History of the Lombards,* 4.21–22, and for more Dennis Trout, "Theodelinda's Rome," in *Memoirs of the American Academy in Rome,* forthcoming.

20. André Grabar, *Les ampoules de Terre Sainte (Monza–Bobbio)* (Paris: Librairie C. Klincksieck, 1958).

21. The text is at Roberto Valentini and Giuseppe Zucchetti, *Codice topografico della città di Roma,* vol. 2 (Rome: Tipografia del Senato, 1942), 67–99, and at *Itineraria et alia geographica* (*CCSL* 175), 305–11. Translations are the author's.

22. Damasus's *elogium* is Ferrua 7. For the epitaph see *ILCV* 2142 = *ICUR* 2.6018. For the fresco, see Deckers et al., *Die Katakombe "Commodilla,"* Textband 61–65.

23. It is partially quoted by the seventh-century *De locis sanctis martyrum* 7 (CCSL 175, p. 316).

24. Bertram Colgrave, *The Life of Bishop Wilfrid by Eddius Stephanus* (Cambridge: Cambridge University Press, 1927); with Colgrave, "Pilgrimages to Rome in the Seventh and Eighth Centuries," in E. Atwood and A. Hill, eds., *Studies in Language, Literature, and Culture of the Middle Ages and Later* (Austin: University of Texas, 1969), 156–72.

25. Nicholas Howe, "Rome: Capital of Anglo-Saxon England," *Journal of Medieval and Early Modern Studies* 34 (2004): 147–71.

Chapter Eight. Personal Devotions and Private Chapels

1. On the chapel, see Beat Brenk, "La cristianizzazione della Domus dei Valerii sul Celio," in William V. Harris, ed., *The Transformations of the Urbs Roma in Late Antiquity,* Journal of Roman Archaeology Supplement 33 (Portsmouth, R.I.: Journal of Roman Archaeology, 1999), 69–84.

2. On the reserved sacrament, see Otto Nussbaum, *Die Aufbewahrung der Eucharistie,* Theophaneia 29 (Bonn: Hanstein, 1979); Henri Leclerq, "Réserve eucharistique," in *Dictionnaire d'archéologie chrétienne et de liturgie* (Paris: Letouzey et Ané, 1907–53), 2385–89; Archdale A. King, *Eucharistic Reservation in the Western Church* (New York: Sheed & Ward, 1964), chaps. 1–8; W. H. Freestone, *The Sacrament Reserved: A Survey of the Practice of Reserving the Eucharist* (London: Mowbray, 1917).

3. Archer St. Clair, "Early Christian Pyxides Carved with New Testament Scenes," PhD diss. (Princeton University, 1977), 2–3, although she suggests the *pyxides* were used only for the *viaticum.*

4. For instance, see P. M. Chaine, "Sermon sur la pénitence attribué à Saint Cyrille d'Alexandrie," *Mélange de la Faulté Orientale* 6 (1913): 493–528; and Paul Hindo, *Disciplina Antiochena Antica Siri,* vol. 4, Codificazione canonica orientale 2/28 (Vatican City: Tipografia poliglotta vaticana, 1943), 300–301.

5. On the cult of relics and the private space of the grave, see Peter Brown, *The Cult of the Saints: Its Rise and Function in Latin Christianity* (Chicago: University of Chicago Press, 1981), chap. 2.

6. See Holger Klein, "Constantine, Helena and the Cult of the True Cross in Constantinople," in Bernard Flusin and Jannic Durand, eds., *Byzance et les Reliques du Christ,* Centre de Recherche d'Histoire et Civilisation de Byzance 17 (Paris: Association des Amis du Centre d'Histoire et Civilisation de Byzance, 2004).

7. Beat Brenk, "Microstoria sotto la Chiesa dei SS. Giovanni e Paolo: la cristianizzazione di una casa privata," *Revista dell'Instituto Nazionale d'Archeologia e Storia dell'Arte,* Serie III 18 (1995): 169–206.

8. See Gary Vikan, *Byzantine Pilgrimage Art* (Washington, D.C.: Dumbarton Oaks Research Library and Collection, 1984).

9. See particularly Hans Belting, *Likeness and Presence: A History of the Image before the Era of Art,* trans. Edmund Jephcott (Chicago: University of Chicago Press, 1994), chap. 3; Leslie Brubaker, "Image, Audience and Place: Interaction and Reproduction," in Robert Ousterhout and Leslie Brubaker, eds., *The Sacred Image East and West,* Illinois Byzantine Studies 4 (Urbana: University of Illinois Press, 1995), 204–20; on icons in the private sphere, see the essays by Charles Barber and Georgia Frank in *A People's History of Christianity,* vol. 3 (Minneapolis: Fortress Press, forthcoming 2006). For eulogia and the function of images, see Cynthia Hahn, "Loca Sancta Souvenirs: Sealing the Pilgrim's Experience," in Robert Ousterhout, ed., *The Blessings of Pilgrimage,* Illinois Byzantine Studies 1 (Urbana: University of Illinois Press, 1990), 85–96; for other objects of holy power bearing images, see Eunice Dauterman Maguire, Henry P. Maguire, and Maggie J. Duncan-Flowers, *Art and Holy Powers in the Early Christian House,* Illinois Byzantine Studies 2 (Urbana: University of Illinois Press, 1989).

10. Klaus Gamber, *Sacrificium Vespertinum: Lucernarium und eucharistisches Opfer am Abend und ihre Abhängigkeit von den Riten der Juden,* Studia Patristica et Liturgica 12 (Regensburg: Pustet, 1983).

11. On Apollonia, Richard Goodchild, "The 'Palace of the Dux,'" in John Humphrey, ed., *Apollonia: The Port of Cyrene: Excavations Conducted by the University of Michigan 1965–1967,* Supplements to Libya Antiqua 4 (Tripoli: Directorate-General of Antiquities, Museums, and Archives, 1976), 245–65; Simon Ellis, "The 'Palace of the Dux' at Apollonia and Related Houses," in Graeme Barker, John Lloyd, and Joyce Reynolds, eds., *Cyrenaica in Antiquity,* Biblical Archaeology Review International Series 236 (Oxford: Biblical Archaeology Review, 1985), 15–25. On Ephesus, Josef Keil, "XVI. Vorläufiger Bericht über di Ausgrabungen in Ephesos," *Jahreshefte des Österreichischen Archäologischen Institutes* 27 (Beiblatt) (1932): 5–72.

12. On Lullingstone, see G. W. Meates, *The Roman Villa at Lullingstone, Kent,* vol. 1: *The Site,* and vol. 2: *The Wall Paintings and Finds,* Monograph Series of the Kent Archaeological Society 1 and 3 (Chichester: Kent Archaeological Society, 1987). On Villa Fortunatus, see Cristina Godoy Fernández, *Arqueología y liturgia: Iglesias hispánicas (siglos IV al VIII)* (Barcelona: Universitat de Barcelona, 1995), 227–37.

13. On Pueblanueva, Teodor Hauschild, "Das Mausoleum von Las Vegas de Pueblanueva (Prov. Toledo): Grabungen in den Jahren 1971/1974," *Madrider Mitteilungen* 19 (1978): 307–39. On La Cocosa, José Serrá Rafols, *La 'villa' romana de la Dehesa de 'La Cocosa'* (Badajoz: Institución de Servicios Culturales, 1952), 108–44.

14. On Loupian, Christophe Pellecuer, "Loupian: Église Sainte-Cécile," in Noël Duval, ed., *Les premiers monuments chrétiens de la France,* vol. 1 (Paris: Ministère de la culture et de la francophonie, 1995), 47–50. On Torre de Palma, Stephanie Maloney and John Hale, "The Villa of Torre de Palma (Alto Alentejo)," *Journal of Roman Archaeology* 9 (1996): 279–94; Stephanie Maloney and Äsa Ringbom, "Carbon-fourteen Dating of Mortars at Torre de Palma, Portugal," in *V Reunió de Arqueología Cristiana Hispánica* (Cartagena: Congreso Nacional de Arqueología, 2000), 151–55. The arguments for a fourth-century phase of this church remain unconvincing.

15. On these regulations generally, see John Philip Thomas, *Private Religious Foundations in the Byzantine Empire,* Dumbarton Oaks Studies 24 (Washington, D.C.: Dumbarton Oaks Research Library and Collection, 1987); L. Pietri, "Évergétisme chré-

tien et fondations privées dans l'Italie de l'antiquité tardive," in Jean-Michel Carrié and Rita Lizzi Testa, *"Humana Sapit": Études d'antiquité tardive offertes à Lellia Cracco Ruggini* (Turnhout: Brepols, 2002), 253–63.

16. See for Gaul, Charles Pietri, "Chiesa e communitá locali nell' occidente cristiano (IV–VI d.c.): L'esempio della Gallia," in *Societá Romana e Imperio Tardoantico, 3: Le merci gli insediamenti* (Rome: Laterza, 1986), 761–95; Françoise Monfrin, "La christianisation de l'espace et du temps: À l'établissement matériel de l'Église aux Ve et VIe siècles," in Luce Pietri, ed., *Les églises d'orient et d'occident* (Paris: Desclée, 1998), 959–1014; for Hispania, Kim Bowes, "*'Nec sedere in villam'*: Villa-Churches, Rural Piety and the Priscillianist Controversy," in Thomas Burns and John Eadie, eds., *Urban Centers and Rural Contexts in Late Antiquity* (East Lansing: Michigan State University Press, 2001), 323–48; Pablo Díaz, "Comunidades monásticas y comunidades campesinas en la España Visigoda," in *Los Visigodos: Historia y civilización,* Antigüedad y Cristianismo vol. 3 (Murcia: Universidad de Murcia, 1986), 189–95; for Italy, Cinzio Violante, "Le strutture organizzative della cura d'anime nelle campagne dell'Italia centrosettentrionale," in *Cristianizzazione ed organizzazione ecclesiastica delle campagne nell'alto medioevo: espansione e resistenze,* vol. 2 (Spoleto: Il Centro, 1980), 963–1158.

17. The Encratites, Saccophori, and Hydroparastate are probably understood here as branches or alleged branches of Manichaeism. See *CTh.* 16.5.9 (382).

18. On the use of private space during two of the century's great controversies, Pelagianism and Origenism, see Peter Brown, "Pelagius and His Supporters: Aims and Environment," *Journal of Theological Studies* 19 n.s. (1968): 93–114; Elizabeth A. Clark, *The Origenist Controversy: The Cultural Construction of an Early Christian Debate* (Princeton, N.J.: Princeton University Press, 1992).

19. Alain Le Boulluec, *Notion d'hérésie dans la littérature grecque: IIe et IIIe siècles,* 2 vols. (Paris: Études Augustiniennes, 1985). On gender and heresy, see Virginia Burrus, "The Heretical Woman as Symbol in Alexander, Athanasius, Epiphanius and Jerome," *Harvard Theological Review* 84/3 (1991): 229–48.

20. Peter Brown, *The Body and Society: Men, Women, and Sexual Renunciation in Early Christianity* (New York: Columbia University Press, 1988), chap. 15.

Chapter Nine. Heresy, Households, and the Disciplining of Diversity

1. *The Octavius of Marcus Minucius Felix,* trans. G. Clarke (New York: Newman, 1974).

2. For a fuller discussion, see Stevan L. Davies, *The Revolt of the Widows: The Social World of the Apocryphal Acts* (Carbondale: Southern Illinois University Press, 1980); Virginia Burrus, *Chastity as Autonomy: Women in the Stories of the Apocryphal Acts,* Studies in Women and Religion 23 (Lewiston, N.Y.: Mellen, 1987).

3. Dennis Ronald MacDonald, *The Legend and the Apostle: The Battle for Paul in Story and Canon* (Philadelphia: Westminster, 1983).

4. I cite here the translation of S. L. Greenslade, ed., *Early Latin Theology: Selections from Tertullian, Cyprian, Ambrose and Jerome,* Library of Christian Classics 5 (London: SCM, 1956).

5. The majority of antiheretical legislation may be found in book 16 of *The Theodosian Code,* a compendium of imperial laws published from 313 CE onward. For

an English translation, see Clyde Pharr, *The Theodosian Code and Novels and the Sir-mondian Constitutions: A Translation with Commentary, Glossary, and Bibliography* (New York: Greenwood, 1952), esp. book 16, 440–77.

6. Ramsay MacMullen, *Roman Government's Response to Crisis, A.D. 235–337* (New Haven: Yale University Press, 1976), 92.

7. For the transformation of ancient cities and their civic cultures through the promotion and monumentalization of sacred sites and the religious celebrations associated with them, see Robert Markus, *The End of Ancient Christianity* (Cambridge: Cambridge University Press, 1990), 137–56; Peter Brown, *The Cult of the Saints: Its Rise and Function in Latin Christianity* (Chicago: University of Chicago Press, 1982); Richard Krautheimer, *Three Christian Capitals: Topography and Politics* (Berkeley: University of California Press, 1983); and especially Charles Pietri, *Roma Christiana: Recherches sur l'Église de Rome, son organisation, sa politique, son idéologie de Miltiade à Sixte III (311–440),* Bibliothèque des écoles françaises d'Athènes et de Rome 224 (Rome: École française de Rome, 1976).

8. Can. 13; J. B. Chabot, *Synodicon orientale* (Paris, 1902), 266; similarly, Can. 58 of the Council of Laodicea in Asia Minor, convened in the middle of the fourth century, condemns bishops and presbyters who celebrate eucharists in households.

9. Augustine, *Against Petilian* 2.108.247; Optatus, *On Schismatics* 1.16, furnishes similar information.

10. *Incomplete Work on Matthew, Homily* 26 PG 56, 770–71 (traveling Arians and Matthew 10); *Hom.* 49, 907 (emperor as Antichrist); *Hom.* 5, 684–85; 23, 755; 24, 756–60; 31, 794; 46, 894 (persecution and true orthodoxy).

11. Hilary, *Against Auxentius* 12, PL 10.616C (love of buildings); 3, 10.611A (secret assemblies).

12. Gaudentius, *Sermon* 21, PL 20, 372B, 999–1000.

13. Thus, Cyril of Alexandria, *Ep.* 11a, 5–7.

14. Canons 1, 2, and 4, PL 84, 315–18.

15. For an English translation, see C. J. Hefele, *A History of the Councils of the Church,* 7 vols., trans. Henry Nutcombe Oxenham (Edinburgh: T. & T. Clark, 1876), 2.326–31.

16. *Ep. Alex.* 1, 13; similarly, Theodoret, *Ecclesiastical History* 5.7.1, depicting Arius as teaching his ideas from household to household.

17. John Chrysostom attacks this practice in two treatises: *Adversus eos qui apud se habent subintroductas virgines* and *Quod regulares feminae viris cohabitare non debeant* (PG 47), both translated by Elizabeth A. Clark in *Jerome, Chrysostom, and Friends: Essays and Translation,* Studies in Woman and Religion 2 (New York: Mellen, 1982). For strutting at eucharistic assemblies, *Adv. eos* 10 (PG 47, 510); for living together celibately as a means of gaining celebrity, *Quod reg.* 6 (PG 47, 524).

Chapter Ten. Jewish Christians, Judaizers, and Christian Anti-Judaism

1. Alan Segal, *Rebecca's Children: Judaism and Christianity in the Roman World* (Cambridge: Harvard University Press, 1986).

2. See Philip S. Alexander, "'The Parting of the Ways' from the Perspective of

Rabbinic Judaism," in *Jews and Christians: The Parting of the Ways A.D. 70 to 135,* ed. James D. G. Dunn (Tübingen: Mohr, 1992), 1–27, and, more recently, Seth Schwartz, *Imperialism and Jewish Society, 200 B.C.E. to 640 C.E.* (Princeton, N.J.: Princeton University Press, 2001), and Daniel Boyarin, *Border Lines: The Partition of Judaeo-Christianity,* Divinations: Rereading Late Ancient Religion (Philadelphia: University of Pennsylvania Press, 2004).

3. Robert L. Wilken, *John Chrysostom and the Jews: Rhetoric and Reality in the Late Fourth Century* (Berkeley: University of California Press, 1983), 10, emphasizes that he was only a priest, not a bishop at the time.

4. Heinz Schreckenberg, *Die christlichen Adversus Judaeos: Texte und ihr literarisches und historisches Umfeld (1–11 Jh.),* Europäische Hochschulschriften 23/172 (Frankfurt: Peter Lang, 1982).

5. James Parkes, *The Conflict of the Church and Synagogue: A Study in the Origins of Anti-Semitism* (New York: Atheneum, 1974 [1934]).

6. Cited from the English translation: Marcel Simon, *Verus Israel: A Study of the Relations between Christians and Jews in the Roman Empire A D 135–425,* trans. H. McKeating, Littman Library of Jewish Civilization (London: Oxford University Press, 1986 [1948]), 217. Curiously, it was not until 1986 that an English version was published.

7. Rosemary Radford Ruether, *Faith and Fratricide: The Theological Roots of Anti-Semitism* (New York: Seabury, 1974). See also John Gager, *The Origins of Anti-Semitism: Attitudes toward Judaism in Pagan and Christian Antiquity* (New York: Oxford University Press, 1984), who builds on Ruether's work.

8. Gager, *Origins of Anti-Semitism,* 120.

9. See Wilken, *John Chrysostom,* chap. 4, "Fourth Century Preaching and the Rhetoric of Abuse."

10. Parkes, *Conflict of the Church and the Synagogue,* 164.

11. That is, Homily 6, Section 6, Column 913; references to the homilies are from *Patrologia Graeca* (PG), the most readily available edition of the Greek text. For a translation I have drawn on Wendy Mayer and Pauline Allen, *John Chrysostom* (London: Routledge, 2000). Wilken explains John's insecurity as based in his inability to read those books: "John, unlike Jerome, was not a scholar. He did not know Hebrew. In the face of the Jewish possession of the Scriptures and the allure of the Jewish books, he felt helpless" (*John Chrysostom,* 83).

12. For the purpose of receiving dream revelations, as suggested by Gager, *Origins of Anti-Semitism,* 119. Daphne is a suburb of Antioch; see Wilken, *John Chrysostom,* 36–37, and Christine Kondoleon, *Antioch* (Princeton, N.J.: Princeton University Press, 2000), 9–10.

13. See also Wilken, *John Chrysostom,* 79ff.

14. Ibid., 80.

15. E.g., *Adversus Judaeos* 1:3, 848: "Jews scare the more simple-minded Christians."

16. Parkes, *Conflict of the Church and the Synagogue,* 189–90. See also Gager, *Origins of Anti-Semitism,* 120, who states, "Here the connection between popular Christian Judaizing on the one side and official Christian anti-Judaism on the other side could not be more apparent." On the issue of the Judaizer, see further below.

17. Wilken, *John Chrysostom,* 92.

18. References to the Didascalia are from Corpus Scriptorum Christianorum Orientalium (CSCO) 402 and 408, *The Didascalia Apostolorum in Syriac I and II*, ed. and trans. Arthur Vööbus (Louvain: Secrétariat de CorpusSCO, 1979), the only complete English translation to date. Vööbus also provided the text-critical edition of the Syriac text in CSCO 401 and 407.

19. See Charlotte Methuen, "Widows, Bishops and the Struggle for Authority in the Didascalia Apostolorum," *Journal of Ecclesiastical History* 46 (1995): 204, who suggests that "the Didascalia condemns the practices of two groups: first, as has long been established, a group of Jewish Christians who observe the Second Legislation, and, second, a group which rejects marriage, prohibits meat-eating, and has a theology of 'blaspheming God Almighty.'"

20. See Simon, *Verus Israel*, 89ff., for references. The Greek term *deuterosis* is a close translation of the Hebrew term *mishnah*.

21. On the futility of observing the Sabbath, see, e.g., *Epistle of Barnabas*, chap. 15; Justin, *Dialogue with Trypho* 12 and 47; Ignatius, *Magn.* 9. On Sunday, see Justin, *First Apology* 67, and Sunday competing with the Sabbath Ignatius, *Magn.* 9. See also D. A. Carson, ed., *From Sabbath to Lord's Day: A Biblical, Historical and Theological Investigation* (Grand Rapids: Zondervan, 1982), and Paul K. Jewett, *The Lord's Day: A Theological Guide to the Christian Day of Worship* (Grand Rapids: Eerdmans, 1971).

22. The Latin translation, however, states the complete opposite. Vööbus comments that the strong prohibition of the Latin version "indicates that something is wrong with the text in Syriac" (CSCO 408; 244 n. 229). He speculates about a missing part of the Syriac text. Shaye Cohen, on the other hand, suggests that "the Latin translator was so offended by it that he emended it out of existence" ("Menstruants and the Sacred in Judaism and Christianity," in *Women's History and Ancient History*, ed. Sarah B. Pomeroy [Chapel Hill: University of North Carolina Press, 1991], 290). Against Vööbus he argues, to my mind convincingly, that the Syriac version fits the argument of the particular paragraph, whereas the Latin does not (298 n. 60).

23. Even the rabbinic texts themselves consider the sin of the golden calf as the collective original sin of the Israelites in the desert. See, for example, *Tosefta Shabbat* 1: 16 and *Tosefta Megillah* 4:31–36. For a comprehensive discussion of the golden calf as an argument in the polemics between Jews and Christian, see Pier Cesare Bori, *The Golden Calf and the Origins of the Anti-Jewish Controversy* (Atlanta: Scholars, 1990). Texts as early as the *Letter of Barnabas* read the incident of the golden calf as an intra-biblical dividing line.

24. According to the Didascalia, "the prayer is heard through the Holy Spirit, and the eucharist is accepted and sanctified through the Holy Spirit. And the Scriptures are the utterances of the Holy Spirit, and are holy" (CSCO 408, 239).

25. For an extended discussion of this radical argument as a critique of early Christian politics with respect to women's bodies, see my *Menstrual Purity: Rabbinic and Christian Reconstructions of Biblical Gender* (Stanford, Calif.: Stanford University Press, 2000).

26. Jerome, for instance, refers to the *iudaizantes heretici*. On Jerome's use of the term, see Hillel I. Newman, "Jerome's Judaizers," *Journal of Early Christian Studies* 9:4 (winter 2001): 421–53.

27. Ibid., 422. See also references there.

28. Ibid., 431, 444.

29. Joan E. Taylor, "The Phenomenon of Early Jewish-Christianity: Reality or Scholarly Invention?" *Vigiliae Christianae* 44 (1990): 313–34.

30. Gager, *Origins of Anti-Semitism,* 117.

31. Boyarin, *Border Lines,* 208.

32. But see also Gager, *Origins of Anti-Semitism,* 118.

Chapter Eleven. Beyond Magic and Superstition

1. Blomfield Jackson, *NPNF* 3 (Edinburgh, 1892), 148n.; George T. Dennis, "Popular Religious Attitudes and Practices in Byzantium," *Proche-Orient chrétien* 43 (1993): 274.

2. Arnaldo Momigliano, "Popular Religious Beliefs and the Late Roman Historians," in idem, *Essays in Ancient and Modern Historiography* (Middletown, Conn.: Wesleyan University Press, 1977), 141–59; Peter Brown, *The Cult of the Saints: Its Rise and Function in Latin Christianity* (Chicago: University of Chicago Press, 1981), 12–22; Jonathan Z. Smith, *Drudgery Divine: On the Comparison of Early Christianities and the Religions of Late Antiquity* (Chicago: University of Chicago Press, 1997); Natalie Zemon Davis, "Some Tasks and Themes in the Study of Popular Religion," in Charles Trinkaus and Heiko Oberman, eds., *The Pursuit of Holiness* (Leiden: Brill, 1974), 307–36, quotation on 311.

3. L.-Th. Lefort, "L'homélie de S. Athanase des papyrus de Turin," *Le muséon* 71 (1958): 35–36.

4. See J. H. W. G. Liebeschuetz, *Continuity and Change in Roman Religion* (Oxford: Clarendon, 1979), 123–39; Hans G. Kippenberg, "Magic in Roman Civil Discourse: Why Rituals Could Be Illegal," in Peter Schäfer and Hans G. Kippenberg, eds., *Envisioning Magic: A Princeton Seminar and Symposium* (Leiden: Brill, 1997), 137–63; and Richard Gordon, "Imagining Greek and Roman Magic," in Bengt Ankarloo and Stuart Clark, eds., *Witchcraft and Magic in Europe: Ancient Greece and Rome* (Philadelphia: University of Pennsylvania Press 1999), 159–275.

5. See William E. Klingshirn, "Isidore of Seville's Taxonomy of Magicians and Diviners," *Traditio* 58 (2003): 59–90.

6. Phrygian religion as heretical: Filastrius of Brescia, *Book of Heresies* 49; Epiphanius of Salamis, *Panarion* 48.14; Macarius of Magnesia, *Remaining Works* 4.15; Augustine, *On Heresies* 26. Athanasius: *Festal Letter* 41, on which see David Brakke, "Athanasius of Alexandria and the Cult of the Holy Dead," *Studia Patristica* 32 (1997): 112–18. John of Paralos: Vienna K 9831ᵛ, ed. A. van Lantschoot, "Fragments coptes d'une homélie de Jean de Parallos," *Miscellanea Giovanni Mercati* I, Studi e Testi 121 (Vatican City: Biblioteca Apostolica Vaticana, 1946), 304 (translation on 320).

7. *Lives of the Eastern Saints,* ed. and trans. E. W. Brooks, *Patrologia orientalis* 17.1 (1923): 233–47; quotation on 236.

8. On "informative" versus "performative" uses of sacred texts, see Sam D. Gill, "Nonliterate Traditions and Holy Books," in Frederick M. Denny and Rodney L. Taylor, eds., *The Holy Book in Comparative Perspective* (Columbia: University of South Carolina Press, 1985), 224–39.

9. See Gary Vikan, "Art, Medicine, and Magic in Early Byzantium," *Dumbarton Oaks Papers* 38 (1984): 65–86.

10. Ed., Tito Orlandi, *Shenute: Contra Origenistas* (Rome: C.I.M., 1985), 18–21; trans. by author.

11. On Shenoute's polemic against the cult of martyrs see L.-Th. Lefort, "La chasse aux reliques des martyrs en Égypte au quatrième siècle," *La nouvelle Clio* 6 (1954): 225–30. Cf. Arietta Papaconstantinou, *Le culte des saints en Égypte de Byzantins aux Abbassides. L'apport des sources papyrologiques et épigraphiques grecques et coptes* (Paris: Centre National de la Recherche Scientifique, 2001), 313–67.

12. See R. Van den Broek, "Popular Religious Practices and Ecclesiastical Policies in the Early Church," in Peter H. Vrihjof and Jacques Waardenburg, eds., *Official and Popular Religion: Analysis of a Theme for Religious Studies,* Religion and Society 19 (The Hague: Mouton, 1979), 26–28; Ramsay MacMullen, *Christianity and Paganism in the Fourth to Eighth Centuries* (New Haven: Yale University Press, 1997), 109–12. Compare Athanasius, *Life of Antony,* 90–91, where Antony is said to eschew (alleged) domestic mummification practices.

13. *Iberian Fathers 1,* trans. Claude Barlow, Fathers of the Church 62 (Washington D.C.: Catholic University Press, 1969), 81–82.

14. Translation from *The Theodosian Code and Novels, and the Sirmondian Constitutions,* trans. Clyde Pharr, Corpus of Roman Law 1 (Princeton, N.J.: Princeton University Press, 1952).

15. Augustine of Hippo, *Serm.* 198 in *Works of Saint Augustine,* trans. Edmund Hill, ed. John E. Rotelle (Brooklyn: New City, 1990–99), 3.11, 201–2.

16. Ibid., 473–74.

17. João de Pina-Cabral, "The Gods of the Gentiles Are Demons: The Problem of Pagan Survivals in European Culture," in Kirsten Hastrup, ed., *Other Histories* (London: Routledge, 1992), 50.

18. Maurice Bloch, *From Blessing to Violence: History and Ideology in the Circumcision Ritual of the Merina of Madagascar* (Cambridge: Cambridge University Press, 1986); Rodney Needham, *Primordial Characters* (Charlottesville: University of Virginia Press, 1978); Pierre Bourdieu, *Outline of a Theory of Practice,* trans. R. Nice (Cambridge: Cambridge University Press, 1977), 81, 82–83; Paul Connerton, *How Societies Remember* (Cambridge: Cambridge University Press, 1989).

19. See Rosalind Shaw and Charles Stewart, "Introduction: Problematizing Syncretism," in Stewart and Shaw, eds., *Syncretism/Anti-Syncretism: The Politics of Religious Synthesis* (London: Routledge, 1994), 1–26, esp. 16–19; and Webb Keane, "From Fetishism to Sincerity: On Agency, the Speaking Subject, and Their Historicity in the Context of Religious Conversion," *Comparative Studies in Society and History* 39/4 (1997): 674–93.

20. Davis, "Some Tasks and Themes," 312.

21. See, for example, William A. Christian Jr., *Local Religion in Sixteenth-Century Spain* (Princeton, N.J.: Princeton University Press, 1981); Michael J. Sallnow, *Pilgrims of the Andes: Regional Cults in Cusco* (Washington, D.C.: Smithsonian Institution, 1987); Robert Redfield, *Peasant Society and Culture: An Anthropological Approach to Civilization* (Chicago: University of Chicago Press, 1956); Victor Turner, "Pilgrimages as Social

Processes," *Dramas, Fields, and Metaphors* (Ithaca, N.Y.: Cornell University Press, 1974), 166–230.

22. On the ecology of local religion: Sallnow, *Pilgrims of the Andes;* Terence Ranger, "Taking Hold of the Land: Holy Places and Pilgrimages in Twentieth-Century Zimbabwe," *Past and Present* 117 (1987): 158–94; Mauno Koski, "A Finnic Holy Word and Its Subsequent History," in Tore Ahlbäck, ed., *Old Norse and Finnish Religions and Cultic Place-Names* (Åbo, Finland: Donner Institute, 1990), 404–40; and Sandra E. Greene, *Sacred Sites and the Colonial Encounter: A History of Meaning and Memory in Ghana* (Bloomington: Indiana University Press, 2002). On the idiosyncrasies of religious expertise in local religion: Matthew Schoffeleers, "Christ in African Folk Theology: The *Nganga* Paradigm," in Thomas D. Blakely, Walter E. A. van Beek, and Dennis L. Thomson, eds., *Religion in Africa: Experience and Expression* (Portsmouth, N.H.: Heinemann, 1994), 73–88; and on late antiquity, Valerie I. J. Flint, *The Rise of Magic in Early Medieval Europe* (Princeton, N.J.: Princeton University Press, 1991), chap. 11; and David Frankfurter, "Dynamics of Ritual Expertise in Antiquity and Beyond: Towards a New Taxonomy of 'Magicians,' " in Marvin Meyer and Paul Mirecki, eds., *Magic and Ritual in the Ancient World,* Religions of the Graeco-Roman World 141 (Leiden: Brill, 2002), 159–78, esp. 167–70.

23. On changes in spirit-contact in circumstances of religious conversion, see esp. I. M. Lewis, *Ecstatic Religion: A Study of Shamanism and Spirit Possession,* 2d ed. (London: Routledge, 1989).

24. Robert Redfield, *Peasant Society and Culture: An Anthropological Approach to Civilization* (Chicago: University of Chicago Press, 1956), and James C. Scott, "Protest and Profanation: Agrarian Revolt and the Little Tradition," *Theory and Society* 4 (1977): 1-38, 211-46.

25. Clifford Geertz, "Thick Description: Toward an Interpretive Theory of Culture," in Geertz, *The Interpretation of Cultures* (New York: Basic, 1973), 3–30.

26. See David Frankfurter, " 'Things Unbefitting Christians': Violence and Christianization in Fifth-Century Panopolis," *Journal of Early Christian Studies* 8/2 (2000): 273–95; Steven Emmel, "From the Other Side of the Nile: Shenute and Panopolis," in A. Egberts, B. P. Muhs, and J. van der Vliet, eds., *Perspectives on Panopolis: An Egyptian Town from Alexander the Great to the Arab Conquest* (Leiden: Brill, 2002), 95–113. Later hagiography: Pseudo-Dioscorus, *Panegyric on Macarios of Tkow,* ed. D. W. Johnson (Louvain: Peeters, 1980).

27. Françoise Dunand, "La consultation oraculaire en Égypte tardive: L'Oracle de Bès à Abydos," in *Oracles et prophéties dans l'antiquité,* ed. J.-G. Heintz (Paris: De Boccard, 1997), 65–84; David Frankfurter, "Voices, Books, and Dreams: The Diversification of Divination Media in Late Antique Egypt," in Sarah Iles Johnston and Peter Struck, eds., *Mantike: Greek and Roman Divination,* Religions of the Graeco-Roman World 155 (Leiden: Brill, 2005), 233–54.

28. *Life of Moses of Abydos,* trans. Mark Moussa, "The Coptic Literary Dossier of Abba Moses of Abydos," *Coptic Church Review* 24/3 (2003): 66–90 (quotation from 83–84). On subsequent archaeology: A. Piankoff, "The Osireion of Seti I at Abydos during the Greco-Roman Period and the Christian Occupation," *Bulletin de la Société d'archéologie copte* 15 (1958/60): 125–49, and René-Georges Coquin, "Moïse d'Abydos,"

Deuxième journée d'études coptes, Cahiers de la bibliothèque copte 3 (Louvain: Peeters, 1986), 1-14.

29. On the relationship of demons to liminal topography, see Charles Stewart, *Demons and the Devil: Moral Imagination in Modern Greek Culture* (Princeton, N.J.: Princeton University Press, 1991).

30. See Victor Turner, "The Center Out There: Pilgrim's Goal," *History of Religions* 12/3 (1973): 191–230, and Aryeh Kofsky, "Mamre: A Case of a Regional Cult?" in Aryeh Kofsky and Gedaliahu G. Stroumsa, eds., *Sharing the Sacred: Religious Contacts and Conflicts in the Holy Land* (Jerusalem: Ben Zvi, 1998), 19–30.

31. Doron Bar, "The Christianisation of Rural Palestine during Late Antiquity," *Journal of Ecclesiastical History* 54/3 (2003): 401–21; compare Bishop Porphyry in Gaza in Mark the Deacon, *Vita Porphyrii,* ed. Henri Grégoire and M. A. Kugener (Paris: Les Belles Lettres, 1930).

32. *The Works of St. Augustine,* 3.11, 277–78.

33. Peter Brown, "Sorcery, Demons, and the Rise of Christianity from Late Antiquity into the Middle Ages," in Mary Douglas, ed., *Witchcraft Confessions and Accusations* (London: Tavistock, 1970), 17–45.

34. See, for example, H. J. Magoulias, "The Lives of Byzantine Saints as Sources of Data for the History of Magic in the Sixth and Seventh Centuries A.D.: Sorcery, Relics and Icons," *Byzantion* 37 (1967): 228–69; Dennis, "Popular Religious Attitudes," 288–93; and Matthew W. Dickie, *Magic and Magicians in the Greco-Roman World* (London: Routledge, 2001), chap. 10.

35. Translation by S. Skiles, in *Ancient Christian Magic: Coptic Texts of Ritual Power,* ed. Marvin Meyer (San Francisco: HarperSanFrancisco, 1994), 108.

36. Coptic corpus: *Ancient Christian Magic;* synthesis in David Frankfurter, *Religion in Roman Egypt: Assimilation and Resistance* (Princeton, N.J.: Princeton University Press, 1998), 257–64. Anglo-Saxon corpus: Karen Louise Jolly, *Popular Religion in Late Saxon England: Elf Charms in Context* (Chapel Hill: University of North Carolina Press, 1996).

37. Translation by Richard Smith in *Ancient Christian Magic,* 130.

38. See Bronislaw Malinowski, "Magic, Science and Religion" [1925], in idem, *Magic, Science and Religion and Other Essays* (Boston: Beacon, 1948). Spells cited in this paragraph, respectively (*ACM* = *Ancient Christian Magic*): London Or. 5525 = *ACM* 64; Coll. Moen = *ACM* 52; Strasbourg copt. 135 = *ACM* 87; London Or. 6172 = *ACM* 93; Michigan 1523 = *ACM* 108; London Or. 6795 = *ACM* 130.

INDEX

Abydos (Egypt), 272–74, 276

Africa. *See* Egypt; North Africa

Alexandria, 4, 13,16–18, 20–21, 30, 32, 34–35, 38, 82, 101, 111, 113, 209, 220, 227–29, 237, 259

Ambrose, 8, 13, 18, 21, 35, 43, 119, 171, 174–76, 232, 237

amulets, 14, 99, 258, 261–62, 266, 269, 272, 276–77, 280, 282

Andrew (the apostle), 46, 51–53, 57–58, 68, Plate B (color gallery)

animals

as amulets, 262, 272, 276

in the arena, 54, 60, 82–84

in images of paradise, 140–41, 298n18

as pets or toys, 98–99, 105

sacrificed and/or eaten, 84, 148–151, 162, 169, 264

as symbols of heresy, paganism, irrationality, 28, 50, 59, 64, 118–19, 227, 259

talking, 46, 59–61, 293nn12,14

anti-Judaism, 234–54, 307n16

Antioch, 4, 13, 20–21, 54, 83, 152, 159, 194, 196, 219–20, 236–43, 261, 263, 269

anti-Semitism. *See* anti-Judaism

Antony, 11, 13, 31, 36

Apocryphal Acts of Apostles, 10, 46–68, 74, 124, 148–49, 153, 156, 159–60, 177, 218–19

apostles, 3, 19, 40, 46–68, 87, 105, 122, 128–29, 159, 174–75, 181, 183, 186, 198, 203, 214, 216–17, 243–45. *See also* Andrew; *Apocryphal Acts of Apostles;* John; Paul; Peter; Thomas

Arians, 4, 6, 17–18, 21, 101, 106, 136, 207, 209, 213, 226–30, 252, 298n17, 299n21

art. *See* visual arts

Artemis, 55–56, 103

ascetics, 8–11, 13–14, 21, 27–44, 52, 65, 72, 86, 87–88, 91, 98, 103–4, 106, 110, 133, 148–50, 153, 161, 163, 168–69, 179, 188–89, 216, 218, 229–33

Asia Minor, 4, 16–17, 46–47, 149, 153, 159, 219–20, 229, 237, 259, 268, 271. *See also* Ephesus

Athanasius, 4, 10, 13, 17, 21–22, 31, 35–36, 38, 113–14, 227–28, 230, 259, 263, 266, 270

Atripe (Egypt), 260, 271–72

Augustine, 13, 17, 22, 28, 35, 40–44, 130–36, 142, 170, 175, 176, 178–79, 195–96, 224, 230, 258, 265, 270, 277

baptism, 2, 11, 14, 76, 79, 81, 95–96, 106, 117–18, 158, 192, 206, 215, 222, 228, 249, 252, 264, 268

archeological evidence, 135–43

in Augustine, 130–35

of blood, 124, 142, 297n8

as children's play, 113

in Cyprian, 124–30

of infants, 130–34, 298n15

and Jewish rituals of immersion, 247–48

of lions, 60

and post-baptismal eucharist, 11, 134, 148

in Tertullian, 3, 118–24

waterless, 119, 121–23

baptisteries, 120, 135–43, 174–75, 204, 207, 224–25, Plates E and F (color gallery)

Basil of Caesarea, 28–29, 31, 35, 40, 42

basilicas, xiv, 157, 167, 189–90, 200–202, 204, 209, 224–28

in Milan, 174–75

in Nola, 168, 170

in North Africa, 121, 125, 127, 131, 137, 139–40, 142

in Rome, 171–76, 183, Plate J (color gallery)

Bloch, Maurice, 267